THE JOURNEY FROM TOLLGATE TO PARKWAY

THE JOURNEY FROM TOLLGATE TO PARKWAY

== *African Canadians in Hamilton* ==

Adrienne Shadd

Foreword by the Hamilton Black History Committee

NATURAL HERITAGE BOOKS
A MEMBER OF THE DUNDURN GROUP
TORONTO

Editor: Jane Gibson
Copy Editor: Shannon Whibbs
Design: Courtney Horner
Printer: Webcom

Library and Archives Canada Cataloguing in Publication

Shadd, Adrienne L. (Adrienne Lynn)
    The journey from tollgate to Parkway : African Canadians in Hamilton / Adrienne Shadd.

Includes bibliographical references and index.
ISBN 978-1-55488-394-3

1. Blacks--Ontario--Hamilton Region--History. 2. Blacks--Ontario--Hamilton Region--Social conditions. 3. Blacks--Ontario--Hamilton Region--Biography. I. Title.

FC3098.9.B6S53 2009   971.3'5200496   C2009-900305-8

1 2 3 4 5   14 13 12 11 10

 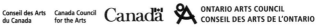

We acknowledge the support of the **Canada Council for the Arts** and the **Ontario Arts Council** for our publishing program. We also acknowledge the financial support of the **Government of Canada** through the **Canada Book Fund** and **Livres Canada Books**, and the **Government of Ontario** through the **Ontario Book Publishers Tax Credit program**, and the **Ontario Media Development Corporation**.

Care has been taken to trace the ownership of copyright material used in this book. The author and the publisher welcome any information enabling them to rectify any references or credits in subsequent editions.

J. Kirk Howard, President

Printed and bound in Canada.
www.dundurn.com

Published by Natural Heritage Books
A Member of The Dundurn Group

Front cover photographs (clockwise from top): Hamilton women's baseball team, 1920s (*Courtesy of Norval Johnson Heritage Library, Niagara Falls, Ontario*); Corinne and Vincent Bryant Jr., *circa* 1930s, great-great-grandchildren of manumitted Tennessee slave Abraham Bryant (*Courtesy of Corinne Bryant Chevalier, Toronto, Ontario*); St. Paul's AME Church, Hamilton, now called Stewart Memorial Church, with Reverend J.W. Crosby (inset) (*From "Negroes in Ontario, 1963," exhibit by Daniel G. Hill. Toronto Public Library (TRL), Special Collections, Baldwin Room*); Port Dalhousie Emancipation Day Celebrations, 1941. From the 1920s to the 1960s, the Port Dalhousie Picnic was a huge affair drawing Blacks from Toronto, Hamilton, the Niagara area, and New York State to a full day of fun at Lakeside Park, Port Dalhousie, Ontario (*Courtesy of Dorothy Hunt Parker Collection, Norval Johnson Heritage Library, Niagara Falls, Ontario*). Back cover photograph: Bird's-eye view of Hamilton, Ontario, in 1859, showing harbour in the distance. Drawn by G.S. Rice (*Courtesy of Library of Congress Prints and Photographs Division, Washington D.C., LC-USZ62-23766*).

Dundurn Press
3 Church Street, Suite 500
Toronto, Ontario, Canada
M5E 1M2

Gazelle Book Services Limited
White Cross Mills
High Town, Lancaster, England
LA1 4XS

Dundurn Press
2250 Military Road
Tonawanda, NY
U.S.A. 14150

To my parents, and all the ancestors who paved the way

CONTENTS

ACKNOWLEDGEMENTS

There is one person who, during the course of the research and writing of this book, went beyond the call of duty in providing information about pertinent people and events, in making herself available for interviews, in furnishing valuable photos, and in doing whatever she could to make sure that I got the straight story. That person is the indomitable Wilma Morrison of the Norval Johnson Memorial Library and Nathaniel Dett Chapel. Her importance to Niagara Falls Black history and that community has been truly remarkable and heralded by everyone from the prime minister of Canada right down to the ordinary citizen. Fortunately for me, however, Wilma grew up in Hamilton, and was both witness to and involved in many activities and initiatives that were important to Hamilton's history and growth over the years, not to mention knowing everyone who lived there. I am tremendously indebted to her and thank her from the bottom of my heart.

I am also indebted to the Hamilton Black History Committee, whose original foresight and vision to pay tribute to some of the key champions of human rights and social justice in Hamilton resulted in this larger book. I thank, in particular, Evelyn Myrie and Vince Morgan, for supplying key information and photographs that were necessary for its completion, and for helping to steer the project to its conclusion. I would also like to thank the contemporary fighters of social justice for providing me with their information, bios and resumés, photos and newspaper clippings. They are Evelyn Myrie, Dr. Gary Warner, Bill De Lisser, Fleurette Osborne and, again, Wilma Morrison. I thank Lyn Royce, as well, for her invaluable assistance with Wilma Morrison's biography and in getting her materials to me.

There were a number of families that were instrumental in providing information on their ancestors who were important to the development of the Hamilton area. I am indebted to Robert Foster Jr. for handing over a ton of information and photographic data on the Berry and Foster families, thus enabling me to recreate the life of his father, Robert Foster Sr., and to Judith Foster Morgan for her memories and insights on the Berry and Foster families. I am also indebted to Joe Rhodes and his cousin Tara Scott of East Lansing, Michigan, for providing valuable details about the Rhodes family, as well as photographs. My aunt Corinne Chevalier's long family history in Hamilton, and her memories and records of her father, Vince Santee Bryant, and his forebears were also incredibly generous and helpful in fleshing out the story of the Black contribution to Hamilton.

I am thankful to Kenn Stanton of the North American Black Historical Museum for steering me in the right direction and providing information on the Lightfoot family. I am also very grateful to Lois Corey, site supervisor of Fieldcote Memorial Park & Museum/Griffin House for sending me research on Ancaster pioneer Enerals Griffin, and to historical interpreter Anne Jarvis for facilitating the process. My cousin Bryan Prince assisted tremendously in giving me helpful tips regarding research on Hamilton as well as his list of Hamilton Black Civil War veterans. Thank you, Bryan! Mr. Eugene Miller, my grade 7 history teacher and one of the premier Canadian collectors of early jazz and memorabilia, has always gone out of his way to help me whenever I have called him for rare photos or audiotape for a project I am working on, and this time was no different. Once again, he came through and sent photos and photocopies of the Famous Canadian Jubilee Singers and their songbook. I will be forever grateful to him for all his assistance over the years.

The Hamilton Public Library Special Collections has done a tremendous amount of work in identifying information related to Black history, and their index files are a treasure trove of individuals, events, newspaper articles, and related data. I salute them for their efforts, as well as the outstanding and very accessible photograph collection that they have amassed over the years. There were also a number of other archival repositories that helped to bring the book alive in terms of images: The Carolina Digital Library and Archives of the University of North Carolina, Chapel Hill; the Collections of the University of Pennsylvania Archives, Philadelphia; and Special Collections and Archives of the Johnston Memorial Library, Virginia State University, Petersburg, Virginia; in particular, Lucious Edwards and Jessica Johnson, who also helped with access to the Colson-Hill Family Papers there.

I began working with the Hamilton community in 2001, when I was hired by the Workers Arts and Heritage Centre to curate an exhibit entitled "… and still I rise: A History of Black Workers in Ontario." Through this project, and through a project entitled "The Souls of Black Folk: Hamilton's Stewart Memorial Community" for the Community Memories program of the Virtual Museum of Canada, I was privileged to get to know many people in the Hamilton community and to interview a number of people who were invaluable to this book, some of whom have passed on. They include Ray Lewis, Jackie Washington, Doris Skorpid, Shirley Brown, Joe Rhodes, Corinne Bryant Chevalier, Marjorie Lake, Clive and Barbara Barnes, Eric Auchinvole, and Reverend George Horton. I am also grateful for the commitment, advice, and wisdom of the individuals of the Black workers advisory committee who oversaw these two projects: Dr. Warner, Carmen Henry, Fleurette Osborne, Eleanor Rodney, Evelyn Myrie, Neville Nunes, Noreen Glasgow, Deborah Brown-Simon, Janice Gairey, Maxine Carter, Winston Tinglin, Lennox Borel, and Renee Wetselaar. The staff of the Workers Arts and Heritage Centre must also be commended for their always helpful and cheery assistance in facilitating my work.

My colleague Karolyn Smardz Frost read over the manuscript and provided much insight, commentary, suggestions, and corrections for the improvement of the text. Her input has been invaluable and I cannot thank her enough for the time and effort she put into it.

I was very pleased that Barry Penhale and Jane Gibson of the Natural Heritage imprint were keen on working on the book and that they, along with the people at Dundurn Press, stuck with me through some ups and downs during the course of its writing. I thank them for their patience and understanding throughout.

Lastly, I am incredibly thankful for my daughter Marishana, who was often an important sounding board for my thoughts, joys and frustrations during the course of the research and writing of this book. Her love and support throughout was vital and something for which I will always be very appreciative.

I am also very grateful to the Ontario Arts Council Writers' Reserve Program for providing much-needed financial support during the project.

⟞⊹ FOREWORD ⊹⟝

In 2007, the Hamilton Black History Committee joined with communities across Ontario to commemorate the 200th anniversary of the passage of legislation in the British parliament to end the trade in enslaved Africans. A coalition of Black cultural community groups were brought together to plan and organize local events in Hamilton to educate the community about the history of slavery in our province, reflect on the contributions of freedom fighters, and celebrate the tenacity of those who survived.

In addition to the commemorative events, the Hamilton Black History Committee received financial support from the Ontario Bicentenary Commemorative Committee on the Abolition of the Slave Trade Act to research and document the contributions of historic and contemporary African Canadians from the Hamilton area who led the way in advancing rights and freedoms.

The Journey from Tollgate to Parkway is the result of that research. For the very first time, the voices of the local Black community in Hamilton are heard in a book-length forum. The book documents the untold narrative of the lives of the local Black men and women who refused to capitulate to power in the face of injustice and racism. It is a story that needs to be heard. Moreover, it is a detailed account of the development of the community, the conditions under which people lived, and the names of some of the key leaders of the community over time. It is an impressive work that should stand for decades to come as the go-to book on Blacks in Hamilton.

The Hamilton Black History Committee would like to extend a special thank you to Dr. Jean Augustine, who headed the Ontario Bicentenary Commemorative Committee on the Abolition of the Slave Trade Act, and to the Ontario Ministry of Citizenship and Immigration, which provided the funding.

This book would have not been possible without the dedicated efforts of the Hamilton Black History Committee which continues to push for Black history in our educational curriculum. Stewart Memorial Church remains a foundational place for Hamilton's Black community and its contribution to this narrative is especially appreciated.

In addition, we are grateful to the Workers Arts and Heritage Centre for its administrative support of this significant historical narrative.

To the men and women in our community who continue to fight for justice and equality, we salute you.

Evelyn Myrie
Chair
Hamilton Black History Committee

Introduction

On January 20, 2009, the world watched the swearing in of the forty-fourth president of the United States, Barack Obama, and in so doing, bore witness to an incredible moment in history — the inauguration of the first African-American president. It seemed almost unimaginable that 150–200 years ago, African Americans were "stealing" themselves and making their way north, guided by the light of the moon and the "drinking gourd" of the North Star, and the Big and Little Dipper constellations. However, people of African descent had not first arrived as African Americans breaking their chains to find freedom from the prison of slavery in the United States. Slavery had also been practised by farmers, merchants, clergy, and colonial leaders right here on Canadian soil in the early years of settlement of what would become the province of Upper Canada. So the stain of the evil, oppressive system that was slavery, buttressed by the African slave trade, also existed here, although it was not as widespread. There were enslaved Africans in Hamilton and their arrival predated the height of the Underground Railroad period by many years. The long journey had already begun.

Gradually, slavery petered out, and the Head of the Lake, as Hamilton was known, began to take off as a town. As more and more free Blacks populated the area, they demonstrated their worth as citizens by distinguishing themselves in the War of 1812 and during the 1837 Rebellion. In fact, in the latter conflict, Black Hamiltonians formed a "Coloured Company" that was highly praised for its defense of British territory and her institutions. In the 1830s, St. Paul's African Methodist Episcopal Church — today's Stewart Memorial — was established, making it the first known *Black* institution in the city, and one of the early Black churches in the province. It was also the means by which other grassroots organizations and self-help initiatives were facilitated. It should not be surprising that Hamilton's Mount Olive Lodge #1, Prince Hall affiliated, formed on December 27, 1852, marked the inauguration of the Black Masonic movement in the province. It remains the longest-running Black lodge in Ontario. Therefore, by the time that Hamilton was incorporated as a city in 1846, people of African descent had already been resident in the area for decades and a flourishing community was already underway. As time went on, what Hamilton represented for people of African descent was a place not only where folks could migrate to take advantage of employment and entrepreneurial opportunities, but also where the foundations of community infrastructure, bold leadership, and a solid record of political and anti-slavery activism, and racial uplift work had been laid.[1]

One African-American expatriate, Reverend W.M. Mitchell, wrote about the Black Hamilton of 1860 as follows:

> Among [the 600 coloured people] are blacksmiths, carpenters, plasterers, and one wheelwright. Many of them own property ... Mr. M. ... who still drives his own hack, is worth 15,000 dollars.... Beggary and pauperism are almost unknown among them. Not a coloured person in this place is supported by the Township ...[2]

William Wells Brown, a writer and abolitionist who had once escaped slavery himself, toured the province about the same time and described Blacks in Hamilton in a similar fashion:

> I found about 500 colored persons in this city, and apparently doing well. They have two churches, a Baptist and a Methodist.... The American Hotel is kept by William Richardson ... Thomas Morton ... has two public carriages, one of which he drives himself. There are four shoemakers, one tailor, three plasterers, one cooper, two carpenters, one blacksmith, and thirteen artists in *water colors*. They have several benevolent societies ... The morals of the people here will compare favorably with the whites. There is considerable wealth here ...[3]

It is quite unusual that among the skilled trades listed by Brown, visual artists are given a nod. Even at that time, it appears that artists were attracted to the larger urban environment, as they so often are in our time.[4] Boston abolitionist, Benjamin Drew, visited Hamilton in 1855 and wrote that "Many of the colored people in Hamilton are 'well off'; are good mechanics, and good 'subjects' ..."[5]

The Blacks who lived in Hamilton clearly took advantage of what the urban world had to offer. Two of the key occupations held by Black Hamiltonians were barber and hotel waiter, jobs that would have been few and far between in rural districts. The Berry family operated the tollgate at the top of James Street. Thomas Morton owned a successful cab business, and other Blacks opened restaurants and taverns. In her study of Toronto's Black history, Karolyn Smardz Frost wrote that Toronto was the only true urban centre in Upper Canada, then Canada West, by mid-century.[6] Certainly, in terms of population, Toronto was by far the largest urban centre, numbering thirty thousand in 1851. By contrast, Hamilton numbered only 6,832 people when it was incorporated as a city in 1846. However, it was the largest and most important centre south and west of Toronto as of 1840.[7]

By all accounts, therefore, African Americans and African Canadians were prospering in the 1840s and 1850s, and jobs were fairly plentiful in the frontier town. Katz's 1975 study of ethnic groups in Hamilton illustrated that a sizeable proportion held skilled occupations in the 1850s and 1860s. The study also indicated that 20 percent owned their own homes, and that the population was fairly stable over the decade.[8] The problem was that their rights as citizens, while extant on paper, were by no means guaranteed, even at the best of times. Thus, from the very beginning, equality and civil rights were issues for which Black Hamiltonians continually sought redress.

As early as 1828, Hamilton-area Blacks joined with others from across the province at Ancaster to protest their exclusion from the public schools, and to request land on which to settle collectively as a group. In 1837, Blacks in Hamilton campaigned to free fugitive slave Jesse Happy, whom his enslavers were attempting to brand as a horse thief so that the Upper Canadian authorities would extradite Happy back to Kentucky. In 1843, Black Hamiltonians again petitioned to be allowed to send their children to the public schools. Forever thereafter, Black children attended the schools in common with all other children, a situation that did not exist for African Canadians in many parts of the province during the nineteenth century. Black Hamilton was a proud, self-conscious, self-empowered community with a vision of freedom and self-determination that tested the promise and the limits of the Canadian haven. These threads of protest and yearnings for equality and social justice were picked up and weaved into a broader cloth with each new generation.

In the decades after the Civil War and into the twentieth century, the status of all African Canadians was under fire. No longer needed as a haven for the slave, Canada appeared to lose interest in the plight of its Black citizens. Events in other parts of the world helped to cement the status of African Canadians at the bottom of the rung of Canada's "vertical mosaic." The Reconstruction Era in the United States, in which African Americans had begun to gain an economic and political foothold in society after emancipation, was abruptly swept aside in the 1880s and 1890s. What became known as the Jim Crow laws, which denied Blacks' right to vote, live and attend schools in the neighbourhoods of their own choosing, and to otherwise partake in the American dream — or segregation

— were ushered in. At about the same time, the 1885 Berlin Conference solidified the European acquisition of most of the African continent. Over the next seventy to one hundred years, Africans would be ruled by a host of European powers, notably Britain, France, Belgium, Portugal, Spain, and Germany. They would be categorized as heathens, unable to govern themselves, a people without a past that had contributed to modern civilization. Africa itself was referred to as the "Dark Continent."

With such a dismal outlook for Africa and its diaspora, the position of African Canadians, as with all peoples of African descent, sank. Winks wrote about this in his epic work *The Blacks in Canada*. In it he maintained that the period from 1865 to 1930 was the nadir in African-Canadian history. "Canadian blacks, once individuals to many whites, now became the stock figures they had been in Southern mythology. No longer addressed by their Christian names, they were hailed affectionately as Lemon John, Black Bill, Pop Eye, Old Shack, Susan's Bill, Taffy Mary ..." and the list goes on.[9] Pseudo-scientific theories of race placed "the Negro" at the bottom of the human hierarchy and, as Winks put it, "the Negro in Canada found himself sliding down an inclined plane from mere neglect to active dislike."[10]

In 1866, a petition with the names of seventy-two Black citizens was sent to Hamilton's mayor, pressing for the enactment of a bylaw prohibiting the insulting and degrading show bills that were plastered on posts and fences throughout the city advertising minstrel shows that periodically came to town. The ads depicted Blacks with huge lips and heels and other such malformations, and less than a week after the petition was delivered to city council, the *Evening Times* reported that the mayor was of the opinion that there was nothing he could do as long as the limits of morality and common decency had not been transgressed by the touring companies. However, some Blacks had already taken matters into their own hands. The show bills were painted over with whitewash.[11]

A wave of negative beliefs and offensive stereotypes was crossing the land. In the 1930s and 1940s, Mable Burkholder's writings on "Little Africa" — a concentration of Black settlers on Hamilton Mountain beginning in the 1840s — was a tribute to exaggeration, half-truths, and outlandish stereotypes.

In a place where Blacks had plied myriad skilled trades and started up thriving businesses, Olympic track star Ray Lewis would state that, in the early decades of the twentieth century, there was practically nothing that Black men in Hamilton could find for employment other than as porters on the railway.[12] Even The Honourable Lincoln Alexander, the first Black to be elected to the Canadian House of Commons, contended that his own wife, Yvonne, worked in a laundry, as an elevator operator, and in helping her mother clean houses in east Hamilton while Alexander was attending McMaster University in the 1940s.[13]

Nevertheless, African Hamiltonians continued to press for equal justice and opportunities. Reverend John Holland and his son, Oliver Holland, were instrumental in helping to change hearts and minds — not to mention open pocketbooks and make available positions of employment — in the mainstream community. Wilma Morrison talked about the sit-ins held by the youth group that was affiliated with Stewart Memorial Church and led by Oliver Holland to ensure that restaurants served all clientele, not just those with white skins. They even staged a sit-in at the Alexandra Skating Rink.[14]

It has been a long journey from the days that a Black woman — Julia Washington Berry — operated one of the tollgates in the 1880s to the opening of the Lincoln M. Alexander Parkway in 1997. Today's movers and shakers within Hamilton's Black community — people like Dr. Gary Warner and Evelyn Myrie — are far more ensconced in the halls of learning, government, and other places of power than ever before. Nevertheless, their alignment with and service to the impoverished, the disenfranchised, the immigrant community, and to the issues of community involvement and social justice are inspirational. However, their concern and dedication is just the latest installment in a long history of community activism and contributions to the city by the bay.

In *Hamilton: A Black Perspective*, published by the Afro-Canadian Caribbean Association of Hamilton and District, the authors lament the fact that "[a]lthough Black people contributed greatly to the history of Hamilton, they are not included in many of the volumes which examine Hamilton's history."[15] Once again, the history of Blacks has become a footnote to the *real* history of the city. It continues to reside on the margins, far removed from the centre of the historical narrative.

In *Journey from Tollgate to Parkway*, the history, exploits, and contributions of people of colour in Hamilton finally take centre stage. It is a history of triumphs, amid disappointment and setbacks; achievements often in the face of serious hardships. But it is a story that must take its place as an important and integral component of the *true* Hamilton story, both for what it reveals about the Black community, and also for what it tells us about the larger Hamilton narrative. Footnotes be damned! It's been a long journey, and it ain't over yet.

SOUTHERN ONTARIO AND EASTERN UNITED STATES, SHOWING WENTWORTH COUNTY INSET

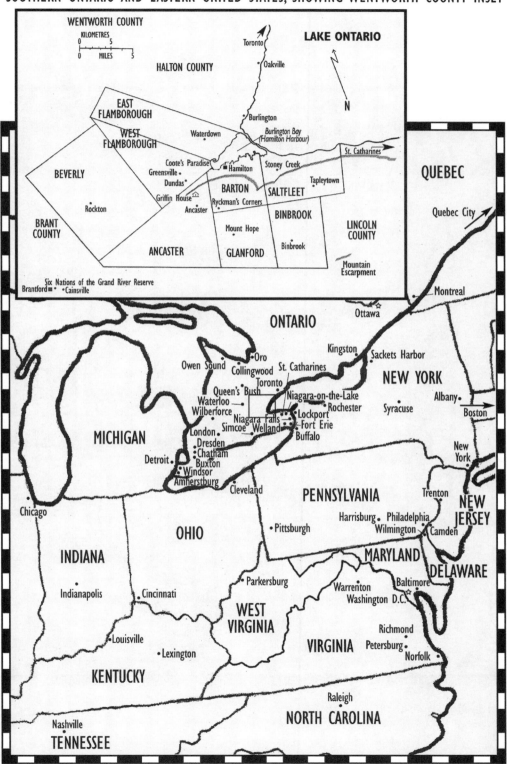

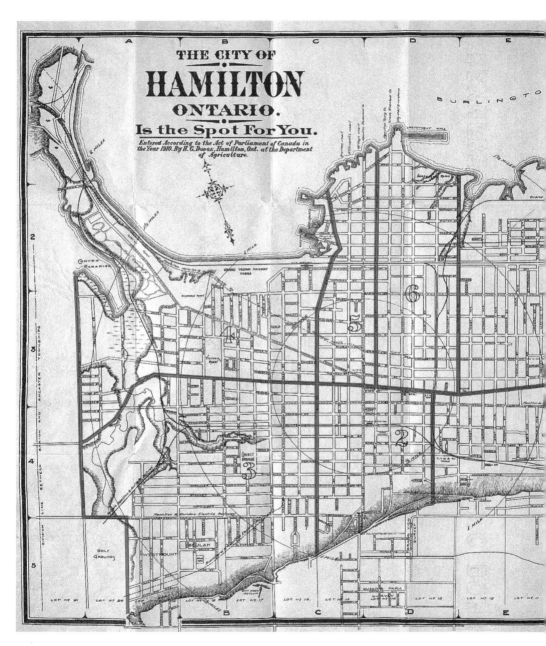

City of Hamilton and Wards, 1910.

CHAPTER 1

The Journey Begins:
Slavery and Freedom at the Head of the Lake

On Wednesday March 21, 1793, Peter Martin, a free Black man employed by Colonel John Butler, entered the Council Chamber at Navy Hall in Newark, the temporary capital of Britain's new province of Upper Canada. His Excellency, Lieutenant-Governor John Graves Simcoe, and members of the Executive Council of Upper Canada were meeting. Present were Simcoe, Chief Justice William Osgoode, and Peter Russell, receiver-general of the province. The man who entered the chamber, Peter Martin, was a former slave of Colonel John Butler and a veteran of Butler's famous Rangers who had served so faithfully in the King's forces in the American Revolution.

Butler and Martin had originally come from New York State, but when the revolution broke out, Butler had sided with the British, and the enslaved Martin and his brother Richard, along with the rest of Butler's "property," were confiscated and sold at public auction. However, the brothers had managed to escape and they later enlisted with Butler, who in the meantime had raised a corps of provincial raiders popularly known as Butler's Rangers. If this seems strange, it was not. It represents the fluid situation in which many enslaved people found themselves during the revolutionary period, particularly after Sir Henry Clinton issued his 1779 proclamation, which promised to free any African slave who fled behind British lines during the war.[1] Untold thousands did just that. When the war ended, the Martin brothers were discharged from the army in 1783. They were given land grants in the Niagara area along with other soldiers and officers of the British contingent.[2]

Peter Martin informed the Executive Council who were present that a "violent outrage" had recently been committed against an enslaved Black woman named Chloe Cooley by her owner, William Vrooman. Martin testified that Cooley, who had been residing with Vrooman near Queenston, was bound and transported across the Niagara River and sold to someone in the United States against her will. William Grisley, a white inhabitant of "Messissague point," witnessed the entire incident and corroborated Martin's story, stating that it had taken three men — Vrooman, his brother, and another man named Venevry (*sic*) — to force Cooley into the boat. He added that once on the American side, "she screamed violently, and made resistance, but was tied [with a rope] ..." and delivered to a man standing on the bank of the river. Grisley added that he had seen another Black man tied up in a similar fashion and had heard other slave owners in the area say that they too planned to sell their slaves in the United States. The Council resolved that Attorney General John White prosecute Vrooman for this "violent breach of the public peace."[3]

In actuality, Simcoe had no grounds on which to prosecute Vrooman because, as a slave owner, the latter was perfectly within his rights to sell Cooley to whomever he wished. Simcoe immediately moved to limit slavery in the new province of Upper Canada. Although Simcoe believed in the abolition of slavery and had wanted to abolish it outright, many in his government did not. At least six members of the Legislative Assembly owned slaves, as did various officials in Simcoe's administration and his Executive Council. This included Peter Russell, who was present when Peter Martin made the initial report against Vrooman.[4]

The seizure and sale of Chloe Cooley, her resistance, and Peter Martin's act to inform the Executive Council changed the course of history in Upper Canada. These events would have an impact on the institution of slavery, particularly its duration, across the new province, including at the Head of the Lake, Hamilton's future home. Most slaves in Upper Canada lived in the Detroit-Windsor area, the Niagara peninsula, the settlements around Kingston, and eastward along the St. Lawrence River. Of course, slavery was first practised by the French regime beginning in the 1500s, and the first people to be enslaved on Canadian territory

The Honourable Peter Russell, president and administrator of Upper Canada, 1796–99, shown in a black and white image of a painting by George Theodore Berthon, circa 1882.

were the aboriginal people, commonly known as *Panis*. The earliest record of Africans being introduced into Quebec was that of a young boy from Madagascar, later christened Olivier Le Jeune, who was sold to a Quebec clerk in 1628.[5] By the early 1700s, there were hundreds, if not thousands, of enslaved Africans in New France, an area that covered much of what is today Ontario and Quebec. French-Canadian historian Marcel Trudel counted 4,092 enslaved people — 2,692 aboriginal and 1,400 African slaves — in his more recent study of slavery in New France. This represented the total number of enslaved people over the entire course of New France's history.[6] When the British took over jurisdiction of France's territory in 1760 after the battle on the Plains of Abraham at Quebec City, slavery was given legal status in the Treaty of Paris. Slaves continued to be bought and sold along with other items at their owners' will. Moreover, slavery came more and more to be identified with a single race — the Africans.

The only area that seems to have kept reliable statistics on slavery was Detroit, which remained part of Upper Canada until 1796. However, the numbers of aboriginal versus African slaves represented by these statistics is not known. The authorities enumerated 33 slaves in 1750, 83 in 1773, 138 in 1779, and 179 in 1782. Included were those located on the south shore of the Detroit River where Windsor is now living.[7] Trudel counted 528 aboriginal and 128 African slaves at Detroit over time, but we have no specific dates associated with his numbers.[8] In Niagara, three censuses were conducted between 1782 and 1783, indicating that the numbers of slaves rose from one to ten in the space of one year.[9] They were most likely all Black. In the Kingston area, a census for the new townships along the St. Lawrence River indicated ninety slaves among the disbanded troops and Loyalists there.[10] These slaves were most likely all African as they were brought in by Loyalists from the American colonies, and slavery there had long since become associated with the African race.

In 1793, Lieutenant-Governor Simcoe moved the capital of Upper Canada from Newark — what is today Niagara-on-the-Lake — to York, on the northern shores of Lake Ontario. The new capital would later be renamed Toronto. With the removal of the government, officials and settlers relocated, moving their household goods and slaves with them. This included Peter Russell and William Jarvis, the first provincial secretary of Upper Canada. Both families were slaveholders.

A "List of Inhabitants" of York, and including the townships of Scarborough and Etobicoke, provides a count of those who were Black, but does not distinguish between slaves and free people. However, based on what is known about the Jarvis and Russell slaves, those Blacks can be counted as part of the enslaved population. In 1799, there were twenty-five people of African descent in York, ten known to be the slaves of Russell and Jarvis. In 1800, there were seventeen Blacks, eleven of whom were Russell's and Jarvis's slaves. In 1801, there were seventeen Blacks, five belonging to Russell or Jarvis, and, in 1802, there were eighteen Blacks at York, six of whom were enslaved in the households of Russell and Jarvis.[11] Beginning in 1801, Blacks in York were listed separately at the end of the list, but by 1804 there was no indication of the race of

York inhabitants. It wasn't until decades later that some Black residents of Toronto were again identified as such in the city directory, with the term "col'd" or "coloured" printed in brackets beside their names.

Most Blacks who first entered the province that became Upper Canada did so during and after the American Revolution. The Imperial Act of 1790, passed by Britain to encourage immigration to her colonies in North America, Bermuda, and the Bahamas, permitted the importation of "Negroes, household furniture, utensils of husbandry or cloathing."[12] Free Blacks were not encouraged. Although some, like Peter and Richard Martin, had fought in British regiments and had obtained their freedom for doing so, the majority of Africans entering the province were slaves. Some of the enslaved came in with drovers, who also brought in horses, cattle, and sheep for the purchase of the troops and the settlers. Colonel Clarke of the 2nd Lincoln Militia recalled that his father was one of a number of people who purchased slaves — three males and one female — from one of these drovers.[13] But as was the case in the Niagara region, York (Toronto), and the settlements along the St. Lawrence River, slavery at the Head of the Lake came into being with the advent of the Loyalists.

The Loyalists consisted primarily of European-American settlers who wished to remain loyal subjects to the British Crown. They left en masse to settle in British North America and other British colonies. The United Empire Loyalists, as they were named, packed up as many of their possessions as they could muster, and made the arduous trek across land, lake, and river to the border and across into Canada. Along with the furniture, livestock, clothing, and other belongings came human property in the form of slaves.

One of these Loyalist families that headed north was the William and Hannah Davis family of North Carolina. They had heard that the new lieutenant-governor of Upper Canada was none other than John Graves Simcoe, whom they had befriended during the British occupation of Yorktown, Virginia. Simcoe, a British officer, had commanded the New York regiment called the Queen's Rangers light infantry unit. In 1792, therefore, they loaded up a covered wagon with carpets, a grandfather clock, and other fine pieces of furniture, and began the nearly eight-hundred-mile journey with twenty horses, their eight children, and "several faithful slaves."[14] They first settled at Chippewa, above Niagara Falls, on the Niagara River. However, the following year, Hannah Davis fell ill with fever and died. Devastated, William Davis moved his family to a drier part of the country, and, on the brow of the Niagara Escarpment now known as Hamilton Mountain, they established a home overlooking one of the most picturesque vistas in the province. The family was given a generous grant of eight hundred acres to compensate them for the loss of their southern plantation during the Revolution. Today, part of this land grant comprises a good portion of the City of Hamilton, including the Glendale Golf Course.[15]

Unfortunately, little is known about the slaves who made the journey with the Davis family. We don't know their names, genders, nor exactly how many made the journey north. We also do not know why they remained with the Davises. However, of the first two log structures that were built on the land, one was inhabited by these enslaved individuals. Much of the work involved in clearing the land, building houses, planting and growing crops, and making sure that everyone was fed and clothed for the harsh winters would have been performed by the slaves. A new home, which was named "Harmony Hill Manor," was soon built to replace the Davis's original log cabin. It was a more palatial residence with colonial pillars and a second-floor ballroom, and its similarity to a Southern colonial mansion suggests the possibility that African slaves were the builders. In addition, the Davis family built a sawmill and gristmill on their property to serve not only themselves, but the surrounding farm community "although," as a descendant of the Davis family noted, "they were neither millwrights nor carpenters ..."[16] The slaves could well have been involved in the building and operation of these enterprises. Fifty years later, former slave and Black leader Josiah Henson and other abolitionists established the manual labour school called the British American Institute at Dawn, where Dresden, Ontario, is today. In that instance, a Black millwright from South Carolina designed and built the sawmill.[17] Therefore, it is quite conceivable that the bondsmen and women on the Davis establishment were not only heavily involved in the construction of the operations, but also in their actual design as well, given that African slaves often were the master builders of these early industries.

Unlike the Davis slaves, the names and ages of two of another early Niagara-area resident, Adam Crysler, were recorded for posterity. Adam Crysler served first as a lieutenant in Butler's Rangers and then joined Captain Brant's Indian Company under Colonel Guy Johnson. Because the Cryslers remained loyal to Britain, they were forced to make a hasty departure from their home in Schoharie, New York. The family settled near St. David's, Niagara Township, in 1784, when it was a vast area of forest. Adam Crysler purchased at least two slaves after he and his wife Ann Mary and their children arrived in the province. "A Negro Wench named Sarah about nine Years old" he purchased for £40 New York Currency, and later added "a Negroe man named Tom aged about Thirty Years" to his inventory for £90 New York Currency.[18]

When they first arrived, the Crysler family was living at Fort Niagara, which was actually located on the American side before the terms of the Treaty of Paris obliged them to move to the other side of the river. However, in 1784, the Cryslers settled on the land grant provided as compensation by a grateful British government, a grant that ended up being a two-thousand-acre allotment. They built a rudimentary log house on the west bank of the Four Mile Creek, just west of present-day Niagara-on-the-Lake, there being no sawmill nearby to cut boards. Compared to their comfortable home in Albany County, New York, their life in this wilderness was a crude existence indeed. Adam Crysler and his slaves and hired help had to cut down and burn trees to clear the land for farming. They had to build not only the main house, but also cabins for the slaves and extra hands, as well as a pigpen and stable for the animals. It took several years before the land began to yield sufficient crops for market. In the meantime, these hearty pioneers, both slave and free, survived on flour, and other necessities supplied by the British administration, not to mention the plentiful supply of fish from the lake and river, and game such as bear, partridge, duck, and other wildfowl.[19]

It is not known how many slaves the family ultimately possessed. What is intriguing is that Cryslers of African descent pop up in Wentworth County archival records decades later. It was common, although not exclusively the rule, that the enslaved took the names of their owners. Two Cryslers (spelled Crisler), Robert and Thomas, enlisted as privates in the Coloured Corps that served in the Niagara region during the War of 1812.[20] This unit helped to keep Upper Canada in British hands and valiantly fought in some key battles, including the Battle of Queenston Heights, Stoney Creek, and Fort George. These soldiers would no longer have been enslaved, but rather were free individuals, and were very likely related to one another.

Canadian-born Black Cryslers were living in Wentworth County in the 1850s and 1860s. According to the 1851 census, for example, a Thomas Chrysler (spelled with an "h") was a twenty-five-year-old servant working in an inn in the Township of Ancaster, situated on the south side of the Stone Road. Another Black servant working at the inn, Julian Frazier, was born in the United States, but Chrysler's place of birth was recorded as Canada West. Both stated that they professed to have no religious creed whatsoever.[21] In 1861, a family of Black Cryslers was living in the Township of Flamborough East. James Crysler, his wife Sarah and their two girls, Emily and Hannah, were living in Concession 1, Lot 2.[22] James was a forty-four-year-old labourer and his wife, Sarah, was twenty-three years old. Their girls were three-year-old twins. The family professed their religious affiliation as Church of England. An additional descriptor beside each name was "m" for "mulatto," a Portugese word meaning "of mixed blood." Could these Cryslers be the children and grandchildren of the original slaves bought by Adam Crysler? Particularly compelling is the fact that James Crysler, as well as his wife and children, originated in "Upper Canada," meaning that James was born in the province around 1817. That James was a "mulatto," or of mixed race, also raises the possibility that he could be the blood offspring of one of the white Cryslers. A cruel aspect of female slavery, as compared with that for males, was sexual exploitation inherent in the master–female slave relationship whereby the slavemaster could force himself on a slave woman and thereby avail himself of a sexual "partner" at any time. The female bondswoman had little recourse to rebuff his advances. Slave inventory could thereby be augmented with no additional outlays of cash.[23] It was a perfect set-up for the slaveowner, and one way to resolve the severe shortage of labour prior to Simcoe's 1793 legislation banning any further importation of slaves into the province.

Adam Crysler left no will, and so his property, including his slaves, was inherited by his eldest son, John. Interestingly, John Crysler received a receipt from Tom Blackman suggesting that the slave Tom, purchased by his father in 1792, was given his freedom in 1800.

> Received May the 3rd 1800
> From Mr. John Crysler My former Master Twenty-five Dollars in Cash and a new suit of clothes and every other demand agreeable to my instructions.
> As witness my Hand this Day above written.
>
> his
> Witness present   Tom x Blackman
> David Secord   mark[24]

This document has the appearance of an agreement between an apprentice and his master, more so than a slave, which begs the question: was this Tom, the slave, or someone else? If it was the slave Tom, the 1793 Act which Simcoe passed to gradually eliminate slavery in Upper Canada had a section (v), which stipulated that if a slave owner manumitted a slave, he or she was obligated to provide indemnity or money to the church or town warden should this person became a public charge. Nancy Butler and Michael Power, local historians who wrote a well-researched monograph on early Black history in the region entitled *Slavery and Freedom in Niagara*, suggest that this clause would have effectively discouraged manumission for many slave owners.[25] Could Tom Blackman have struck a deal with Crysler and the town officials to obtain his freedom, which included the clause requiring that an outlay of cash and a new suit of clothes be given directly to him? We will probably never know.

There are many mysteries surrounding the Crysler name. For instance, who were the African-Canadian Cryslers recorded in the census? Were they descendants of Tom Blackman, but now using the Crysler name, or perhaps the descendants of nine-year-old Sarah, purchased in 1786? Could they also have been blood descendants of one of the white Crysler men? There are so few known descendants of Canadian slaves on record that these are intriguing questions to contemplate.

As elsewhere in Canada, and due to the shorter growing season requiring no need for the huge agricultural workforces of other slave-holding nations, many bondsmen and women were household servants. The Richard Beasley family owned several slaves. Richard Beasley is credited with being one of the first, if not the first, white settlers at the Head of the Lake. Prior to this, an aboriginal people known as the Attiwandaronks, numbering about forty thousand, lived in the territory which included the Niagara Peninsula in the early 1600s. The French called them the Neutrals because they remained neutral between the Iroquois (or Five Nations) of south of Lake Ontario and the Hurons who lived along Georgian Bay. They were agriculturalists, and their lands abounded with corn, squash, beans, and other vegetables, and their forests and rivers were full of game and fish. They were described as fine physical specimens and great warriors and hunters. However, this population virtually disappeared, in part because of a smallpox epidemic of 1638–40, and also because of a war that took place between the Iroquois and the Hurons. After the Iroquois destroyed the Hurons, they turned on the Attiwandaronks. The Iroquois had acquired firearms from the Europeans, and the bows and arrows and clubs of the Attiwandaronks were no match for this superior weaponry. By the 1700s, the Mississaugas of the Ojibway Nation had moved on to the lands around Lake Ontario.[26]

Richard Beasley, a Loyalist from Albany, New York, arrived in the province in 1777 at the age of sixteen. He began working as an assistant commissary for the British forces at Fort Niagara. In the early 1780s, he went into partnership with Peter Smyth of Kingston, and the two men set up a trading post in the interior. Beasley received a land grant of two hundred acres in 1791 near today's intersection of Paradise Road and Main Street West in Hamilton. With James Wilson, he established a gristmill and sawmill on a stream that flowed down from the Ancaster Hills into Coote's Paradise, the natural wetland at the west end of Burlington Bay (now called Hamilton Harbour). Beasley then set about importing settlers' supplies, forwarding flour and other agricultural produce to Montreal, and speculating in land. Eventually, he acquired thousands of acres of choice government terrain, including a property in Burlington Heights at the west end of Burlington Bay, where he built a substantial home. It is this house whose front and foundation were later incorporated into the famous historical landmark of Dundurn Castle. Beasley also served in the Legislative Assembly of Upper Canada from 1791 to 1804 and was elected speaker of the assembly in 1803. He was appointed justice of the peace in 1795, magistrate in 1796, and advanced to colonel of the York Militia.[27]

Beasley's dealings have been well-documented in the annals of Hamilton history. However, the fact that he and his family of nine children owned slaves is not usually mentioned. According to family lore, when Britain abolished slavery, the Beasley slaves "were generously provided for and given a start in life." However, one man, named Wilson, "while glad to own his own body, would not leave Beasley."[28] Newspaper columnist Richard Butler later wrote in *Saturday Musings*, a series of weekly articles in the *Hamilton Spectator* dealing with the early history of Hamilton, that a slave named Jackson was a house servant in the family of Colonel Henry Beasley, son of Richard Beasley. In this version, Jackson was nurse and guardian to members of the Beasley family, including Thomas C. Beasley, who later became well-known as a lawyer and Hamilton city clerk, and his son A.C. Beasley. In his old age, the white-haired Jackson lived in a frame cottage near the Delta, an area in central-east Hamilton. There he raised vegetables, chickens, and some fruit. Jackson died in 1868 at the approximate age of one hundred years old.[29] It is unclear whether Wilson and Jackson were one and the same man, because both were described as having remained in the service of the Beasley family long after slavery was abolished.

Another enslaved person came to the Head of the Lake with James Durand in 1805. James Durand emigrated with his wife from England at the turn of the nineteenth century and settled in the County of Norfolk, Upper Canada. In 1805, the couple bought a one-hundred-acre farm at the Head of the Lake that extended from what is today the top of the Mountain to King Street, and from James Street on the west to Wellington Street on the east. In his 1897 memoir, *Reminiscences*,[30] Charles Durand, the son of James Durand, told the story that one day his father, his father's wife, and their baby were descending the Mountain when tragedy struck. The baby, who was one year old, was in the care of an enslaved woman on horseback. Peter Desjardins, a clerk in his store who would later build the Desjardins Canal between Coote's Paradise and the town of Dundas, was also descending the Mountain on horseback with the family. Mr. and Mrs. Durand were in a "curricle," or two-wheeled carriage drawn by two horses. There was an accident and Mrs. Durand was thrown out of the vehicle and onto the rocks, dying not long thereafter. The enslaved woman, whose name has been lost to history, became nurse to the children of James Durand's second marriage.[31]

There is also evidence of a few enslaved persons being brought into the Hamilton district of Upper Canada illegally. John Thomas, of what today is known as Brantford, was a Loyalist persuaded by Joseph Brant to come to Canada and settle on part of the land grant given to the Six Nations. John Thomas and his wife Eleanor, his father-in-law, John Smith Sr. and Smith's five other children, all journeyed to the Grand River and settled there with the Mohawks. In 1809, Thomas took a trip to Tennessee and brought back two slaves, a husband and wife, who lived in a log house

at Cainsville.[32] Unfortunately, again, the names of this husband and wife couple were not recorded for posterity by the Thomas family.

Slavery was practised not only by European American Loyalists and immigrants from the British Isles, but also by the First Nations. Joseph Brant or Thayendanegea, the Mohawk leader of the Six Nations at Brantford, was said to possess many slaves. Brant was originally from Ohio, but had relocated to the Mohawk Valley of New York State with his family. He had fought as a British ally in the Indian and Revolutionary

Thayendanagea, also known as Joseph Brant, leader of the Six Nations.

Wars, and had taken Black slaves as prisoners. Upon the close of the American Revolution, Sir Frederick Haldimand, governor of Quebec (which included Ontario at the time), granted Brant a huge tract of land along the Grand River, and it was here that he and part of the Six Nations clans transplanted their homes. Estimates of the number of slaves owned by Brant vary from twenty to forty.[33]

When a Scottish traveller named Patrick Campbell journeyed through Canada and the United States in 1791–92, he stopped at the home of Joseph Brant and described in great detail the Native leader, his family, and living conditions, all of which greatly impressed him. He noted that Brant received him with great politeness and hospitality, and served up sumptuous meals, accompanied by fine wines, brandies, and rums. He also regaled his guests with scintillating conversation and entertainment. On the second day, when Campbell's party returned to Brant's home:

> Dinner was just going on the table in the same elegant
> stile (*sic*) as the preceding night, … the servants dressed
> in their best apparel. Two slaves attended the table, the
> one in scarlet, the other in coloured clothes, with silver
> buckles in their shoes, and ruffles, and every other part
> of their apparel in proportion.[34]

When Mrs. Brant appeared dressed in elegant Native attire, Campbell was mesmerized by her striking beauty. In fact, she was so beautiful, according to Campbell, that she put the two European ladies who were visiting to shame. Campbell went on to report that: "Her person about five feet nine or ten inches high, as streight (*sic*) and proportionable as can be, but inclined to be jolly or lusty. She understands, but does not speak English. I have often addressed her in that language, but she always answered in the Indian tongue."[35]

Sophia Burthen Pooley, one of Brant's female slaves, gave a very different account of Catherine Brant. Interviewed by Quaker abolitionist Benjamin Drew in 1854–55, she has provided our only first person narrative of slavery in Upper Canada.[36] Sophia Pooley reported that she was born in Fishkill, New York, of slave parents, Oliver and Dinah Burthen. An old woman by the time Drew interviewed her, her date of birth was probably about 1771–72. One day, at the age of seven, Sophia and her sister were playing among the currant bushes when her master's sons-in-law, Daniel Outwaters and Simon Knox, grabbed them and tied handkerchiefs over their mouths. They carried the girls down to a boat, placed them in the hold and sailed up the river. The two girls were sold at Niagara to Joseph Brant.[37]

Pooley was probably brought to Upper Canada in 1779, after Brant bought a farm on the Niagara River. Pooley reasoned that she must have lived with Brant about twelve or thirteen years. She described in detail some of her duties in the household.

> While I lived with old Brant we caught the deer. It was at Dundas at the outlet. We would let the hounds loose, and when we heard them bark we would run for the canoe — Peggy and Mary, and Katy, Brant's daughters and I. Brant's sons, Joseph and Jacob, would wait on the shore to kill the deer when we fetched him in. I had a tomahawk, and would hit the deer on the head — then the squaws would take it by the horns and paddle ashore. The boys would bleed and skin the deer and take the meat to the house.[38]

Pooley expressed a great deal of admiration for Brant, describing him as a peacemaker and statesman. However, this feeling did not extend to Brant's wife, Catherine:

> Brant's third wife, my mistress, was a barbarous creature. She could talk English, but she would not. She would tell me in Indian to do things, and then hit me with any thing that came to hand, because I did not understand her. I have a scar on my head from a wound she gave me with a hatchet; and this long scar over my eye, is where she cut me with a knife … Brant was very angry, when

he came home, at what she had done, and punished her as if she had been a child. Said he, "you know I adopted her as one of the family, and now you are trying to put all the work on her."[39]

Eventually, Pooley learned to speak Mohawk. As she told Drew, at one point she could speak it better than English. She also stated that she came to like living among the Native people. Brant himself believed that given the choice of being enslaved by Native people or whites, his slaves would prefer to remain with him. He once told Jeromus Johnson, a New York merchant and later United States Congressman who visited him on the Grand River in 1797, that his bondsmen "… appeared to be happy, and entirely willing to live with him … [and were] pleased with the Indian habits and customs …"[40]

Of Brant's other slaves, Pooley remembered:

> Brant had two colored men for slaves: one of them was the father of John Patten, who lives over yonder [referring to her current residence in the Queen's Bush] the other called himself Simon Ganseville. There was but one other Indian that I knew, who owned a slave.[41]

Thankfully, Pooley put names and faces to people whom others described simply as "slaves" or "servants." In many of these accounts of slavery, the enslaved are treated as faceless and nameless persons, identified only by their colour and condition. It took a fellow former bondsperson to remind us that the enslaved were human beings with personal histories and families, with first and last names, hopes and dreams for their future and that of their children.

When she was in her late twenties or thirties,[42] Pooley was sold to an Englishman named Samuel Hatt of Ancaster for $100. Hatt had immigrated to Upper Canada from England in the 1790s and established a considerable business enterprise with his brother Richard. In fact, the Hatt brothers are considered to be the founders of Dundas, because they cleared a road from Ancaster to the town now known as Dundas in order to gain more customers for their business. The family had been granted 1,200 acres, and when they emigrated from England, they brought six indentured servants with them, each of whom also received two hundred acres. Hatt's brother, Richard, was granted an additional four hundred acres on top of this.[43] The Hatts' establishment included a huge farm and extensive livestock, two gristmills, a sawmill, store, blacksmith shop, cooper's shop, distillery, and numerous houses.[44] There would have been a tremendous amount and variety of work for Sophia to do. In addition to cooking, cleaning, washing and ironing clothes, and looking after children, she may also have made soap, candles, and other needed household items, tended to the farm animals, worked in the fields, ran countless errands, and helped out in the stores.

It was unlikely, therefore, that Pooley was Hatt's only slave. A deposition sworn by innkeeper and merchant George Rousseau in 1821 claimed that in the summer of 1812, "Samuel Hatts (sic) Servants or Coopers did cut take and carry away a quantity of oak timbers for Staves" from his father's property, for which Hatt had agreed to pay the elder Rousseau £8.[45] As we have seen, the term "servant" was often used as a euphemism for "slave." If the individuals who removed the timber from Rousseau's property were servants, they may have been African slaves.[46]

Sophia Pooley lived with Hatt for a number of years,[47] during which time, she stated, slavery was abolished, "Then the white people said I was free, and put me up to running away. [Hatt] did not stop me — he said he could not take the law into his own hands. Then I lived in what is now Waterloo."[48]

Sophia Burthen married Robert Pooley, but he left her for a white woman. Sophia endured nonetheless, and lived through the War of 1812, the emancipation of the slaves throughout the British Empire, the 1837 Rebellion, the coming of a new wave of Black immigrants during the Underground Railroad years, and many other events of her life and times. She completed her interview by stating that she was entirely dependent on her neighbours for her subsistence, and that there were many good people in the Queen's Bush who helped her.

Apart from Sophia Pooley's first-person account of her days in slavery at the Head of the Lake, much of the knowledge we have of slavery in the Hamilton area has been anecdotal. In the recordings, by their descendants, of the first Loyalist families who settled in the area, some of these stories of slave ownership have come to light, but very little information about the enslaved people themselves — who they were, their names, ages, duties, personal histories, or skills — has been retained for posterity. Furthermore, very few documents seem to have survived in the archives of actual enslaved individuals being left in wills, being bought or sold, and so forth. There are frustrating gaps in the records. For instance, Richard Butler, in his article of 1916 about slavery in Hamilton, mentioned that he knew of a box of legal papers that contained the sales and transfers of slaves in the area then known as the Head of the Lake.[49] The box, he added, had been taken to Toronto by the owner many years prior to his writing the article. Unfortunately, he did not identify the owner or say what became of the box. What additional information about slave owning and the enslaved might come to light in the Hamilton area is anybody's guess.

Nevertheless, the following surviving document hints at the extent of slave ownership at one time or another by the prominent business people and families of the Hamilton area. James Crooks, owner of W. & J. Crooks in the Niagara District, advertised for the following in the *Upper Canada Gazette*, October 11, 1797:

> Wanted to purchase,
>   A NEGRO GIRL, from 7 to 12 years of Age, of good disposition. — For further particulars Apply to the Subscribers.
> W. & J. CROOKS
> West Niagara

Crooks who emigrated from Scotland in 1791, later purchased four hundred acres in West Flamborough Township at the Head of the Lake in 1811, and established a substantial business operation there. It included a gristmill, sawmill, paper mill, carding mill, general store, cooperage, and blacksmith's shop along the Spencer River near what is today Greensville. In 1818, Crooks acquired a lot in Coote's Paradise

The Honourable James Crooks (1778–1860) who won election to the Legislative Assembly of Upper Canada in 1820 and was appointed to the Legislative Council in 1831, advertised for the purchase of a "Negro girl" between the ages of seven and twelve in 1797.

on Burlington Bay, and his growing industrial interests led him to gain a seat in the House of Assembly in 1820. Three years later, he sponsored a bill authorizing the construction of the Burlington Bay Canal, and became its commissioner.[50]

Slavery was just another fact of life for the people who settled at the Head of the Lake in the latter days of the 1700s and early 1800s. A significant number, it seems, either owned slaves themselves, or knew people who did. Robert Hamilton, the father of George Hamilton, from whom the city by the bay earned its name, was a wealthy merchant from Queenston (Niagara) and a slave owner.[51] George Hamilton's wife, Maria Lavinia Jarvis, also came from a prominent slave-owning family. As has been noted, her father, William Jarvis, was the provincial secretary and a well-documented owner of numerous slaves.

Despite the fact that there is little information about slavery in Hamilton, the portrait painted by the slave owners and their descendants — either that the slaves were happy, willing servants only too ready to do the bidding of their masters, or that they were hapless victims who needed their slave-masters to survive — was a very paternalistic and one-sided perspective indeed. Moreover, it was far from the reality. Studies show that slaves acted as independent agents and practised varying levels of resistance in their everyday lives.[52] Newspaper advertisements requesting the return of slaves to their owners were commonplace. The case of

Marie-Joseph Angélique, probably the most spectacular example of slave resistance on record in Canada, took place in Montreal. She was a slave woman from Portugal who was accused, tried, and hanged for burning down her mistress's home. The fire, which took place in 1734, caused forty-six other buildings to be lost. Afua Cooper's masterful work of historical resurrection of the life of this woman, in *The Hanging of Angélique: The Untold Story of Canadian Slavery and the Burning of Old Montreal*, has exposed her story to a wider audience.[53] Whether Angélique indeed set the fire is a question that historians are still debating, but based on the court transcripts, Angélique was a very headstrong woman who threatened people and who ran away at least twice.

In another case, Reverend John Stuart, minister of St. George's Anglican Church of Kingston, expressed shock and disbelief in a letter to his son James that his "Negro Boy" had run away. However, the young man's determination to escape his bondage and remain in freedom was quite evident, even though his hand and foot had been frozen in the process:

> Kingston, March 6, 1802
> Dear James,
> A Domestic occurrence has deranged us very much. On 22 of last month, the coldest day experienced here for several years, my Negro Boy, without any pretended reason whatever, ran away. He went on skates by the way of Carleton Island. — On the 3rd I heard that he was at a house about 30 miles distant, with a hand and foot frozen. I dispatched a person to bring him back — the people where he was, told my messenger, that they would neither prevent nor assist him in bringing the negro back. Upon this, he returned here and took a horse and slay (*sic*), as the fellow could not walk. But a few of the bandits of the place collected, and said that if the Negro would not go voluntarily back, they would not allow him to be compelled. Of course, he said he was not willing and the man returned without him. And what

mortifies me more than the loss, I hear that the fellow is at work publicly with the republican [American] Rascal who keeps the Ferry in sight of Carleton Island. I have advertised and written to a magistrate on the Black River [New York] on this subject, but I have very little expectation that I shall ever recover the fellow — these democratic villains are not contented with ruining me once.[54]

Exactly one year later, Stuart wrote another letter to James expressing regret at the loss of his "Negro Boy." It is unclear whether the young man had returned and then run away again, or whether Stuart was referring to the previous year's escape. One thing is certain — that he had made more than one escape attempt.

Perhaps the most interesting letter about an Upper Canadian fugitive slave was written from the perspective of the slave himself to his former owner, William Jarvis, on May 3, 1798. The author, Henry Lewis, offered to purchase himself:

Schenectady May 3, 1798
Sir
My desire to support my self as free man and enjoy all the benefits which may result from my being free in a country whear a Blackman is defended by the laws as much as a white man is induces me to make you an offer of purchasing myself. I am a black man and am not so able to pay you all the money down which you may ask for me but upon these conditions I will purchase myself ten pounds this year and every year after sixteen pounds untill the whole sum is payed. I should wish to pay the money to Joseph Yates the man of this sitty becaus he is the most proper man that I can think of at presant ...[55]

One might ask why, if Lewis had successfully escaped, would he contact Jarvis with his whereabouts and offer to purchase his freedom. Perhaps Lewis was seeking peace of mind, something that would elude him if Jarvis were attempting to track him down. In any case, in the letter Lewis also tried to enlighten his former master about the reasons why he fled his domain:

> The reason why I left your house is this your woman vexed me to so high a degree that it was far beyond the power of man to support it it is true and I will say in all company that I allways lived as well in your house as I should wish.
>
> Pleas to write to Joseph Yates what you will take in cash for me and let him be the man to whom I shall pay the money yearly …[56]

So as not to come across as too haughty and demanding, Lewis added a touch of the obsequious:

> In a supplicant manner I beg your parden ten thousand times and beg that you would be so kind as to permit me to purchase myself and at as a low a rate as any other person. My mistress I also wish long life and good health and pleas to tell her I beg her parden ten thousand times my mistress I shall always remember on account of her great kindness to me
> I remain your affectionate servant
> Henry Lewis[57]

Slaves resisted in other ways as well. One slave, Jack, took his master, John Croisdale, to court in 1793 at the Quarter Sessions held at Adolphustown. Croisdale was ordered to "keep the peace and in particular to Jack his Negro Boy." In 1794, Jack again charged Croisdale with assault and battery. Croisdale was found not guilty by the jury.[58]

Joseph Gutches was another slave who took his owner, Richard Cartwright of Kingston, to court. Cartwright was the former business partner of Robert Hamilton of Niagara and an important member of Simcoe's Executive Council. Gutches was attempting to prove that he was being held illegally as a slave. In the minutes of the Civil Board on August 12, 1787, Joseph claimed that "he was taken by the Indians and sold for a slave for life, but that he was at the time of his capture bound only to serve until twenty-one years of age. Cartwright's reply to the Board on August 16, 1787, asserted that Joseph had always been a slave:

> The original Proprietor of him was one Jonas Vrooman of Schohary, in the State of New York. — In an Incursion of the Indians during the late War, this man was killed, and the Negroe brought to Niagara, he was there sold to a Mr. Dunn at that time belonging to the Indian Department, by him resold to a Mr. Allen, and from Mr. Allen I purchased him for an hundred and twenty five pounds New York currency —
>
> I have every reason to believe that he was always legally a slave, from the testimony of people who knew him when in the possession of Vrooman some of whom are still at Niagara ...[59]

Cartwright prevailed, illustrating once again the difficulties the enslaved encountered in going up against a slave owner in court.

Peter Russell's family of slaves included Peggy, her husband Pompadour, a free Black who worked for the family for wages, and the slave children, Amy, Milly, and Jupiter. The following letter written by Russell to Matthew Elliott reveals his utter exasperation with Peggy as he tries to sell her off.

> York, Septr 19, 1801
> My Slave Peggy, whom you were so good to promise to assist in getting rid of, has remained in Prison ever since you left this (in expectation of your sending for her) at an Expence of above Ten pounds Halifax, which I was obliged to pay to the Gaoler — and release her last Week by order of the Chief Justice. She is now at large, being not permitted by my Sister to enter this House,

and shows a disposition at Times to be very trouble-
some, which may perhaps compel me to commit her
again to Prison. I shall therefore be glad that you would
either take her away immediately, or return to me the
Bill of Sale I gave you to enable you to do so. For tho I
have received no money from you for her, my property
in her is gone from me while you hold the Bill of Sale;
and I cannot consequently give a valid Title to any other
who may be inclined to take her off my hands. I beg to
hear from you soon ...[60]

It appears that Elliott himself was planning to sell Peggy to none
other than Joseph Brant, but the deal fell through. Thus Peggy remained
with the Russell family.[61]

Peggy and her family represented major nuisances for the Russells. In
her diary, Elizabeth Russell, Peter's sister, described Peggy, Pompadour,
and Milly as dirty, idle, and insolent. She also portrayed Amy and Milly
as addicted to pilfering and lying, owing, she felt, to the bad example of
their mother. In another entry, Pompadour was described as drunk and
impertinent, and Jupiter, who was sent to jail for threatening the life of
another family, was called a thief and everything that was bad.

This was classic dissembling behaviour, otherwise known in today's
parlance as "slave resistance," whereby slaves lied and invented schemes
or excuses to get their own way.[62] Unable to sell Peggy, Peter Russell
advertised on September 2, 1803, in the *Upper Canada Gazette*, warning
readers that "The subscriber's black servant Peggy not having his permission to absent herself from his service, the public are hereby cautioned
from employing or harbouring her without the owner's leave. Whoever
will do so after this notice may expect to be treated as the law directs."

Studies of female slavery reveal that truancy — another form of resistance — was actually common among slave women since it was far less
likely for bondswomen (as compared with bondsmen) to permanently
flee. For many enslaved women with children, flight was not an option.
Truancy represented a way of reconciling their desire to flee with their
need to remain with their families. For some women, as it would appear

Ran away from the subscriber a few
weeks ago,

A Negro Wench,

named SUE :—this is therefore to fore-
warn all manner of persons from harbor-
ing said wench under the penalties of
the laws.

JAMES CLARK, senior.

Niagara, August 17, 1795.

This ad first appeared in the Upper Canada Gazette *on August 19, 1795, and is one of numerous ads for the return of slave runaways or slaves for sale in Upper Canadian newspapers of the period.*

in the case of Peggy, truancy became a way of life, a way to disappear for a while, but never permanently.[63] Of course, the Russells didn't quite see things that way. They continued to try to unload their "problem" on other unsuspecting slave owners. In February 1806, an ad appeared in the *Upper Canada Gazette* for the sale of Peggy and her son Jupiter.

These cases of slave resistance were more than just nuisances for their owners. Slaves who ran away dealt a blow to slavery because it meant an economic loss to the slave-master in terms not only of the value of the slave, but also the value of his or her labour. Moreover, these slave owners had to spend time and money in an effort to track down their "property." Likewise, when slaves took their masters to court or otherwise caused them "trouble," it could be time-consuming and costly to deal with. The more resistance that slaves demonstrated, the less attractive a system it must have appeared to the slave-owning class.

The distinction between slave and free was often a very blurred line. Five years prior to the founding of the town site by George Hamilton in 1815, an orphaned Black boy named Eli Brackenridge was apprenticed to Elijah Secord until he reached the age of twenty-one years. The child was required to "faithfully serve in all such lawful business as the said

Eli Brackenridge shall be put unto by the command of his master, ... and honestly and obediently in all things shall behave himself towards his said master and honestly and orderly towards the rest of the family ..." For his part, Elijah Secord promised to "get and allow unto the said Apprentice meat, drink, washing, lodging and all other things needful ... for an Apprentice during the term aforesaid ..." When the term of apprenticeship expired, Secord was also bound to give the young man a complete new suit of clothing, including a "coat, waistsash (*sic*), overhauls, hat, shoes, stockings, with suitable linen ..." The indenture was signed January 25, 1810, by two wardens of the Township of Ancaster, and given consent by two justices of the peace on March 3, 1810.[64]

Apprenticeship, also known as pauper apprenticeship, was the principal way that orphaned and abandoned children were dealt with by the province in the first half of the nineteenth century. The apprenticeship took effect by written indenture, a legal document that was signed by the mother in cases where she could not support the child, or by the town warden, in the case of true orphans, as it perhaps was in Brackenridge's circumstances. It was in addition countersigned by two justices of the peace. This type of apprenticeship, derived from English Poor Law, was provided for by provincial legislation as early as 1799.[65]

Interestingly, another child orphan named Ann Thayer — a white female child — was apprenticed in 1803 to a farmer named Andrew Templeton of Ancaster Township. Ann Thayer was nine years of age at the time, and her apprenticeship was to last until she was eighteen. The age of eighteen or twenty-one was the usual point at which an apprenticeship ended. In addition, the indenture required that Templeton instruct the child in "the craft, mastery and occupation of cooking, sewing, spining (*sic*) and such other qualifications."[66] This was a typical requirement for girls because these activities would be important skills that a woman would need in the home, or if she worked in service for a middle- or upper-class household. However, the indenture also specified that Templeton "at some convenient time within the term aforesaid shall cause the said Ann Thayer to be taught to read and write."[67] These indentures always mandated that the apprentice be taught to read and write, and, by the late 1830s, to learn basic arithmetic. In fact, an indenture was nullified in 1789 in Kingston because it failed to provide for the education of the child.[68] So why had Eli Brackenridge been denied this right? Was it because town officials felt that a Black child would not need to know how to read and write? It would appear that there were different expectations placed on white children compared with Black children, and the terms of apprenticeship reflected this.

There is another twist in the apprenticeships of these two children. One of the justices of the peace who signed both indentures was none other than Samuel Hatt, who owned the slave woman, Sophia Burthen Pooley. Obviously, the existence of slavery and the slave-owning class had a tremendous impact on the fate and circumstance of all Blacks, whether they were enslaved or not. The fact that five-year-old Eli Brackenridge was denied his right to a basic education illustrates in stark terms the fundamental inequality of opportunity for Black children right from birth. This is echoed later in the century with the exclusion of Black children from the schools that white children attended. Notably, too, at the end of her apprenticeship, Ann Thayer was to be given "one complete new suit of apparel," as was Brackenridge, but also "one good feather bed and one good cow four or five years old ..."[69]

On July 9, 1793, Simcoe and his colonial government passed An Act to Prevent the Further Introduction of Slaves, and to Limit the Term of Contracts for Servitude in this Province. This compromise piece of legislation did not abolish slavery outright, but was passed to end the practice gradually over time. It meant that any enslaved person brought into the province would automatically be freed. However, enslaved men, women and children already living in the province, unless manumitted, would remain slaves for life. Children born after passage of the Act would remain in slavery until the age of twenty-five, and the children of these children would automatically be free at birth.[70]

In actuality, slavery and slave ownership continued to be an important part of the society and culture of Upper Canada among the members of the Family Compact — the ruling elite. In fact, five years after Simcoe's compromise legislation passed, a majority of members revisited the issue of importing slaves into the province. By this time, Simcoe had returned to England and the province was governed by Peter Russell, pending the appointment of a new lieutenant-governor by the Crown. On Saturday, June 16, 1798, "Mr. Robinson seconded by Mr. Jessup moved for leave to bring in on Monday next a Bill to enable persons migrating into this Province to bring their negro slaves into the same."[71] Christopher Robinson and Edward Jessup were former American Loyalists. Robinson, from Virginia, was the father of future chief justice, Sir John Beverly Robinson. The labour shortage in the new province of Upper Canada was critical. In fact, when Simcoe's Act to Prevent the Further Introduction of Slaves ... was being debated in 1793, those opposed argued that the cost to hire whites as labour-

Courtesy of Archives Ontario, Government of Ontario Art Collection Acc No. 694156.

Colonel John Graves Simcoe, lieutenant-governor of Upper Canada, 1791–1796, artist, George Theodore Berthon, circa 1881.

ers to perform the work and clear the land was very high. French noble-man François-Alexandre La Rochefoucault visited Simcoe at Navy Hall in 1795 while gathering information for his *Travels Through the United States of America* and made similar observations about the shortage of labour and the difficulty of retaining servants.

> The scarcity of men servants is here still greater than in the United States. They, who are brought hither from England, either demand lands, or emigrate into the United States. A very wise act of the Assembly declares all negroes to be free, as soon as they arrive in Canada. This description of men, who are more or less frequent in the United States, cannot here supply the want of white

servants. All persons belonging to the army employ soldiers in their stead. By the English regulations, every officer is allowed one soldier, to whom he pays one shilling a week; and this privilege is extended, in proportion as the officers have need for a greater number of people. The Governor [Simcoe] ... is attended in his house, and at a dinner, merely by privates of this [Queen's Rangers] regiment, who also take care of his horses. He has not been able to keep one of the men servants, he brought with him from England.[72]

The second reading of the proposed bill took place on Tuesday, June 19, 1798, moved by Robinson and seconded by none other than Richard Beasley, a slave owner and also a member of the Executive Council. A third reading took place the following day, June 20. Solicitor General Robert Isaac De Gray moved that the bill not pass third reading. A vote was taken and the assemblymen in favour were eight members, including Beasley. Those in opposition numbered four and included Solicitor General De Gray.

The bill went to the Legislative Council where it was given a first and second reading and then passed to a committee. Then something remarkable happened. The chairman of the committee was Robert Hamilton, slaveholder and father of George Hamilton, who later purchased much of the land that became the city of Hamilton. He and Richard Cartwright Jr. — first cousin of Richard Beasley and also a slave owner as already noted — effectively killed the legislation. Cartwright moved, and Hamilton seconded that the bill be read in three months' time. This was the three-month hoist, a legislative devise used to halt a piece of legislation. Interestingly, it is not known why these two men acted to abort the new bill. Butler and Power suggest that perhaps "Russell, in his capacity as administrator [Simcoe had left the province in 1796 due to ill health] felt that his career would have been ruined if the bill was passed into law, and consequently he appealed to the nobler instincts of Hamilton and Cartwright to conserve the 1793 act, which had meant so much to Simcoe."[73]

In 2007, a plaque to honour the role of Chloe Cooley and Lieutenant-Governor Simcoe's legislation limiting slavery in Upper Canada was erected in Niagara-on-the-Lake on the east side of the Niagara Parkway near Vrooman's Point.

Whatever the motivation, in the short term, the lives of those enslaved individuals of African descent did not alter substantially. Those who were enslaved in 1793 would remain so ostensibly for the remainder of their lives. Peter Martin, the man who played such a pivotal role in bringing the status of Chloe Cooley and other enslaved people to the attention of Simcoe, and who was therefore so instrumental in the subsequent passing of the landmark anti-slavery legislation, continued to pursue his own agenda. He petitioned the government for his deceased brother's land grant owed to him for his military service under the British. His reason was that he wished to purchase the freedom of his son George who, ironically, remained enslaved in the household of his own employer's son, Thomas Butler. Martin was lame and figured that the best way to raise the £60 required would be to sell his brother's land grant, if he could gain possession of it. On August 21, 1797, the administration recommended that "the Military Lands of Richard Martin a dec'd Soldier amounting to 300 Acres issue to Peter Martin his Sole Surviving next of Kin ..."[74] Martin must have been extremely gratified.

The end result of Martin's attempt to obtain his son's freedom is not known. However, George Martin was sooner or later freed, because he enlisted in the Coloured Corps and fought in the War of 1812, no doubt to the utter pride and joy of his father.[75] After the war, George Martin received a land grant in Mono Township, Dufferin County, roughly 180 miles northwest into the interior. He had no desire to move there from the Niagara area, and sold his grant in 1831 to another Niagara resident, David Thorburn.[76]

CHAPTER 2

Routes to Freedom

As has been shown, an enslaved population already existed in the earliest years of the development of Hamilton, when it was known as the Head of the Lake. Almost equidistant between Toronto and Niagara Falls, the Head of the Lake consisted of Hamilton proper, as well as associated towns and villages, the principal of which were Dundas, Ancaster, and Stoney Creek. The area was a nexus for trade, for Hamilton was blessed with a major deepwater port as well as a highly defensible position at the foot of the Niagara Escarpment — of which Hamilton's "Mountain" forms a part. Watered by several important streams flowing down the banks of the escarpment to the bay shore below, feeding mills and other industries that relied on water power, and with a rich agricultural hinterland of Niagara that possessed relatively mild climatic zones, Hamilton was geographically destined to play a very important role in the early growth of what is now Ontario.

Given such advantageous natural circumstances, settlers were drawn to the area in increasing numbers in the early decades of the nineteenth century. They encompassed not only the well-heeled elite of British society, but also merchants and farmers, immigrants from other European origins, Euro-American colonists, and people of African descent primarily from the United States.

Enslaved Africans in Upper Canada ultimately received their freedom after the passage of the Emancipation Proclamation decreed by the British Parliament in 1833, and which took effect on August 1, 1834. The fight against slavery in the British Empire by those who were enslaved and their allies in England and North America is a whole chapter in the anti-slavery annals. However, the immediate result of the 1833 Act, not to mention Simcoe's earlier 1793 bill, was a growing movement of African Americans seeking their personal liberty by escaping to British *terra firma* on Canadian soil. The vast majority of Blacks to arrive in Hamilton, therefore, came from the United States either as escaped slaves, or if they were already free, as freemen fleeing the severe handicaps often faced as African Americans in that country. In the latter case, Ohio Black Codes or laws were instituted in free states where the Black population was increasing in numbers and power due to the sheer volume of people escaping their servitude from nearby slave states. The codes were intended to curtail their mounting numbers and economic clout, and to restrict their movements and opportunities at every turn. Severe penalities could be exacted if the laws were violated.

Despite the common American origin of these émigrés, the circumstances under which Africans in Hamilton came were incredibly diverse. The stereotype of the illiterate slave fleeing a large southern plantation, running through the bushes with only the clothes on his or her back, and making it to Canada continues to be the prevailing view of how African Americans got here in the nineteenth century — and such images have been incredibly powerful in shaping notions of what these people were like, and what they brought to Hamilton in terms of skills, education, capital, and the like. Certainly, many Black people were ex-slaves, but often they were not coming directly from the slave plantations, but rather had been living in freedom in the northern United States for some time before moving to Canada.

Places of birth of different family members reported to census takers betrayed the circuitous route many had taken to get to the city by the bay. Henry Fields, for example, was born in Virginia, and his wife, Sylvia, in Kentucky. Virginia and Kentucky were slaves states in the upper South and Henry and Sylvia were likely born into slavery. However, their children Melford, William, and Sarah, ages nine, five, and two, had all come into the world in Buffalo, New York, a free state as of 1799. What this means is that the family had been living in western New York as free people for at least nine years prior to arriving in Hamilton.[1] Likewise, William Linch (*sic*), a blacksmith, hailed from Jackson, Maryland, and his wife Rebecca from Baltimore. Their daughters, Celestine and Malibar, ages nine and three, were born in the free state of Pittsburgh, Pennsylvania.[2] Another family that passed through Pittsburgh on their way farther north was the Willson family. A cook by trade, John Willson, and his wife Sarah, had originally come from Maryland and Virginia respectively, and were most likely former slaves. However, their ten-year-old son, Isaac, was born in Pittsburgh and their daughter, Mary Jane, aged eight, and younger son, John Junior, aged two, both reported their birthplace as Hamilton, Canada West, in the 1840s.[3]

Abraham Bryant was another cook living in Hamilton. However, a little more insight into his background and circumstances is available. His freedom was purchased for meritorious service from his owner, James H. Bryan, in Robertson County, Tennessee, in 1831. This is known because his "freedom papers" were discovered among some old family documents by his great-grandson Vincent Bryant 150 years later. "Freedom papers" referred to a court-issued document that proved a Black person was legally free. They were especially needed after the passage of the first Fugitive Slave Act in 1793, when slaves who had fled their masters could be brought before a judge and remanded back into slavery so long as there was proof of ownership on the part of the master. There was a $500 penalty for obstructing an owner's attempts to recover a slave, or for concealing or otherwise harbouring a fugitive. Bryant's papers were housed in a tin box with a waterproof lid and built-in belt loops, suggesting he

Abram Bryant's freedom papers being held by great-grandson Vincent Bryant, 1979.

was able to carry the document with him at all times. There were many cases of Blacks who had never been enslaved being illegally obtained that way, so he likely carried them on his person wherever he went. After his manumission, Abraham, or Abram, as he was named in the document, subsequently moved to Buffalo, New York, where he met Eliza Dixon, an Irish-born woman. They married in 1837 and had three children — George, Violet Ann, and James Thomas. Violet Ann was born in Hamilton in 1844.[4]

By contrast, Daniel Sweet, a chimney sweep, originated in New Jersey and was a free-born African American. His wife Maryanne, a washerwoman, was born in Norfolk, Virginia, and very likely into slavery. Their fifteen-year-old daughter, Rebecca, was born free in Sackets Harbor, New York, and their eleven-year-old daughter, Charlotte, in Pickering, Canada West. A third child, Mary Burns, only two and a half, was likely a relative of the family or had otherwise been taken in by them. She was a Hamiltonian by birth.[5] Another New Jersey native was Ann Smith, a nineteen-year-old servant living in the Watkins household, immigrants from Ireland.[6] Still another family reported that they were all from Ohio.

Joseph Kere, eighty, his wife Elizabeth Kere, sixty, and their son, George, twenty-nine, were farmers from that free state.[7]

One of the best-known members of Hamilton's Black community in the nineteenth century was a curious character by the name of Paola Brown. He has variously been described as a leader of the community, as well as an imposter. He was certainly outspoken, led a colonization movement and various protests, wrote a pamphlet against slavery based on a speech he delivered at city hall, and, as town crier and bell ringer, was a very visible member of Hamilton society. According to census records, Brown was born in Pennsylvania in 1806 and therefore was a freeborn African American.[8] His first name, which contemporaries noted was pronounced "Pe-o-lee," suggests that he hailed from Paoli, Pennsylvania, in Chester County, about twenty-four miles from Philadelphia.

Brown first made his appearance in Upper Canada's historical record in the late 1820s. In June 1828, a meeting of two hundred Blacks from around the province was held at Ancaster to discuss concerns about education, and about the problem of kidnapping and the forcible removal of African citizens to the southern states. It was indeed a momentous occasion. The group, likely presided over by Paola Brown, among others, proposed to move together into a settlement as protection against such recent frightening occurrences. They drafted a petition to Lieutenant-Governor Sir Peregrine Maitland, which was published in the *Gore Gazette* on June 21, 1828, and reprinted in the *Kingston Gazette and Religious Advocate* of July 25, 1828. Printed petitions were forwarded to the different communities to gather signatures, which would then be submitted to the Lieutenant-Governor.[9] The petition, dated November 9, 1828, was signed by Paola Brown and Charles Jackson, another Upper Canadian resident of African descent, on behalf of 237 inhabitants. It read, in part:

> To His Excellency Sir Peregrine Maitland, Knight Commander of the Most Honorable Military Order of the Bath, Lieutenant Governor of the Province of Upper Canada, and Major General Commanding His Majesty's Forces therein, &c.&c.&c.

The Petition of the under-named People of Color, residing in different parts of the Province, Humbly Sheweth, that your Petitioners duly appreciate the excellent constitution of the Province, and anxiously desire to enjoy more fully the many privileges it confers, and from which they are, in their present situation, in a great measure excluded. One of the many, and perhaps the greatest disadvantage under which they labor, is the want of means of educating their children — which desirable object they fondly cherish the hopes of being able to accomplish, should they be formed into a settlement, where they could combine and unite their means and exertions for so laudable a purpose as that of securing to their posterity the means of obtaining a moral and religious education, with all its happy consequences; and your petitioners hope that it will be the means of preventing the system of kidnapping which is now carried on through His Majesty's Provinces by the Georgia and Virginia kidnappers, from the southern states of America ...[10]

The petition referred to two cases in 1827 and 1828 in which Black men were bound, gagged, and carried across the border. One of them was James Smith, who lived in the Niagara District. He was seized in the dead of night and taken to New York State. He managed to escape and make his way back to Upper Canada by swimming across the Niagara River. The other unnamed kidnapping victim was unfortunately never heard from again. The petitioners thus requested a block of land on which to settle as a group to prevent such kidnappings, as well as to set up their own churches and schools, to allow them to become productive citizens.

Your petitioners therefore humbly pray, that your Excellency will be so graciously kind as to grant your Petitioners — contiguous to the main road leading from Burlington to Lake Huron — such portion of the waste lands of the Crown, as to your Excellency shall seem meet,

on which to establish a settlement of Colored People, and
your Petitioners as in duty bound will ever pray.[11]

The petitioners were aware that a tract of land had been set aside for
Black settlers beginning in 1819 on Wilberforce Street in Oro Township
on Lake Simcoe. In that case, individual Black families or military veterans who had petitioned for land were granted one hundred acres each in
Oro Township, even though they had not requested to be placed together
in a separate Black settlement. The petition specifically referred to the
Oro Settlement, stating that there were "many disadvantages" preventing
them from getting to it. Thus, they were asking for a tract of land to be
set aside in a less remote location in the province.[12]

As mentioned above, the petition did not reach the lieutenant-governor
until November 1828. In a handwritten appendage to the petition, Brown
and Jackson added that if Maitland was not agreeable to such a settlement,
perhaps his government would at least provide some assistance in getting
to Lake Simcoe.[13]

Provincial authorities did not grant the request of the petitioners,
citing the already-existing Oro Township appropriation, and the fact that
there were still many lots available there on which to settle, as well as in
the adjacent townships of Vespra, Flos, and Tiny.

> [T]he Board do not deem it expedient to advise the selec-
> tion of Lands in any other part of the Province with a view
> to the formation of a Settlement of Coloured People —
> Nor can they advise any special assistance to those desir-
> ous of establishing themselves on Wilberforce Street not
> shewn to other casual Emigrants coming to the Country.[14]

The Executive Council also noted that in providing land as the
government had done, it wished only to "promote the welfare of those
already in the Province, not to encourage an influx of Coloured People
from other Countries."[15]

Undaunted, the group, led again by Paola Brown as agent, immediately
followed up this application with a second petition requesting permission

to *purchase* a block of land on the Grand River in the clergy reserves of the Six Nations land bounded on the south by Wilmot Township, on the east by Woolwich Township, and on the south by Garafraxa Township (the west side being unsurveyed). The group felt that this tract would be perfect for cultivating tobacco. This petition was signed by Paola Brown and twenty-three others at St. Catharines on December 20, 1828. Abraham Top and thirty-three individuals from Ancaster signed the petition on December 24, 1828. Joseph Smith and twelve people from Brantford did so on December 27, 1828, and Jonathan Wright and nine others from Waterloo and Dumfries signed it, presumably on the same date. Charles Jackson represented two hundred from Amherstburg, and Nicholas Matthews represented another two hundred African residents of Sandwich.[16]

This second petition was read in Council on January 17, 1829. Unfortunately for the petitioners, the Executive Council replied that the land in question on the Grand River had not been surveyed, and was therefore not for sale. It continued: "The Petitioners if not disposed to settle on Wilberforce Street [in Oro] may purchase from the Commissioner of Crown Lands as Ordinary Settlers — but the Council cannot recommend them to any special consideration in any other situation than the one already assigned to them."[17]

Over the course of the next couple of years, several additional petitions penned by Blacks representing various groups of settlers or potential settlers made their way to Government House in Toronto, the seat of provincial authority. For example, Charles Jackson made another representation dated September 22, 1829, on behalf of people desiring to emigrate from the United States, as well as people already residing in Upper Canada. This group wished to purchase ten thousand acres of unsurveyed land in the clergy reserves in Lincoln County just to the east of the Hamilton-Wentworth region. Once again, they were denied assistance.[18] However, when a large group of Cincinnati Blacks, represented by J. C. Brown, wrote to the new lieutenant-governor, Sir John Colborne, and in July 1829 sent a two-member delegation to meet with him about forming a settlement, the prospect of a Black colony was suddenly welcomed by provincial authorities. Colborne himself reportedly advised the delegation: "Tell the Republicans on your side of the line that we

Royalists do not know men by their colour. Should you come to us, you will be entitled to all the privileges of the rest of His Majesty's subjects."[19]

Why had the government's tune changed so dramatically? These Cincinnati African Americans were being pushed out of the city by punitive Ohio Black Codes. An 1804 law, for example, required that Blacks had to obtain a certificate of freedom to live and work in Ohio. Three years later, they were required to post a $500 bond, signed by two white men, guaranteeing good behaviour. In addition, Blacks could not testify in court against a white person. Although these laws had never been particularly enforced, in 1829, when white workers and city officials voiced their disapproval of the increasing numbers of African Americans settling in Cincinnati, these laws were dusted off and reinvigorated. The delegation of Israel Lewis and Thomas Crissup that met with Colborne may have impressed upon him the unjust plight of their fellow Cincinnatians and their desire simply to live in a free society on equal terms with other citizens. Upper Canadian officials could also have been taking the welcome opportunity to embarrass the Americans in regard to the treatment of their African American population. To make matters worse, before the group could ready themselves to leave, a riot broke out in which white mobs stormed through Black neighbourhoods, beat the residents, and burned down their homes on a rampage that lasted for three days. Whatever the motivation of Sir Colborne and his government, with their blessing, 460 eventually left Cincinnati and settled in various parts of the province. Only five or six of the original Cincinnati families moved to the proposed colony located in Biddulph Township, Middlesex County, where present-day Lucan is located. Several weeks later, fifteen families from Boston also moved there, and there were migrations from Rochester, Albany, New York, and Baltimore, as well. It was named Wilberforce, after William Wilberforce, member of the British Parliament and a champion of anti-slavery. Families purchased twenty-five to thirty acres each for a total of 1,220 acres at $1.50 per acre. Because many families did not have the funds to purchase their land outright, J. C. Brown and Stephen Dutton obtained donations from Ohio and Indiana Quakers and bought an eight-hundred-acre tract with the money.[20]

Meanwhile, Brown and a number of families eventually found the perfect spot for a settlement on Crooks Tract in Woolwich Township, northern Waterloo County. It was located east of the Grand River on Six Nations land which had been sold to William Wallace in 1797. Brown and his group called the settlement Colbornesburg in honour of Lieutenant-Governor Colborne, who had responded so favourably to Blacks from Cincinnati desiring to settle in the province. Ironically, this land had been purchased by William Crooks in 1821, and according to some sources, was acquired by his brother James Crooks, who divided it into small lots and sold them.[21] This was the same William and James Crooks who, as merchants of Niagara, had advertised to buy a young "Negro Girl, of 7 to 12 years of age," in the *Upper Canada Gazette* on October 11, 1797. It would be interesting to know how William and James Crooks felt about dealing with these free Africans from the United States. After all, they presumably had come to Canada with money and skills and very likely lacked the subservient manner to which he was accustomed on the part of his own slaves. Perhaps he was more interested in the colour of their money than their skin. James Crooks alone owned a total of forty-five thousand acres of land in the province, which he advertised for sale in 1832 to help finance his many business ventures and clearly wanted to unload his property.

By 1831 four individuals and three families totalling twenty-four people, a number of whom would later move to Hamilton, had settled on 720 acres in Crooks Tract. Paola Brown was a single man who had recently come from St. Catharines. Other members of this group included: John Brown from Brantford and his family of three; Jacob Williams, who, like Paola Brown, had been living in St. Catharines; Joseph Mallot and his family of three; Solomon Connaway and his seven family members; John Johnson, also from St. Catharines; Daniel Banks; and Lewis Howard, who had moved from Brantford with his family of seven.[22]

Conditions regarding the settlement appeared to be progressing nicely. Abolitionist Benjamin Lundy mentioned "Woolwich" in his travel diary when he visited Upper Canada in January of the following year. He wrote that there was a Black settlement on the Grand River just a few miles north of Brantford where emigrants from the United States were said to be doing well. However, he was not able to travel there himself and provide a first-hand account of the colony.[23]

Fortunately, the tax assessment for 1832 provided a more detailed snapshot of the Colbornesburg Settlement. John Brown inhabited one hundred acres, twenty-six of which were cultivated, and owned two oxen and two cows. He was assessed at £63, the highest amount in Colbornesburg for that year. Joseph Mallot had 150 acres, four of which were under cultivation. Likewise, Solomon Connaway had four acres under cultivation out of a total of one hundred acres, although Connaway had the added benefit of an ox and a cow to his name. Their property was assessed at £33 and £30 respectively. John Johnson, whose family of eight had since joined him, was living on one hundred acres, none of which was cultivated. His property, which included two cows, was assessed at £26. Three of Paola Brown's seventy acres were now under cultivation, and he was assessed at £16.8. Daniel Banks had no acres attached to his name, although he did own two oxen and one cow. He was assessed at £11. Lewis Howard was settled on one hundred acres, three of which were under cultivation and he was assessed at £22.8. Jacob Williams also had one hundred acres, but none had been cultivated and his assessment stood at £20. Griffith Hughes, who had just moved to the community with a family of five, was apparently too recently arrived to be assessed.[24]

The intellectual and spiritual wants of the colony were not to be neglected. That same year, the residents of Colbornesburg managed to erect an "African church and School-house." A meeting of the community was called to celebrate the achievement, and give thanks to Lieutenant-Governor Sir John Colborne and all who assisted in the venture. At the gathering, Paola Brown moved that the African Church be called Brown Church in honour of Bishop Brown of the African Bethelite Societies. The minutes of the meeting were reported by Paola Brown on June 26, 1832, and appeared in the *Colonial Advocate* newspaper on August 2. The editor of the paper noted that the building had been suspended for lack of funds to complete the job, but that the "Philanthropic and persevering" Brown deserved "the encouragement and patronage of the benevolent of all denominations for his zealous and praiseworthy endeavours to better the condition of the people of Colour in this country."

On October 4, 1832, the *Colonial Advocate* copied a notice from the *Quebec Gazette* informing the public that Paola Brown was acting as agent for the Colbornesburg Settlement in Quebec City and was soliciting funds for the completion of the church and school there. He had also presented a petition to His Excellency Lord Aylmer, governor general of British North America, requesting aid for the same purpose, which he published in the abolitionist press. A "Circular Address to the Free People of Color Throughout the United States," appeared in the *Liberator*, a Boston abolitionist newspaper dated October 27, 1832. It informed American readers of the settlement at Colbornesburg and described the freedom and equality that African Americans could expect in their adopted province:

> We find ... that under this limited Monarchy more real freedom and real republicanism exist than in a professed Republic. We are here, my Brethren, in all respects, upon an equality with the whites — we are as much entitled to our elective franchise as they are, and in a Court of Justice it is not inquired of what color a witness is, but whether he is worthy of credit. Most of you, my countrymen, have been educated in the principles of liberty and equality. Do you find them exemplified around you? It is far from my wish, wherever you are not persecuted and oppressed, *on account of your color*, to estrange you from your native country; but if you are so persecuted and oppressed, here is an asylum, here is a refuge, where persecution and oppression, by reason of a wholly different colored skin are wholly unknown ...

Brown described the thousands of acres available for sale at moderate rates and on easy terms of payment in Upper Canada, the towns, canals, and waterways that led to markets near and far, and the fact that, again, there was no impediment to industry and enterprise based on race against those willing to take of advantage of them. In a final appeal, Brown stated:

> Countrymen, Friends, Brethren! I have no interested
> motives for this address. We invite you to settle amongst
> us, because we ourselves feel happy and contented — if
> you feel happy and contented where you are, for God's
> sake remain there — but to those who are oppressed
> and miserable, on account of their degraded state in the
> different parts of the Union, we should be wanting in
> Christian charity and humanity, were we not to point out
> to them the way we have followed ourselves, and invite
> them to partake of the benefits we ourselves experience.

Such was the promise that British North America held in the eyes of these Black settlers from the United States. Such was the faith they maintained in British justice and ideals.

Unfortunately, the high esteem in which Paola Brown was held by the public was short-lived, because the following February, Brown was excoriated in the press. Under the heading LOOK OUT FOR AN IMPOSTER, the *Montreal Courant* of February 2, 1833, reported that Brown had called a meeting in the town of Hamilton to obtain signatures on a petition to be presented to the Upper Canadian Parliament. The purpose, again, was to solicit funds to assist in the building of a school at Colbornesburg. However, during the meeting, Brown was asked to produce an account of the monies he had collected, and of his expenditures in travelling, lodging, and incidentals, as well as the balance of funds that remained. Apparently, Paola was either unable or unwilling to do so. Participants at the meeting signed a resolution, which was printed at the bottom of the article, stating that they considered Brown unfit to be entrusted with any money, because he had not used the funds for the purposes that he claimed. The *Hamilton Free Press* of February 23, 1833, copied the piece in the *Courant*, and the editor added that he had already met with Brown and proposed that he show his list of funders to two reputable people and then hand over the money for deposit in the Bank of Montreal. Brown refused. However, he did promise to submit a list of subscribers to the *Courant* for publication. Interestingly, this all appeared in the American abolitionist press, in a Boston *Liberator* article of February 23, 1833, washing the dirty laundry of the African Canadian community in public.

Surprisingly, in a couple of years, the question of whether Brown had committed fraud would be moot. By 1840, almost every Black settler at Colbornesburg had left Woolwich Township. Only four of the original seven Black households were still in the settlement in 1833, although two new ones were added to the list of the assessment rolls for the township. Morris Jackson and his family of four and Lewis Crague (*sic*) were now living at Colbornesburg, along with Lewis Howard, Paola Brown, John Johnson, and John Brown. Between 1832–33, Paola Brown had also apparently taken a bride, for he is shown on the tax assessment roll as having a female aged sixteen or older living in his household. The 1851 census recorded that Catherine Brown was fifteen years his junior, and hailed from the United Kingdom.[25] By 1837, only John Brown, Lewis Craig, and Lewis Howard of the original inhabitants were left, and the latter two were recorded as having no land either cultivated or uncultivated. Another Black settler, John Jackson, was also on the list with no land.[26] In 1840, only John Jackson and Jonathan Butler were still living in Woolwich Township, neither of whom had been in the original settlement. Moreover, Butler was located west of the Grand River, clearly not on Colbornesburg land. Colbornesburg was no longer.[27]

Of the original settlers who dispersed to other areas, one family was Joseph or Josephus and Lucinda Brown Mallot and their children. They relocated to Bloomingdale, near the village of Waterloo. Several families moved and joined the scattered settlements throughout the Queen's Bush Settlement, about eighteen miles north of Waterloo. This included Lewis Howard and his family and Daniel Banks.[28] Solomon Connaway and his family moved to Hamilton and settled on the Mountain.[29] As for Paola Brown, he also moved to Hamilton, where he became a leader and very visible member of the Black community there. It is unclear why the Colbornesburg Settlement that began with such promise disbanded so quickly. For one thing, no record of any land deals exist for Crooks Tract involving the families. Perhaps, as with the case of the Queen's Bush, the families squatted on land hoping to establish productive farms that would enable them to eventually purchase their lots. Paola Brown hinted at the transient nature of the settlement in his above-mentioned circular in 1832. Referring to the other Black settlement of Wilberforce, he noted: "Though our two settlements are at present separate, I believe there is a great likelihood, from my having lately met with Mr. Nathan (*sic*) Lewis, the Agent for Wilberforce Settlement, of both being united, which will form a bond of harmony and strength, that cannot fail to be of benefit to both ..."[30]

It is certainly understandable that these rural inhabitants might feel more comfortable banding together in one larger settlement, rather than existing apart in two smaller ones. In this way, there would be more families upon which to rely in times of need. However, the original inhabitants of Colbornesburg did not end up joining the Wilberforce community, but rather split up and went in several different directions. Moreover, the Wilberforce community itself was having its own problems. Charges of fraud on the part of agent Israel Lewis, who was supposed to solicit funds in the United States, and disappointment with the meagre fundraising results of Reverend Nathaniel Paul, who was sent to Britain, led to serious divisions within the Wilberforce leadership. Lewis was later thoroughly

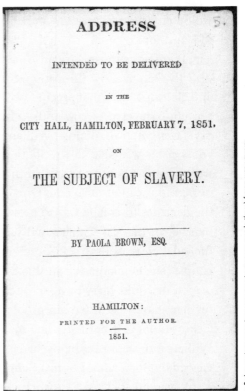

Bell-ringer and town crier Paola Brown's speech delivered at Hamilton City Hall, February 7, 1851. A tall, stout, dark man who dressed immaculately in black coat and pants, plug hat, white ruffled shirt, kid gloves, and kid boots, Paola Brown had a deep booming voice that could reportedly be heard past the town limits. Brown's speech was interrupted by pranksters who set off firecrackers, forcing him to end the event prematurely, but he later published the speech in this booklet.

discredited and removed as its agent. It is not known whether this played into the events at Colbornesburg as they unfolded.[31]

Thus was the interesting and somewhat controversial route by which Paola Brown arrived in Hamilton. If he had made mistakes, he had made them in the service of others as a proud, confident, racially conscious actor. He had come to Canada seeking freedom and the right to self-determination, not only for himself, but for others of his race. And he would continue to make a contribution in that regard in his new town of Hamilton.

There were those African Americans in Hamilton who had escaped directly from slavery. They too were coming from a variety of situations and circumstances that precipitated their fleeing. Henry Williamson was born into slavery in Maryland. Although he stated that his owner treated his slaves better than most, Williamson felt he had a right to be free. His wife's sister was sold down South at a private auction and her parents were so upset about the sale of their daughter that they became determined to escape to Canada. One of the chief reasons that slaves made the decision to escape was to prevent their families from being split up by sale. In this case, anger and resentment about their daughter's sale fuelled their reasons to leave. Williamson went with them. In all, eighteen people left the plantation in this escape party, carrying everything they owned or could carry away on their backs, "like terrapins." Williamson further stated that the main problem the fugitives encountered was the lack of money. Eventually they made it to Canada. By 1854–55, Henry Williamson would be living in Hamilton when he agreed to be interviewed by Boston abolitionist Benjamin Drew.[32]

Reverend Richard S. Sorrick was also a slave in Maryland, born in about 1815 in a place two miles from Washington, D.C. At the age of one, he was sold along with his parents to someone who lived near Hagerstown. He was later sold back to his first owner, then to a man also close to Hagerstown. At about twenty-five years of age, he was sold to yet another slave owner. But Sorrick obviously possessed a gift that his latest master could not tolerate. In 1841, this slave owner had him imprisoned for preaching the gospel to his fellow slaves. Fortunately for Sorrick, his previous owner took pity on him, bought him back, and obtained his release from prison. Sorrick spent a total of three months and eight days in jail.[33]

Richard Sorrick was grateful for the chance to be released from prison. According to the good reverend, his owner felt that his calling to preach the gospel was genuine, and so the man made him a deal and offered him his freedom on condition that Sorrick send him $400 once he had an opportunity to earn that amount as a free man. Sorrick moved to Pennsylvania on October 11, 1843, and thereafter sent his former owner a portion of the money. By 1845, however, Sorrick was in Canada, never sending the balance that he had agreed to pay. He first settled in Toronto, then Oro, a Black community on the northwestern shores of Lake Simcoe in the south-central part of the province. In 1847, Sorrick found himself in Hamilton as a preacher in the AME Church there.[34] In the 1851 census, Reverend Sorrick was listed as living on Hughson Street in St. Andrew's Ward with his wife, Jane. They were both thirty-six years old and living in a one-storey frame house on almost a half acre of land. She was born in Tennessee and was most likely a former slave.[35]

Some ex-slaves had lived lives of incredible adventure, albeit under the thumbs of their slave masters. Williamson Pease, for example, was born into slavery in Tennessee. What should also be known about Pease, which speaks to the incredible diversity of skin colour of incoming Blacks, is that he could "pass," meaning pass for white. In fact, interviewer Benjamin Drew noted that in appearance, Pease was "a white man with blue eyes."[36] This was not that unusual, due to the huge numbers of children being fathered by slave-masters across the South.

When talented novelist and abolitionist William Wells Brown, himself a former slave of mixed heritage, toured Canada West in the fall of 1861, he wrote about his travels in the *Pine and Palm*, the official journal of the Haytian Emigration Bureau. Brown was helping this organization promote Black immigration to the Caribbean island of Haiti. He observed that in Toronto, every shade of colour from the purest white to the darkest dark was represented among the Black population there and that perhaps as many as five hundred were passing for white in that city. He jokingly added, "Many of these pass for foreigners, and under that guise, almost any mulatto may push himself through the crowd, if he can rattle off a little French, German, or Spanish. With some of our class, this is an inducement to study the languages."[37] In Hamilton, he noted that the American Hotel was kept by William Richardson, "a colored white man."[38]

According to his 1855 interview with Drew, as a boy, Pease ploughed in the fields and also served in the main house when needed. At the age of eighteen, his master died and the man's property, including his slaves, was inherited by the deceased's grandson. After a year and a half, this young man moved to Arkansas. At first the slaves were put to work picking cotton, but some time thereafter, he rented the land out and sold all his slaves, including Williamson Pease's mother and sisters — everyone except Pease himself. The two set off for California in search of gold.

Pease's goal was to earn enough money to purchase his freedom. In fact, his master had encouraged him by saying that if they made enough money, he would free him after two years. But the two only mined about $80 in gold, not enough to pay expenses. They moved to San Francisco, where Pease was offered a job as a waiter at $40 a month. However, Pease's master persuaded him that it wasn't enough money. His master dangled the promise of free papers before him while begging Pease to accompany him back to Arkansas because he was ill and needed company on the trip back. Pease countered that if he returned, he might have his own freedom, but his mother would still be enslaved. On the other hand, if he remained in California and worked for wages, he might be able to purchase his mother's freedom. The young slave owner put forward every argument in the book. He stated that if Pease returned with him, he would buy his mother back and ensure that she was well taken care of. Against his better judgment, Pease agreed.

They boarded a ship for Panama, on which Pease worked for his passage. However, the vessel was thirty days at sea and landed at Acapulco, far from their destination. They made the next leg of the trip on horseback, travelling through Mexico City to Vera Cruz. Again, Williamson Pease requested his freedom papers. His master agreed. Pease went out for a walk to sightsee. Upon his return, his owner began to cry, explaining that if he gave the freedom papers, and they passed through New Orleans, they would both be imprisoned. The freedom papers were not forthcoming, but, his owner said, if he returned with him and waited until he was settled and married, he could then leave if he wished.

The two set sail for New Orleans in a Spanish schooner, and upon their return home, his master opened a dry goods store, and enlisted Pease's labour in running it. Again, Pease demanded his freedom papers and was promised them in a day or two. Of course, they never materialized. This was in the spring. Pease never again asked for his freedom papers, realizing that this master would never hand them over. By July, however, he was hired out to a saloon owner to tend the man's saloon.

Not too long afterward, Pease's master married. It began to be rumoured that he had been sold to his father-in-law. When confronted, of course, he denied everything. But the father-in-law later confirmed the worst. Pease went to his young master, who continued to lie, promising that if he would come back with him, he would put him in charge of a store in Texas, and give him one-third share of the profits. The saloon owner also offered to purchase him, but the father-in-law refused. Pease returned to work with his new owner and family.

The following March, Pease was asked to get ready to go to New Orleans the following morning. He was to accompany the father-in-law there. Pease immediately knew that the plan was to sell him. Of course, the young master laughed and bet him fifty dollars that Pease would be back. Pease rode over to see his mother and tell her the situation. She was very upset, and told Pease in no uncertain terms that it was his own fault, that he should never have returned from California. This must have been a bitter pill to swallow for the naive young bondsman.

Pease left for New Orleans by boat with his new owner, his previous owner's father-in-law. During the trip by boat and steamer, the man was already attempting to sell him, although there were no takers. In New Orleans, they went to numerous places that traded in slaves, but to no avail. The problem was that Pease could pass for white and would be too great a flight risk. One trader asked, "Can you read and write?" When Pease answered in the affirmative, he replied, "I don't want you in here, — I should have to chop your fingers off."[39]

Eventually, a cotton merchant paid $900 for him in partial payment for a debt that the father-in-law owed. But, this was not the end of the twists and turns in the life of this young "white" slave. The cotton merchant informed Pease that he lived in a free state, and that if he were to take him there, he could not prevent him from leaving. So after only four or five days, he was again sold to a man from Arkansas who employed him in the "big house." This plantation had one hundred slaves working on it, and the owner was part owner in two or three other estates.

However, the slave-master was cruel and determined to teach his new "acquisition" a lesson or two. Pease recalled, "He said, so I heard from others, that I thought I was white: that I was a good boy, but would have to be whipped to let me know that I was a 'nigger;' for 'niggers always should be whipped some, no matter how good they are, else they'll forget that they are niggers.'"[40]

But apparently, a whipping was not all he had in mind. Pease figured out that he was being measured for stiff-legs:

> These are, one iron ring around the ankle and one up on
> the thigh, joined together by an iron rod behind. When
> these are put on a man, he cannot bend his knees at all,
> and so cannot run away ... My master's plan was to whip
> me, as I have the best reasons to believe, then put on the
> stiff-legs, and chain me to work in the smith's shop.[41]

After all the lies, broken promises and excuses, it took the threat of real, horrific torture to finally provoke Pease's escape. He ran and never looked back, grabbing his clothes and some biscuits that were being served for supper, as he made his getaway. "I walked forty miles through the Arkansas Swamp to the Mississippi, along a muddy road, and at 2 o'clock the next day, got to Napoleon, on the Mississippi River. Nobody questioned me."[42]

One might ask why it took so long for Williamson Pease to make his escape. He was young and naive, and obviously unaware of what the world could hold for him, particularly as someone who did not even look like a Black person. Moreover, through most of his life up to that time, he maintained a fair amount of freedom to move around, and he was given jobs that required some degree of autonomy. Most importantly, even though his masters had lied to him repeatedly, it does not appear that they physically abused or tortured him in any way.

Pease fled in January 1854, and briefly stopped in London before moving on to Hamilton. A W. Pease was first identified in the 1858 directory working as a "hair dresser" in the establishment of well-known Black barber and community leader John H. Bland on Upper James. The barbering trade would be his livelihood for the rest of his days, as Pease appeared in the censuses of 1861, 1871, 1881, and 1901, listed as a barber, going into business for himself at 2 Hughson Street at least by the 1870s. It appears he added a store to his barber's establishment by 1881 as well, because his African Canadian-born wife, Eliza, was reported as a storekeeper in the census of that year. In terms of his personal life, in 1861, the twenty-seven-year-old Pease and Eliza, aged twenty-one, were already married with a one-year-old child, Sarah, all recorded as "mulattoes," and living in a one-and-a-half-storey frame house. There was another barber living with them by the name of W.B. Van Horn. They would go on to have ten more children, some of whom were adults still living with them in 1901 at 32 John Street. At that time, his son Archibald was working in his business as a barber, and five daughters, Sarah, Nina, Nita, Cassandra, and Elsie were living in the household. Interestingly, Pease's old mentor, John H. Bland, named Nina Pease in his 1884 will, and in that will it is confirmed that William Pease and Williamson Pease were one and the same person, stating: "I give devise and bequeath to Miss Nina Pease, daughter of Williamson Pease of Hughson Street in the City of Hamilton Barber one fourth part in cash for her own use and behoof forever …"[43]

Breathing in the fresh air of freedom in Canada, as Pease told Drew in 1855, he liked it much better than America. He would now utter with absolute certainty, "I could not be pulled back into Arkansas — I would have my head pulled off first."[44]

Studies of fugitive slaves indicate that the majority of those who ran — an estimated 75–80 percent — were male. This was true for a variety of reasons that relate to the nature of female slavery in America. Women were less mobile and less likely to have travelled off the slave owner's property. Male slaves were more likely to have been off the plantation for work-related purposes. Hence, men were often more familiar with the surrounding countryside than were women, and therefore, more likely to escape without recapture. Most importantly, however, was the fact that

Philadelphia abolitionist and Underground Railroad agent William Still met and assisted hundreds of fugitive slaves to Canada and freedom, some of whom settled in Hamilton and environs.

women were more likely to have children, or to be pregnant or nursing an infant, and therefore less likely to risk their safety and that of their children in attempting to flee. Black abolitionist and Underground Railroad agent, William Still, observed that it was far more risky for women with children on the Underground Railroad, and thus, very unusual when they did run with their offspring. When Ann Maria Jackson fled her Maryland slave-master with seven children, it was quite a noteworthy event. Still recorded the story of the miraculous family when he met them upon their arrival in Philadelphia.[45] She was sent on to St. Catharines and then Toronto, where she made a home for her children as a laundress. Her descendants still reside in Toronto and other parts of Ontario to this day. Unfortunately, there are no first-hand accounts on record of women who escaped alone and settled in Hamilton.

Male slaves who fled often left behind wives and children in slavery. Two brothers, Anthony and Albert Brown, escaped from Tanner's Creek, Norfolk, Virginia, and their owners, John and Henry Holland. They were accompanied in this flight by Jones Anderson and another man, who went simply by the name of Isaiah. John and Henry Holland were oystermen and described as brutal slave owners. Albert and Anthony decided they had had enough of this treatment and seized one of their masters' oyster boats, sailing north toward what they hoped were the shores of a free state. The party first landed twenty-five miles north of Baltimore, which was still slave territory. Eventually, they discovered their error and made their way to Philadelphia and the Philadelphia branch of the

Underground Railroad. Anthony and Albert Brown ultimately jour-
neyed on to Hamilton, Canada West, where they found jobs as waiters.
As elated as they were to be free in Canada, they missed their wives,
Alexenia and Ellen Brown, and hoped against hope to see them again.
They wrote to Still and offered their reflections about what they had been
through and their hopes for the future.

> Hamelton (*sic*) March 7th 1856
> Mr. Wm. Still: — Sir —
>   I now take the opportunity of writting you a few lins
> hoping to find yourself and famly well as thes lines leves
> me at present, myself and brother, emploied in the new
> hotel, name Anglo american, wheare we wintered and
> don very well, we also met with our too frends ho came
> from home with us, Jonas Anderson and Izeas, now
> we are all safe in hamilton, I wish to cale you to youre
> prommos, if convenient to write to Norfolk, Va., for me,
> and let my wife mary Elen Brown, no where I am, and
> my brothers wife Elickzener Brown, as we have never
> heard a word from them since we left, tel them that we
> found our homes and situation in canady much better
> than we expected, tel them not to think hard of us, we
> was boun to flee from the rath to come, tel them we live
> in the hopes of meting them once more this side of the
> grave, tel them if we never more see them, we hope to
> meet them in the kingdom of heaven in pece, tel them
> to remember my love to my cherch and brethren, tel
> them I find there is the same prayer-hearing God heare
> as there is in old Va ; tel them to remember our love to
> all the enquiring frends, I have written sevrel times but
> have never reseived no answer, I find a gret meny of my
> old accuaintens from Va., heare we are no ways lonesom
> … Nothing more at present, but remane youre frends,
> Anthony & Albert Brown[46]

The Anglo American Hotel, where escaped Virginia slaves Anthony and Albert Brown obtained jobs as waiters in the mid-1850s, was located at 61 King Street East between John and Catharine Streets. It was converted to the Wesleyan Female College, an exclusive school for women, in the 1860s and later reconverted into the Waldorf Hotel in 1898.

It seems one brother's prayers were answered, as is evident from the following letter sent to Still just four months later.

> Hamilton, June 26th, 1856
> Mr. Wm. Still: — kine Sir: —
> I am happy to say to you that I have jus reseved my letter dated 5 of the present month, but previeously had bin in form las night by Mr. J. H. Hall, he had jus reseved a letter from you stating that my wife was with you, oh my I was so glad it case me to shed tears.
> Mr. Still, I cannot return you the thanks for the care of my wife, for I am so Glad that I dont now what to say, you will pleas start her for canaday. I am yet in hamilton, C.W, at the city hotel, my brother and Joseph anderson is at the angle american hotel, they send there respects to you and family my self also, and a greater part to my wife. I came by the way of syracruse remember me to Mrs. logins, tel her to writ back to my brothers wife if she is living and tel her to com on tel her to send Joseph Andersons love to his mother.
> i now send her 10 Dollers and would send more but being out of employment some of winter it pulls me back, you will be so kine as to forward her on to me, and if life las I will satisfie you at some time, before long. Give my respects and brothers to Mr. John Dennes, tel him Mr. Hills famly is wel and send there love to them, I now bring my letter to a close, And am youre most humble Servant, Anthony Brown
> P.S. I had given out the notion of ever seeing my wife again, so I have not been attending the [post] office, but am truly sorry I did not, you mention in yours of Mr. Henry lewey, he has left this city for Boston about 2 weeks ago, we have not herd from him yet.
> A. Brown[47]

On occasion, men did escape with their wives. On August 2, 1855, the Philadelphia Vigilance Committee met Robert Jones and his wife, Eliza. They had fled bondage in Petersburg, Virginia, Robert from Thomas Lee, whom he described as "a very hard man." Eliza belonged to a different owner, an Eliza Richie, whom she described as "moderate" toward her slaves. Robert himself was portrayed as "about thirty-five, chestnut color, medium size, of good manners, [and] intelligent." Eliza was "about forty years of age, chestnut color, nice-looking, and well-dressed."[48]

The couple was sent onward on their Underground Railroad journey, where they disembarked at Hamilton. They immediately set about to make themselves useful in their new home. In 1858, the Joneses were living on Rebecca Street between West Avenue and Wellington and Robert had found work as a carpenter. The two attended the Baptist church and Robert, who had learned to read and write quite well before coming to Canada, wrote numerous letters back to William Still. Still published one of these letters, revealed in Chapter 4, which outlines some of the useful activities Jones had engaged in since his arrival in Hamilton.

Robert Jones continued to earn his living as a carpenter until the 1870s, when he was listed as a Baptist clergyman. Tragically, his beloved Eliza had passed away, and the forty-six-year-old Jones was now living in the Ephraim Reddick home. He apparently did not earn his living as a man of the cloth for the remainder of his life. He was recorded as a clothes cleaner by the census year 1881.[49] His story is just another of the interesting tales that can be told of Hamilton's nineteenth-century Black citizens.

Another long-time Hamilton resident, bearing the name Henry Criel, recounted his story of escape from slavery to a local journalist.[50] It is one fugitive's story, but it is testament to what many bondsmen and women endured in fleeing their oppression.

Criel was born in Parkersburg, West Virginia. He was the son of his master's son, from whom he received his last name. When his master died, Criel's father, a medical doctor, inherited the property — including his slaves — but, unfortunately, he was not as kind as the elder Criel. Dr. Criel worked his "chattel" much harder than his father, and it was only a provision in his father's will that prevented the son from putting his slaves up for public auction. However, our protagonist was hired out,

Underground Rail Road Records (Philadelphia: William Still, 1883), 470.

"Suspended by the hands with block and tackle" woodcut image.

meaning that someone paid his owner for his labour. He worked over-time in the nearby salt mines and was allowed to keep a portion of his earnings, from which he saved $80, putting it aside little by little.

Not surprisingly, Criel was not happy in his enslavement, and quietly began to plan his escape. One of the occurrences that helped to make up his mind took place when a fellow slave, who was in charge of a number of ovens used to dry the salt, was brutally punished. Either through careless-ness or some other cause, one of the ovens became overheated, and the grate inside was ruined. For this relatively minor infraction, the man was stripped to his waist and his hands were tied to a beam, his toes barely able to touch the ground. Another slave was ordered to give him two hundred lashes under the close watch of the overseer and the other slaves. Upon completion of the order, the man, half-dead, bleeding and wounded, was taken down, washed, and essentially bedridden for a month.

Parkersburg was conveniently located just south of the Ohio River, which separated West Virginia from the state of Ohio and freedom for those in chains. The work of the abolitionists and the Underground Railroad (UGRR) appeared to be well-known in the area, because Criel obtained the names of certain individuals who would be able to help him once he made his getaway. He also held secret meetings with several oth-ers who wished to take leave of their owners. In all, four men, including Criel and his brother, made preparations over a period of time and set a specific date and time to make their bid for freedom. On the designated night, the four men met near a small boathouse and began their journey. They pushed a canoe into the Ohio River and floated away. Either they were destined for freedom or capture and a return to bondage, possibly even death. Fortunately, an Underground Railroad operative was wait-ing for them on the other side. Once they had completed the difficult boat ride across the Ohio, he met and led them to his house, where they remained hidden for a brief period.

At the house, a young woman named Rachel who had escaped from a nearby farm was there waiting for the opportunity to make the next leg of her own journey on the Underground Railroad. It was decided that she would accompany the four men disguised as a man herself. The party of five set out, escorted by the UGRR activist for a time, and then left to carry on by themselves. There were several stops at safe houses or *stations* along the way before arriving at Cleveland, their second to last destination prior to arriving in Canada. However, just before leaving them, the abolitionist warned them to be careful when passing a certain house at which a dance was being held.

The house was spotted in due time, and just as our group was passing the house, the party was breaking up. Ten men and several women were outside, spotted the fugitives, and questioned them in no uncertain terms. Some quick thinking on Criel's part enabled the group to continue on their way.

One hundred miles north of Zanesville, Ohio, and approximately halfway to Cleveland, Rachel began to suffer terrible soreness in her feet. Having reached another safe house, they decided to leave her behind to rest. This girl eventually reached Windsor, Ontario. When last heard of, she was married and living in Buffalo. Meanwhile, the four males journeyed on unencumbered, and eluded their pursuers, who were close on their tracks. They sought refuge in a hotel kept by an abolitionist, and were received with hospitality. However, someone recognized Street, one of their companions, and accused him of being an "escaped slave." The hotel keeper came to his rescue, but advised them to leave before daybreak, or they would not be safe. He also instructed them to stop about three miles outside Cleveland at a Dr. Stone's, who lived in a stone house near a wood.

The party pressed on, passing through village after village, and putting on a bold front if anyone questioned them. Eventually, they spotted a house near a wood, similar to the one described to them, but it was brick, not stone. This caused considerable consternation. Had they been misinformed, or were they on the wrong track? They decided to conceal themselves until dark, when one of them knocked on the door and asked who lived there. A servant girl confirmed that it was indeed Dr. Stone's residence.

After resting for several days, Dr. Stone arranged their passage, undoubtedly by boat, to Detroit and then Windsor. The year was 1837. Newly freed, the men prospered in their new home. Street became a labourer, and, with his earnings, purchased a farm near Cayuga, which was passed down to his family upon his death many years later. Henry

Criel worked in a warehouse in Amherstburg and witnessed some of the conflict related to the 1837 Rebellion. He moved to Queenston (now part of Niagara Falls) and became a servant to Mrs. Catherine Hamilton, the mother of George Hamilton after whom the city was named. In time it became apparent that although he was a free man, he did not possess all the rights of other people in this society: he could not vote. Therefore, after the seven-year waiting period was up, he became a naturalized British citizen. Criel could now vote his staunch Conservative conscience. His biographer noted that he still possessed his naturalization papers, dated December 30, 1845, and was proud of them.

Although Criel could not read or write, with the help of an acquaintance, he learned to sign his own name. While he was not able to calculate with pen and ink, he had a remarkable head for figures, witnessed by his financial success after coming to Hamilton. Criel arrived in the city in the mid-to-late 1840s and, with the $80 in savings that he brought with him, purchased the lot at 229 North MacNab Street when the area was still relative wilderness, and lived there for the rest of his life. He also speculated in real estate and purchased a number of other lots over the years. He even provided the mortgage for a two-acre property purchased by well-known barber Josiah Cochrane and his wife Amelia, on Hamilton Mountain, later dubbed "Little Africa."[51] Criel worked as a cook on the lake boats, and later, after the railways usurped the lakes as an important form of transportation in the 1850s, he worked as a waiter for Sir Allan MacNab at Dundurn Castle. His first wife, Jane, was Irish and worked as a cook at the Castle, as well.[52] Criel was also employed at the Hotel Royal by a Mr. Davidson of Welland. He stated that this particular hotel was a well-known stomping ground of Americans, many of whom despised Blacks and never hesitated to let their antipathy be known, making for a rather uncomfortable work environment for Black staff.

After the death of his first wife Jane, Criel remarried a younger African-Canadian woman named Barbara, born in Quebec, and adopted her five-year-old son, Henry. At the time of the 1881 census, he was earning an income as a market gardener.[53] According to Criel's biographer, the lifelong Baptist maintained a comfortable income and lived in a well-furnished home in his final years. After the death of Barbara, he was married again to a Mary Geisel. He died on October 17, 1904, at the age of eighty-seven in his home at 229 MacNab, after residing in Hamilton for over sixty years. He was survived by his widow and adopted son.[54]

At the time of his death, Henry Criel possessed two additional lots on the west side at 231 and 233 MacNab Street between Colborne and Barton Streets, which included his two-storey brick house and a garden, and he owned a frame cottage at 45 Barton Street East. He also owned a vacant lot at the corner of MacNab and Barton Streets. The combined value of these properties was $4,500, which was split between Henry Jr. and Mary Criel, and the total value of his estate was $4,750. Among his personal items was a photo album which he bequeathed to his son, except for seven photos of her choosing which were handed down to his wife.[55] It is indeed unfortunate that these photos have been lost to history. Although a fugitive slave, he had managed to bring enough money to buy property and although uneducated, always managed to find employment, earn a decent living, and build up his portfolio.

Whether Canadian-born, educated freeborn African Americans, escaped slaves, or former slaves looking for a life free of racial intolerance and bigotry, the Black population that arrived in Hamilton came from a variety of circumstances, albeit the same root of racial oppression. Flying in the face of slaveholder propaganda, however, they were a self-sufficient people who contributed the knowledge and skills they had learned in slavery and in freedom in the northern United States to help build new lives in this city. However, in the world of British North America, they were lumped into one category, and the "myth of the fugitive slave," fleeing servitude and arriving destitute, in need of charity and benevolence, became the stereotype by which all were judged.

CHAPTER 3

On Course: Settling in By the Bay

Quaker abolitionist Benjamin Lundy travelled through Upper Canada in the dead of winter from Queenston to Hamilton, Brantford, London, the Wilberforce Settlement, and then down through the countryside of the "Western District" to Detroit in January 1832. His sole purpose was to inform African Americans about the conditions of Blacks in this country to the north so that they could make an educated decision about whether or not to migrate there. He described Hamilton as "truly, a beautifully situated village … laid off on a kind of secondary elevation, a short distance from the foot of the 'mountain' …" He had observed a "neat Court House and Jail, several pretty good inns, about a dozen mercantile stores, a fair proportion of mechanics' shops, etc."[1] There were two weekly newspapers, and the stagecoach routes from near Niagara to Hamilton and York (Toronto) to Detroit met there. The stage ran daily in the summer, and tri-weekly in the winter. The country around Hamilton, he noticed, was heavily settled and many of the inhabitants, wealthy. However, so far, wrote Lundy, he had seen "very few of the African race in Canada."[2]

In just a few short years, however, a vibrant Black community would take shape in Hamilton, with a church established under the banner of the African Methodist Episcopal (AME) body that had been founded in the 1790s and spread across America and into Canada. With the construction of that first modest log structure on Rebecca Street, the foundations of the first and most significant institution in the Black community was complete. It facilitated the growth of political and anti-slavery activism and a host of self-help, fraternal, and racial uplift organizations that would improve the lives of people of African descent in the city.

Escaped slave Jermain Loguen arrived in Hamilton sometime between 1834 and 1835. Loguen remembered it as a "cold wilderness for the fugitive." At that time, according to Loguen, it was not a thriving depot of the Underground Railroad, as it would become in the 1850s. There were few Blacks living there, "no thriving colored farmers, mechanics and labourers" who could give him shelter, advice, or assistance in finding employment. The whereabouts of the thirty-three people from Ancaster who signed the 1828 petition requesting a block of land for a Black settlement are not known. Perhaps they were scattered across the township or no longer living in the area. Fortunately, Loguen met a white farmer in the vicinity who agreed to hire him to clear his

Courtesy of Carolina Digital Library and Archives, University of North Carolina, Chapel Hill, NC.

Jermain Loguen was born a slave in 1813 in Davison County, Tennessee, about sixteen miles from Nashville. He was the son of his slavemaster, David Logue, and his mother "Cherry." In 1834, Loguen escaped, and, after a long and dangerous journey, arrived in the Hamilton area. He later resettled in Syracuse, New York, and became a leading Underground Railroad agent, AME Bishop, founder of schools, and anti-slavery activist.

land by chopping, rolling, and burning logs. The farmer and his wife also introduced him to a local church, where he learned to read and write in the Sabbath school. The following summer, he graduated as a Bible reader at Ancaster.[3]

But not everyone Loguen met was helpful to him. In his third year after settling in the Hamilton area, he leased a farm of two hundred acres. The farm was quite successful, and he partnered with someone who he hoped would help him augment his enterprise and therefore his bottom line. Unfortunately, it was not to be. Apparently, this individual was heavily indebted, and as soon as they harvested their first crop as partners, everything, including the land, crops, and farm implements, was seized to pay the man's debts. According to Loguen, had he known his rights, he might have retained his farm. However, left with only his clothing, some money, two horses, a wagon, and harness, Loguen was so disgusted that he moved to St. Catharines and purchased a house and lot there. But his stay in St. Catharines, too, would be short-lived. Loguen crossed back over the border and ended up in Rochester, eventually settling in Syracuse, New York. He graduated from Oneida Institute as a teacher and founded several schools for African-American children. He also became a minister and later bishop in the AME Church. Loguen was one of the most ardent Underground Railroad activists and stationmasters in the region, openly flouting the Fugitive Slave Act by aiding and transmitting 1,500 escaped slaves to Canada. He was even active on the lecture circuit and contributed to various anti-slavery newspapers. Jermain Loguen, a refugee from bondage himself, was touted as the "Underground Railroad King."[4]

Although Loguen stated that there were virtually no Africans living in Hamilton and vicinity when he arrived, he might well have come into contact with Enerals Griffin at some point during his stay in the area. Griffin came to Canada in approximately 1829. He was born between 1784 and 1798, and his "fugitive slave" story, as told in *Ancaster's Heritage: A History of Ancaster Township*, was that he was a slave in Virginia[5] who had been well-treated and educated by his master. The latter promised him his freedom, but we have already seen that slaves could not take much stock in such assurances. Owners routinely reneged on their promises to bondspeople. After keeping watch at the owner's deathbed, Enerals realized that he might very well end up on the auction block, so he decided to become the master of his own fate."Therefore, he got some paper and ink from his master's home and wrote himself a pass, signing his master's name: 'This nigger belongs to me. He has my permission to go to town and visit the sick negras on my place. Edward Lee.'"[6]

Griffin took off one night on one of his master's horses, following the main road north to the Canadian border. He had only one close call in Harrisburg, Pennsylvania, when he was stopped and questioned. He was asked to write his master's name to prove that he had not written the pass himself. He was shaking so hard that his writing did not match the writing on the pass, and he was let go.[7]

Interestingly, the above story has been called into question by the discovery of a report written by Reverend Hiram Wilson, a well-known missionary who devoted his career from 1836–64 to Black refugees in Canada. Wilson would soon become one of the architects of the British American Institute and Settlement at Dawn with Josiah Henson, the man who came to be known as the "real" Uncle Tom of *Uncle Tom's Cabin* fame. Wilson routinely penned articles and letters to anti-slavery newspapers describing his work in the field. A letter to the editor of *The Emancipator*, printed in the June 15, 1837, issue reported the following:

Visited Ancaster — called on Mr. Griffin, formerly in the service of Gen. Finlay of Cincinnati, an enterprising farmer who was driven from Ohio in 1829 by oppression. He cultivates one of the best farms in the country. White farmers were at first unwilling to trust their land to him, but have since found him capable of teaching them the art of husbandry. Year before last he and his son raised a thousand bushels of wheat, a thousand bushels of corn and over four hundred of oats, and his landlord is unwilling to let his land to any other as long as he will cultivate it.[8]

Whether Griffin was an escaped slave from Virginia or a free Black from Ohio has not been definitively determined. He could very well have been both, and have escaped to Cincinnati before pulling up stakes for Canada. Hiram Wilson noted that Griffin was employed by General James Findlay, the prominent Cincinnati merchant turned mayor who was elected to the United States Congress and served as major-general of the State Militia's First Division. If Wilson's account is indeed accurate, Griffin was probably one of the group of Cincinnati African Americans who exited the state during the repression of 1829. Like most who emigrated, Griffin had not settled in the Wilberforce colony, but had instead staked out his own picturesque territory on the Niagara Escarpment in Ancaster. But it would certainly help to explain how Griffin was able to act as one of two bondsmen for married couple Patrick McNamara and Catharine Finlan in 1832. This meant that he would have had to possess a sizeable amount of money, because if anything happened to the husband, Griffin would be partially responsible for supporting the widow and her children. In that regard, he purchased a fifty-acre lot in Concession 1, Lot 40, for the sum of £125 in 1834, although it has been shown that an enslaved Henry Criel saved $80, which he used to purchase a house and lot upon his arrival in Hamilton. But, once again, it is probably an indication of the extent to which the "narrative of the fugitive slave" has captured the imagination of Canadians, to the detriment of a more honest and nuanced portrayal.

Griffin's wife Priscilla came the same year, so they may have come together. It is speculated that she was white, because their only child James, born in 1833, was described as a mulatto in the census. Priscilla herself died in 1850, just prior to the first Canada-wide census, when her racial origin would have been specified. Whatever the case, by 1832, the family had settled in Ancaster, and began clearing the land for cultivation. Griffin leased and farmed more land than he actually owned. In the coming years, he grew a wide variety of crops and raised cows, sheep, horses, and pigs, and, by 1861, his farm was valued at $2000. As Enerals Griffin aged, his son James took over the running of the farm, and inherited the estate upon his father's death in 1878. The census and assessment rolls indicate that James was a veterinary surgeon as well as a farmer. The land

Griffin House, located near the intersection of Mineral Springs Road and Sulphur Springs Road in Ancaster Township, was designated a National Historic Site in 2008.

and original house remained in the hands of Griffin descendants, some of whom continue to live in the area. Because of the historic nature of the architecture, particularly because it was owned by an early Black pioneer, the Griffin House was designated a National Historic Site in 2008. Interestingly, through intermarriage, the family gradually became white, and were unaware of their African heritage when the Griffin House was first excavated and restored in the 1990s.[9]

In addition to the Griffin family of Ancaster, there was apparently a large enough community in Hamilton for numerous individuals were mentioned in city council minutes in the first years that minutes were recorded. Some Blacks were in business for themselves. Mr Andriss, a "blackman," was ordered to pay his grocery licence of £1.3 shillings to the city clerk, and £5 to the police, which he paid in order to have it transferred regularly. This appeared in the minutes of December 13th, 1834.[10] On June 33rd (*sic*), 1835, it was recorded that John Brown, "a coloured man" was fined £2.6 shillings for driving his milk cart on the sidewalks.[11] There were very few cases of disorderly conduct involving Blacks and only one of petty theft. The world's oldest profession, however, was alive and well in Hamilton. The minutes show two Black men being convicted of keeping a house of ill repute at different times in these early records.

There were enough people to form St. Paul's AME Church in the 1830s, the longest-surviving Black congregation in Hamilton, now known as Stewart Memorial Church. City council minutes contain the record of an assault case involving some young boys and "much insulting behaviour" directed towards "some respectable coloured people returning from chapel ..." on October 22, 1838, in which two boys, aged twelve and fifteen, were fined.[12] Austin Steward, formerly a leader of the Wilberforce colony, remembered an important AME conference held in Hamilton led by Bishop Morris Brown of Philadelphia in 1838 or 1839. In Steward's account, the Black population of Hamilton was larger than that in New York City, obviously a great exaggeration. He found none of the extreme poverty that he observed in New York nor any of the drunken rowdiness amongst the Blacks that was so common in eastern United States cities. The conference delegates met many African Hamiltonians who were doing well, including a number of mechanics. "Some of them took us about the place, showing us the different buildings they were engaged in erecting; quite a number were employed in building a church which appeared to be done in a workman-like manner."[13]

Steward found the conference, which was well-attended by both Blacks and whites, to be a whirlwind of networking and social activities, and far more

Born a slave in Virginia, Austin Steward (1793–1865) moved to upstate New York with his slavemaster. He eventually escaped and established a prosperous grocery business in Rochester, New York. In 1831, Steward moved with his wife and children to lead the Black settlement of Wilberforce, Upper Canada, where he remained for six years. They returned to Rochester and Steward resumed his business and career as a Black activist. He published his narrative Twenty-two Years a Slave, and Forty Years a Freeman *in 1857.*

interesting than the one he had just attended in New York. The group explored the city and were given a tour of Sir Allan MacNab's palatial grounds and residence by his wife, Mary Stuart MacNab. Sir Allan MacNab was Hamilton's representative on the Legislative Assembly. A staunch Tory and friend of the Black community, he would later build the Great Western Railway and become prime minister of the Province of Canada (as it was known before Confederation). On the evening of their last day, some Black families put on a "grand soiree" in honour of Bishop Brown's first visit to Hamilton. Steward described the main hostess in some detail, although he unfortunately did not provide her name:

> She was very beautiful and very dark; but a complete model of grace and elegance, conversing with perfect ease and intelligence with all, both black and white ministers, who surrounded the festive board, as well as our Irish friends, not a few of whom were present.[14]

Dundurn Castle, circa 1925, named after Sir Allan MacNab's ancestral area in Scotland, was purchased by the City of Hamilton and opened as a public park in 1900.

Courtesy of Hamilton Public Library, Special Collections.

By the late 1830s, Hamilton had become a bustling town, and fugitive slaves and free Blacks were increasingly taking advantage of the opportunities it offered. They were settling in, forging key institutions such as churches, and establishing a definite presence in the city. The church became the locus not only of religious worship and activity, but also of a great deal of organizing around issues such as the anti-slavery cause, the reception of incoming fugitive slaves who needed assistance, not to mention a host of other matters of concern to the community.[15] The stage was set for a series of events which galvanized the community and spurred it into action. Hamilton Blacks, for example, rallied around a fugitive slave whose case was to become another bone of contention between the United States of America and the British colony of Upper Canada. His name was Jesse Happy.

Jesse Happy had escaped on his master's horse from Kentucky in May 1833. His whereabouts were only discovered four years later, when he was found living and working in Hamilton. Paola Brown, John Brown, and Solomon Connaway, all Colbornesburg Settlement alumni, were now in Hamilton and part of the lobby to have Happy released. Jesse Happy's owner, Thomas Hickey, swore out an affidavit stating that he was residing "probably in the Town of Hamilton" and described him in considerable detail:

> [A man] about thirty-nine years old and about five feet nine Inches high, well made and muscular, but not fleshy; likely healthy, active, and remarkably shrewd, the loss of one of his upper fore teeth is easily noticed when he smiles. He has a good forehead, I think a little scarred above one of the eyes, prominent cheek bones, straight and sharp nose, and cheeks somewhat sunk, black bushy hair, a little sun burnt which comes out straight, but is inclined to curl, and is usually long. His color is generally red, or which some call between a light and dark gingerbread, and has a natural mark called a flesh mark, on one of his cheeks, which shews at some seasons more than at others. His eyes are yellow as hazel, and he has

a fierce look. He had a cut on the back of his head to the Skull in 1833, which left a scar of more than an inch long, hid by his Hair. The little finger of one of his hands is crooked at the middle joint, and stiff; and he plays on the violin. He uses the word submit for permit.[16]

Interestingly, Hickey never mentioned anything about the supposed crime of horse stealing. He merely stated that Happy "absented himself from the State of Kentucky."[17]

The person who appeared in Hamilton and swore out an oath that the Jesse Happy in Hamilton was the same man who had been indicted by a Grand Jury in Kentucky was none other than David Castleman. Castleman was a wealthy horse breeder from Lexington, whose nephew John Cabell Breckinridge became vice-president under James Buchanan and lost to Abraham Lincoln in the 1860 presidential election. Castleman owned another fugitive slave from Kentucky named Solomon Moseby, who was living in Niagara. One day after he filed a claim for Moseby, he travelled

Crossing the River on Horseback in the Night, a woodcut image from William Still's Underground Rail Road Records.

to Hamilton and filed an affidavit against Happy. It would seem that Castleman and the four men that accompanied him were trying to stage an all-out slaveholder assault on Canada's status as a haven for fugitive slaves.[18]

What happened in the Moseby case was nothing short of incredible. He was arrested and imprisoned for stealing a horse in the attempt to escape. He sat in jail awaiting the order for extradition under the Fugitive Offenders Act that had been passed in 1833 to mollify the American government. An Act to Provide for the Apprehending of Fugitive Offenders from Foreign Countries, and Delivering Them Up to Justice, required that reasonable proof of a crime be presented to the Lieutenant-Governor, that it be of a capital nature, or one punishable by death, flogging, or incarceration at hard labour. The final decision to extradite a criminal would be made "at the discretion of the Lieutenant Governor." Thornton and Lucie Blackburn, fugitive slaves from Kentucky, were discovered living in Detroit just months after the act was passed and became the first test case for fugitive slaves under the new law. They managed to escape to Upper Canada, albeit after a riot broke out in Detroit over the matter, but were arrested and detained in the gaol at Sandwich to await their fate. Attorney General Robert Simpson Jameson gave the opinion that escaping from slavery could not be considered a crime in Canada because slavery did not exist in Canada. Moreover, if the punishment for a crime — in this case, escaping the custody of an officer of the law — was more severe than what the British colonial government would impose for the same offense, then the accused would not be returned. A return to slavery was far more severe than punishment for a misdemeanour offense, and the Blackburns were released to live their lives in freedom in Canada.[19]

Solomon Moseby's case was not that simple. Obviously, the charge of stealing a horse was indeed a capital crime both in Canada and the United States. Numerous petitions on behalf of Moseby were delivered to the government on the part of both Black and white citizens. A petition from "persons of colour" in the Niagara District argued that the "horse thief" charge was just a ruse to drag Moseby back into slavery and that Castleman had refused $1,000 for him, proving that, in his owner's eyes, he was a very valuable piece of "property."[20] The Black community, led by teacher Herbert Holmes, decided that it was not going to stand for Moseby's extradition and return to slavery under any circumstances.

For three weeks, several hundred Black men were alerted and some camped outside the jail. Sentrys were posted at all times to make sure that the prisoner was not removed from jail in the dead of night. When Lieutenant-Governor Bond Head gave the order for extradition, Moseby was finally escorted out in handcuffs and placed in a horse-drawn wagon, surrounded by constables. Two hundred Black men crowded on both sides and in front of the emerging procession, and a group of Black women stood on a nearby bridge singing hymns and forming a solid mass of humanity. The time taken to disperse the women would hopefully create a diversion and allow the prisoner to escape. At least one woman stuffed a stone in her stocking to use as a weapon and an eyewitness reported seeing that other women had aprons full of stones ready to hurl at the officers.[21]

Holmes rushed the horses and they came to a standstill. A man named Green stuck a fence rail into the spokes of the back wagon wheel, and locked them. Moseby's handcuffs somehow came off and he jumped out of the wagon and disappeared into the crowd. Meanwhile, the sheriff, on horseback with a drawn sword, had been arguing with a large Black woman who refused to move. When he realized that the wagon was stopped, he yelled "Fire!" and "Charge!" Holmes was shot dead and Green was gored with a bayonet and later succumbed to his wounds. Because of the riot, several dozen men were incarcerated and released just in time to form part of a Black regiment in the 1837 Rebellion.[22]

This was not exactly what Castleman had in mind when he entered the province to claim his slave. In the meantime, however, his affidavit caused the arrest and imprisonment of Jesse Happy in the Hamilton city gaol.[23] The following day, Attorney General Christopher Hagerman found the evidence sufficient enough to deliver Happy up to the State of Kentucky.[24]

However, Happy's guilt was not quite so clear cut. First, a petition from the "Coloured Inhabitants of Hamilton" was sent to Lieutenant-Governor Sir Francis Bond Head, signed by nine men: Peter Snowden, Leonard Neal, Paola Brown, Stephen Balden, Benjamin Harris, Jefferson

Grissom, Josiah Davis, John Brown, and Solomon Connaway. These men were the leaders of Hamilton's African community, and well-established in the city. Paola Brown had led a province-wide colonization movement almost a decade earlier, and was an educated free Black from Pennsylvania. Leonard Neal and Stephen Balden were also literate, evidenced by the fact that they too signed their names on the petition as opposed to marking an X as the remaining six had done. Benjamin Harris was a skilled gunsmith and the man who later brought the complaint against the two teenage boys in the assault case related to a group of Black churchgoers in October 1838.[25] The men informed His Excellency that a forty-year-old Happy escaped to Canada using the horse "lent to him by his Master" and that before crossing the border into Canada, he left the horse in the Perrysburg, Ohio, and immediately wrote to his former master informing him of its exact whereabouts. The petition also stated that they had proof that Hickey had retrieved the horse and had it in his possession. Happy had conducted himself with propriety since arriving in Hamilton, and deserved to be granted a fair trial.[26]

A second petition was also fired off from a broader constituency of African Canadians. It was signed by Peter O'Banyoun and ninety-eight other "Men of Color." O'Banyoun was a "Kentucky-born mulatto" and person held in high regard in Brantford. He became a respected minister of the African Methodist Episcopal Church in Brantford in the 1840s and 50s.[27] The Hamilton men no doubt decided to take their case beyond the Hamilton arena to a wider community of African Canadians, and almost one hundred people had signed that petition. They asserted that this case was nothing more than an attempt to re-enslave Happy, and had nothing to do with the theft of a horse. This time, they also raised the prospect that an extradition of Happy would have chilling repercussions for all persons of African descent who had previously been enslaved in the United States. They strongly urged Sir Francis Bond Head to order a full examination of the Happy case, as well as to "make such arrangements in regard to similar cases that may yet occur …"[28] In other words, they were asking that the government make an exception to its extradition agreement with the United States for fugitive slaves whose true crime was that they had stolen their own bodies in a bid for their freedom.

A third petition came from a group of "Gentlemen Freeholders and other white Inhabitants of the aforesaid Province." It read almost word for word the same as the previous petition and was signed by "Alfred Digby and 125 others."[29] The Executive Council of the legislature met and filed a report to the lieutenant-governor, advising in effect to allow time for the accused to provide affidavits supporting his innocence. It also advised Sir Francis Bond Head to inform the British Secretary of State for the Colonies, Lord Glenelg, of the case and to request his opinion in the matter.[30]

One month later, Bond Head sent the facts of the case as he knew them to the British Foreign Office. However, much had taken place in regard to the Solomon Moseby case that reflected very badly on the province. Bond Head was candid in his letter to Lord Glenelg, admitting only a few days prior to his being informed of this case that he had ordered the extradition of Solomon Moseby for the same offence, a decision that had ended in chaos, two deaths, and the wounding of numerous others. Ultimately, the prisoner had also escaped, and the entire debacle was under judicial investigation. Obviously weighing his decision more carefully this time, he argued powerfully on behalf of Jesse Happy and all other fugitive slaves in similar circumstances.

> ... it may be argued that a slave escaping bondage on his master's horse is a vicious struggle between two guilty parties, of which the slave owner is not only the aggressor, but the blackest criminal of the two. It is the case of the dealer in human flesh versus the stealer of horseflesh; and it may be argued that, if the British government does not feel itself authorized to pass judgment on the plaintiff, neither should it on the defendant ...
>
> ... the republican states have no right under the pretext of any treaty, to claim from the British Government which does not recognize slavery, beings who by slavelaw are not recognized as men and who actually existed as brute beasts in moral darkness, until on reaching British soil they suddenly heard for the first time in their

lives the sacred words *"Let there be light*, and there was light." From that moment it is argued they were created *men*, and if this be true, it is said they cannot be held responsible for conduct prior to their existence ...[31]

In the meantime, Happy supplied an affidavit sworn before Justice of the Peace Colin Ferrie (who would go on to become Hamilton's first mayor), stating that he was "born a Negro slave in Bedford County, Virginia. At eleven years of age he was traded by Presley Wilkinson, who took him to Kentucky, and loaned him to James Happy." He was a slave of Mrs. Happy after her husband's death, then to her daughters, then traded to Thomas M. Hickey of Fayette County, Kentucky for a woman. He remained with Thomas Hickey for five years. In 1833, his master granted him leave to visit a daughter and gave him a pass to protect him from "patrollers." Hickey also loaned him a horse and saddle for his trip. Thus equipped, he headed for what he termed "The Land of British Freedom and British Law."[32]

In Happy's letter regarding the whereabouts of Hickey's horse, he also thanked the Council and apologized for taking so long to provide this testimony. Attached to this document was another:

> Hamilton, Upper Canada
> 28th September 1837
> Personally appeared before me, one, Daniel Sweets who Made solemn oath that he witnessed the receipt of the Horse by the above-mentioned Thomas M. Hickey by the Above. Sworn by me September 28, 1837
> [Signed] Colin C. Ferrie, JP[33]

Sweets was likely the New Jersey-born chimney sweep Daniel Sweet who was later enumerated in the 1851 census living in Hamilton with his wife and children.

The Executive Council met on October 12 to review the case. The members included Robert Baldwin Sullivan, William Allan, Augustus

Baldwin, and John Elmsley. They decided that there were insufficient grounds to surrender the prisoner to the State of Kentucky and that Jesse Happy should be released. On November 14, Happy was freed and the case was closed.[34]

Tensions were mounting between Canada and the United States immediately preceding the outbreak of the 1837 Rebellion in Upper Canada later that year. But the actions of the community on Happy's behalf were absolutely critical to the favourable outcome of his case, as they had been in the Moseby affair. The determination of the Black community of Niagara in preventing the return of Moseby, and the resulting riot and deaths of two of its members, contributed to a climate of apprehension or uncertainty on the part of the government and to Lieutenant-Governor Bond Head's hesitation in surrendering Jesse Happy. In July 1841, however, another fugitive slave extradition case came before the authorities when Nelson Hackett, an escaped slave from Arkansas, stole *his* master's fastest horse and made a mad dash to the Canadian border.

Hackett settled in Chatham, Canada West — in the same year, Upper and Lower Canada were united under one government in the Act of Union and Upper Canada was now known as Canada West. Unfortunately, by September, Alfred Wallace, Hackett's master, had tracked him down and discovered him living in Chatham. Hackett was arrested and admitted his guilt. In addition to the horse, he had taken a beaver topcoat, a gold watch, $100, and a saddle that belonged to two white families. The prisoner was moved to the Sandwich gaol where he awaited his fate.[35]

Upper Canadian officials did not take action immediately. They advised Wallace that Hackett had not been indicted in Arkansas, prompting Wallace to obtain the indictment in November. Hackett was put on trial, and then secretly transferred to the Detroit prison by night, where he was later turned over to his owner. Many suspected collusion between the slave owner and the prosecutor, as well as the defense attorney, judge, and jailor in Canada. Back in Arkansas, Hackett was publicly and unmercifully whipped and sold away to Texas, where he was never heard from again.[36]

Needless to say, the Hackett case sparked alarm and outrage on both sides of the Atlantic and in Black communities across Canada.

Emboldened by their victory in the Happy case, Hamiltonians voiced their concerns in an address to Allan MacNab, their representative in the legislature. The group was once again led by Paola Brown and Benjamin Harris, as well as William Robinson, and was signed by 178 people. MacNab responded that he was already aware of the Hackett case and that it had been brought to the attention of the British government. He added that he would be "happy to peruse the papers you have already prepared on the subject, and you may rely on my using every exertion in my power, to procure a full measure of justice for the injured parties."[37] Of course, there was really nothing that MacNab, or anyone else, could do to help Hackett at this point. But it was important that Canadian officials realize what was at stake for future cases of fugitive slaves indicted for supposed crimes.

With the release of Happy and one successful campaign behind them, Hamilton Blacks were buoyed for another battle mounting on the horizon — the segregated school issue. But before this came to a head, the community became embroiled in another major conflict of the day that erupted in actual fighting — the Rebellion of 1837. There was growing dissatisfaction with the small group of officials, known as the Family Compact that led the government of Upper Canada. Their political patronage and favouritism toward the Church of England and recent British emigrants, their land-granting policies, economic priorities, and educational system were becoming increasingly unpopular, particularly among American-born settlers who migrated prior to the War of 1812. In late fall 1837, newspaper editor and politician, William Lyon Mackenzie, led a group of Reformers in an attempt to take over the government by force.

The new lieutenant-governor, Sir George Arthur, who succeeded Sir Francis Bond Head, directed his officers to "get hold of any loyal man you can, no matter from Militia Regiment or of what colour."[38] Of course, people of African descent unanimously sided with the Tories and against the rebels, and Black men signed up to stand guard for Britain and, they believed, their way of life as free people.

The Black community was so loyal to the Crown that rebel leader William Lyon Mackenzie expressed his disappointment in that regard. "…

nearly all of them are opposed to every species of reform in the civil institutions of the colony — they are so extravagantly loyal to the Executive
that to the utmost of their power they uphold all the abuses of the government and support those who profit by them." Mackenzie acknowledged
that the province's African citizens were an industrious, temperate group,
and not inclined to criminality, but that "an unfounded fear of a union
with the United States on the part of the coloured population should have
induced them to oppose reform and free institutions in this colony, whenever they have had the power to do so." This fact he chalked up to the reality that they had not been educated as freemen.[39] One loyal settler by the
name of George Coventry, who was living in the Niagara District at the
time, substantiated this view when he related that Harry, a Black servant,
"had heard that in the event of the rebels succeeding, he would be immediately sent out of the country and sold in slavery again."[40]

But was this loyalty to the British cause so irrational? Jermain Loguen,
who had spent some years in Upper Canada in the 1830s, didn't think so.
When so many African Canadians were former slaves, how could they
possibly be "passive, when the success of the invaders would break the
only arm interposed for their security, and destroy the only asylum for
African freedom in North America."[41] Before his departure, Lieutenant-
Governor Bond Head, in a sarcastic poke at the rebel stance, paid tribute
in a speech before the House of Assembly to the province's Black citizens
and their support of the government:

> When our coloured population were informed that
> American citizens, sympathizing with their sufferings,
> had taken violent possession of Navy Island, for the
> double object of liberating them from the domination
> of British rule, and of imparting to them the blessings of
> republican institutions, based upon the principle that all
> men are born equal, did our coloured brethren hail their
> approach? No! On the contrary, they hastened as volun-
> teers in wagon-loads to the Niagara frontier to beg from
> me permission that, in the intended attack upon Navy
> Island, they might be permitted to form the forlorn

hope — in short they supplicated that they might be allowed to be foremost to defend the glorious institutions of Great Britain.[42]

Several units of a Coloured Corps were in fact raised at Niagara under Captains Robert Runchey, Thomas Runchey, and Captain James Sears. There were additional "Coloured Companies" in Essex County along the Detroit–Windsor corridor, and two companies stationed at Chatham. The Black men of Hamilton were no less willing to respond to the call to arms. When Allan MacNab organized an army of men to lead the Tory charge against the rebels, the Hamilton *Gazette* reported that "… from 150 to 200 additional volunteers left town to join Col. MacNab on the frontier, amongst whom, we are happy to say, almost every coloured man in town appeared."[43]

Born in Newark, Upper Canada, Sir Allan Napier MacNab (1798–1862) established a law practice in Hamilton in 1826 and made a fortune in real estate speculation. Elected to the Legislative Assembly in 1830, he led the government forces during the 1837 Rebellion and was knighted for his success in defeating the rebels. MacNab became premier of the united Canadas from 1854 to 1856.

For the men, their allegiance to their government was about much more than preventing a rebel takeover, although that in itself was critical. It was also about proving their bravery and worth to their fellow citizens, who did not always regard them as equals. Paola Brown said as much in an address before a group of people gathered at City Hall in Hamilton almost fifteen years later. At that time, Brown remembered that "every colored man, as soon as he heard the Canadas were to be invaded, fled to arms under their brave leader

Sir Allan McNab (*sic*), and other officers. Therefore, I say to our Canadian friends, fear not, we can work and make good soldiers too, in times of troubles or war."[44] The men's actions on behalf of the government were a source of tremendous pride that the community could point to as proof of their value as citizens, and Brown could utter with certainty "... let the drum beat for an invasion, or rebellion, to-morrow morning, hundreds and thousands of my color would fly to arms at a moment's warning. This I know to be true."[45]

Austin Steward wrote with obvious pride about the regiment of Black soldiers stationed in Hamilton when he came to attend the AME Church Conference there in the late 1830s. "It was common in passing through the streets of Hamilton, to meet every few rods, a colored man in uniform, with a sword at his side, marching about in all the military pomp allowed only to white men in this *free republic*" (sarcastically referring to the United States).[46]

The company distinguished itself and was well regarded, as the following letter indicates:

> Hamilton, 24th Jany., 1838
> This is to certify that the Colored Company commanded by Captain Allan [*sic*] and attached on the 26th Decr. last to the 5th Gore Militia under my command did their duty while on the Frontier in every respect to my satisfaction, and I do not hesitate for a moment to say that should they again be employed (as they desire to be) they would not disgrace Her Majesty's Service, and I strongly recommend that Captain Allan [*sic*] be allowed to raise a volunteer corps to Serve until the 1st day of July next.
> Wm. M. Jarvis, Coll.
> 5th Regt. G.M.[47]

MacNab himself wrote that "The men under Captain Allan [*sic*] were always ready and willing and conducted themselves to my entire satisfaction."[48]

The Hamilton unit was also distinguished for another rather unusual circumstance at the time — its captain was a Black man. Captain William Allen was born in Barbados, West Indies, around 1795. He came to Upper Canada in approximately 1821 and was living in York working as a labourer. Allen must have heard about grants of land being given to Blacks on Wilberforce Street in Oro Township beginning in 1819, because he petitioned Lieutenant-Governor Sir Peregrine Maitland for a plot of land there, and was granted a ticket of location on one hundred acres on August 9, 1825. However, he did not end up settling in Oro Township. Apparently he left York in order to retrieve his family, and, during his absence, someone else informed the commissioner of Crown lands that he had left for good, and located on the property instead. Allen moved to Hamilton.[49]

When the Rebellion broke out in 1837, William Allen was instrumental in raising a Coloured Corps in that city, and he boasted with pride that he was the first Black captain of a company in British North America. He also confirmed that he and his men had volunteered to storm Navy Island, where Mackenzie was located with his rebels.[50]

While it was considered acceptable by British army officers and soldiers to have separate units of Black and Native fighters, it was felt that they should generally be led by white officers.[51] On occasion, however, Black captains were endorsed. In fact, Jermain Loguen wrote in his narrative that after he moved back to Rochester, New York, he returned to St. Catharines in the winter of 1837–38 to sell his house and property. An official from the government of Canada urgently requested that Steward accept the captaincy of a unit of Black troops. He declined. Most of the danger had subsided and he was profitably employed in Rochester and did not wish to interrupt his enterprise.[52] Josiah Henson, another impassioned leader of his people, was appointed captain of the 2nd Essex Company of Coloured Volunteers. This company was involved in the capture of the schooner *Anne* and all its provisions at Malden, thereby assisting in the ultimate defeat of the rebel forces there.[53] In any case, William Allen and his Hamilton African-Canadian unit were so highly regarded that Captain David MacNab, sergeant-at-arms in the House of Assembly, captain in the militia, and younger brother to Sir Allan MacNab, presented Allen and his company with a sword as a gift.[54]

The special connection that the MacNabs had with the Black community extended to Lady Mary MacNab. When she passed away in 1846 of a lung disease, her thirteen-year-old daughter, Sophia, wrote in her diary that "there was an immense procession. They reached from here [Dundurn Castle] down to the Grave. There were people from a great distance and also a great many women black and white."[55]

Of course, not all Black enlistees in the 1837 forces entered the Coloured Companies. A man named Joseph Harris living near Chatham told a newspaper reporter years later that he, along with a number of other Black men, served under Colonel MacNab in No. 1 Company of the Grenadiers. The brief entry under "King St. East Notes," in the *Chatham Daily Planet* of May 10, 1892, stated:

> Joseph Harris, eighty-one years of age and living near Chatham in the Township of Harwich, is one of the few surviving colored hereas [*sic*] of the war of 1837. He is yet hale and hearty, Canadian by birth, and a life long resident of this country. He served under Col. McNab [*sic*], and belonged to No. 1 Company of the Grenadiers. He says there were altogether eight hundred in the regiment including a number of colored soldiers.

After the cessation of fighting, the Legislature decided to construct a road from Niagara to the Detroit frontier, something that had been needed for agricultural and commercial purposes, as well as military defence. A corps of Black men was assembled in May 1840 to build the "Cayuga Road" between Drummondville (Niagara Falls) and Simcoe, under Captain Alexander MacDonald. The company was engaged in forging the road through vast areas of forest, and they had to fashion their own living accommodations alongside the construction route, since they were so far from any settlements. By the fall of 1841, they had reached Walpole Township in Haldimand County. At the end of the year, they marched to military headquarters in Hamilton, arriving on January 4, 1842. At this time, the strength of the unit was one captain, two subalterns, three sergeants, three corporals, one drummer, and fifty-two rank and file. When six Blacks from the 1st Battalion at Penetanguishene were accepted for re-enlistment, they were absorbed into the company stationed at Hamilton.[56]

At one point, one of the men was convicted of theft. He was deserving of severe penalty, but was let off with a reprimand because "the high character which the Colored Company holds in the estimation of Lieut.-General Clitherow has been the means of saving the prisoner from the degradation and punishment which the serious nature of his offence so loudly calls for."[57] It is not known how long this regiment continued to be active, but it may have been the one utilized to keep the peace on the second Welland Canal construction site not long thereafter. The canal, which runs between Lake Erie and Lake Ontario, was constructed to allow ships to bypass Niagara Falls. Captain MacDonald was in command of this unit, as well, which was stationed at Port Robinson.[58] The Coloured Corps was retained on permanent service until April 1850, when the government decided it was no longer financially expedient to maintain the unit. It had been the only incorporated militia company to be employed in Upper Canada after the militia reductions of 1844, and its soldiers were "a fine set of fellows, very jealous for the honor of their company and exceedingly proud of the trust reposed in them."[59]

Robert Jones, the man who escaped slavery with his wife Eliza in the mid-1850s, may not have been aware of Hamilton's history with Black men in uniform. A letter he sent to William Still in Philadelphia and preserved for posterity detailed his effort to set up a militia under the name of the Queen Victoria's Rifle Guards. Perhaps, however, he *was* told by one of the old-timers of the glory days of the Coloured units during the rebellion and its aftermath. Perhaps Jones was trying to recapture the honour and respect garnered by these men in uniform.

Hamilton, C.W., August 9th, 1856.
Mr. Wm. Still: — Dear Friend:
    I take this opportunity of writing you these few lines to inform you of my health, which is good at present, ...
    I was talking to you about going to Liberia, when I saw you last, and did intend to start this fall, but I since

looked at the condition of the colored people in Canada. I thought I would try to do something for their elevation as a nation, to place them in the proper position to stand where they ought to stand. In order to do this, I have undertaken to get up a military company amongst them. They laughed at me to undertake such a thing; but I did not relax my energies. I went and had an interview with Major J.T. Gilepon, told him what my object was, he encouraged me to go on, saying that he would do all he could for the accomplishment of my object. He referred me to Sir Allan MacNab, ... I took with me Mr. J.H. Hill to see him — he told me that it should be done, and required us to write a petition to the Governor General, which has been done ... The company is already organized. Mr. Howard was elected Captain; J.H. Hill, 1st Lieutenant; Hezekiah Hill, Ensign; Robert Jones, 1st Sergeant. The company's name is, Queen Victoria's Rifle Guards. You may, by this, see what I have been doing since I have been in Canada. When we receive our appointments by the Government, I will send by express, my daguerreotype in uniform.

My respects, ... Robert Jones.[60]

As for William Allen, after the rebellion he left for the West Indies, but later returned to Hamilton for health reasons. He again attempted to receive a land grant, this time in any available location, but his petition was rejected outright by the Council. [61]

Black Hamiltonians fought battles that took place not only in the military theatre, but in the educational arena, as well. As elsewhere in the province, Black children in Hamilton were barred from attending the common schools. The issue of access to education was a longstanding one in the province, and a source of tremendous anger and frustration. The 1828 meeting in Ancaster of Blacks from across the province had been held in part to discuss concerns about education, as has been seen. The early attempts to settle together in a larger colony and establish schools did not remedy the situation, since most Blacks did not end up relocating to them, or, in the case of Wilberforce and Colbornesburg, the settlements did not last. African Canadians continued to grapple with the separate school issue in many parts of the province for the rest of the nineteenth century.

In Hamilton, frustrated members of the community took action. A petition to Sir Charles Metcalfe, governor general of British North America, dated October 4, 1843, made a request for equality before the laws of the land:

> May it please Your Excellency
> We the Coloured inhabitants of the town of Hamilton District of Gore and province of Canada West — As loyal Subjects of Your Excellency on your arrival amongst us as her majestey's representative … In behalf of Your petitioners offspring who are denied Of the privileges of being admitted into any of the free Schools of this town Your pettrs having all taxes to pay and assessments and now being denied the priviledge [sic] of Education as adopted by the government Your pettrs humbly entreats Your Excellency that your pettrs children may be admitted into the free Schools of this town.[62]

The petition was signed by Reverend Amsted Brown, "minister of the babtist [sic] Church Hamilton."

Church ministers have always played an important leadership role in Black communities and as the minister of the Black Baptist Church in Hamilton, Brown took on the responsibility for this issue. He was born in Virginia but not much is known about his career and educational attainments or how he came to reside in Hamilton. He was listed in the assessment rolls for Hamilton in 1848–49 as living on the east side of MacNab Street and the census of 1851 indicated he owned a one-and-a-half-storey frame house on one-fifth of an acre. At that time, the fifty-two-year-old Brown and his wife, Susan, employed as a housekeeper, were living with Henry and Sylvia Fields and their three children.[63] The

Fields, as previously noted, hailed from Virginia and Kentucky, by way of Buffalo, New York.

Records indicate that Brown was presiding over the First Baptist Church in 1847 when it joined the Amherstburg Regular Missionary Baptist Association, the umbrella group for Black Baptist churches in Ontario. The church was founded by Reverend Washington Christian, who had come to Toronto in 1825, founded the very first Baptist church there in 1826, and had gone on to establish churches in Hamilton and St. Catharines, as well as serving as the pastor in Niagara.[64] The exact year that the Hamilton church was launched is not recorded, but it had come into existence by the late 1830s.[65] At the time of its entry into the Amherstburg Association there were thirty-six members. The church reached its zenith in 1861 with eighty members, but withdrew from the association in 1868, perhaps due to a precipitous decline in attendance after the Civil War.[66]

Following more closely on the heels of the first one, a second, more strongly worded petition regarding the segregation of their children, dated October 15, 1843, conveyed the deep sense of injustice felt by the community. This time it was not signed by any one person, although it was obvious that it had been penned by a single individual:

> We the people of colour in the Town of Hamilton have a right to inform Your Excellency of the treatment that we have to undergo. We have paid the taxes and we are denied of the public schools, and we have applied to the Board of the Police and there is no steps taken to change this manner of treatment, and this kind of treatment is not in the United States for the children of colour go to the Public Schools together with the white children, more especially in Philadelphia. And I thought there was not a man to be known by his colour under the British Flag ... we are grieved much, we are imposed on much, and if it please Your Excellency to attend this grievance.... Sir, I have left property in the United States and I have bought property in Canada, and all I want is

justice and I will be satisfied. We are called nigger when we go out in the street, and sometimes brick bats is sent after us as we pass in the street. We are not all absconders. Now we brought money into this Province, and we hope never to leave it, for we hope to enjoy our rights in this Province, and may my God smile upon your public life and guide you into all truth which is my prayer and God bless the Queen and Royal Family.

The Coloured People of Hamilton[67]

The author of the letter made reference to schools in Philadelphia being integrated because of an 1834 law that technically allowed Black children to attend the school of their choice. However, as was the case across the northern United States, Black students continued to be excluded from the schools in Philadelphia despite the law.[68]

Nevertheless, as a result of the two petitions, Governor General Metcalfe asked Reverend Robert Murray, superintendant of education for the province, to inquire into the matter and report back to him. Murray wrote to George S. Tiffany, president of the Board of Police for Hamilton, and requested information regarding the number of "coloured children" in Hamilton between five and sixteen years of age, the prevailing feeling regarding their attendance in the schools, the "religious body or bodies to which they belong," Tiffany's recommendations as to how to get them admitted into the schools, and whether the school assessment had been collected from their parents.[69]

Tiffany's reply indicated that, at least in Hamilton, if not very many other localities around Canada West, the rights of these children and their parents would be respected.

Hamilton 9th November, 1843
Sir,

I am favoured with your letter dated the 19th ultimo, respecting the Petition of the Coloured inhabitants of this Town upon the subject of their exclusion from the benefits of the Established Common Schools.... First, there appears to be about 20 coloured children within the ages of five and sixteen years. Second, I regret to say that there is a strong prejudice existing amongst the lower orders of the Whites against the coloured people. The several teachers as well as others acquainted with the extent of this prejudice fear that if coloured children are admitted into the Schools the parents of the greater part of the White children will take them away. Third, the coloured population belong chiefly to the Methodist and Baptist persuasions. Fourth — the Board of Police are unanimous in the opinion that whatever may be the state of feeling at present with respect to the admission of the coloured children into the same Schools with the whites, it would not be advisable to yield to it, but that the law ought to be enforced without distinction of colour. They think that if a firm stand be taken at first, the prejudice will soon give way.

I have the honour to be

Your obedient servant

George S. Tiffany

President Board of Police[70]

From that time forward, there were sometimes conflicting reports about racial segregation in Hamilton schools, such as Thomas Morton's lament to Reverend W.M. Mitchell in 1859 that he would have to move to the West Indies to educate his children because his two daughters were refused admission to the "Female Academy."[71] Morton was referring to the Burlington Academy of Hamilton, a private school for girls located at Bay and King Streets, which taught "reading, writing, and French, along with painting, embroidery, waxing flowers, etiquette and manners."[72] Morton was a well-to-do cab owner in Hamilton who could easily afford to send his daughters to the elite finishing school. It is difficult to find another reason for the girls' exclusion apart from race. But most observers reported that Black children were not officially barred from the public schools. An 1848 survey of the African population of Canada West indicated that Hamilton was one of only four locations out of twenty where Black children were able to attend the public schools with white children, the others being Gosfield, Toronto, and Niagara.[73]

In 1850, the provincial legislature passed a Separate School Act that gave any group of five or more Black families the right to open a separate school, if they so desired. This legislation was supposedly meant to give families choice in the way their children were educated. However, the act was used to justify the actions of whites in many localities who prevented Black children from attending the common schools.[74] Fortunately, this was not an issue in Hamilton after 1843. However, the students sometimes experienced racism from white students. Often, the result was that they did not attend school at all. Paola Brown lamented that even those who attended school were not learning what they needed to learn, and that they were not being adequately prepared.[75]

As elsewhere in the province, Black educators tried as best they could to fill the gap and set up private learning facilities in their homes or other public buildings and locations. For example, Susanna Brice opened a school in her family's rental flat on Hughson Street in St. George's Ward in Hamilton. She was eighteen years old and from Pennsylvania. Her parents, Charles and A.M. Brice, were born in Baltimore, Maryland, and her eight brothers and sisters, ranging in age from fourteen down to two, had all been born in Pennsylvania like their sister. This means that the family was only recently arrived in the province. The Brice school was kept in the cellar flat of the home, but nothing else is known about it.[76] Likewise, Reverend Robert and Mrs. Robinson moved from Hamilton to Windsor with their family in late 1852 and Mrs. Robinson promptly opened a select school for females that taught reading, writing, arithmetic, and geography, as well as needlework, drawing, and music.[77] It is tempting to suggest that Mrs. Robinson was carrying on the important work she had begun in Hamilton to uplift the young girls of that town.

When Boston abolitionist Benjamin Drew toured Canada West in 1855–56 to interview the Black population and determine the condition in which they were living, he learned that there were 1,700 pupils in all of the Hamilton schools, of whom only twenty-five were Black. At Central School, there were eight hundred students in attendance on

Courtesy of Hamilton Public Library, Special Collections.

Central School, located on 75 Hunter Street West, was a ground-breaking facility when it opened in 1853. Built for one thousand students, it was the largest graded, multi-roomed school in the province and boasted an excellent curriculum. Six hundred students enrolled initially, and in a few years, it was already overcrowded.

June 12, 1855, when he visited the school, and only seven of them were of African origin. Of the seven, six were girls. Drew stated that it was a shame that the community did not take advantage of the educational system more than it did, but that the reasons were not unanticipated. The prejudice against these students "prevails to too great an extent," concluded Drew.[78]

What was required was leadership. The principal of the high school in Hamilton stated that he was not aware of any case where the white children refused to play with or come into contact with the Black children. He noted that some parents did not want their children sitting at the same desk with them, but that in his school, seating went according to marks and not colour. Principal McCullum set an excellent example, commenting that "at first, when any new ones came, I used to go out with them in the playground myself, and play with them specially, just to show that I made no distinction whatever; and then the children made none."[79]

Again, however, the African-Canadian churches in Hamilton also did double duty as educational facilities. The AME Church Conference of July 1852 reported in its minutes that there were forty-eight scholars in its Hamilton Sabbath school, and two teachers. Reverend Henry Dawson presided as the preacher that year.[80] These classes filled part of the void left by the fact that some African-Canadian children were not attending the public schools. Many a child received lessons in reading, writing, and other subjects to help bridge the gap. So did their parents. Edward Patterson declared that although he never attended a day school in his life, he was able to pick up "a knowledge of reading, writing, and ciphering [because] I went to a Sabbath school four Sundays."[81]

CHAPTER 4

Gathering Speed: Anatomy of a Community

In the 1840s, the African population was steadily streaming into the city by the bay. There were two churches, a Baptist and an AME Church that had been established to serve the rising numbers. The community had garnered a measure of respect from government officials with their unwavering support during the 1837 Rebellion, and leaders like Paola Brown, Reverend Amsted Brown, and others had emerged to take the grievances of the community forward. They could point to successes in the Jesse Happy case and the school desegregation issue.

However, a storm was gathering on the horizon in the United States, which erupted in the passing of the controversial and highly oppressive legislation known as the Fugitive Slave Act of 1850. This act, designed to appease southern slave interests in the United States Congress, tightened the 1793 Fugitive Slave Act by making it easier to retrieve escaped slaves. It set up a force of federal commissioners empowered to pursue slaves across state lines and to compel ordinary citizens to assist in their capture. Those who did not co-operate could be fined or imprisoned. Once apprehended, a slave did not have the benefit of a jury trial to prove his or her innocence and the word of a slave against that of a slave-holder meant nothing. Commissioners were awarded a fee of $10 for every suspected runaway returned to slavery, but only $5 if they were freed. The law was hated by many white northerners, and many African Americans who had escaped years earlier and were living in freedom in places like Pennsylvania, Ohio, and New York suddenly were liable to be whisked away down South in chains. Even free Blacks, who had never been enslaved, could and were forced into servitude on the strength of one white person's testimony. Cases like these appeared routinely in the anti-slavery press. The freeborn, the manumitted, and those who had previously escaped slavery flocked across the border into Canada.

The Canadian anti-slavery newspaper, the *Voice of the Fugitive*, founded by a fugitive slave turned anti-slavery lecturer named Henry Bibb and his educated freeborn wife, Mary (Miles) Bibb, had recently been launched in Sandwich (Windsor), Canada West. The Bibbs' *Voice* made numerous reports about free Blacks streaming into the province. Some of the newcomers came with both educations and the means with which to purchase land. One account stated that several families from Indiana had just arrived with wagons, teams (of horses), and money with which to buy farms.[1] At an anti-slavery meeting held in Toronto, noted American abolitionist and speaker, Reverend Samuel J. May, told the crowd that there were many Blacks in his city of Syracuse, New York, who were waiting for his return with instructions as to the best way to proceed in moving to Canada West.[2] One farmer in Pennsylvania, because of his fear of the Fugitive Slave Act, asked how to get to Canada, and questioned whether or not he should bring his beds and other furniture with him. It turned out that, while furniture and goods were duty-free if brought with migrating families, it made more sense to purchase house-hold goods and furniture upon arrival.[3]

Moreover, the Underground Railroad into the province began to do a brisk business. Activists in the United States helping the enslaved reach freedom were no longer content to send their passengers to northern United States termini. To ensure that fugitives would not be tracked down and recaptured, vigilance committees and other UGRR organizers had a whole network of agents and safe houses ready to assist these people all the way to Canada.[4] In fact, thousands were arriving in Canadian communities between 1850–63. One observer estimated that three thousand African Americans alone had arrived between September and December of 1850.[5]

In the midst of this turmoil and confusion, Henry Bibb and a number of others organized a North American Convention of Colored People in Toronto in September 1851. Although there was initially some talk of holding it in Hamilton, delegates from across Canada West and the northern United States soon converged on Toronto's

Courtesy of Carolina Digital Library and Archives, University of North Carolina, Chapel Hill, NC.

Anti-slavery activist, newspaper publisher/editor, and former slave Henry Bibb was born in Shelby County, Kentucky, in 1815. After attempting to escape on numerous occasions, he finally succeeded, settling in Detroit. He married Mary Miles, a freeborn abolitionist and teacher, and the couple moved to Sandwich, Canada West, after the passage of the Fugitive Slave Act of 1850. They established a newspaper, founded a school, and made their home a constant site of fugitive slave reception and assistance.

St. Lawrence Hall from the 11th through to the 13th to register their protest and condemnation of slavery and the most recent disturbing developments. The convention was truly international because there was a representative from Jamaica and another from England in attendance. Hamilton sent Frances Russell and John Burns as delegates to the convention.[6] Although successful cabman Thomas Morton had endorsed the call for the convention in the *Voice of the Fugitive*, he was not a delegate.[7] However, there were many people who attended who were not delegates.

Frances Russell was a forty-four-year-old labourer and active in the AME Church. He served as district book steward of the AME Conference that was held in St. Catharines the following year. In this role, Russell was responsible for purchasing Bibles, hymn books, et cetera for the various churches.[8] John Burns was a forty-six-year-old "saloon keeper" who owned a four-storey brick enterprise valued at $1,000. Hamiltonians writing in the early twentieth century remembered that Burns was a large, dark man who owned a cookshop as early as 1840 on King Street just west of James. His skills as a chef were apparently unsurpassed and his establishment was crowded every night with people clamouring for his delicious pastries, sandwiches, and coffee. Burns was born in Upper Canada, and, although he did not attend the Baptist or African Methodist churches — he professed to be a Church of England convert — he was nonetheless a leader in the community. It was Burns, according to Richard Butler, who was marshal of the annual Emancipation Day celebrations held on August 1 each year.[9]

The first resolutions on the floor of the North American convention of 1851 dealt with the ramifications of the Fugitive Slave Act, described as "an insult to God, and an outrage upon humanity, not to be endured by any people." Central to the convention's deliberations was the issue of emigration, in particular, immigration to Canada. Although some prominent delegates from the United States, like Dr. Martin Delany of Pittsburgh, Pennsylvania, opposed African Americans leaving the United States for Canada or other countries, the majority adopted a very clear statement that Canada was "by far the most desirable place of resort for colored people to be found on the American Continent." On the second day, they highlighted the centrality of the issue by strengthening the resolution on emigration: "Resolved, that the convention recommend to the colored people of the U.S. of America, to emigrate to the Canadas instead of going to Africa or the West India Islands, that they, by doing so, may be better able to assist their brethren, who are daily flying from American slavery."[10]

The problem that many Black abolitionists in the United States had with the exodus of American Blacks to Canada and other places was its association with African colonization, or the wholesale removal of Blacks back to the African continent. The American Colonization Society (ACS) was founded in 1817 to send free African Americans back to Africa as an alternative to emancipation. Many viewed the goals of the ACS as a "smokescreen," in Afua Cooper's words, "to 'deport' them from their native land and break their connection with their enslaved sisters and brothers. This would give the slaveholders more opportunities to oppress … the enslaved."[11] However, the Canadian delegates made the argument that Canadian immigration was a "wonderful compromise" because from here, African Canadians "could easily support their enslaved brethren and agitate on their behalf."[12] Burns and Russell must have had a great deal to report back to the community in Hamilton from this exciting and important conference.

Black Hamilton was part of a larger network of people and organizations objecting to American slavery that spanned the entire breadth of the province. Speakers regularly toured the province, stopping in Hamilton and various other locales. *Provincial Freeman* editor, H. Ford Douglas, already a noted anti-slavery speaker before immigrating to Chatham, Canada West, wrote about one of his speaking tours in the May 16, 1857, edition of the paper. He described large gatherings in London (Canada West), Paris (Canada West), Brantford, Dundas, and Hamilton. In Hamilton, moreover, there were over one thousand people in attendance for his lecture at the Mechanics' Hall. Douglas thanked William Berry, J.H. Bland, Charles J. Carter, and Josiah Cochrane for their kind assistance during his stay there. Also active in Hamilton was the Anti-Slavery Society of Canada (ASC), founded in 1851 in Toronto. In its *Second Annual Report* of 1853, the ASC informed its audience that branches of the organization had been formed in Kingston, Hamilton, London, Windsor, and Grey County.[13] Another association formed by Hamiltonians was the Black Abolitionist Society. By 1860, it was sponsoring anti-slavery speakers and protesting discrimination.[14]

The *Provincial Freeman* newspaper, published by Mary Ann Shadd, was an example of an enterprise that brought people from across the province together in a common cause of anti-slavery, Canadian equality, and racial justice. Mary Ann Shadd, who had attended the

Mary Ann Shadd, abolitionist, teacher, founder, and editor of the Provincial Freeman, *is considered to be the first Black woman to edit a newspaper in North America, and one of the earliest women to do so in Canada. She went on to become the second Black woman to graduate from a law school in the United States in 1883.*

North American Convention of Colored People with her father, Abraham D. Shadd (although, as a woman, she was not an official delegate to the conference), came to Canada at the invitation of Henry and Mary Bibb. They had asked her to set up a school for the fugitive slave population in Windsor. However, she soon became embroiled in a well-publicized feud with the Bibbs that spilled onto the pages of the anti-slavery press. Ideological differences over whether the school should be a "separate colored school," that is, one that served the needs strictly of the fugitive slave population, or a school that observed no "complexional differences," as Mary Ann advocated, may have sparked the dispute, but when the Bibbs mentioned in their paper that Shadd was receiving money to the tune of $125 per annum from the American Missionary Association (AMA) to support her school, this merely added fuel to the fire. Mary Ann was angry because she felt that this acknowledgement would discourage parents from paying their school fees, and the AMA stipend alone would not be enough to carry on her work. She also felt it was deliberate. Shadd was then chastised in the *Voice* for being unladylike. She hurriedly assembled a meeting with the community to explain the situation. When the American Missionary Association subsequently fired her from her teaching post, one could rightfully suppose that it was not for the reason that her religious views were not sufficiently evangelical — the explanation they had offered — but because of her public dispute with the Bibbs and their endeavours. The outspoken Shadd had butted heads with the male establishment and overstepped the bounds of accepted female behaviour of the time. Although it was a severe blow, she suddenly gained an entirely new focus. It was the establishment of a literary vehicle by which she could disseminate her own views on her own terms.[15]

To this end, Shadd produced the first edition of a new newspaper named the *Provincial Freeman*, which she used to sell subscriptions and generate interest. The paper was fiercely anti-slavery, pro-temperance, and called for Black Canadians to integrate into the larger society as yeomen and skilled tradesmen and women.

After the paper began to appear weekly in March 1854 out of Toronto, with anti-slavery lecturer and ASC representative Samuel Ringgold Ward as its editor, agents in the various towns and localities were needed to sell subscriptions. J.W. Taylor and Robert Brown acted as agents in Hamilton.[16] Later that year, a province-wide organization was formed to help raise funds and the profile of the paper. Among the primary goals of the Provincial Union were the encouragement and support of any press that stood up for equality and against "exclusive communities" (all-Black colonies), West Indian emigration, and the condition of one race being the "hewers of wood and drawers of water" for another. It took an aggressive stand against slavery, and aimed to promote literary, scientific, and mechanical development among the younger generation. Finally, the *Provincial Freeman* was to be the official organ of the Provincial Union. A Ladies' Committee was also an important component of the organization. Its aim was to make items for sale and to organize bazaars in Toronto, Hamilton, London, Chatham, and other towns and cities, which would help support and assist in the running of the "people's organ," the *Provincial Freeman*. Once again, restaurateur John Burns and barber and community leader Josiah Cochrane, in addition to Robert Brown of Dundas, were listed as vice-presidents along with representatives from Toronto, London, Chatham, Dresden, Windsor, and Amherstburg.[17]

A sign of the maturity of the Hamilton community was the sheer number of groups and the level of organizing activity that took place. The Emancipation Day commemorations were an annual ritual in

Hamilton, just as they were in many African-Canadian communities across the province, and had most likely commenced from the first day that every enslaved person on British territory was finally set free. The momentous date was August 1, 1834, one year after the Slavery Abolition Act of 1833 was passed. The first record of an Emancipation Day event taking place, however, was in 1837, when the city council minutes of July 31 read that "A coloured man applied on the part of his brethren for protection while they celebrated the anniversary of their emancipation from slavery, and was referred to the bailiff."[18] Was the request for police protection because the organizers had experienced harassment from the broader community in the past, or was this routine? The answer to this question is likely to be found in the account of the 1853 celebration. After the usual street procession, with music and banners attended by about one thousand people, the parade ended at Christ's Church, where a sermon was delivered, and then a "festival" was held at the Mechanics' Institute.[19] Unfortunately, a number of teenage "rowdies" disrupted the occasion when tea was about to be served and "rushed to the table and prevented the possibility of persons retaining their seats recovering any refreshments whatsoever ..." Despite the fact that the police force had not sent enough officers, that no one was injured, the reporter noted, was due to "the wise and judicious conduct of the colored persons present."[20]

In the mid-1850s, Hamilton and Toronto's communities celebrated the day together, one year in Hamilton and the next in Toronto. The *Provincial Freeman*, based in Toronto at the time, reported extensively on the festivities in 1854. That year Toronto citizens hosted the event. The day began bright and early at 5:00 a.m. with a prayer meeting at the Sayer Street BME Chapel, after which a procession was formed led by Scott's Brass Band and the Oddfellows fraternal order, which marched from the Government House grounds to Browne's Wharf to meet the steamer *Arabian*, which transported the Hamiltonians. Thomas Smallwood, president of the day, gave a speech and the assemblage proceeded to St. James' Cathedral to hear a sermon by a Reverend Grasett. They then marched through the principal streets of Toronto back to the Government House grounds that surrounded the home of the lieutenant-governor, where everyone "partook of a sumptuous dinner." G. Dupont Wells read an address to the queen and the crowd gave three cheers to Her Majesty, the governor general, and the *Provincial Freeman* newspaper. Mr. Blue, president of the Hamilton delegation, "followed in a neat speech," and there were three cheers for the Toronto and Hamilton bands, after which it was resolved to celebrate next year's event in Hamilton. Finally, a soiree was held in the evening followed by a fireworks display.[21] In 1857, the *Freeman*, which had relocated to Chatham, published a report from the *Canadian Mail* that the "colored population of Toronto and Hamilton celebrated ... the emancipation of the negroes ... at the latter city by a procession to and from the church; and a very creditable display of oratory at the Mechanics' Hall in the afternoon."[22]

On August 1, 1859, the twenty-fifth anniversary of Emancipation Day, a special invitation was extended by the member of provincial parliament, Isaac Buchanan, Esquire, for the ceremonies to be held at the grounds of his estate at Claremont Park on Hamilton Mountain. After a procession through the streets, and a sermon delivered by Reverend Geddes at Christ's Church, the main Anglican Church in town, some three or four hundred people from St. Catharines, Niagara, Brantford, and Toronto (and spots in between) climbed the Mountain on foot or took cabs to the grounds. Seated under the fruit trees, they partook of a sumptuous feast of "roast beef and fowls, and pies and pastry of all kinds." Boxes of oranges and huge tubs of lemonade were also on hand for thirsty revellers. Dinner was followed by "orations" on the subject of slavery, freedom, and strategies for American emancipation.[23] Participants gave thanks to Britain and professed the loyalty of her African subjects. The occasion was concluded by a soiree at Price & Carrols, a local establishment.

During the 1850s, the Black population in Hamilton, just as it did in the rest of the province, swelled to its highest levels of the nineteenth century. In 1851, the year of the first Canada-wide census, the population numbers totalled 244 in the city of Hamilton proper, and forty-three additional people in Barton Township. The latter was located both on the outskirts of the city spanning the area from Burlington Bay to the

Auchmar Manor, Claremont Park, the location of the twenty-fifth anniversary of Emancipation Day celebrations in Hamilton in 1859.

foot of the Mountain and the top of the escarpment above the city. The numbers in the five wards broke down as follows: St. Patrick's Ward: 20, St. Mary's Ward: 22, St. Andrew's Ward: 90, St. Lawrence Ward: 84, and St. George's Ward: 28. Clearly, the majority of Black citizens were living in St. Andrew's Ward, followed closely by St. Lawrence Ward. It is easy to understand why. The "Colored Baptist Church" was located on MacNab Street, between Cannon and Mulberry Streets in St. Andrew's Ward and St. Paul's AME was located on Rebecca Street, between John and Catharine Streets in St. Lawrence Ward just east of the border between these two wards.[24]

By 1861, the numbers had doubled to 498 in the city. St. Lawrence Ward counted the highest number of Black residents that year, at 171. St. Andrew's Ward was next at 111. St. George's Ward came third, at 86, and St. Patrick's Ward and St. Mary's Ward counted 55 and 53 respectively. In the rest of Barton Township, there were 140 inhabitants of African descent.[25] The range of origins of people of African descent who lived in Hamilton paints a fascinating portrait of a cultural mosaic.

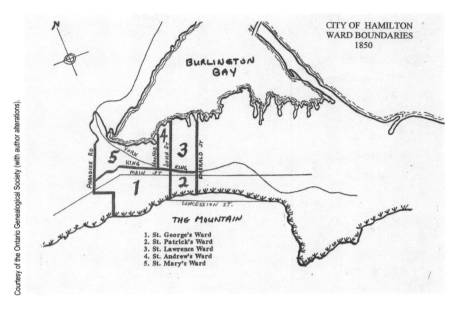

Courtesy of the Ontario Genealogical Society (with author alterations).

Place of Birth of Black Residents of Hamilton, 1861

Place of Birth*	Number
United States	219
Maryland	22
Virginia	14
New York	8
Pennsylvania	8
Kentucky	5
Alabama	1
Delaware	1
Massachusetts	1
South Carolina	1
Wisconsin	1
Subtotal	**281**
Canada	2
Upper Canada/Canada West	172

* Indicates how people responded to the census question "What is your place of birth?" Source: 1861 Census of Canada, Canada West, City of Hamilton.

Hamilton	24
Toronto	3
Chatham	1
Lower Canada	4
Subtotal	206
West Indies	5
Santo Domingo	1
Subtotal	6
England	1
Scotland	2
Germany	1
Subtotal	4
Africa	1
Subtotal	1
Grand Total	498

Place of Birth of Black Residents of Hamilton by Region, 1861

Region	Number	Percentage
United States	281	56%
Canada	206	41%
West Indies	6	1%
Europe	4	0.8%
Africa	1	0.2%
Total	498	99%

Source: 1861 Census of Canada, Canada West, City of Hamilton.

The large increase in the numbers had a lot to do with the passage of the Fugitive Slave Law of 1850 and occurred in many localities across the province. By the same token, a sizeable percentage (41 percent) of Blacks in Hamilton were not from the United States, but had been born in Canada. Again, this was a far cry from the stereotype of the panting fugitive recently arrived from the bowels of slavery. But what impact did this increased flow of Black migrants have on the older residents and the community as a whole? Samuel Ringgold Ward, a Black Congregational minister who moved to Canada West

Samuel Ringgold Ward, Congregational minister, anti-slavery lecturer, and first editor of the Provincial Freeman.

and was hired by the Anti-Slavery Society of Canada as a lecturer, visited Hamilton many times during his tenure at the ASC. He stated that in Toronto and Hamilton, "extreme suffering is scarcely known among the black people …"[26] Boston abolitionist Benjamin Drew observed that many Hamilton Blacks were "'well-off,' good mechanics and good 'subjects' in the English sense of that word."[27]

In terms of the occupational structure of the community of 1851, one-quarter of men reported that they were labourers. However, there was a sizeable number in the skilled/semi-skilled trades and a number who owned their own businesses. Black men held jobs as shoemakers, blacksmiths, carpenters, and barbers. There was also a cooper (barrel maker), a dyer, a gunsmith, saloonkeeper, and bricklayer. The gunsmith was none other than fifty-eight-year-old Benjamin Harris, one of the men who had signed the initial petition on behalf of Jesse Happy some fourteen years earlier, and the same person who had brought the assault complaint to the Board of Police, a case involving the harassment of some Blacks returning from church in 1838. Harris, who was from Kentucky, owned a shop and a sleeping room. He worked with a thirty-eight-year-old Irish man named Richard Wynne.[28] The men in the skilled/semi-skilled trades and those in business for themselves constituted 42 percent of the total number of men.

In the unskilled category were the labourers, as well as whitewashers, waiters, butlers, carters, a porter, driver, sailor, and a chimney sweep. This represented 52 percent of the total. Five percent reported no job or trade. This could have meant that they were unemployed, elderly and retired, apprenticing with someone, living off rental income (although usually such an individual would be described as a "Gentleman"), or sick that year.[29]

In 1861, those in the unskilled job category had decreased to 46 percent, although 11 percent of all men had no occupation listed beside their name. The percentage of Black men in skilled/semi-skilled jobs was 43 percent. Of this number, at least one-third (14 percent) owned their own business. In 1861, it was much easier to determine if someone was a business owner, because there was a category in the census for "Name of business or manufacture" and "Capital invested in business in real and personal estate." John Randle, for example, had invested $1,000 in his cooperage business, which was housed in a two-storey brick edifice on MacNab Street between Cannon and Vine.[30] Robert Browne claimed to have invested $5,000 in his grocery business. Perhaps his wife's dressmaking income gave them enough of a cushion to enable them to plough large sums into their gocery store.[31] W.H. Howard owned a tailor shop in a two-storey frame building on John between King William and Rebecca Streets, in which he had invested $400.[32]

Interestingly, the number one skilled occupation held by Black men in 1861 was that of barber: there were fifteen men who listed barber as their occupation, which represented 10 percent of all Black men employed. Many of these barbers owned their own shops and thus, were small business owners. H.F. Gardiner remembered that when he came to Hamilton in 1870, most of the barbers in town were Black.[33] The Black barber came out of the history of slavery, when Black men worked in

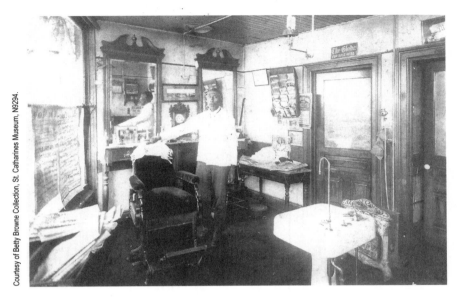

Courtesy of Betty Browne Collection, St. Catharines Museum, N9294.

Barber William A. Barnes of Cayuga, Ontario, in his barbershop, circa 1915.

personal service as butlers, valets, servants, and the like. In freedom, they turned this tradition into a business opportunity, which not only gave them a sense of independence and control over their own lives, but enabled them to amass considerable wealth. One historian has noted that "On the eve of the Civil War, one out of eight African Americans in the upper South worth at least $2,000, the standard for affluence at that time, owned a barbershop."[34] For a dozen generations, Black barbers in the United States dominated the profession. Most worked in the "white trade," exclusively cutting the hair of white clientele and combining elements of the luxury hotel, spa, and clubhouse in their barbershops, which were usually located in upscale downtown commercial districts and adorned with first-class furnishings: carpeting, chandeliers, lace draperies, matching upholstered furniture, and so forth. They also offered customers hot baths and a range of items for purchase, such as perfumed soap, cigars, and suspenders. With the rise of Jim Crow segregation, the tradition of the Black barber gradually died out and in the twentieth century most Black barbers catered primarily to a Black clientele. These barbers then parlayed their success into other ventures, catering to Black customers in segregated neighbourhoods. African-American barbers brought their skills and business acumen with them to Canada.[35] In Hamilton, Black barbers were a successful subgroup of the skilled class and among the leaders of their community.

In terms of the women's job profile, the practice by the census enumerators of omitting women's occupations, particularly when the husband was present in the home, effectively masked the large numbers of women who, in addition to their work cooking, cleaning, and rearing children, were engaged in waged work. Therefore, the women who had no occupation listed beside their names represented by far the largest category for women. In 1851, this was 73 percent. There was one school-teacher, two cooks, and one in sewing, jobs that have been classified as middle-class occupations or which required knowledge and skill. These women comprised 8 percent of the total. The rest of the Black female residents of Hamilton were listed as servants, housekeepers, domestics, and washerwomen, and this represented 18 percent.[36] In 1861, 83 percent of women did not report an occupation. Of the rest, six (5 percent) held skilled occupations as dressmakers, seamstresses, fancy workers or tailoresses, and cooks. Twelve percent were in the unskilled job category, working as servants, laundresses, or hucksters.[37]

The lower employment figures in 1861 for both Black men and women may be explained by a financial crisis brought on by massive city debt. The building of the Great Western Railway, which was launched in 1854, and the construction of the city waterworks incurred huge tax hikes and a temporary exodus of thousands from the city because of it. This resulted in a major recession by the late 1850s and early 1860s.[38]

On the whole, however, Hamilton appeared to be a place of opportunity for Blacks. In terms of good jobs in the skilled trades, there were opportunities for men and women to utilize the skills they had acquired in Southern slavery and as free men and women living in northern cities. Henry Williamson, a former slave from a town in Maryland, told Benjamin Drew that he first found work in Canada on the railroad. Since his experience was as a waiter, he was unused to this kind of labour, but Williamson persisted until, he said, he found something he liked better. Apparently, this was waiting tables, because he was listed in the *1856*

Hamilton City Directory living at 65 East Market working as a waiter.[39] The fact of the availability of jobs and opportunities had a significant impact on other indicators of security and well-being. Michael Katz's study, *The People of Hamilton, Canada West: Family and Class in a Mid-Nineteenth Century City*, revealed of Black families that:

> [I]n 1851 about 20 percent and in 1861 about 24 percent owned their own homes, very respectable proportions, and 50 percent of Black household heads present in 1851 remained in the city a decade later, a figure higher than that of any other ethnic group and a clear indication of Black stability and modest prosperity. Among Blacks, moreover, there were fewer female-headed households than among either the Irish Catholics or the population as a whole, again a sign that the Black community fared relatively well in urban Canada.[40]

There are few studies of this kind that look at the occupational breakdown, levels of home ownership, and family structure of nineteenth-century Black Ontarians. An 1840 survey of Toronto's Black community, which numbered 528 in that year, showed that 43 percent of workers were in skilled/semi-skilled trades or owned small businesses, and 48 percent were labourers or in other unskilled work. These figures included both men and women. Eight percent were widowed, retired, or otherwise unemployed.[41] However, Chatham is one centre where detailed information exists on the nineteenth-century socioeconomic status of Blacks, thanks to the 1979 Ph.D. thesis of Jonathan William Walton entitled "Blacks in Buxton and Chatham, Ontario, 1830–1890: Did the 49th Parallel Make a Difference?"[42]

Chatham was a much smaller town than either Toronto or Hamilton in terms of its population. There were 2,070 residents in Chatham in 1851 compared to 14,112 in Hamilton, and this number had increased to 4,466 by 1861, compared to 19,096 for Hamilton.[43] Chatham, however, was arguably the mecca of Black settlement in the province. It boasted the largest Black population in an urban centre in Canada West, as well as a high number of the educated elite, including medical doctors, teachers, newspaper editors, writers, business people, skilled tradesmen, and a number of high-profile abolitionists. Among the latter were Dr. Martin Delany, the Shadds, H. Ford Douglas, and poet James Madison Bell. One reason that Chatham attracted these people was the considerable employment prospects the town offered, as well as the fact that it was the largest town in Kent County, which held by far the largest population of Blacks in the province, owing to the location of the Black colonies of Buxton and Dawn within its borders.[44]

In Chatham's case, the 1851 census showed that 51 percent of Black men were engaged in skilled and semi-skilled employment that year. Forty-one percent were unskilled and 8 percent reported no job or were otherwise unemployed.[45] Ten years later, the comparable numbers were 48 percent in skilled or semi-skilled trades, 50 percent unskilled, and 2 percent listed no occupation.[46] Like Hamilton, Black women in Chatham were largely absent from the paid workforce according to the census, although this masked those who did work for wages. In Chatham, 5 percent of women listed (five in number) were employed in 1851, and of this number three were servants and two were labourers. In 1861, the numbers were 29 percent employed, 51 percent of those in skilled or semi-skilled employment, 4 percent in independent or self-employed positions, and 45 percent in unskilled jobs.[47]

When compared to workers in major United States cities at this time, Blacks in the British colony to the north seemed to have superior advantages. In American counterparts like New York, Washington D.C., Pittsburgh, and Cincinnati, according to Walton, barely one-fifth of Black workers held skilled or semi-skilled positions. In Philadelphia, not only was there a very limited proportion in this category, but they were being displaced by Irish immigrants. Only in Detroit were Black workers employed in the higher-skilled positions at a comparable rate to those in Hamilton and Chatham.[48]

John Bland, or J.H. Bland as he preferred to be called, was one of those men in the skilled trades who was interviewed by the American Freedmen's Inquiry Commission in 1863. This commission was set up to collect the testimony and make recommendations about what was to be done for the newly freed slaves whose emancipation had just been proclaimed by President Lincoln on January 1, 1863. In addition to interviewing white army officers, slaveholders, government officials, and missionaries, the commission collected the testimony of former slaves in South Carolina, Kentucky, Louisiana, and Canada. The report of the commission helped to form one of the most important early blueprints for Reconstruction, and it is also an important source on Blacks in Canada West in this time period.[49]

Bland had been a slave in Warrenton, Virginia. Although he maintained that his slave-masters had been rather mild compared to some, he noted that they were "not half mild enough for me at that." At the age of twenty-one, therefore, he fled to New York City and remained there until the passage of the Fugitive Slave Act, after which he did not consider it safe to stay. Bland moved to Hamilton with his wife, Saharta, a native New Yorker, and established himself as one of that class of men who dominated the barbering trade. Over the years, he opened his own barbershop and was doing well. In 1861, the couple was living in a two-storey brick home with an eight-year-old boy named Charles. Their business was reportedly worth $7,000, and another barber, Thomas Sinclair, lived with them. At the time of the interview in 1863, Bland had been in Canada for twelve years.[50]

Bland told the Freedmen's Commission interviewer that he was doing "a very good business," but that it had required a great deal of perseverance. From his description, he probably worked in the "white trade," as most Black barbers would have done in Hamilton at that time.

> It is hard to get the confidence of the people. I have had people walk by my shop for five or six years and never look in; but some day they would come in, looking as if they were half frightened to death, and then, if they got a good shave, they would come again, and be among my best customers.[51]

Was there any difference between Americans and Canadians in this regard?

[Canadians] are very different from the Americans. There, when a man opens a new shop, everybody comes to see what he has got; but here, a man will go half a mile out of his way to patronize the old place. I like this country very well since I have got acquainted.[52]

John Henry Hill was an escaped slave whose harrowing journey to freedom was documented in Underground Railroad activist William Still's book, *The Underground Rail Road*. Hill penned numerous letters to abolitionist Still detailing his new life in freedom. Initially, he settled in Toronto, but by 1855 he had relocated to Hamilton. In 1856, he was living at 25 James Street. Two years later, he was joined by his uncle Hezekiah Hill, who had also escaped slavery after buying himself several times over and being cheated out of his freedom. The two resided on East King Street and earned a living as carpenters.[53] Hill went on to establish a successful tobacco-manufacturing business with three other Black men. By 1861, he, his wife, who had joined him in December of 1853, and three children lived in Barton Township just outside the eastern city limits. A sixteen-year-old younger sister of Rosetta named Martha McCray, also lived with the family in Barton Township. Their location would have been just east of Wentworth Street somewhere between Barton and Main. They owned five pigs valued at $15.[54]

Courtesy of Special Collections & Archives, Johnston Memorial Library, Virginia State University.

John Henry Hill, captain, Petersburg Guard 187, 1873. Hill escaped from a Richmond, Virginia, slave auction and hid for nine months in the free Black community before forging a pass to Norfolk and stowing away on a steamer bound for Philadelphia. There he met with William Still and the Vigilance Committee, who sent him on to Toronto in October 1853. In 1855, he moved to Hamilton.

Hill was also interviewed by the Freedmen's Inquiry Commission in 1863. His interviewer, Samuel Gridley Howe, was suitably impressed with Hill and his tobacco-manufacturing operation. The business was housed in a building that had been leased for $250 per year and most of the woodwork for the machinery had been built by the men themselves. Howe noticed when he visited Hill's establishment that there was a quiet hum of activity as each man went about his task, some pressing the tobacco with iron levers, some filling boxes, others nailing them up; some were sorting the stock, and others rolling it into plugs. The grown men were doing the heavier lifting and pulling, and the younger boys were picking and sorting the tobacco leaves.[55] Hill commented on his business:

Born a slave in Petersburg, Virginia, Rosetta McCray Hill acquired her freedom through her father, John McCray, who purchased her in 1840. She married John Henry Hill and bore him two sons, whom she brought with her to Canada in 1853. Their sons died, but she gave birth to seven more daughters. After the Civil War, the family returned to Petersburg and became prominent members of the Black community.

> We employ twelve or fourteen hands now, and have white & black boys at work: there is such a demand for boys, that we have to take anybody we can get.... Our business is paying about $26 a day, and we hope to make it pay $50 a day. We mean to succeed....[56]

Hill stated that the wages were good, and that some men made between $20 and $25 a week in the tobacco factories. When asked if he suffered from prejudice or racist treatment, Hill maintained that:

When we came here in 1855, we found no difficulty
in getting into the best shops of the city; and after we
had worked here a while, I believe we were preferred,
because we were steady & stuck to our work. I never
heard of any objection being made to taking a colored
boy into a shop to learn a trade. One of the best machin-
ists in the city will take colored boys into his shop. There
is no difficulty in a good colored mechanic getting work
among white men. I think the colored people, after a
while, will surmount the prejudice against them.[57]

Hill's Uncle Hezekiah, named Henry in the 1861 census, also resettled in Barton Township with his family.[58] In addition to his tobacco
business, John Henry Hill personally helped many fugitives once they
arrived in Canada, and, as was noted in Chapter 3, he was active in
Robert Jones's Queen Victoria's Rifle Guards as 1st lieutenant along with
Uncle Hezekiah, who was the ensign.[59]

As stated earlier, not all Blacks who migrated to Hamilton were escaped
slaves or former slaves. One free African-American family who moved
to Hamilton in the 1850s was the Aaron Mossell family. Aaron and Eliza
Mossell and their eight children were living in Barton Township on five
acres in Concession 2, Lot 21, just outside the western city limits in 1861.
They would later become one of the most prominent African-American
families of their day. This is known as Dr. Nathan Mossell, who was five
years old in 1861 when the census enumerator interviewed the family,
wrote a memoir in 1946 at ninety years of age. He shed light on the history
of the Mossells and their remarkable journey through the nineteenth and
early twentieth centuries, including their brief stay in Hamilton.[60]

Nathan Mossell's father, Aaron, was a free Black and brick-maker
living in Baltimore, Maryland. His paternal great-grandfather had been
stolen from the coast of West Africa, and his grandfather had purchased his freedom and that of his wife from his master, moving from
the Eastern Shore of Maryland to Baltimore. Nathan Mossell's mother,
Eliza Bowers Mossell, was also a freeborn African American. Her family
had been involved in a colonization scheme in Trinidad, West Indies.

However, they ended up returning to the United States, where Eliza met and married Aaron Mossell.[61]

According Dr. Mossell, his father's exceptional skill as a brick-maker enabled him to save enough money to purchase a home for his new wife. However, he decided to uproot his family and move to Hamilton because there were no schools in Baltimore for Black children. "Father disposed of his Baltimore holdings about 1853, from which he secured enough money to buy a small tract of clay-land in Hamilton, Canada. There, he established a brickyard of his own."[62] They lived on Ray Street in the city for a time with their two children, Charles and May. Nathan Mossell was born on July 27, 1856. His father was engaged in his brick-making business, and demonstrated a "strong propensity for mathematics as he was able to estimate the number of bricks he needed for any size contract, with amazing accuracy."[63] He was also philanthropic, as he donated the brick that was used to build the AME Church in Hamilton.

One of young Nathan's early memories was the visit of the Prince of Wales to the city in 1860. During the procession, the African contingent passed, all adorned in white hats:[64]

> Father took the day off with his family to participate in the parade. I sat in our carriage with our father, my two sisters, and mother with baby in her arms. My two older brothers rode horse back on either side of the carriage. I think that the whole thing would have gone from my memory had it not been for the vast scene of soldiers in red uniforms.[65]

Nathan also wrote that his father attended night school in order to learn to read and write. However, according to Nathan, "the young lawyer who supervised father's purchase of the Canadian property; and father, from a lack of training — overlooked some of the intricacies of the British entail system, causing father to lose his property." He continued:

> I recall also the visit to our home of the old British lady who claimed the land on which we built our home and

established our business. Had we met the amount of her claim, it would have wiped us out of everything we possessed; for under the law, her claims covered not only the land, but all of the improvements and much of our personal effects.[66]

As a result, Aaron Mossell secretly sold a horse to the Union Army and used the proceeds of the sale to move the family to Lockport, New York. After twelve years in Barton Township, the Mossells moved back to the United States.[67]

The British entail system of inheritance did not apply in Upper Canada (Canada West) so Dr. Mossell's statement in that regard is not accurate.[68] Land Registry records reveal that the Mossells purchased five acres in 1855 from William Hill in Lot 21, Concession 2, just west of Paradise Road North, taking out a mortgage of £250 on the property. By 1861, the land and business were valued at $1,000. In May 1864, the property was confiscated because of default of payment of £150 plus interest that was due December 1, 1856. Hill was deceased and the niece who now claimed the property was widow Emma Garret Wyth of the City of Hamilton. It must have been she whom Nathan Mossell described as the "old British lady" who came to the house to take possession of their land and everything on it.[69]

Despite this setback, the Mossells went on to excel. Nathan attended college and graduated second in his class at the University of Pennsylvania Medical School. He became a prominent physician and surgeon who founded the Frederick Douglass Memorial Hospital in Philadelphia. He was also, among other things, a member of the Niagara movement and founder of the National Association for the Advancement of Colored People's (NAACP) Philadephia chapter.[70] Mossell married Gertrude E.H. Bustill, a teacher and noted journalist who authored two books and became heavily involved in charity work.[71] His brother, Charles, was a minister and missionary in Haiti, and his younger brother, Aaron Jr., a lawyer in England. Aaron Jr.'s daughter, Sadie Mossell Alexander, became a practising attorney with her husband, Raymond Pace Alexander in Philadelphia. Her brother, Aaron, was a pharmacist in Philadelphia and their

Mossell Family, circa 1875. Nathan Mosell is seated on the far right.

sister, Bessie Mossell Anderson, became dean of women at Wilberforce University. Nathan's younger sister, Alberetta, died while doing missionary work with Charles in Haiti; his older sister, Mary, married Professor Parker Denny and *her* only daughter was the wife of attorney A.T. Walden of Atlanta, Georgia. Most interestingly, Gertrude Mossell's nephew was Paul Robeson, the legendary singer, actor, and social activist. [72]

Some Hamilton area families clearly preferred to live in the semi-rural or suburban locations just outside the city proper. Farming and land ownership remained a goal of many in mid-century Canada because it offered independence and was considered one of the best ways to get ahead in a province that was still largely unsettled and heavily forested. George Johnson and his family of fourteen were enumerated in the 1861 census as living in Barton Township on twenty-one acres.[73] Fortunately, Johnson was also interviewed by the Freedmen's Inquiry Commission in 1863. Johnson stated that he was born a slave in Maryland and escaped when he was fifteen years old. He lived in Pennsylvania, a free state, for twenty years before coming to Canada. The census shows that he came with a family of eight children plus his wife, Harriet, and an older relative named Ruth Johnson — most likely his mother. The family would have also brought some cash and other personal property. Why did the Johnsons make the move to a new country? "I concluded I would go where I could possess the same liberty as any other man," said Johnson.[74] He reported on his life since coming to Canada: "I have got along very well here, farming and carrying on different businesses for myself. I have one place of 135 acres and another place of 21 acres. I rent both these places. I have had twelve children, but have lost three since last April."[75]

The information from the census corroborates this. In 1861, the family owned two horses, one cow, and six pigs, all together worth $150. They had five carriages for hire, also worth $150, and farmed spring wheat, oats, Indian corn, hay, and potatoes that were sold to the local market.[76] In 1871, the Johnsons were still living in Barton Township on Concession 1, Lot 10, and now owned 11.75 acres. The family was considerably reduced to five members, including wife, Harriet, the elder Ruth Johnson, and sons James and Edward, ages seventeen and sixteen, both of whom were attending school. In addition to the tragic deaths of three of his children, the older children had most likely married and moved out of the household.[77]

Just as Blacks settled on the outskirts of Hamilton proper *below* the Mountain so that they could take advantage of more land and space to engage in farming and other business operations, a number of families settled on Hamilton Mountain. Many bought lots of land from William Bridge Green, a British émigré who owned one hundred acres on the Mountain, Lot 9, Concession 4. Green was born in London, England, in 1814, emigrated to Upper Canada, and purchased his one hundred acres from Peter Hunter Hamilton in 1826.[78]

Green sold land to at least seven Black families on the Mountain and some of these families subsequently divided up the land they had purchased and resold smaller plots to other Blacks. The families who purchased land in Lot 9, Concession 4, included Daniel Johnson, William and Sarah Calamese, Henry and Martha Johnson, Marianne Connaway (likely the widow of Solomon Connaway), William and Mary Nelson, Lewis Miles and Anna Johnson, Charles J. and Ann Eliza Carter, Edward

Strongman's Road, located on the brow of Hamilton Mountain, overlooking the picturesque city and harbour below, has awed onlookers for generations.

and Annie Caroline (or Hannah) Johnson, George Santee, George and Elizabeth Morton, John and Rachael Johnson, Josiah and Amelia Cochrane, and William and Ann Elizabeth Mallory. A number of other families were tenants on this tract along Concession Street or on other lots in Concession 4, many of them renting from those Blacks who had bought land there. Not everyone who purchased land on the Mountain brow was living in Canada. George Santee actually lived in Port Clinton, Schuylkill County, Pennsylvania, when he made his land transaction with Isaac Dixon of Barton Township. George's son, Ephraim Santee, Ephraim's wife Mary Jane, and their six children lived on the property.[79]

It would be interesting to know why Green sold parcels of land to so many Black families. Whatever the motives, he was not the only catalyst for property ownership among Blacks on Hamilton Mountain. As noted, once Blacks gained a foothold on the Mountain through William Bridge Green and others, the door was now open for additional families to buy into the area. For example, Pennsylvania native Charles J. Carter, a dyer and clothier turned clergyman who ran his establishment at the corner of King and Park in Hamilton, bought an acre from Lewis Miles and Anna

Johnson in 1855 for £50, and another from Henry and Martha Johnson for £75 in 1857. Carter, in turn, sold his two acres to well-known barber, Josiah Cochrane, and his wife Amelia for $400 twelve years later, making a tidy profit.[80] Others, like William and Ann Elizabeth Mallory appear to have bought land on the Mountain strictly as an investment, because there is no evidence they ever actually lived there. Several Black individuals provided mortgages to Black landowners and earned the interest from these transactions. Henry Criel, the former slave from West Virginia whose life and escape was outlined in Chapter 2, held the $80 mortgage of George and Elizabeth Morton, who purchased two acres from William Bridge Green in 1862. William L. Simpson of Buffalo, New York, whose racial origin is not known but who may well have been Black, was another mortgage lender.[81] By the mid-1860s, when the Black population in Barton Township was at its peak, the number of Blacks living in Concession 4 on the Mountain was at least forty-six.

At another location on the Mountain — Lot 12, Concession 4 — several additional families purchased land, this time on the basis of one initial transaction that occurred between William Kirkendall and Reverend Joseph P. Williams and his wife Violet. Lot 12 in Concession 4 was originally granted to Philip Crips by the Crown, in 1801. James Durand, an important figure in Hamilton affairs and provincial politics — not to mention a slaveholder — purchased it from Crips in 1808, and he sold it to George Hamilton, the founder of the city, in 1815. Hamilton split up the property by selling smaller lots to a number of different people, and, upon his death, his son Robert Jarvis Hamilton continued to do the same. William Kirkendall was one of the people to whom the younger Hamilton sold a tract of land in 1844, and two years later, Kirkendall sold five acres to the Williams, both transplanted African Americans, for £65/12/6. They then sold one acre to John and Rosanna Spellman, both from the "West Indies," for £25 in 1849, and another half acre to the African-born Pompey Lewis for £12/10 in 1852.[82]

Joseph P. Williams was a minister of the Methodist faith. In 1854, he sold 816 square feet of his property to William Calamies (Calamese), John Spellman, and Henry Johnson, described in the deed as the "Trustees of the African and Methodist Episcopal Society of the Township of

Barton." This property bordered on that of Pompey Lewis and John and Rosanna Spellman, and on it was built a modest frame structure capable of accommodating one hundred persons. Mabel Burkholder wrote about this church, stating that it stood where the old Jolley homestead was subsequently located at the top of the Jolley Cut. This was quite true, for James Jolley ended up buying the land on which the church stood, as well as that of the Williams and Pompey Lewis, and, in 1864, built a home called "Bellemont" at what is today the corner of Concession and East Fifteenth Streets. A Scotsman who owned a successful shop selling saddles and harnesses in downtown Hamilton, Jolley also bought up lots from a number of other families and in 1869 received permission from city council to construct what became known as the "Jolley Cut," a free road from the Mountain to the city, because he had no desire to use the toll routes. This road was later donated to the city in 1873. Although it would appear that the AME Church was not in operation for very long, its existence is a strong indication that a vibrant Black community was being forged on the Mountain.[83]

Whether as landowners or tenants, residents of African descent on the Mountain engaged in a variety of occupations and means of earning a living in order to get ahead. Many farmed and sold their produce to the city, as well as holding down other jobs as labourers. Joseph P. Williams was the resident minister on the Mountain, as already noted. Some inhabitants, such as Lewis Miles Johnson, and William Nelson also had carriages for hire that they either rented or drove themselves for people in need of transportation and John Johnson made his living as a carter. Julia Berry was the toll keeper for the tollgate at the top of James Street in the 1880s.[84]

Beginning in the 1930s, a descendant of a Swiss-born Mennonite who settled at the Head of the Lake after the American Revolution,[85] Mabel Burkholder, began a regular column in the *Hamilton Spectator* called "Out of the Storied Past." In it she recounted a story of Black settlement on the Mountain and called the community "Little Africa." Although Burkholder claimed that this was the name of the settlement, no records of the period ever referred to a Black community on the Mountain by this name. Unfortunately, her articles were full of romantic myth, half-truths, complete untruths, and patronizing stereotypes. In a nutshell,

Courtesy of Hamilton Public Library, Special Collections.

Mabel Grace Burkholder (1881–1973) was a local historian who, for many years, wrote a column about Hamilton history for the Spectator *entitled "Out of the Storied Past." Her misleading and patronizing articles on "Little Africa," the community of Blacks on Hamilton Mountain, were quoted for decades.*

Burkholder stated that the Green family donated land *free of charge* to numerous destitute Black families recently escaped from slavery. These settlers, "with meagre possessions ... had to be helped in establishing homes" because they were "illiterate, childish and rather dependent in their attitude toward life, as was only natural to a people reared in servitude, but they responded readily to kindness and gave very little trouble."[86]

According to Burkholder, families that comprised this community were several Johnson households, the Berry family who operated the tollgate at Concession and Wentworth, the Atkins, Banks, Greens, Murdocks, Nelsons, Peter Carey, and Frankie Waters. She suggested that these names were aliases chosen after the fugitives escaped from their slave-masters, so as to elude recapture. She wrote that *Daddy* Nelson and Henry Johnson were the gravediggers for the Burkholder cemetery. Eventually, she stated, the community disappeared because the winters proved too cold for these "children of the south." With slight alterations here and there, this story of "Little Africa" was repeated almost word for word in several articles and later books that Mabel Burkholder published. She rarely gave any sources for the information contained in these various incarnations of the history of "Little Africa."[87]

This narrative of "Little Africa" came to be repeated by writers, historians, and the public without question. One sociologist postulated that civic leaders *planned* the "Black colony" because they were anxious to find a use for the sparsely settled mountain and its tollgate.[88] However, there was no evidence that this was a planned settlement by the authorities. Rather, it was simply the case that William Bridge Green had no problems selling parcels of his hundred-acre tract to African Americans and African Canadians who had the wherewithal to buy the plots of land in the first place. William Kirkendall and others did the same on a smaller scale. A concentration of Blacks along Concession Street also occurred as those who bought plots subdivided them and sold the subdivisions to other Blacks.

The history of Julia Berry and her family is quite interesting. Granddaughter Viola Berry Aylestock remembered that her grandmother "was born just outside of Hamilton; when she was a child in the 1800s, she used to open and close the toll gate at the top of James Street.... The farmers used to bring their wares down to the Hamilton market, and she would open and close the toll gate and take their money."[89] Julia Berry was born in Canada sometime between 1855 and 1856. Her father was George B. Washington, who, according to family lore, came to Canada in 1832. In the 1861 census, a six-year-old Julia was living with her parents George and Rachel Washington, and a sister named Matilda, one year old. George was a labourer and the family lived in a one-storey frame house in St. Patrick's Ward in Hamilton. In the next census, Julia was fifteen years of age, with a brother Isaac, aged six. It would appear that her younger sister, Matilda, passed away during this period. She continued to live with her family in St. Patrick's Ward. Her father earned his living at that time as a saw sharpener. Vi Aylestock stated that her grandmother operated the tollgate when Julia was a child, suggesting that she may have done so before her marriage to Henry Berry, as well.[90]

Henry Berry was an escaped slave who had come on the Underground Railroad through St. Catharines. He was very likely from the same Berry family said to have been brought up on the Underground Railroad by Daniel Servos from Virginia to the Niagara area. By 1881, he and Julia had married and were living on the Mountain in Lot 10, Concession 4, Barton Township. At that time, the couple had three children: Mary, Rachel, and Julia, ages five, three, and one. Henry worked as a labourer, and Julia was recorded as the "toll keeper."[91]

Henry (top centre) and Julia Berry (seated to the immediate right) and family. The Berrys lived on Hamilton Mountain when Julia was the toll keeper for the tollgate on James Street, then later moved to Catharine Street below the Mountain. After Henry's death, the family lived on Oxford Street. Their descendants continue to live in the Hamilton area as well as other cities in Ontario and the United States.

In the early days of highway travel, roads were often constructed and maintained by private entrepreneurs who had the right to collect tolls. Toll houses and tollgates were erected at which a tollgate keeper would monitor traffic and lift the gate to allow the traveller to pass once the toll had been paid. There were numerous tollgates surrounding the city in the 1880s so that it was virtually impossible to come into or leave the city without paying a toll. There were tollgates on York Street, John, James, Main, and Barton Streets, and at both ends of King Street. One tollgate keeper commented that city dwellers generally paid the toll with no problem, but the famers coming into town always cursed at him as they paid their money. At the Barton Road Company tollgate during Julia Berry's day (now Main Street east of Wentworth) every vehicle drawn by two horses paid six cents every time they passed, and twelve cents for a return ticket. For a vehicle drawn by one horse, four cents and eight cents, and for a lone rider, two cents and four cents. Julia Berry wasn't the only female tollgate keeper. Mary, the sister of blacksmith William Allison, ran

150

the tollgate at Ryckman's Corners and made $12 per month, which was not very much considering she was on call twenty-four hours a day. Men leaving the hotels at night might pass through well after midnight, and the farmers and milkmen used the roads before dawn. The long hours, plus the fact that people sometimes tried to pass without paying were some of the problems she faced in her duties. One can well imagine that Julia dealt with these same issues in her role as a tollgate keeper. Another woman, Mrs. Jane Rose who was the first tollgate keeper on the Barton Road toll, received a salary of $15 per month plus a rent-free house.[92]

According to family records, there were ten children born to Julia and Henry: Doll (1872), Hiram (1894), Irene, Charlotte, Mabel, Clayse, Emma, Julia E. (1880), William, and Matilda. Daughter Julia E. died as a young child. The family were staunch members of St. Paul's AME Church, later renamed Stewart Memorial, where Henry Berry was a deacon. When Henry died in 1912 at the age of sixty-six, he was working as a polisher, and the family owned a home at 193 Catharine Street North. The surviving children were Mary Lucinda (nicknamed Doll), Rachael Matilda Johnson, Julia Charlotte Morton, William Henry, Emma Harrigan, Elizabeth Clayse, Hiram Nelson, Mabel Isabella, and Alverta Irene. Julia, the matriarch, lived well into her nineties, and was taken care of in her later years by Doll, who never married. For years, they lived at 90 Oxford Street in a two-storey brick house with a verandah.[93]

Julia Berry's son, William Berry, the father of Viola Berry Aylestock, got a job on the railway, and he and his family moved to Toronto. Other children left for greener pastures in the United States. However, Doll and Hiram remained in Hamilton and their descendants continued to reside there well into the twenty-first century. They went on to contribute in a variety of professions, including singing and the entertainment fields, the correctional services, banking, the military, and many other endeavours. Vi Ayelstock's daughter, Joan Waite, for example, studied at Sarah Lawrence College and L'École Des Sciences Politiques in Paris and became a professor at Sarah Lawrence. She was also director of education at the African Art Museum of the SMA (Society of Missions in Africa) Fathers in Tenafly, New Jersey. Many Berry descendants also made vital contributions to the community and in the area of civil rights in both Canada and the United States.[94]

Courtesy of Robert Foster Jr., Kingston, Ontario.

Julia Berry and granddaughter Barbara Berry Foster at their home on 90 Oxford Street in Hamilton.

One of the points of interest on the Mountain mentioned by Mabel Burkholder was the Mission Church. It was a modest sanctuary built in 1860 on land donated by a white couple, Mr. and Mrs. Richard Bray, and located on the south side of Concession Street between East 22nd and East 23rd Streets. It catered to all denominations as well as doubling as a school. In a public meeting held December 7, 1860, George Kirkendall was appointed treasurer, John H. Green agreed to hold the communion set for the new church, and "William Nelson (coloured)" was hired to be the caretaker, opening the building, providing light and fuel, and keeping it clean. The very first church service was held Christmas morning 1860. Black children and white children attended the school, which began operation in 1867, and in the evenings, adults also apparently learned to read, write, and do arithmetic. It seems that many African Canadians attended this church after the demise of the modest AME sanctuary.[95]

Contrary to the stereotype, the Blacks who bought land on Hamilton Mountain were a diverse group of people. Some, like Charles Carter, Marianne Connaway, and the Santee family were from free states in the United States prior to coming to Canada. Pompey Lewis was born in Africa. The Spellmans were from the Caribbean. In fact, after the death of her husband in 1857, Rosanna Spellman sold the Mountain property, moved to Hamilton proper, and earned a living as a huckster. It was in the 1861 census that she specified her birthplace as Santo Domingo, the present-day location of the Dominican Republic.[96] Moreover, the vast majority of Hamilton Mountain residents did not leave for warmer climates, but remained in the area. In fact, many of them or their descendants were still in Hamilton well into the twentieth century, or had moved to towns and cities in the vicinity, like Oakville, Brantford, and Toronto. A few remain in Hamilton in the twenty-first century. Some mountain residents took the money earned from the sale of their property and purchased a house and lot in the city. Marianne, or Marian Connaway died on her half-acre plot in 1884, after deeding her property for $1 to John and Rachael Johnson, "who supported and maintained the said Marian Connaway for some time past and [have] agreed to further support and maintain her (in the same manner as heretofore) during her natural life."[97] After the death of Marian in 1884 at the age of eighty-eight, the Johnsons sold their 1.5 acres for $400 and moved to Hamilton proper where they purchased a house and lot at 317 Emerald Street North for $1,150.[98] Pompey Lewis lived on the Mountain for at least twenty years before he sold his property to James Jolley in 1874 and moved back to the city. He bought a parcel of land fronting on Rebecca, King William, John, and Catharine Streets, and, when he died in 1877, the proceeds of the sale of his property were bequeathed to the "Methodist Episcopal Church."[99] The only family in which there is concrete evidence to show they relocated back to the United States after the Civil War was that of Charles and Ann Eliza Carter. They were living in Harrisburg, Pennsylvania, by the time they sold their two acres to Josiah and Amelia Cochrane in 1869. A measure of their prominence in the community was the fact that the deed of sale was signed by the mayor of Harrisburg and another city official.[100]

In the mid-1800s, people of African descent moving into the Hamilton area had many opportunities. Unlike in American cities that were largely segregated, they had some choice in where they could live, whether this was downtown in an urban environment or just outside the city in a more suburban milieu. Some moved downtown first before purchasing plots of land on the outskirts. Owning and running a farm was still the number one goal of many new immigrants in the mid-nineteenth century. Black men and women also had opportunities to engage in skilled and semi-skilled employment at decent wages. Some preferred to exercise their right to become entrepreneurs and work only for themselves. They could not always avail themselves of these same opportunities, based on the evidence, in American cities of the same time period.

What were relations between the races like in Hamilton in the period before the Civil War? On the one hand, many Black citizens were engaged in successful careers in business and the skilled trades. Even those in labouring positions were finding work, although the recession of the late 1850s led to higher unemployment levels that showed up in the 1861 census. On the other hand, blatant discrimination also occurred. The minister of the Sayer Street Church of Toronto who, with his wife and child, attempted to enter the dining area on the boat *America* at Hamilton in the summer of 1855 got a taste of it up close. Although they paid the first-class fare, which should have enabled them to be seated for dinner, they were denied entry on the pretext that white patrons would refuse to sit with them and stewards might refuse to serve them. Edward Barrass, an incensed friend of the family, wrote a letter of complaint to the Toronto *Globe* about the incident that was reprinted in the *Provincial Freeman* of September 29, 1855. In another article in the *Voice of the Fugitive*, the November 4, 1852, edition, Reverend Samuel Ringgold Ward also wrote about an incident in which he was denied lodging at the "Yankee Hotel" in Hamilton by its proprietor Mr. Weeks, in December 1851.

In addition to this kind of outright discrimination, a climate of disrespect was evident. A classic example occurred when the minstrel shows or circus "freak shows" came to town. A description of a circus "act" in the *Hamilton Express* portrayed two albino boys in a lurid and sensational manner:

> The two White Negro boys, which were exhibited here during the week are great natural curiosities, and attracted much attention during their stay. They are perfectly white, with Negro features, white woolly heads, hazel sleepy eyes, and are the offspring of black parents. They are six and eight years old, and afford much amusement by the manner in which they dance and sing à la Jim Crow.[101]

Minstrel shows typically involved a variety show of songs, dancing, and skits performed by whites in blackface. Blacks found them quite offensive, so much so that when these shows came to Toronto, a deputation of Blacks went to the city council and complained about them several years in succession.[102] In Hamilton, Black citizens for years had been incensed at the billboard advertisements, which represented the African race with "pouting lips of enormous dimensions, unnatural elongation of heels and other uncouth malformations."[103] By October 1866, they had had enough. Seventy-two people signed a petition to force city council to enact a bylaw that would refuse to grant licences to any shows or exhibitions that represented the Black race in such a demeaning manner. A few went a step further. They whitewashed over the signs, causing the proprietors of the show to threaten legal action.[104] While in Toronto the mayor and city council eventually refused to let a travelling circus perform there unless it would guarantee that it would not sing "Negro songs" or otherwise offend the Black community, Hamilton's mayor was of the opinion that the local authorities had no power to prevent this kind of advertising so long as it did not overstep the bounds of decency and morality.[105]

There was no shortage of opinion about the state of race relations in Hamilton. Reverend Richard Sorrick, who came to Hamilton from Oro in 1847, naturally focused on the moral rectitude of his people:

> In regard to the colored people in Hamilton, I found them not in a very good condition, when I first came here, although some were wealthy. I never saw so much spirit consumed by the colored people as at that time, but most of those who were among the vicious are dead and gone. Now the evil of drinking ... is pretty much done away with, and those who have come in within a few years, are generally well behaved and industrious.[106]

However, Sorrick concluded by observing that "the main obstacle is a prejudice existing between colored and white.[107]

Edward Patterson also spoke of prejudice, but his perception of the problem was more nuanced:

The prejudice in Canada is amongst the whites to the colored, and amongst the colored to the whites. The colored fancy that the whites are a little against them, and so they do not treat the whites as they would otherwise, — this brings back a prejudice from the whites.[108]

But, according to Patterson, the real problem arose from a lower class of people: "When the colored people here are insulted, it is by the *ruffians* in Canada."[109]

As with all people, the population of African descent was a diverse and heterogeneous group comprising all levels of society. Some were well-to-do, some poor, some industrious and others were of no account. Henry Williamson observed: "In all places and among all kinds of men here are some loafing characters: so with my color.... But the better part are disposed to elevate themselves."[110] Williamson expressed what most, if not all, former slaves in Hamilton felt at that time. It put everything else in perspective: "I would rather be wholly poor and be free, than have all I could wish and be a slave. I am now in a good situation and doing well, I am learning to write."[111]

On the eve of the American Civil War (1861–65), therefore, observers generally offered favourable reports about the state of things where Blacks in Hamilton were concerned. William Wells Brown toured the province in the fall of 1861 and found about five hundred people of colour living there, apparently doing well. He noted that they had two churches, a Baptist church and an AME, presided over by Reverend Benjamin Stewart, who was originally from Trenton, New Jersey. The American Hotel, reported Brown, was kept by William Richardson, "a *colored* white man." This was another way of saying that Richardson was probably *passing* for white or was at least light enough to do so. There were numerous skilled tradesmen and thirteen artists in watercolours. Brown also mentioned that there were several benevolent societies that Black Hamiltonians had formed for their benefit, and that the morals of the people in Hamilton compared favourably with those of the whites.[112]

Two years earlier, Reverend W.M. Mitchell had also toured Canada West. The American-born Mitchell was a Black abolitionist and minister of the Coloured Regular Baptist Church in Toronto. Mitchell subsequently wrote a book about his life and his tour of Canada West. Of Hamilton's Black community, Mitchell wrote that it numbered approximately six hundred out of a population of 24,000, among whom were blacksmiths, carpenters, plasterers, and a wheelwright. Many owned property. Of the morals of the people, Mitchell cited statistics that of 1,982 arrests and summonses to appear in Hamilton court in 1858, eighty-one were African Canadians or 4 percent of the total. Beggary and pauperism were almost unknown and there was not a single Black who was supported by the Township.[113]

Black abolitionist Reverend William M. Mitchell. From the frontispiece of The Under-Ground Railroad (London, UK: W. Tweedie, 1860).

Both Mitchell and Brown made note of Thomas Morton, one of the wealthiest men of the period. He owned two cabs, one of which he drove himself. Morton had come to Hamilton in approximately 1842 and obtained a job as a porter in a store and continued in this position for twelve years before going into the cab business for himself. His cabs consisted of two horse-drawn carriages and four horses. He was said to be worth $15,000.[114] In 1861, the forty-three-year-old Morton lived with his wife, Mary, their six children ranging in age from twenty to four, and four other adults. Their home was a two-storey frame building on a one-quarter acre on MacNab between Colborne and Sheaffe Streets, with two pigs in addition to the horses. In that year, Morton's business was valued at $2,000.[115] Another indication of the Morton family's prominence in the community was the fact that his home was the location of well-known teacher and activist Mary Bibb's second marriage to Isaac N. Cary on May 6, 1859. Her first husband, abolitionist and newspaper editor Henry Bibb, had passed away on August 1, 1854, after a long illness.[116]

Life in Canada was far from perfect, but it afforded African Americans the freedom of self-determination — to live and work and raise their families as independent, self-reliant citizens. They were also free to shape the foundations of community, and to replicate the institutions they had known in their American homeland. In Hamilton, by the late 1830s, Black residents had exercised the right to protest inequality and unjust conditions where they existed, and they had shown that they could come together with one collective voice and take action, effect change, and improve their circumstances.

It is fair to say that no one foresaw the changes that would take place in just a few short years as a result of the election of Abraham Lincoln, and the outbreak of the American Civil War. Lincoln had swept into the presidency on a campaign that stood against the expansion of slavery beyond the states in which it already existed. Seven slave-owning states seceded from the Union and formed the Confederate States of America even before he took office. When Fort Sumter in Charleston Harbour, South Carolina, was attacked by Union forces in April 1861, four more states joined the fledgling Confederacy and the Civil War had begun.

Tens of thousands of Canadians felt that they had a stake in the American conflict. Many white Canadians had close relatives in the United States, being only one or two generations removed from the American Loyalists who had retreated to Canada after the American Revolution. The recession of 1857 that had pushed Canadians from Ontario and Quebec to the United States for employment saw some of these men being swept up in enlistment fever. As the war dragged on, others were attracted by bounties that were offered to encourage enlistment. A few were abolitionists who fervently believed that their actions would result in the total abolition of slavery.[117]

African Canadians watched with baited breath as events unfolded. After eighteen months of war, a policy against Black fighting units was repealed and thousands of African Americans enlisted to fight on the Union side. African-American anti-slavery activists such as Frederick Douglass, Martin Delany, William Wells Brown, and Henry Highland Garnet assisted in recruiting volunteers. Douglass's two sons were among the first to sign up for military service. Dr. Delany, who at one time had advocated against emigration to Canada, had changed his tune and moved to Chatham from Pittsburgh in 1856. Delany's son, Toussaint L'Ouverture Delany, left school at age fifteen and joined the Massachusetts 54th. Former anti-slavery lecturer and *Provincial Freeman* editor, H. Ford Douglas, joined a white unit, the 95th Illinois Regiment of Infantry Volunteers. However, many more recruits were needed. Delany Sr., who was instrumental in raising the 54th Massachusetts Colored Infantry, hired Mary Ann Shadd Cary as a recruiting agent for Black soldiers. She operated in Connecticut and Indiana, making her one of the rare, if not the only,

Tintype of unidentified Union soldier, 1860–70. Close to 200,000 Black soldiers joined the Union Army during the Civil War and proved their valour in all-Black regiments. Thousands came from Canada, at least 1,300 of whom were Canadian-born Blacks.

Black women involved in recruitment as a paid agent. She earned $15 for every slave and $5 for every free Black she persuaded. Delany himself became the only Black major to serve in the Civil War.[118]

As for African Canadians, thousands — both those born in Canada and those originally from the United States — flocked south to fight on the Union side. At least 1,300 Canadian-born Black men alone fought for the Union cause. Of this number, 348 Canadian-born Blacks joined the United States Navy.[119] George Douglas, a twenty-year-old waiter born in Hamilton, joined the United States Navy in Baltimore on April 23, 1864.[120] A number who volunteered for the United States Colored Troops (USCT) were Hamiltonians. Benjamin Morey and Charles Holmes, a twenty-year-old waiter, signed up for the 54th Massachusetts Infantry (USCT). Yet another waiter, John Williams, joined the 18th USCT, Company F. John Fletcher, a twenty-one-year-old farmer, joined the 5th

Massachusetts Cavalry in 1864, and twenty-year-old shoemaker, William E. Howard, also enlisted in the 5th Massachusetts Cavalry that same year. However, Howard deserted after seventeen months. John Jackson was twenty-one and a barber from Hamilton who enlisted in the 14th Rhode Island Colored Heavy Artillery (also known as the 11th USC Heavy Artillery) at Providence, Rhode Island. William Noden, an assistant surgeon with the 10th USCT was reported to be from Hampton, Canada West.[121] Very likely this was a misspelling of Hamilton. There are also the United States Pension Bureau records of Mary Rhodes, which indicate that she was first married to a Civil War veteran named Henry Jackson living in Hamilton.[122] It is not known in which regiment Jackson served.

Other enlistees from Hamilton had been American-born fugitive slaves or otherwise freeborn in the United States. The father of Reverend John Holland, Thomas J. Holland, a former slave from Maryland, enlisted in the Union army and returned to Hamilton from Washington D.C. at the end of hostilities.[123] Nelson Stevens, also a former slave who was born in Lynchburg, Virginia on a tobacco farm in 1832, enlisted in the 25th United States Colored Troops, Company B, at Buffalo in 1865 and saw active service in Florida. After the war, he also returned to Hamilton. He died in 1890 and was buried in an unmarked grave. Many years later, his grave site was rediscovered, and, in November 2007, he was honoured with a tombstone by the United States Department of Veterans Affairs and a proper ceremony fit for a war veteran.[124] William Diggs, another escaped slave from Virginia, made his way to Hamilton, arriving approximately in 1842. He married Louisa Howard in 1846 and the couple had seven children. He reportedly enlisted in the 26th United States Colored Infantry, Company K, in New York State, and was promoted to corporal. After his death, his widow, Louisa, received a pension from the United States government. Interestingly, later in life she was said to be living with Julia Berry, whom she had nursed as an infant.[125] Another man who received a pension for three years' service in the Union Army, according to Richard Butler, was William Moore, although no more is known about him.[126]

Finally, William Mallory was another Civil War veteran about whom there is a more detailed biography. Mallory was born in approximately 1825–26 near Raleigh, North Carolina. He was sold at the age of seven to a Louisiana planter named Susten Allen. Sometime between 1859 and 1860, Mallory escaped from the Louisiana plantation, and, after crossing the Detroit River at Malden (Amherstburg), found his way to Hamilton where he decided to make his home. Mallory joined the Union Army and was involved in a number of battles, including the Battles of Bull Run, Vicksburg, and Gettysburg. Years later, he wrote about his experiences in slavery, his escape, and participation in the Civil War in *Old Plantation Days*. Of the war, Mallory proudly wrote:

We had taken part in an honorable struggle for supremacy, honorably had we conducted ourselves, and honorably were we rewarded with the consciousness that we had assisted in liberating millions of our brethren from bondage and had freed them forever from the hand of the oppressor and the whiplash of slavery. It is no wonder that Victory perched upon our standards and that white-winged Peace could at last fold her wings and rest over the whole nation.[127]

Old Plantation Days

THIRD EDITION

COL. W. MALLORY

EX-SLAVE

Courtesy of Carolina Digital Library and Archives, University of North Carolina, Chapel Hill, NC.

After receiving an honourable discharge, Mallory returned to Hamilton, married Ann Elizabeth, purchased a small lot on John Street, and "carried on a

William Mallory may have served in the 109th Regiment, United States Colored Infantry. A William Mallory was recorded as serving with that unit, which fought a battle on the Rio Grande, a fact which coincides with Mallory's recollection in his narrative. Another William Mallory served with the 15th Regiment, USCT.

business in hay, straw and wood." In the 1875 directory, the Mallorys were listed at 103 John Street and carrying on a second-hand store on the premises. In that year, they dabbled in real estate when they bought two acres on Hamilton Mountain in Lot 9, Concession 4 from the executors of the estate of James Gage, later selling it to lawyer and local politician Frank Russell Waddell in 1881. That year the census recorded that their family had increased to five, including Caroline, aged six, Alice, aged one, and Mary, seventeen.[128]

William Mallory was a well-known man about town. He held a prominent position in the church and his Masonic Lodge, and was appointed a missionary of the BME Church by Bishop Nazrey. He also claimed to have been twice appointed marshal for the day when both the Prince of Wales and Princess Louise, daughter of Queen Victoria, visited Hamilton. Moreover, when the Duke of York came to the city, Mallory boasted that he was selected to represent the Black community on the reception committee. He was reportedly also known for having saved the young daughter of another Hamilton resident, John White, from being crushed by a runaway team of horses. He wrote about his meetings with Sir John A. Macdonald and numerous other Canadian politicians, for whom he apparently campaigned. Mallory acted as a book agent, according to the 1901 census, presumably for his own narrative. He died on April 18, 1907.[129]

The brave individuals mentioned in these pages were probably just a subset of the true numbers of Black men who came from Hamilton to fight for Lincoln and the abolition of slavery. On January 1, 1863, the Emancipation Proclamation issued by Lincoln freed all slaves in the Confederate States and the 13th Amendment, ratified on December 6, 1865, freed the slaves in the remaining border states that had supported the Union (Kentucky and Delaware). Church bells rang in Black churches across Canada.

CHAPTER 5

Eyeing the Summit, 1870–1900

In the latter part of the nineteenth century, the increasing pace of industrialization led to a rapid growth of the urban centres of Ontario. Under Sir Allan MacNab's leadership and influence, the Great Western Railway was built from the Niagara River below the escarpment, through to Hamilton, London, and Windsor, opening in 1854. It had enhanced the economic prospects of the city, but the advent of the railway did not make Hamilton the major centre of the province that some had hoped. The Great Western was quickly usurped by the Grand Trunk Railway, which ran from Montreal along Lake Ontario's north shore through Toronto and Stratford to Sarnia, completely leaving Hamilton out of the mix. As Bill Freeman wrote, "The Grand Trunk became the principal railroad in Canada until the CPR was built in the 1880s. Hamilton merchants and financial institutions that had hoped to use the Great Western to capture trade found themselves in direct competition with companies from Toronto and even

Montreal."[1] Hamilton would never become a major trading and financial centre. As a result, manufacturing became its *raison d'être*.

Industries engaged in such enterprises as metal fabrication; clothing manufacturing, as in Sanford's ready-to-wear clothing empire on King Street east; textile making, such as the Hamilton Cotton Company on Mary Street; or Tuckett's Tobacco manufacturing located at York and Queen Streets. Despite the disappointment at the loss of the railway, the port continued to make Hamilton a viable location for the manufacturing industry. The 1881 Census revealed that there were 212 factories in the city employing thousands of workers. Hamiltonians were now proudly calling their town "The Birmingham of Canada." In 1895, the city became the primary producer of steel in the country when Stelco opened its plant on the harbour just outside the city limits.[2]

Meanwhile, after the American Civil War, the Emancipation Proclamation, and the ratification of the 13th and 14th Amendments, which freed *all* Blacks in the United States and gave them the same constitutional rights as other Americans, a new era of promise and possibility opened up for the oppressed African American. During the period of Reconstruction, new state governments were created in the South in which African Americans voted for the first time, and were elected as state legislators and officials at all levels. Federal troops were sent into the South to restore order and protect the rights of Blacks. The Freedmen's Bureau, set up by the federal government to assist the formerly enslaved in their transition to freedom, distributed rations, and built hospitals and schools for the newly freed across the south.[3] For many Blacks in Canada, there was now a viable choice of whether to remain in Canada or return to the United States. Some exiles in the African-American community who wished to reunite with long-lost relatives and friends back in the United States took a "return trip on the Underground Railroad." For the educated elite, it was also an opportunity to assist in the massive undertaking that was needed in the education and resettling of newly freed slaves during Reconstruction.[4] Former Underground Railroad agent William Still noted, for example, that John Henry Hill and his Uncle Hezekiah, moved south after the Civil War. Despite the fact that John Henry Hill had taken the oath of allegiance for "Canadian" citizenship in

Courtesy of Special Collections & Archives, Johnston Memorial Library, Virginia State University.

James Major and Kate Hill Colson and family, circa 1906. Kate Hill Colson (seated far right) was born in Hamilton, the eldest of seven daughters of John Henry and Rosetta Hill. After returning to Virginia, Kate was one of the first African-American schoolteachers in Petersburg, and became principal of the Normal Preparatory Department of the Virginia Normal and Collegiate Institute (now Virginia State University). She married James Major Colson Jr., graduate of Dartmouth College and the first science teacher at the Virginia Normal and Collegiate Institute. Two of their daughters, Edna (standing far left) and Myra (standing far right), also taught at Virginia Normal and Collegiate Institute. Edna Meade Colson earned her Ph.D. in education from Columbia University.

1859, he took the first opportunity to move his family back to the United States where he became a successful businessman and the first Black justice of the peace in Petersburg, Virginia, while Hezekiah moved to West Point, Virginia.[5] The Hills were not the only ones to leave.

By 1871, the Black population in Hamilton proper was 354, and in the rest of Barton Township numbered at forty-five.[6] This represented a reduction of 29 percent in the city. While certainly a significant drop in the numbers, it was not the vast return trek of all African Hamiltonians back to the United States that historians have traditionally represented as taking place during this period. Michael Wayne's examination of the

1861 census led him to conclude that this mass exodus of Blacks from the province was grossly overstated, because the Black population in Canada West had often been overestimated in the first place by contemporaries. Therefore, the figures of those who remained appeared to be considerably smaller, by contrast, than they really were.[7] To date, no one has done an extensive study of the returnees and their actual numbers. Clearly, however, Hamilton and environs lost their share of the Black population.

It is also true that some residents showed considerable staying power over time.[8] And many never gave up trying to find lost loved ones. Black newspapers, such as the *Christian Recorder*, published out of Philadelphia, were flooded with ads that could bring a tear to the eye of the most cold-hearted soul. One, appearing in the August 5, 1865, issue, read as follows:

> INFORMATION WANTED
>
> Can any one inform me of the whereabouts of Emily Wilson, the Mother of Amanda Jane Wilson? She belonged to John K. Wilson, who lived in Montgomery County, Tennessee, four miles from Clarksville. She was sold and taken to Mississippi, in 1856; or of Eveline Wilson, who belonged to the same John K. Wilson, who, after selling my mother, removed from Montgomery County, Tennessee, to Marshal County, Kentucky, eighteen miles from Paducah. Harriet Wilson, another sister, was sold to Joseph Dear, and taken to Texas. My name was Amanda Jane Wilson. I left Kentucky in 1861 or 1862. My name now is Amanda Jane Bass. Any information of the above named persons will be thankfully received.
>
> AMANDA JANE BASS
>
> Hamilton, C.W.

The September 26, 1868, issue of the *Christian Recorder* published no fewer than four ads from Hamiltonians looking for long-lost relatives. For example, Peter Boone sought information about his mother, Sucky

Boone, his brothers, Jordan, William, and Frederick, and his sisters, Matilda and Harriet. Boone noted that they had all belonged to Captain Samuel Boone of Callamy County, Missouri, prior to the Civil War. Readers were asked to contact him in care of barber and community stalwart Josiah Cochrane of King Street. Ruth Gray inquired as to the whereabouts of her two sons, Merryman Gray, known as Peter Hicks, who lived with Aaron Sparks of Baltimore County, Maryland, as well as America Eli Gray. Information was to be sent to her on May Street in Hamilton.[9]

Some families actually managed to reunite with their loved ones and bring them back to live with them in Canada. For example, Reverend Sorrick, the AME minister who was interviewed by Benjamin Drew, had his seventy-seven-year-old relative, David Sorrick — most likely his father — living with him and his wife in 1861. He went back and retrieved the elder Sorrick even before Lincoln's Emancipation Proclamation of 1863 made it completely safe to do so.[10]

While Hamilton's economic prospects were bright, how did those of people of African descent compare? In 1871, Hamilton Blacks' job prospects were even more favourable to those in skilled, semi-skilled, and entrepreneurial pursuits. The census revealed that 64 percent of Black males held jobs in the skilled/semi-skilled trades or were independent businessmen. Of particular note was the fact that a sizeable number were barbers, as there had been in 1861. Fifteen men made their livings as barbers (including one man who reported his income as "hairdresser"), tying with tobacconist as the job that engaged the most number of Black men in Hamilton. What this means is that 12 percent of the total number of Black males were barbers and 12 percent were tobacconists. In addition, there were ten plasterers, six shoemakers, and six tailors. Other jobs held in the skilled category were those of mason, carpenter, farmer, and cook. There was also a mail carrier, a bookkeeper, and a printer — positions not previously listed as jobs held by Black males in Hamilton. Independent entrepreneurs represented a thriving group, but it is difficult to know exactly how many owned their own businesses, although many of the barbers owned their own barbershops. There was one tavern keeper and one who owned a "refreshment saloon." Thomas Morton's cab business continued to be a going concern. Thirty-two percent were in unskilled jobs such as messenger, carter, and food cutter. In addition, there were twenty-four labourers, four waiters, four whitewashers, and three hucksters or peddlers. Four percent had no job listed, that is, they were either retired, sick, or otherwise unemployed.[11]

In Chatham, the only other urban centre for which there are available statistics, the occupational breakdown of skilled and unskilled workers indicated that opportunities for Blacks in the most populous centre of African Canadians was not growing, but perhaps shrinking. In 1871, 45 percent of Black males held skilled/semi-skilled and entrepreneurial professions, down from 51 percent and 48 percent in 1851 and 1861.[12] Compared to Chatham, the mecca for Blacks prior to the Civil War, Hamilton was doing well as a place where Black males could find employment in a variety of skilled and semi-skilled jobs and as independent businessmen. For women, the majority, 74 percent did not have an occupation reported, but 10 percent were in skilled occupations such as seamstress and cook. One was a grocer, and one, an innkeeper. Seventeen percent held unskilled occupations, either as servants or washerwomen. This represented an increase over 1861 of 5 percent as skilled workers and 12 percent as unskilled workers. In 1861, more women (83 percent) reported no occupation.[13]

After the great celebration and rejoicing that accompanied Lincoln's freeing of four million enslaved brothers and sisters in America, and the period of tremendous hope and optimism during Reconstruction, the forces of tyranny and repression were mustering a comeback. The laws protecting the freedmen after emancipation were rolled back beginning in 1877 and a fragile equality was replaced by segregation and brutality in all aspects of life. Globally, the situation was no better. Almost simultaneous with the termination of the historic era of Reconstruction, Europe was masterminding the division of virtually every inch of African territory for itself in what has been termed the "Scramble for Africa." At the 1885 Berlin Conference, this massive land grab resulted in an additional 9 million square miles being added to the various colonial empires of Britain, France, Portugal, Germany, and Belgium, among others. Africans of all tribal and ethnic backgrounds were subjugated, the wealth of the continent sucked out at a rapid pace, and the smug air of superiority over the African was stifling. As a result of these international developments, the position of people of African descent worldwide sunk to new lows.[14]

In 1881, the census indicated that the population of Hamilton had crept back up to 476 people, almost as high as it had been at its pre–Civil War heyday. The 1881 census indicated, moreover, that the bustling and commercial economic base of Hamilton continued to provide opportunities for the majority of Black males. Fifty-one percent of Black males held skilled, semi-skilled, or entrepreneurial positions, although this was down from the percentage in 1871. This time there were twenty-one barbers, nine tobacconists, nine plasterers, six bricklayers and brick makers, and four shoemakers. There was a restaurateur, a storekeeper, a saloonkeeper, and four ministers, not to mention a number of other skilled and semi-skilled trades in which Black men were employed. Forty-two percent of the men held unskilled positions, including thirty-six labourers, ten waiters, eight servants, and seven whitewashers. Six percent had no job listing, indicating retirement or illness, as well as unemployment.[15]

In Chatham, data from the city directory indicated that 38 percent of Black males were skilled, semi-skilled, or in the independent category, and 59 percent were in the unskilled category.[16] These statistics suggest, as in 1871, that employment opportunities for Blacks were on the decline in Chatham. At the same time, Jonathan Walton's study pointed out that Blacks in northern American cities experienced both positive advancement and negative developments in the area of civil rights and employment opportunities. For example, Washington, D.C. passed some anti-discrimination ordinances in the 1870s, but city schools remained segregated. Competitive civil-service exams increased the number of Blacks on the federal payroll, which benefited the small middle class, but exclusion from labour organizations, such as the carpenters' unions, and the hostility of white workingmen who viewed Blacks as competitors meant that working-class Blacks could not practise or learn trades, and could only obtain menial jobs.[17] The situation in Cleveland, Ohio, revealed both positive and negative developments similar to those that transpired in Washington. Schools, both students and faculties, were integrated in 1870–90. Public facilities such as restaurants, theatres, skating rinks, and hotels were generally open to everyone. However,

Cleveland's industrial expansion tended to exclude Blacks. For example, the growing steel industry employed only three Blacks in 1890 and there were virtually no Black males working in a semi-skilled capacity in factories.[18] Conditions in Detroit reflected this same "duality" of experience, in which the legal status of Blacks was almost on an equal footing with whites by 1890, but industrial expansion in the city excluded them. Immigrants benefited from the growth of jobs in industry, and Blacks, for the most part, did not.[19] In Indianapolis, no rapid industrialization occurred, and there was no large European immigrant population with which to compete. However, the colour line effectively kept the doors of opportunity closed to Blacks. Most obtained employment in unskilled and semi-skilled labouring and service positions.[20]

In Chatham, while job opportunities appeared to be dwindling, prejudice and discrimination continued, and indeed, racial antagonism and conflict may have been on the increase. In the 1870s, African Canadians held conventions and staged political demonstrations on August 1 instead of celebrations because they felt that they were not accorded freedom and justice there. Part of the rationale given was that when guests came to Chatham for Emancipation Day they were barred from most restaurants and hotels in town, whereas when Chathamites visited Windsor or Detroit, they could eat in good restaurants and sleep in respectable hotels without difficulty. Other issues that sparked the ire of Blacks in Chatham and the region were the exclusion from jury duty, the unequal allotment of public works to Black taxpayers, and the outright discrimination against Black children in the schools.[21]

In 1891, Black Chathamites formed the Kent County Civil Rights League, which was dedicated to stamping out inequality in all its manifestations. However, its first task was to deal with the separate school issue, against which the Black community had fought for decades. The League first delivered a petition to the school board demanding that children be allowed to attend the school in the district in which they resided. This, if brought about, meant that the segregated school system would effectively end because the children would no longer be forced to attend the one school set aside for them, the King Street School, on the east side of Chatham. When that failed to bear fruit, several parents sent letters to the board requesting that their children be allowed to attend the nearest school in their wards. Again, the board voted against the motion. Next, the league hired a lawyer who fired off a letter threatening a protracted lawsuit. At the same time, several parents took their children to the front doors of the schools in their wards and requested admittance, an action reminiscent of the twentieth-century civil-rights movement. They were refused. On April 4, 1893, the school board met and tabled a Majority Report and a Minority Report to the board. The Majority Report basically recommended that the children in question remain at the King Street School. Then the secretary read the opinion of the school board's lawyer about its legal options in the matter. The exact contents of this letter are not known, but school board trustees voted to allow the children to attend the school in their respective wards after it was read. Clearly, the trustees grasped the tenuous legal position in which the board found itself. On April 5, 1893, the board announced that Black children would be admitted to all the public schools of Chatham, to the utter elation of its Black citizens. It was a stunning achievement, even though it had been decades in the making. What was different in the early 1890s, however, was that the strategy was elevated. The momentum was kept up with a series of actions that demonstrated that the community was not going away, that it was going to keep up the pressure until the offensive policy was finally changed.[22]

In Hamilton, the separate school issue had been laid to rest decades earlier. There had never been a separate government school in operation, but at the same time, there had been no access for Black children to the regular school system until the 1840s. After the community protested, official policy was changed to admit them. However, there is evidence that children continued to experience discrimination on the school grounds. The result was that some children simply did not attend the public schools or they did not attend on a regular basis.

To fill the gap, a number of private facilities were set up by Black teachers in the city. Moreover, Sunday schools in the Black churches offered basic remedial classes in reading and writing along with their Bible studies. In 1868, when the BME Church held its annual conference in Hamilton, it issued a report through its education committee. The British Methodist Episcopal Church was established in the province in 1856, when many of the AME churches decided to split off from the American AME body. Given the passage of the Fugitive Slave Act in 1850, members of the church who had been fugitive slaves felt safer as British citizens under an all-Canadian organization.[23]

The BME committee lamented the pitiable state of education for African Canadians in Chatham, Windsor, Colchester, Buxton, Dresden, and St. Catharines where their children were "not privileged to enter the Grammar Schools or even the Common Schools." In Hamilton, Toronto, London, and other places, however, the opposite was true. Students were "received ... without distinction." According to the report, this was having a positive impact not only in these communities, but as far away as the southern United States, where Black graduates of Canadian schools were teaching among the freedmen and bringing great credit to themselves as well as the British North American educational system. The BME education committee recommended that Black residents in the disenfranchised areas appeal to their local municipalities to rescind the discriminatory policies and if that didn't work, to make their power felt at the polls during election time.[24] For whatever it was worth, while the situation regarding education in Hamilton was not perfect, it had gained the endorsement of the BME Conference.

Despite a semblance of equality in education, the same was not true in employment. Although Hamilton's Black males were in a superior position to Blacks in northern American cities in terms of holding a majority in skilled, semi-skilled, and independent positions, they did not appear to be gaining a foothold in the expanding industrial base of the city. They continued to be heavily represented in service positions like barber, waiter, hotel worker, and servant.

One of the areas from which African Hamiltonians were blocked access was appointments at the city. On December 24, 1889, a deputation of four men — Richard Gwyder, Hiram Demun, George Morton, and James L. Lightfoot — appeared before the city's Market, Fire and Police Committee to protest this discriminatory treatment:

> Your petitioners regret to say that positions of public trust and usefulness in the city have not hitherto been

awarded and distributed with regard to the colored people, as a class of citizens, whom, we respectively submit, are entitled to a fair share of the public trusts of the city.[25]

Mr. Gwyder and Mr. Morton asserted that not a single public position was held by a Black person, although there were many of the community who were "efficient, capable, sober, energetic, courageous, vigilant and painstaking" who could "faithfully guard the interests of the public."[26] The delegation viewed the fire department, which had moved from being a volunteer force in the early years, to one that was hired and paid salaries by the city, as a logical place to begin to redress the situation.[27] The deputies submitted a petition timed to coincide with the opening of a new fire hall on John Street North, and proposed that a "full company of colored men" be appointed "as firemen in charge of the new fire station …"[28] Twenty-seven people signed their names to it.

The four men elected to appear before the city department in question were leaders in the community. Richard Gwyder was a Virginia-born husband and father of four daughters working as a whitewasher. He lived with his family at 110 MacNab Street North in Hamilton and was involved in the Commandery of Knights Templar, a Black fraternal order in Ontario.[29] African-born Hiram Demun was also involved in the Black Masonic movement in the province, including the Grand Chapter of Royal Arch Masons of Michigan and Ontario and Mount Olive #1 Lodge of the Prince Hall Masons of Hamilton. Demun ran a used-goods store at his home at 53 King William Street.[30] Hamilton native George Morton, barber, was the son of George Morton Sr. and Elizabeth Morton, one of the families to buy a lot and move from the city to Hamilton Mountain in the 1860s and then sell out and move back to the city in the 1870s. George Jr. was active in the Mount Brydges Lodge of Oddfellows of Hamilton, and, in 1893, was elected grand secretary of District Lodge No. 28 of the Grand United Order of Oddfellows of Canada. This was not his first involvement with civil rights, as he had been part of a delegation that met with Sir Oliver Mowat, premier of Ontario, on the issue of segregated schools in the province.[31] James L. Lightfoot had a successful boot-and-shoe business on James Street North and was a member of the prominent

Lightfoot family who had settled in West Flamborough Township in the 1840s. Lightfoot was also past grand master of the Prince Hall Masons of Ontario in 1885–86.[32] His community interests included being manager of the Union Cornet Band, which performed at various events in the area.[33]

In response to their protest, Alderman John Kenrick assured the delegation that the Market, Fire and Police Committee did not discriminate on the basis of race, and he encouraged all the young Black men of the city to submit applications and they would be duly considered for positions.[34] The department nixed the idea of a separate brigade of Black men, however, and did not appear to take very seriously the concerns of the community. Gone were the days of the "Coloured Company" commanded by William Allen that honourably protected the colony against Mackenzie's rebel Reformers, or that kept the peace on the Welland Canal during its construction in the 1840s. When, on the day after Christmas, a reporter went over to the Central Fire Station and asked some of the men what they thought of the proposal, they made sure to remind the public that a Black man, Ned Willet, had served for years in Company No. 1 and another, Dave Jackson, in No. 3, both having done good all-round work. But the idea of an entire brigade of Black men was mocked by the firemen. "They expressed the opinion that the colored firemen could stand heat all right, but the smoke and bitter cold of a winter's night would prove too much for them."[35]

The accompanying editorial in the *Herald* newspaper took the side of the Black men. It confirmed that colour was a major impediment to getting a position with the city, and that the community had every right to demand its fair share of hires. However, in supporting the petitioners, the *Herald* editor offered an argument that was questionable at best. He reasoned that an all-Black fire brigade would be an excellent way to address the situation because:

> If the colored people are entitled to, say, six public or municipal positions, it is much preferable that these six positions should be in connection with one department than ... scattered among several ... it would be more satisfactory to see a fire hall manned by a colored

Courtesy of Hamilton Public Library, Special Collections.

Strathcona Fire Station #5, circa 1905, was located at 37 Strathcona Avenue North in Hamilton.

brigade than to see the same men scattered in other departments — one a policeman, one a letter carrier, one an assessor and so on.[36]

Nevertheless, the petition and the deputation of George Morton and his group sparked some heated controversy within the Black community. In the same issue as the editorial and the report about the opinions of the white firemen appeared a letter from "Professor" Jesse Gant, a well-known Black barber in town, stating that there should be no colour line observed in hiring. What everyone wanted, he believed, was "good firemen and good policemen — good men, no matter what color, so long as they were competent."[37] Gant did not believe that Blacks had any problems gaining positions with the city and felt no remedial help was needed.

George Morton was livid. The very next day, he was quoted in the paper as saying that Gant was jealous. "He wasn't asked to sign the petition or to take an active part in getting it up, and he feels sore ... I don't suppose he could get the support of half-a-dozen coloured people in the ridiculous stand he takes."[38] Moreover, in the same issue, Morton contributed a lengthy treatise, taking Gant and the public to school on the subject of how slavery and its aftermath had negatively impacted the lives of the African race. Entitled "Justice is Not Blind: The Color Line Drawn Even at the Sacred Altar," Morton wrote, in part:

> We are habilitated in a flimsy garment, which yields to the fierce blasts of prejudices, and leaves us naked and exposed to the storms of race and color caste. We are told that justice is blind. It is not true, for the blind goddess raises her bandage from the eyes to ascertain the race and color of those kneeling at her shrine before she dispenses her benefits. And when we murmur, complain, cry aloud and demand our inalienable rights and privileges, they tell us we are drawing the color line. It is false. The Caucasian draws the color line. He has always drawn it. He drew it when he enslaved us. He drew it when he robbed us of our labor. He draws it when he practically says we are good enough to vote, but not to hold office. The color line is drawn in public, in private, in pleasure, in business, in life, in death, in the busy marts of trade, and at the sacred altar.[39]

The editor of the *Herald* thought the letter was dead on, employing "the eloquent language of the orator and the penetrating philosophy of a thinker."[40] However, the editor wrongly concluded that the existence of Black churches, organizations, and other associations was due strictly to Blacks' own preference rather than to their exclusion from the churches, clubs, and organizations of the city's whites. For their part, Hamilton's Black citizens were collectively uttering a "Thank you and amen."

On December 28, 1889, Chief Alexander Aitchison, who had done more to modernize the fire department than any other fire chief in the nineteenth century, declined to give his opinion on the establishment of a "coloured fire company" or the controversy that had ensued since the petition was delivered to the committee. When pressed, he was reported to have said that of 130 names, two Black men were listed as applicants

for jobs: Leander Slaughter, who had applied on February 7, 1889, and an
H. Crawford, whose name had been placed on the list since early 1888.[41]

Unfortunately, the city council minutes do not reflect the fact that
council had been visited by the deputation of Gwyder, Demun, Morton,
and Lightfoot, nor do they mention that a petition had been delivered
asking to set up a Black fire company. On January 13, 1890, the Market,
Fire and Police Committee reported that seven appointments had been
made to the fire department, none of which coincided with the sixteen
names put forward by the Black community. Nor were Leander Slaughter
and H. Crawford on the list.[42] It appeared there would be no Black men
hired by the Market, Fire and Police Committee.

This episode was in some ways a defining moment in the late
nineteenth-century period. With jobs for Blacks in the skilled trades and
opportunities for business entrepreneurship slowly dwindling, as the
employment figures for the 1901 census will suggest, the importance of
gaining a foothold in a burgeoning city-government bureaucracy was not
lost on the Black community. Also not lost was the fact that opportunities
for employment with the city were effectively closed to Black citizens,
something people were intensely aware of and about which, apparently,
they were prepared to put up a fight.

By the latter decades of the nineteenth century, Hamilton had long
been established as a place of settlement for Blacks, and the city was
still attracting them from parts far and wide. African Americans continued to be drawn to Hamilton — albeit in much smaller numbers —
years after the Civil War and the Emancipation Proclamation. Wesley
Rhodes was born into slavery in Bedford County, near Lynchburg,
Virginia, "on or about March 15, 1839."[43] Although it is not known
how he attained his freedom, he enlisted at the age of twenty-five in the
5th Regiment (Company L) of the Massachusetts Volunteer Colored
Cavalry in Springfield, Massachusetts, travelling as far as Clarksville,
Texas. He was involved in some merriment on Thanksgiving Day,
November 26, 1864, at Point Lookout, Maryland, while his regiment
was guarding prisoners away from the front lines. The men engaged in
competitive games like sack and wheelbarrow races, greased poles (the
object being to climb up the pole and get a prize of a goose or a plug

of tobacco), pig chases, jig dances, and turkey shoots. Rhodes was one of six men who shot a turkey for their prize. The men enjoyed a fine turkey dinner and the band played throughout the day and evening.[44] After serving as a private for over a year, he was honourably discharged on April 22, 1865.

Wesley Rhodes moved to Buffalo where he worked as a plasterer before immigrating to Toronto in 1878. He eventually put down roots in Hamilton in 1889. He boarded with a widow named Mary Roth. Roth had emigrated from Württemberg, Germany, first travelling to New York City before settling in Hamilton in 1877. She met and married Black Civil War veteran Henry Jackson in 1886, but this man died a year later, leaving her with a young infant daughter, Annie, to care for. Soon enough, a relationship blossomed between Roth and her boarder. By 1901, the couple had married and had six children spanning the ages of three to fourteen: Doherty, Norman, Pearl, Sylvia, Mamie, and Annie, the oldest. Wesley Rhodes worked as a whitewasher and his earnings, which he did not report to the census enumerator, were based on eight months of work during the previous year. The family rented a four-room dwelling at 376 King Street East and stated that they were Methodists.[45]

Wesley Rhodes's attempt to get the pension to which he was entitled as a Civil War veteran was met with delays. He sent a strongly-worded letter to the United States Pension Bureau dated October 6, 1898, written on his behalf by attorney Martin Malone. In it Malone wrote:

> He thinks it strange to say the least of it, that many of his Comrades, who served in the War of the Rebellion, have got their pensions ... He is a Colored Man, and hopes that his Color had nothing to do with equal justice being meted out to him, who shed his blood for our Country the same as his brother White man.[46]

Wesley Rhodes died of heart failure on March 13, 1910, just days before his seventy-first birthday. His wife Mary continued to press for an income for her children from the Pension Bureau. She, too, expressed

This image of Jesse Gant, barber and well-dressed man about town, appeared in an article about Gant in the Hamilton Herald, *November 2, 1895.*

in a letter dated February 23, 1913, her frustration with the bureau and wondered in her correspondence whether it had to do with the fact that she was white and her husband was Black. The family applied to the Pension Bureau and received money to cover Mary Rhodes's funeral expenses when she died in 1929, but it is not clear whether the family received ongoing support or that a pension was ever awarded to the children.[47]

Some of those moving to Hamilton came from farms and rural areas in nearby townships. James L. Lightfoot, for example, one of the community leaders who met with the Market, Fire and Police Committee, was the son of Samuel Jackson Lightfoot. Samuel Lightfoot had escaped slavery from the Maysville, Kentucky area many years earlier with the aid of Josiah Henson, the irascible soon-to-be leader of the fugitive slave population at Dresden. Samuel Lightfoot's brother, James Louis Lightfoot, met Henson at a revival meeting and asked if he would personally conduct his family out of servitude. Henson agreed, and was able to lead four brothers and a nephew out of slavery, one of whom was Samuel Jackson Lightfoot. Eventually, the entire family was able to join the brothers, who settled and purchased land in West Flamborough Township in Wentworth County.[48] James Louis Lightfoot Jr., the second son of Samuel, was born in Ontario in 1842. He moved to Hamilton and went into business as a shoemaker. Another Lightfoot, Levi Wilson Lightfoot, was a cousin of James L. and also a shoemaker. He married Hannah Casey, the daughter of Thomas Powers Casey, owner of a successful barber/hairdressing shop in St. Catharines and later Toronto. Hannah was the sister of Mary Ann Casey, who married Dr. Anderson Ruffin Abbott, reputed to be the first native-born Black doctor in Canada. The Levi Lightfoots lived in Toronto.[49] The Lightfoots and Abbotts were closely aligned with Toronto city councillor William P. Hubbard and his family. Dr. Abbott's daughter, Grace, married William's son, Fred Hubbard. They were also associated with prominent African Americans like Amelia Loguen Douglass and her husband Lewis H. Douglass. Amelia was the daughter of Reverend Jermain Loguen and her husband was the son of the famed abolitionist and orator, Frederick Douglass.[50]

Jesse Gant was another migrant to Hamilton in this period. He was born in 1850 to a Methodist clergyman and had come to Hamilton from Toronto by way of Chicago. While managing a large barbershop in Chicago, Gant dabbled in a variety of other ventures. He boxed, took up the "terpsichorean art" (he was a dance instructor), and was also the advance man for a number of burlesque troupes. While in the States, Gant travelled and lived not only in Chicago, but also in Washington, D.C. There, according to the "Professor," he was asked to run as a senator of Louisiana during Reconstruction. Declining that offer, Gant returned to Canada, set up shop in Hamilton, and, by 1875, when he opened up his barber establishment at 55 John Street South, he was already being described as "that well-known tonsorial artist, Professor Gant ..."[51] In reality, Gant missed his true calling, which was to be a learned and highly respected university professor *or* an influential politician, *or* perhaps a world-renowned impresario. His neverending quest for prominence and recognition led him to be used by the local newspapers, who mocked him repeatedly in articles over a period of thirty years.[52] His letters to the editor always found space, it seems, and his various endeavours, which included a debating club, kite flying, and his always dapper dress — a subject of some interest in and of itself — made him a perfect subject for the amusement of a Hamilton readership. Gant indeed had talents as a public speaker and as a vocalist, and he "long held the reputation for the being the best-dressed man in Hamilton."[53] Unfortunately, his penchant for reading about himself in the press led to sometimes ridiculous stances on issues and he clashed with numerous people on its pages over the years.

Part of journalists' predicament in covering Gant and his activities was the fact that whenever there was an event in which he was involved, a group of people would attend who, it seems, were simply bent on disrupting the proceedings. There would be catcalls at his debates and the audience would erupt in laughter, all of which was reported in detail in the papers. One of the worst cases on record was a wedding that Gant was involved in organizing. One Black person, John Johnston, was described as a "darkey," and another singing group of five boys sang a "plantation song" followed by a few samples of "buck dancing." For some unknown reason, there was a watermelon-eating contest after the wedding, and it erupted in a huge fight with watermelon flying about and Gant and many others being hit by the fruit. It appears that some Hamilton boys who entered the contest were responsible for starting the melee.[54] Black readers were undoubtedly livid at this kind of insulting coverage.

As a businessman with a wife and four children, Gant stood up for his rights. One time he took a neighbour to court for calling his son, Oscar, a "nigger." There were charges and counter-charges, which the judge dismissed with some words of advice for both parties.[55] Another time, he successfully defended against some inebriated cotton-mill workers who were bent on tearing up his shop and fighting everyone in it.[56] And he was very generous with his time, often giving kite-flying demonstrations for the children of the community, such as the Boys' and Orphans' Homes. He even made a call at the residence of the Earl of Aberdeen. Lord Aberdeen was the governor general of Canada from 1893 until 1898. Prior to his appointment, however, he and Lady Aberdeen went on a world tour in 1890, which included an extensive visit to Canada. While they were in Hamilton, Gant paid his respects on behalf of the "coloured citizens of Hamilton," dressed to kill as usual, and presenting the following card to the Earl and his Lady:

> Prof. J. Gant
> Representative coloured man of Hamilton
> 155 Victoria avenue north

Unfortunately, the *Hamilton Spectator*'s account of the visit reported Gant speaking in a southern drawl, making light of the whole affair.[57]

Gant's refined appearance, his donning of the title "professor," and his taking it upon himself to represent the Black community before Canadian officialdom were all part of a one-man campaign, it seemed, to "increase the acceptance of Blacks in the community," as one commentator has noted.[58] Put another way, Gant was trying to raise the spectre of middle-class respectability of Blacks in Hamilton by dispelling the myth that Blacks were ignorant, uneducated people, suited only for menial work and second-class status. Unfortunately, judging from the reporting, he probably did not achieve his goal.

The Hamilton press was often relentless in its coverage of Black people and events, if it meant that they could be made the butt of laughter and ridicule. If "Professor" Gant offered fodder for this kind of journalism, the press struck gold with Charles Augustus Johnson, otherwise known as "*Professor* C.A. Johnson" or "C. Astronomical Johnson," two of the names often attached to him. Johnson was a BME minister who

Mount Olive #1 brothers, circa 1965, of the Prince Hall Grand Lodge Free and Accepted Masons, Province of Ontario and Jurisdiction.

Courtesy of Joe Rhodes.

in the 1870s was lecturing to raise money for the building fund of the Baptist Church on Villanova Street. In 1879, he left the BME Church and in the early 1880s, was lecturing on scientific subjects, and advocating theories that were decidedly against the current thinking of the day. Johnson believed that the earth did not move around the sun. Rather, it was the other way around. This, he claimed, was based on Biblical scripture in the tenth chapter of Joshua. He also felt that the earth was flat, a reversal of centuries of established science on the subject. In later years he professed to know about the inhabitants of Mars, who stood twenty-five feet, ten inches tall.[59]

In 1881, Reverend Johnson lived with his wife Henrietta in Ward 3; both of them had been born in Ontario. The couple had two school-age children, Hiram, nine years old, and Lilly, seven, and two younger ones, George, six, and Russell, four.[60] Beginning in 1883, Reverend Johnson began publishing the *British Lion* in Hamilton, and, by 1884, an American version of the paper, called the *American Eagle*, rolled off the presses in New York. Both papers, neither of which has survived, were free of charge. One of Johnson's goals in publishing them was to help reunify families that had been torn apart by slavery. The *British Lion* was reportedly still being published in 1897.[61]

Charles A. Johnson was another self-styled leader of the Black race in Canada, and offered the Canadian government two hundred Black volunteers to fight against Louis Riel in the Métis rebellion.[62] He wrote open letters to Sir John A. Macdonald and Governor General Lord Stanley, expressing the loyalty of the African-Canadian people to the British government and the Conservative political cause.[63] His actions, and those of Gant, showed that African Canadians continued to be incredibly wary of any party but the Conservatives if there was even a remote possibility of Canadian annexation with the United States, an issue that surfaced periodically in Canada–United States relations. However, he offended his primary constituency when he wrote in his paper that Blacks aspired only to be waiters, barbers, coachmen, jubilee singers, and whitewashers and the elevation of the "coloured race" should involve aspiring to be bankers, real estate agents, editors, and so forth. One African American in Buffalo wrote a letter to the *Buffalo*

Express wondering how Johnson was allowed to "defame the African working classes."[64] Perhaps the ongoing platform he was given by the media was partly to blame.

With the constant barrage of negative reporting, under the guise of poking innocent fun at "colourful characters," the Hamilton press painted a portrait of Blacks that was insulting and demeaning. Sure, Blacks could attend the schools, and they lived in all wards of the city, although they tended to be clustered heavily in certain wards and sections of town. Yes, they found work in a variety of skilled and semi-skilled jobs, and some established their own businesses. But it was also true that both Black men and women were over-represented in the service industry. And when a Black youth stole a bicycle and received a year in prison, news of the theft and sentence appeared on the front page of the August 24, 1907, edition of the *Hamilton Herald* under the title "Bicycle Thief Got One Year: Coloured Youth, with a Past, Sent to Central Prison by Police Magistrate." It was particularly unnerving for Black readers of the article to realize that Police Chief Smith had been unable to learn anything about the boy's past. Headlines like these were not simply accusing one Black youth, but implicating an entire race. The problem was that a climate of derision and disrespect hovered like an ominous cloud over race relations to the point where just walking around in a dark skin was becoming an untenable proposition.

Under the circumstances, membership in the Black church and in Black clubs and organizations thrived. Given the choice between being a part of something in which one was accorded little clout or respect — if accepted at all — and one in which one felt at ease and welcomed, it is no wonder that African Hamiltonians flocked to the latter.

Fraternal organizations had played an important role in the life of Black communities in Canada since the 1850s, and Hamilton was no different in that respect. Indeed, Hamilton was a *key* centre of these fraternal orders in the province and such organizations were clearly a vital component in the health and well-being of Black Hamilton society. The birth of Mount Olive Lodge #1 of Hamilton signalled the dawn of Prince Hall Masonry in Canada West. Prince Hall was the founder of Black Masonry in the United States when African Lodge #1 was established in

Massachusetts on July 3, 1776. Years later, one of the people most influential in setting up Mount Olive #1 was George Shreve, the first Black schoolteacher to be hired in Trenton and Camden, New Jersey, and the first grand master of the New Jersey Grand Lodge. It was Shreve who asked Deputy Grand Master P.T. Harmsley to erect lodges in Canada West. By the early 1850s, Shreve himself had moved to Canada West and settled in Raleigh Township near Chatham along with his in-laws and a number of other families. Shreve's wife, Elizabeth, was the sister of Mary Ann Shadd, the *Provincial Freeman* editor, and the daughter of abolitionist Abraham D. Shadd, who had been active in the Masonic order in Pennsylvania and who had made the decision to relocate to Raleigh Township at that time.[65]

Mount Olive #1 received a warrant on December 27, 1852, for fourteen master Masons to open the lodge, signed by George Shreve and Reverend Joshua Woodlin, secretary, of the New Jersey parent body. Edmund Crump, an older shoemaker originally from Virginia and living on Mulberry Street, was one of the key founding members of Mount Olive. Following closely on the heels of Mount Olive, Victoria Lodge #2 and Olive Branch #3 were established in St. Catharines and Windsor in 1853.[66]

It is not clear why Harmsley went to Hamilton to set up the first lodge. However, Benjamin F. Stewart, an AME minister and deputy grand master of the New Jersey Grand Lodge moved to Hamilton and became a member of Mount Olive #1. Stewart, by the way, had been ordained at the AME Conference held in Chatham in 1854, and it was he who presented a resolution that began the movement to have the AME churches in Canada break away and become BME (British Methodist Episcopal) churches in 1856.[67] The census record showing his residence in Hamilton in 1861 indicates that he was living with and was a member of the William and Annie Davis family.[68] Stewart could very well have influenced the New Jersey Masons to come to Hamilton on the strength of his relatives' discussions and invitation. It is very likely that the Davises, the Crumps, and many other families in Hamilton had been active members in the Masonic orders in the United States before migrating to Canada, and wished to bring these fraternal bodies to their new hometown.

A second Grand Lodge was created in 1856 with the Widow's Son Grand Lodge. Many of Hamilton's skilled workers and entrepreneurs were elected officers of this lodge. Well-known barber John H. Bland became grand junior steward. Willis Reddick, another barbershop owner, became grand senior steward, and Philip Broadwater, a shoemaker turned Baptist minister, was elected grand chaplain.[69] The Baptist Church's ban on those belonging to a "secret organization" had apparently been lifted by this time.[70] Josiah Cochrane, another well-known Hamilton barber and leader of the community as we have seen, was grand secretary and recorded the first minutes.[71] Members of Victoria #2 of St. Catharines, and Mount Olive #1 were present at the inauguration of this Grand Lodge. Olive Branch #3, transplanted from Windsor, was a second lodge from Hamilton also present. By 1866, Reverend Benjamin Stewart was the worshipful grand master of this order, and he would remain so for seven consecutive terms.[72] Yet a third lodge, variously known as Hamilton, Downsview, or Progress #12, made a brief appearance in Hamilton in 1869. It was established by the United Grand Lodge of New York.[73]

In 1872, the Widow's Son Grand Lodge, which had established ten lodges in the province, including the two lodges from Hamilton,[74] amalgamated with all three other Grand Lodges that had been formed in the province by this time. It was J.H. Bland who had made the proposal at the 1871 proceedings to call a convention for the purpose of uniting the several Grand Lodges that were operating in the province. Reverend Stewart, Brother Bland, and E.P. Hilton attended the convention at which the amalgamation took place. The reasons for the amalgamation had first and foremost to do with the loss of population after the Civil War, when a proportion of expatriate African Americans returned to the United States. This population loss was particularly felt among the leadership of these communities, the same group that fed the membership of the lodges. A united Prince Hall Grand Lodge of Free and Accepted Masons was the result. Reverend Stewart was again elected grand master of this body. John Bland was elected grand treasurer, and Josiah Cochrane was appointed district deputy grand master.[75]

Over the ensuing years, Mount Olive continued to thrive in terms of membership relative to other local chapters. Hamilton would also send numerous men to the grand master position of this order. John H. Bland, an active member of the lodge, was elected to the highest post in 1870 and 1881. Shoemaker James L. Lightfoot who had petitioned the Market, Fire, and Police Committee to create a Black fire brigade, received the nod in 1885. George F. Hughes was elected in 1887, and Hiram Demun, another leader of the movement to establish a Black fire brigade, was elected in 1898. As Buxton historian Arlie Robbins observed, Demun "would have the unique honour of being the last Grand Master of

Courtesy of Robert Foster Jr., Kingston, Ontario.

Worthy Matron Judith Foster Morgan, great-granddaughter of Eastern Star stalwart and toll keeper, Julia Berry, dressed in the Eastern Star regalia, circa 1985. Ms. Morgan became a manager with the Royal Bank.

the old century as well as the first Grand Master of the new century."[76] The twentieth century would see many more leaders of the Prince Hall Masons coming from Hamilton.

Black women were also a part of the Masonic movement. The women's arm of the Masons was made up of the wives, sisters, and daughters of the male Masons and had existed since the late 1850s as auxiliaries to various local lodges. On August 30, 1889, however, the Grand Chapter of the Order of the Eastern Star was officially established with five chartered chapters: Electa Chapter #1 of Chatham, Willard Chapter #2 of Detroit, Esther Chapter #3 of Hamilton, Martha Chapter #4 of Grand Rapids, Michigan, and Victoria Chapter #6 of Windsor, Ontario.[77] As in the case of the men, Esther Chapter #3 of Hamilton has been a long-surviving and important

Courtesy of Eugene Miller, Toronto, Ontario.

Front cover of the Canadian Jubilee Singers and Imperial Orchestra songbook. The Royal Paragon Male Quartette, shown on the cover, was a sub-group of the company prominently featured on the tour.

chapter in the order. Julia Berry, the well-known toll keeper, was an active member of Esther Chapter #3, and, in fact, was selected to represent her Chapter at the inaugural meeting in 1889. Some of the important business of the order over the years has been visiting the sick and elderly in hospitals and nursing homes, helping fire victims and those in distress, and awarding youth scholarships.[78]

The various lodges of Prince Hall Masonry were not the only fraternal orders that sprang up in Ontario in the latter decades of the nineteenth century, although they were certainly the most prevalent and longstanding. The Royal Arch and the Provincial Commandery of Knights Templar were upper houses of Masonry that made themselves felt in Ontario's Black communities. From August 16 to 17, 1892, the Eleventh Hamilton Conclave was held, and Knights Templar from across Ontario and Michigan were present in the city. It was billed as "one of the greatest Masonic celebrations for many years" in the "Ambitious City." One of the highlights of the two-day event was the Detroit City Band, which gave a grand concert in Dundurn Park. G.H. Hughes of Hamilton was elected grand junior warden, and Richard Gwyder, grand guard. Reverend Josephus O'Banyoun, formerly of Hamilton, but currently preaching in Chatham, was installed as the eminent grand prelate.[79]

It has already been noted that some people were members of two or more Masonic orders. These fraternities offered fellowship and a sense of belonging that played a similar role to the churches in bringing people together and helping them withstand the difficult racial climate of those years. An article in the *Hamilton Spectator* of August 29, 1884, described in some detail what took place at one of these annual meetings. In 1884, the annual meeting of "Coloured Oddfellows" of Ontario was held in Toronto. The Mount Brydges Lodge of Oddfellows of Hamilton, numbering 175, and the Peter Ogden Lodge of Toronto were the only two groups that met that year, the groups from Amherstburg, Dresden, and Chatham having been defunct for some time. The Hamilton Oddfellows travelled to Toronto where they were met by their Toronto brothers and formed into a procession led by Jesse Gant and the Hamilton Union Cornet Band, marching along York, Chestnut, Elm, and Queen Streets to Queen's Park. There, some of the members had a friendly game of baseball. At 4:00 p.m., they met in the Temperance Hall for the annual meeting, where election of officers took place and reports from the "Households of Ruth" of Hamilton and Toronto were read. This was the female adjunct of the Oddfellows. J.T. Bryant, of Hamilton, was elected deputy district master and George Morton was re-elected secretary of the organization. The officers were installed by W.E. Pearman of Hamilton. In the evening, there was a concert of vocal and instrumental music in Albert Hall and dancing afterwards.[80]

The importance of music and dance to the celebration of fraternal orders demonstrates the important role that music played in Black Hamilton life. The city has had a long history of producing great Black musical artists. Hamiltonians are surely familiar with the Washington family of singers and musicians, and Jackie Washington, who became a well-known blues singer in his own right. They may have heard of renowned jazz guitarist Sonny Greenwich or outstanding blues musician and composer Harrison Kennedy whose hit "Give Me Just a Little More Time" during his stint with the group Chairman of the Board took him to the heights of the music business in the 1960s and 70s. They may even be aware that Grammy- and Tony-nominated recording artist and songwriter Brenda Russell grew up in Hamilton. However, long before these modern-day troubadours, Hamilton was a thriving centre of great entertainment. As early as 1851, a "House of Entertainment" was kept by Peter and Lucinda Price and their family on Hughson Street. Peter Price, a cab driver with his own carriage for hire, had five additional adults — three butlers, a cook, and labourer — also living on the premises and probably employed in his enterprise.[81]

Beyond these kinds of establishments that existed to bring people together for some merriment and relaxation, a number of choral groups of renown came out of Hamilton. The O'Banyoun Jubilee Singers was one such group. Founded by Josephus O'Banyoun in the early 1860s in Halifax, Nova Scotia, over the years the group toured across North America and throughout Europe. In 1892, the group was reconstituted for a Canadian and possible future world tour. It comprised seven singers and an accompanist, all but one of whom were from Hamilton, Ontario.[82]

African-Canadian choral ensembles were prevalent in the latter decades of the nineteenth century. Choral music in the Black Canadian community was largely centred in the church and numerous groups were making the rounds of the churches and concert halls of Canada and the United States to favourable reviews. They patterned themselves after the acclaimed Jubilee Singers of Fisk University of Nashville, Tennessee. The Fisk Jubilee Singers were an a cappella group that started out on a small fundraising tour for the school in 1871 and rose to international prominence, performing in Europe before Queen Victoria of England, as well as at the White House for President Ulysses S. Grant. Although initially they sang a couple of "slave songs" or Negro spirituals as encores, they quickly realized that these songs had a powerful impact on their audience and these became the mainstay of their program.[83] The Fisk Jubilee Singers influenced a whole generation of African-American and African-Canadian singing sensations, and Canadian groups like the Ball Family Jubilee Singers and the O'Banyoun Singers were part of this culture of singing troupes that were immersed in church music and Negro spirituals.

Reverend Josephus O'Banyoun was born in Brantford, Upper Canada, in 1838. His father was the Reverend Peter O'Banyoun of the African Methodist Episcopal persuasion who had pastored a church of that denomination in Brantford during the 1840s and 1850s, and who later joined the BME body. Josephus O'Banyoun followed his father into the profession, and led both BME and AME congregations. In terms of his musical prowess, he was described as a "thorough vocalist" and one of the most experienced and successful concert company managers in the country. He had even conducted a solo tour through England and Wales a few years prior, which was quite successful.[84]

Professor Cockbin of Hamilton possessed a rich bass voice and was also a noted soloist, having recently sung with the Canadian Jubilee Singers and finished a tour in England, Ireland, Scotland, and Wales. Hamiltonian Maud Young was a soprano with a "wonderful compass." She was a former student of Mrs. Martin Murphy of Hamilton and was also recently engaged with the Canadian Jubilee Singers. Alice Dowden, also from Hamilton, was a soprano and experienced member of jubilee groups. She was a student of Professor Jones from England. Mrs. Bland-O'Banyoun, a mezzo-soprano, was a member of the original O'Banyoun Singers and Josephus O'Banyoun's wife. Ernest O'Banyoun, the son of the leader, possessed a magnificent baritone instrument. His signature number, "A Jolly Good Laugh," was adapted from the "Picnic" cantata composed by J.R. Thomas, a popular American composer and singer of the day. O'Banyoun the son had recently been a member of the Dominion Jubilee Troupe under the directorship of Albert Harris. Minnie Parker was the only singer not from Hamilton. The Chatham native was well-known in that city for her rich, highly trained voice. Mrs. Cockbin, wife of Professor Cockbin and another Hamilton native, was accompanist to the group. She was a student of Mrs. Harriet A. Wilkins, and a "thorough musician." The "highly-refined Jubilee Company's" first engagement was at St. Andrew's Church of Chatham on October 21, 1892. They intended to visit Europe, Asia, Africa, and Australia in the coming years.[85]

The Canadian Jubilee Singers and Imperial Orchestra, already mentioned in connection with several O'Banyoun singers who had been members of this company, was reportedly established in 1879, and performed before the Royal Family and toured England, Ireland, and Wales for five years during the 1880s. In the 1890s, it combined a brass orchestra and a first-rate jubilee chorus, and featured a male vocal quartet, a soprano soloist, and the celebrated "Boy Basso," James Escort Lightfoot, who was also its orchestra director and mandolin virtuoso. Lightfoot,

VERINA M. GILLIAM LEWIS
ELOCUTIONIST
WITH THE
CELEBRATED COLORED CANADIAN CONCERT CO.

This handbill of unknown date advertising the Colored Canadian Concert Company featured elocutionist Verina Gilliam Lewis.

who had been with the company since 1890, was apparently the son of the shoemaker and Prince Hall grandmaster, James L. Lightfoot. James E. later joined the Williams and Walker Glee Club, a noted American company, for the 1904–06 seasons. Canadian Jubilee performances also included guitar and mandolin duets and various instrumental solos, such as that of slide trombonist Nathan Warner.[86]

The proprietors and managers of the Canadian Jubilee Singers and Imperial Orchestra were William and Sadie Carter, both Canadian-born from Hamilton. They had been members of the 1890 edition of Thearle's Original Nashville Students, an American jubilee concert company founded in 1878, and proved to be concert managers *par excellence*. In the 1894–95 season, the Canadian Jubilee Singers toured nonstop in New York, Pennsylvania, Ohio, Indiana, and Michigan for forty-seven weeks, closing July 26, 1895, in London, Ontario. In addition to the Carters, the company included Jimmie Lightfoot; J.A. Cockbin and his wife; W.T. Cary and his wife, Fanny Stewart; Hattie Butler; Nathan Warner; and James Thomas. J.V. Carter was added as a tenor soloist beginning in the 1895–96 season. In 1901, the Carters were listed in the census as living at 100 Cannon Street with seventy-three-year-old William Carter Sr., head of the household, and owner of the six-room house. Elizabeth and Julia Lightfoot, his daughters, had both married Lightfoot men and were both vocalists. William Carter, vocalist and manager, and Sadie Carter, pianist, were also listed. It is quite possible that Elizabeth and Julia had joined the

Canadian Jubilee Singers, given their occupations as "vocalists." They and William and Sadie appear to have been touring eight months of that year. Two grandsons, William Lightfoot and Vernon Lightfoot, ages eighteen and six, were also living in the home.[87]

The Canadian Jubilee Singers were a very popular troupe that toured for many years. The *Indianapolis Freeman*, described as one of the "central headquarters" of news on Black professional musicians and entertainers, noted that on July 9, 1897, they "closed a very successful season of forty-two weeks and four days, missing only two days out of the entire season." Ten years later, the *Freeman* reported that they closed a "successful season of forty weeks at Omaha, Neb." on June 15, 1907. As Lynn Abbott and Doug Seroff concluded in *Out of Sight*, their goldmine of information on Black popular music in the late nineteenth century, "The Canadian Jubilee Singers remained in demand for many years. It seems they had come up with a practical formula for stability and longevity on the road."[88]

The Carters managed another Hamilton-based singing sensation at the turn of the century known as the Canadian Colored Concert Company. It is not clear if this was the exact same company as the Jubilee Singers with a new name, or a separate group with an entirely different roster of performers. Both the Canadian Jubilee Singers and the Canadian Colored Concert Company published songbooks with the exact same contents. They consisted of "Plantation Lullabies" and included some music and words, such as "I'm a Rolling," "My Lord Delivered Daniel," "Roll, Jordan, Roll," and "Zion's Children." Other songs consisted of just the words, such as "De Massa ob de Sheepfol," "I Ain't Got Weary Yet," "In My Father's House," and "Oh! Mary Don't You Weep."[89]

William Carter died on the road in 1906. The *Indianapolis Freeman* reported that Carter had been connected with the Canadian Colored Concert Company for almost twenty-five years. His body was shipped to Hamilton for burial.[90] His Canadian Jubilee Singers and Colored Concert Company continued on for some years after his death.

The first decades following the Emancipation Proclamation, passage of the 13th and 14th Amendments, and the end of the Civil War held immense promise for African Americans and African Canadians alike.

Many must have felt that the end of racism and discrimination were close at hand and that a new era of justice and equality was now possible. Blacks had seen the mountaintop, had perhaps felt it was within their grasp. But they did not get there. The twentieth century would usher in a further decline in the prospects of its citizens of African descent in terms of job opportunities, income and social equality.

CHAPTER 6

At a Crossroads: The Turn of a New Century

When "Professor" Jesse Gant died of Bright's disease in 1905 at the age of fifty-four, his obituary in the *Hamilton Spectator* stated that he was survived by four children. His son Oscar was now living in Pittsburgh, and his daughter Rose in Chicago.[1] This seems typical of the choice of many first- and second-generation African Canadians to bypass their own country in preference for cities in the northern United States in search of opportunities. And as Canadian Blacks moved south, tens of thousands of southern Blacks began the same trek north to urban centres like New York, Chicago, and Detroit after the failure of Reconstruction.

In 1901, the Black population in Hamilton remained about the same, at 450, as it had been in 1881, according to the published census records. Compared with 1861, when the majority of Blacks in Hamilton were born in the United States (56 percent), by the turn of the twentieth century the vast majority of African Hamiltonians — 82 percent — were recorded as having been born in Ontario. Seventeen percent were immigrants from the United States. One person reported his birthplace as Jamaica and two were from the British Isles.[2]

The lack of growth of the Black population of Hamilton between 1881 and 1901 can largely be attributed to this population attrition to urban centres in the United States. Historian James Walker has written about the irony that Black Canadians found more opportunity in segregated America than in a Canada that was supposedly devoid of racial animus:

> In the "segregated" United States there was a full black society from top to bottom, with black universities, black newspapers, black hospitals, black lawyers and doctors and tradesmen, as well as waiters, labourers and small farmers. But in "non-segregated" Canada blacks tended all to fit into one level of society, for the higher institutions and higher professions were tacitly reserved for whites.[3]

Viola Berry Aylestock, granddaughter of Julia Berry, operator of the tollgate in Hamilton, commented in a 1988 interview that "It was hard being a Black person: the fact that you had the education and you still couldn't get the jobs really you were qualified for — it was frustrating and that's why so many Blacks left. I can remember my mother saying that in the early 1900s some friends of our family left, and they went and settled in Cincinnati."[4] One man gave notice of his leaving in the Black newspaper of the day, the *Canadian Observer*, published out of Toronto by J.R.B. Whitney. John Preston practically apologized for his decision in the January 9, 1915 issue:

> Mr. John Preston is leaving the city for Buffalo. Mr. Preston is a bricklayer, and intends working at building on the other side. As he is one of the prominent members of the new amateur minstrel troupe, it is probable his going away will hinder the progress of the company, and cause some delay in their starting on the road.

The young and the not so young alike went south. Shoemaker and past grand master of the Prince Hall Masons of Ontario, James L. Lightfoot, left for Michigan some years prior and had joined Pythagoras, a lodge in Detroit. He died at his daughter's home in St. Paul, Minnesota.[5] Dr. Charles Roman was one of many who left in the flower of their youth. Charles Victor Roman was born on July 4, 1864, in Williamsport, Pennsylvania.[6] He was the son of Captain James W. Roman, a canal-boat owner, and Ann Walker McGuin Roman. The family moved to Canada and settled in Dundas, Ontario, where the young Roman began working in a Dundas cotton mill at the age of eight. He then obtained the opportunity of a lifetime. The Reverend Featherstone Osler, rector of the Church of England

Courtesy of Robert Foster Jr., Kingston, Ontario.

Viola Berry Aylestock moved up the occupational ladder, holding positions as a domestic and then secretary in a tanning factory during the Second World War. After receiving a practical nurse's diploma, she worked in that capacity and then as food supervisor at Toronto General Hospital. She later served as a correctional officer at the Vanier Centre in Brampton, Ontario.

for Ancaster and Dundas, established a night school for the benefit of the boys who worked at the mill. Reverend Osler was the father of Sir William Osler, the famous physician and teacher who was knighted for his contributions to the teaching of medicine. Charles Roman took full advantage of this lucky happenstance. Even at an early age, he had announced to his fellow young cotton-mill workers that he would someday be a doctor. When the Romans moved to Hamilton several years later, he entered the Cannon Street Public School. He sustained an injury to his right knee that required amputation of his leg, but this did not

From Charles Victor Roman, Meharry Medical College: A History (Nashville, TN: Sunday School Publishing Board of the National Baptist Convention Inc., 1934).

Dr. Charles Roman was a professor of medicine at Meharry Medical College and set up a new Department of Ophthalmology and Otolaryngology there. He broke barriers when he was hired as a lecturer for the United States Army during the Second World War.

seem to stop his upward trajectory. During his convalescence, Roman planned his future.

As soon as he was able to move around on crutches, Roman entered Hamilton Collegiate Institute. He was apparently the first student of African descent to enter the school, but he was so accomplished that he graduated from the four-year course in just two years. This was in the year 1885. He later wrote that there was much discussion and gossip at the school about his future prospects and that one of his teachers made a suggestion: "Go South and teach school." This teacher was well aware that Black teachers were desperately needed in the southern United States to educate the large population of former slaves and their children. Accordingly, Roman headed south and taught in Cadiz, Trigg County, Kentucky, and in Columbia, Tennessee. In his history of the Meharry Medical College, he wrote, "By a streak of fate I went to board with Dr. John C. Halfacre, a graduate of Meharry College. I told him of my ambition and he told me of Meharry. Up to this time I had no other thought than saving up sufficient money to enter the Medical College of McGill University in Montreal ..."[7] Roman then began the fulfillment of a childhood dream. He obtained a teaching position in Nashville and entered Meharry Medical College there, taking his courses after school hours and obtaining his medical degree in 1890.

It seems that the brilliant young medical student was torn between teaching and a medical career. In 1889, he became assistant to Dr. R.F. Boyd in his medical practice in Nashville. As Dr. Roman wrote:

> [This association] counteracted the discouraging advice of [my] friends and offset the example of two of [my] classmates who stuck to their jobs as city teachers. Decision was difficult as [I] was both popular and successful as a teacher ... [My] desire was to practice but according to [my] friends, [my] duty was to teach. Desire won.[8]

When Dr. Boyd left for Chicago to upgrade his medical resumé, he left his understudy in charge of the practice. Roman observed that "The experience of those two summer months gave the writer confidence in his own ability to practice medicine. Upon the doctor's return [I] tendered [my] resignation as city teacher and hung out [a] shingle in Clarksville, Tennessee."[9]

After practising medicine in Tennessee and Texas, Dr. Roman studied at the Royal Ophthalmic Hospital and Central Nose, Throat, and Ear Hospital in London, England, in 1904. Upon his return, he was appointed to his alma mater, Meharry Medical College, and set up a new department of Ophthalmology and Otolaryngology there. Roman served as fifth president of the National Medical Association (1904–05) and was first editor of the *Journal of the National Medical Association* (*JNMA*), serving in this latter capacity from 1909 until 1919. These associations were African-American entities, made necessary by segregation. Dr. Roman gave a statement of purpose of the National Medical Association:

> Conceived in no spirit of racial exclusiveness, fostering no ethnic antagonism, but born of the exigencies of the American environment, the National Medical Association has for its object the banding together for mutual cooperation and helpfulness the men and women of African descent who are legally and honorably

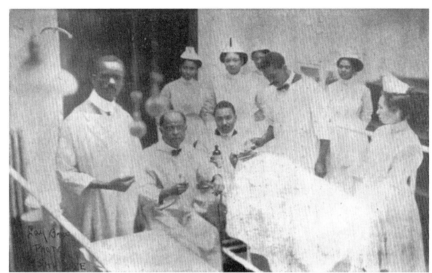

From Charles Victor Roman, Meharry Medical College: A History (Nashville, TN: Sunday School Publishing Board of the National Baptist Convention Inc., 1934).

Dr. Charles Roman in the operating theatre.

engaged in the practice of the cognate professions of Medicine, Surgery, Pharmacy and Dentistry.[10]

Dr. Roman also became director of health at Fisk University and, during the First World War, was appointed medical lecturer for the army. In addition to his medical career, Dr. Roman was a popular teacher of Bible class at St. Paul's AME Church in Nashville. In 1911, he was one of five lay delegates of the AME Church at the Methodist Ecumenical Conference in Toronto and took time out to speak at the First Methodist Church in Hamilton. His homecoming was quite a sensation, and he was surprised by the attendance of a group of former students of the night school that he attended so long ago.[11]

Apart from his stint in the army, his entire career had essentially operated in a segregated environment, from medical school to his teaching career, medical practice, and appointments at various universities and associations. When Dr. Roman died of a heart attack in 1934 at the age of seventy, he was able to look back on an illustrious career conducted with the highest level of professionalism. During his reign as editor of the *JNMA*, the journal was known for its scholarly competence,

prompting the *Nashville Globe* to comment that it "easily leads the literature produced by Negroes."[12] Roman also published several books, most
notable among them, *American Civilization and the Negro* and *Meharry
Medical College: A History*, the latter published in the year of his death.[13]

One biographer, in summarizing Dr. Charles Roman's incredible
accomplishments, observed that the segregated Black environment in
which he became immersed after graduating high school in Hamilton
was an important feature of his life:

> It seems reasonable to infer from his own accounts
> that during his twenty-one years in the North and in
> Canada, he had been so oppressed with a feeling of
> social loneliness that when he left a white environment
> which he was in but not of, and entered the Negro
> environment which for the first time gave him the
> emotional security of a sense of "belonging," he could
> never quite bring himself to dissociate even temporar-
> ily from that new environment.[14]

But one thing that Canada gave him was an excellent preparation:
"such preparation as he had had gave him an advantage over most of his
associates and he quickly became a hero."[15]

Reading between the lines, one might infer something else from the
biographer's comments. One of the most persistent legacies of slavery
was the continuing belief that people of African descent were intellectu-
ally inferior to those of European origin. Roman's life and career was an
indisputable refutation of that belief, and showed what could be accomplished in a supportive environment in which white supremacy and the
never-ending questioning of a person's intelligence and competence were
not the subtext of one's day-to-day routine.

Writing in the Canada of 1930, economist Ida Greaves summarized
the situation for Black workers in the 1920s as compared with the late
1800s. She observed that there had been a "marked shrinkage in the field of
employment for Negroes and a retrogression in the economic position of
the race during the present century. Until twenty or thirty years ago there

were coloured waiters in the best hotels, and several Negroes carried on businesses of their own. All waiters are now white, and except within the limitations of a Negro community a coloured businessman is very rare."[16]

The 1901 census indeed showed that the percentage of skilled workers and those in business had dipped to 32 percent of Black males. The barbering trade still employed the most number of any skilled/semi-skilled occupation, but in 1901, that meant that only six barbers worked in Hamilton, as compared with more than triple that in 1881. In addition, there were four plasterers, three cooks, two carpenters, and one brickmaker. In contrast, those in the unskilled class had jumped to 63 percent. This category included seven whitewashers, six waiters, and six porters, comprising one railway porter and several hotel porters. Additionally, there were four other hotel employees, three of whom were bellboys. Seven tobacco workers employed in a factory were probably Tuckett's Tobacco employees. Five percent cited no employment.[17]

The occupational breakdown for women indicated that 17 percent were in skilled jobs, including three teachers — two of whom taught music — eleven dressmakers or tailoresses, one cook, and three vocalists. In the unskilled category, there were 21 percent employed. These included thirteen domestic servants, six washerwomen, one tobacco worker, one peddler, and one charwoman. Sixty-three percent reported no occupation. The trend for women was that those working in skilled/semi-skilled jobs more than doubled from 8 percent in 1851 to 17 percent in 1901. This may not have been a reflection of increased job opportunities, but rather that more women were reporting an income from some form of waged work. In 1851, 27 percent stated that they were employed outside the home or in some form of waged work. In 1861, 17 percent reported an occupation, in 1871, the figure was 26 percent, and, in 1881, 41 percent were engaged in waged work. Finally, in 1901, it was 37 percent. For men, the overall trend was a decline over time in the proportion of skilled/semi-skilled tradesmen and entrepreneurs.

After his well-publicized bid to open up city jobs for Blacks, George Morton, the articulate leader of the campaign, received a job as a letter carrier in 1891. By 1901, he probably was the only African-Canadian

Letter carriers, 1910. Civil rights leader George Morton Jr. is standing third from right. One other Black postman, whose identity is unknown, is visible in the photograph.

letter carrier with the city, and, in 1910, was one of two letter carriers in Hamilton. There were no Black firemen or policemen. Interestingly, there was one Black woman who obtained the position of police matron in 1894. Martha Lewis had worked for the police department for fourteen years on an intermittent basis. Her principal duty was to inspect female prisoners to see if any poison or dangerous weapons were concealed on their bodies. However, the Women's Christian Temperance Union (WCTU) agitated for a permanent position of police matron to help counsel the women, as well as young boys, and bring them into contact with appropriate women's organizations and agencies. When Mrs. Lewis was given the position, the WCTU wrote a letter to the *Evening Times* protesting the move. Their argument was that a good, *white* Christian woman was more suited to such an appointment in a *white* community such as Hamilton because they would have a greater influence on these wayward girls and women than would a *Black* woman. The letter referred to "agitation" caused by the raising of the colour question, suggesting a possible protest on behalf of Mrs. Lewis by the Black community. No evidence of such protest has been found except for a letter to the editor of the *Hamilton Spectator* by Jesse Gant. This time Gant put his support behind Mrs. Lewis and slammed the WCTU, stating, in part,

Courtesy of Corinne Bryant Chevalier, Toronto, Ontario.

Postal worker Vincent Bryant (standing left), Corinne Bryant (seated right), with baby Corinne and godparents Mr. and Mrs. Seeley, circa 1935. Bryant started out as a letter carrier in 1929 and eventually was promoted to supervisor of city delivery, retiring after forty-three years. His last position came toward the end of his career after he protested being passed over for a promotion for years. Better known as Hamilton's "Dean of Football," Vince Bryant coached winning high school and junior football teams from the 1920s through the 1950s. A number of his players went on to play professional football in Canada.

"Solomon was black, Bishop Niger, an African, ordained Paul the Apostle, Moses married a coloured woman, and she did not belong to the WCTU."[18]

George Morton kept his position as letter carrier for thirty-six years, and for the last twenty-one of those years he was treasurer of the local letter carriers' association.[19] Mr. Morton obviously held a high degree of trust with his fellow letter carriers. But the fact still remains that there were precious few in these steady, secure positions. And even when a Black person, by chance, did receive such an appointment, it was not particularly regarded with approval by the white community. When Sir Adam Beck, chairman of the Ontario Hydro-Electric Power Commission (of which he was founder) hired a Black person as a clerk in the London office, North Hamilton's Member of Parliament attacked him for doing so.[20]

To stem the tide of immigration to the United States, Hamilton continued to draw partly from the small town and rural areas of Ontario. Ray Lewis, known for his 1932 Olympic bronze medal achievement in the 4 x 400-metre relay in Los Angeles, was born in Hamilton on October 8, 1910. His mother, Emma Green, was from Collingwood, Ontario, one of the areas settled by former African-American slaves. She had moved to Guelph where she was working as a maid when she met Ray's father,

Cornelius Lewis. He had relocated to Hamilton from Simcoe, Ontario. Although Cornelius was a skilled builder, the racism of the day dictated that he work as a dining-car waiter on the Grand Trunk Railway and later as a janitor at Westinghouse and Canadian Porcelain companies.[21]

Other families continued to be drawn to Hamilton from the United States at the turn of the century. One American family who arrived was that of Shirley (Wade) Brown. Shirley's mother and grandmother, Evangeline Day and Mary Ellen (Logan) Day came to Canada from Danville, Virginia, at the turn of the century.

> … My grandmother had asthma very bad, and my grandfather burned the tobacco and [his employer] sent him to Canada [where] he worked at Tuckett's [Tobacco Factory]. But the weather was better for my grandmother. My mother was only between five and seven when she came to Canada.[22]

Shirley's father, Byron Kenton Wade, was born on an Indian Reservation near St. Paul, Minnesota. He came to Canada as a boy with his father — Reverend George Harrison Wade. Between 1910 and 1912, Reverend Wade pastored at Hamilton's St. Paul's AME. Byron Kenton Wade later became a vaudeville entertainer who sang, danced, and played the guitar and banjo. He married Evangeline Day when the two were quite young. They had seven children, but eventually the marriage dissolved. Both Mrs. Wade and her mother supported the family doing housework and Mrs. Wade later worked as a matron at the Tivoli and Century theatres. These were the only types of jobs available to many Black women in the decades leading up to the Second World War:

> She looked after the washrooms and made sure that there was no one there bothering any of the kids or anything. She used to walk up and down the aisle … and when they were really busy, she used to be an usher and used to sit people in their seats. And that's how she made her living, and then she finally retired from the Century

Theatre. But that's how she and my grandmother raised us, between my grandmother doing housework too, because she retired from Tuckett's Tobacco Co. but she would still go out and do housework …[23]

Because of the rampant racism of the day, life could be hard for Black families in the early twentieth century. Black men couldn't catch a break when it came to getting a decent job. Many were relegated to stereotypical service jobs on the railway as porters, or other low-status occupations such as janitor, in far greater numbers than they had been in the nineteenth century. Black women, as was the case with Shirley Brown's mother and grandmother, often worked as maids, washroom matrons in hotels or theatres, and elevator operators.

Despite the fundamental injustices of the time and the denial of opportunities, the Black church was a place of respite and solace. According to Ray Lewis, who chronicled his life story in the book *Shadow Running*, published in 1999, the members of his family were long-standing members of the church. His parents married at St. Paul's AME Church on July 4, 1900. The church was now located at 114 John Street North with a four-hundred-seat capacity. At the time of their marriage, there were ninety-eight communicants and eighty Sunday school scholars, with sixteen Sunday school teachers.[24] Lewis, himself a life-long member, was secretary of the Sunday school at age twelve and served on the Board of Trustees until his death in November 2003. As he reminisced in his autobiography:

> Stewart Memorial Church [the former St. Paul's AME] was one of the vital cornerstones of our family life. My parents were regular churchgoers and took us to church regularly … I was christened at Stewart Memorial and I recall sitting in the northeast corner pews as a young child. While Stewart's community was predominantly Black, I recall one or two white families who were happily accepted by the congregation.[25]

Henry Berry was a deacon in the church and many Black families were members of St. Paul's AME Church. The original minute book from 1910–35 contained the names of many of these families, such as the Hollands, Wades, Downys, Johnsons, and many others. Mrs. Louisa Diggs, the widow of Civil War veteran William Diggs, also attended the church, and Sylvia Rhodes, daughter of Mary and Wesley Rhodes, was received into full membership on March 27, 1911.[26]

The entire Rhodes family was quite active in the church, as this *Canadian Observer* notice entitled "Old Folks Dinner" documented in the March 20, 1915 issue:

Shadow Running, *by Ray Lewis as told to John Cooper, is a brutal but honest look at life through the eyes of a Black person in the early twentieth century. Another book about Lewis's life,* Rapid Ray, *was written for a younger audience.*

> On Friday evening the old folks of the city and the widows and widowers were royally entertained to dinner by Mrs. Mary Rhodes of 27 Greig Street … At 7:30 the invited guests sat down to an elaborate dinner prepared by Mrs. Rhodes in the Sunday-school room of the church, and afterwards a lunch was sold to the patrons of the occasion. This was a unique and most worthy undertaking, and the greatest credit is due to the patroness for her generosity in gladdening the hearts of the many guests. A large proportion of the viands were contributed by kind merchants

and the proceeds of the entertainment are for the use
of the Missionary Society in relieving the distressed
among the church congregation.

Clearly the church and its missionary adjunct were important in the
lives of congregants and had a vital stop-gap role to play for its less for-
tunate members.

Although Black people were excluded from many trade unions and
the better jobs in factories, and were subjected to discriminatory treatment — or perhaps because of it — Black males again sought to prove
their worth and valour at war. Calvin Ruck, author of *The Black Battalion,
1916–1920: Canada's Best Kept Military Secret*, phrased it another way.
At the outset of the First World War, Black Canadians, he wrote, were
"caught up in the patriotic fervour of this conflict, which was being hailed
as the 'war to end all wars,' 'a war to make the world safe for democracy.'"[27]

All across the nation, Black men appeared at recruiting stations only
to be turned away. Sometimes they were bluntly told that this was "a white
man's war." Often, they were politely told to wait until they were called,
although the call never came. Voices of protest began to mount from community leaders in various parts of the country. Arthur Alexander of North
Buxton, Ontario, wrote a letter to the minister of Militia and Defence, Sir
Sam Hughes, demanding to know why African Canadians were not being
allowed to enlist in the Canadian Expeditionary Forces.[28] The response
was that the selection of recruits was handled by the commanding officers in the field, and their selections or rejections were not interfered with
from headquarters. The fact was that a few African Canadians had been
allowed to enlist on an individual basis in various units across the country. However, most were being rejected by field officers.

Letter carrier and community leader George Morton sent a letter to
the minister a year later:

September 7, 1915
Dear Sir,
... The reason for drawing your attention to this matter,
and directly leading to the request for this information,

is the fact that a number of Colored men in this city (Hamilton) who have offered for enlistment and service have been turned down and refused solely on the ground of color and complexional differences, this being the reason given on the rejection or refusal card issued by the recruiting officer.

As humble, but loyal, subjects of the King trying to work out their own destiny, they think they should be permitted in common with other peoples to perform their part and do their share in this great conflict. So our people, greatly remembering their obligations in this respect, are most anxious to serve their King and Country in this critical crisis in its history, and they do not think they should be prevented from doing so on the ground of the hue of their skin.[29]

The letter was sent by way of Hamilton's MP at the time, T.J. Stewart. Brigadier-General W.E. Hodgins, who was acting adjutant-general, sent Stewart a similar response to that Mr. Alexander had received:

There are no regulations or restrictions which prohibit or discriminate against the enlistment and enrollment of coloured men who possess the necessary qualifications … The final approval of any man, regardless of colour or any other distinction, must of course rest with the officer commanding the particular unit which the man in question is desirous of joining.[30]

More and more inquiries began to pour into the authorities. Then there was the case of twenty Black volunteers in New Brunswick, who, after great persistence, were finally accepted into the army. However, when they reported to military camp at Sussex, they were rudely insulted and sent home to Saint John. They had families and had apparently quit their jobs so they could enlist. The situation was becoming increasingly uncomfortable for the military, not to mention for those who had given up jobs to serve their country. Toronto-based Black newspaper publisher, J.R.B. Whitney of the *Canadian Observer*, proposed to raise a Black platoon. He was given the okay by Sir Sam Hughes, and went on a recruiting tour to London, Chatham, and Windsor, accompanied by a Black enlistee from the 80th Battalion. The problem was that Hughes forgot to mention that this Black platoon would have to be accepted by a commanding officer of an authorized battalion. Needless to say, no battalion would accept one.

After this considerable embarrassment, and the indignation of more men with families who had given up jobs to enlist, Major-General G.W. Gwatkin finally proposed a compromise. The Army, while still opposed to a Black fighting unit in the European theatre, decided to form a Black labour battalion, the No. 2 Construction Battalion, C.E.F.[31] "On May 11, 1916, the British War Office in London cabled the governor general expressing its willingness to accept such a unit."[32] Over six hundred men enlisted from across Canada, including at least 165 from the United States. Sixteen men also served in the 106th Battalion, C.E.F. Included in the ranks of the No. 2 were the following Hamilton men: Ernest Bell, Charles Bryant, Frederick Lewis, Joshua Miller, Samuel Thornton, and George Wimbish. Lieutenant Leslie Bruce Young, also from Hamilton, was one of nine Black lieutenants who served in this unit.[33]

The No. 2 Construction Battalion embarked from Halifax on March 28, 1917, for Liverpool and in early May proceeded to the French-Swiss border where it was attached to the Canadian Forestry Corps. A film about this battalion entitled *Honour Before Glory* was made by the great-nephew of the only Black commissioned officer in the British forces during the First World War, Reverend Captain William A. White, of Truro, Nova Scotia. It was based on the diary of Reverend White and provided an insight into the character of the men and dramatized their experiences during the war. Filmmaker and actor Anthony Sherwood, played the role of his great-uncle.

Calvin Ruck concluded his history of the No. 2 by stating:

> The unit was commended for its discipline and faithful service while attached to the Forestry Corps. Some of the men were eventually assigned to line units and

participated in trench combat. In early 1919, following the Armistice of November 11, 1918, the unit returned to Canada, where it was officially disbanded in September 15, 1920. The No. 2 Construction Battalion thus faded away into the dusty annals of Canadian military history.[34]

The men who had proudly served their country returned home with honour. The situation to which they were returning at home was not an honourable one, however. Job opportunities continued to elude Black Canadians, and a segregation of the races in worship, club membership, and fraternal organizations was the order of the day. Freemasons of the white Grand Lodge of Canada, for example, refused to even recognize their Prince Hall brothers, although numerous attempts to contact them were made by the African Canadian order over the years.[35] As historian Robin Winks observed, "… a once vague mythology about what the Negro could and could not do had taken on a more exact form. Language, literature, the theatre, science, and even history had informed generations of Canadians of the Negro's inability to adapt to the north, of his love of pleasure, of his sexual appetites, his unreliability, laziness, and odor."[36] There was a federal government policy to keep hopeful Black immigrants out of the country, and restaurants, hotels, bars, skating rinks, tennis clubs, swimming pools, and a host of public facilities often did not welcome Black customers. It was all perfectly legal. James Walker's discussion of Canadian segregation in *"Race": Rights and the Law in the Supreme Court of Canada* was blunt:

> In his classic description of American racial segregation, *The Strange Career of Jim Crow*, C. Vann Woodward identified the areas of life where legalized segregation tended to apply following the end of slavery in the United States. He listed "churches and schools," "housing and jobs," "eating and drinking," "public transportation," "sports and recreations," "hospitals, orphanages, prisons and asylums" and, in death, "funeral homes, morgues

and cemeteries." In virtually every one of these areas of life and death, African Canadians too experienced exclusion and separation from mainstream institutions, amounting to a Canadian version of "Jim Crow."[37]

Another more frightening consequence of the racist climate of the times was the formation of the Ku Klux Klan in Canada. The Ku Klux Klan was founded in Tennessee after the Civil War by several white officers of the Confederate Army, who derived the name from the Greek word for circle, or *kuklos*. Initially, it was intended as a social club, and fashioned itself after other fraternal orders, using names like "Grand Wizard," "Grand Dragon," "Hydra," "Fury," and "Cyclops." Members donned white gowns and conical hoods with eyeholes cut out so that their faces were completely hidden. However, the hatred and deep-seated resentment over the emancipation of African Americans and their new status as equal citizens resulted in the organization beginning a reign of terror on the newly freed Black population through intimidation, physical and sexual assaults, property damage, and murder. This first phase of the organization's existence was stifled when Congress passed legislation making it a crime to appear in disguise in order to deprive others of their constitutional rights. Anyone with foreknowledge of Klan violence could be held liable to the victims for any suffering they could have prevented.[38]

Although there is only negligible evidence of its activity beforehand, after the re-emergence of the Klan in the United States in 1915, branches of the KKK began to appear in numerous Canadian towns and cities in the 1920s. Historians attribute the reinvigoration of the Klan in the United States to the publication of a novel entitled *The Clansman* and its subsequent interpretation on film in *The Birth of a Nation*, directed by D.W. Griffiths. In it, Black men are depicted like monkeys as they take over state governments during Reconstruction, and white-hooded men come to the rescue of white women being raped by these "animals" in their midst. *The Birth of a Nation*, which was the first blockbuster of its day, "began to premiere to very mixed reviews in Canadian theatres. Sir John Willison, writing in *The Canadian Magazine* in 1923, described the movie as 'a glorified representation of the Klan as an agent of order and security."'[39] However, as early as September 18, 1915, the *Ottawa Citizen* condemned the film and the directors of the Central Canada Exhibition for screening it in Ottawa, saying that they showed "poor judgement," and that the film's intent was to "excite prejudice against, if not hatred of, the negro race ..." Moreover, The *Canadian Observer* reported on September 25, 1915 that a deputation was successful in pressuring Premier William Howard Hearst to have some of the more highly objectionable scenes from the film cut before it could be screened again.

Among the doctrines professed by the local Canadian Klan were Protestant Christianity, the belief in "good citizenship in an unswerving allegiance to the British Crown and patriotism to the Empire," and the upholding of "British justice in the promotion of law and order."[40] However, a more sinister aspect of the organization was its belief in white supremacy, and that there should be absolutely no race mixing. What made the Klan different from other organizations was that it was willing to act on these fears in a way that some people, particularly Blacks, Jews, Catholics, and people of colour generally, found absolutely terrifying.

In addition to branches in Montreal, Vancouver, across New Brunswick, and in Nova Scotia, Klan activity became evident in Toronto, London, Barrie, Sault Ste Marie, Welland, Ottawa, and Niagara Falls.[41] In the summer of 1925, cross burnings, which had become the frightening calling card of the Klan, occurred at Chatham, Dresden, Wallaceburg, Woodstock, St. Thomas, Ingersoll, London, and Dorchester.[42] A division of the organization was active in Hamilton for at least a decade from 1925–35, and it listed some influential Hamiltonians as members.[43] The public became aware of active recruitment in Hamilton when the organizer, Almond Charles Monteith, was arrested for carrying a loaded revolver in 1924. He was in the act of initiating two female members in the Orange Hall at 177 James Street North. In his pocket was a list of thirty-two names of local citizens who had joined. There had been two recent cross burnings on the Mountain — for which Monteith refused to take responsibility. However, an item on an expense account list showed $200 for two fiery crosses. The police also retrieved correspondence referring to thirty-six white robes and hoods. Monteith was not from Hamilton, but responded that he was a Canadian citizen, and that his wife lived in Kingston. An adjacent article in the Toronto *Globe* made it known that Monteith was a Niagara Falls resident, but that he had no connection with the Klan there, or in the United States. Several days later, the arresting officer in the case received a threatening letter stating, in part: "Beware. Your days are numbered." It was signed "K.K.K."[44]

For its part, the executive committee of the Orange Lodge, a popular fraternal order that promoted Protestantism, issued a disclaimer stating that it was in no way connected with the KKK and had no knowledge of any of its activities on lodge premises. It seems that many members of the community were well aware of the danger of being associated with such an organization and its brutal tactics. A statement read, in part, that Orange Association "members are loyal, law-abiding citizens, who believe in equal rights to all and special privileges to none. They are all strong supporters of our laws as administered by a regularly constituted Government, and do not believe that it is necessary in this country to recognize, or in any way support, such an organization as the Ku Klux Klan, or its methods."[45]

Nevertheless, Klan organizing in Hamilton continued.[46] A shocking article in the *Hamilton Herald* of March 20, 1925, indicated the extent of Klan support in the area. A women's order entitled the Women's Canadian Ku Klux Klan was headquartered in Hamilton and had huge support, to the tune of over one thousand members. There were also branches in Toronto, Brantford, Kitchener, and Windsor. One of the members also indicated that the men's order had many more members than the women's. A photograph of the Grand Executive of the women's Klan, decked in full robe and hood regalia, appeared on the front page of the *Herald*.[47]

By 1930, the Toronto *Globe* reported that Hamilton and the surrounding area continued to be a stronghold of the Klan. The proof given for this assertion was that in the fall of the previous year, the Klan held a parade through the streets of the city to a ceremony in nearby Saltfleet Township and an estimated four to five hundred people took part.[48] On another occasion, a ten-by-five-foot cross was burned in Ancaster where, according to the local police commissioner, "a Chicago-based organization known as the African Brotherhood of America was considering the erection of a home for 'colored children and aged colored folk.'"[49]

Women's Canadian Ku Klux Klan, from a front page article in the Hamilton Herald, March 20, 1925.

These activities must have sent a shudder down the spine of every Black resident in town. Ray Lewis and Reverend Bob Foster later remembered the Ku Klux Klan parading down the streets of Hamilton and staging cross-burnings in 1929.[50] Lewis witnessed a burning cross on the Mountain one evening that year about 9:00 p.m. as he was walking along Barton Street and crossing Ferguson. On another occasion, Lewis was studying at Marquette University in Milwaukee, Wisconsin, and his brother wrote him a letter informing him of a parade held by the Klan. Not only were Klan members in robes, but their horses wore robes with hoods as well. According to Lewis, the horses from a local bread company had been loaned to the Klan, and some spectators recognized them during the parade route through an Italian section of town. "Given the Klan's anti-Catholic views, the entire neighbourhood was incensed. The resulting boycott of the bread company drove it out of business a year later." For Ray Lewis, this was just another manifestation of what he had to face every single day of his life — the abject stupidity of racial bigotry.[51]

In 1930, the Ku Klux Klan staged an act of intimidation and coercion

Local Ku Klux Klan marching south past the Lister Building on James Street North, circa 1930. Photo by Milford Smith.

that was even more shocking than previous events. Its actions resulted in a highly publicized trial of three of its participants. At 10:30 p.m. on February 28, a large group of seventy-five to one hundred men, dressed in white robes and hoods, marched through the streets of Oakville and appeared at the door of a Black man and his family. The man, whose name was Ira Johnson, was visiting his aunt and uncle with his white fiancée, Isobel Jones. The Klan knocked at the door, asked if Johnson was looking for work, and led him out to a car in which four or five men were seated. The Klan then went back to the house and demanded the girl, Isobel Jones, and hustled her off to her mother's in another car. Mrs. Jones had been trying to get her daughter away from Johnson, but to no avail. Isobel was later taken and placed in the care of Captain W. Broome, an officer of the Salvation Army. The intruders then returned to the home of Ira Johnson's aunt and uncle, nailed a large cross to a post in front of their door and set it on fire, with the Johnsons looking on. Before dispersing, the Klan warned them that if Ira Johnson was ever caught walking down the street with a white girl again, he would hear from them.[52]

Police Chief Kerr of Oakville stated that when he learned of the incident, he rushed over to the demonstration and spoke to the leaders, recognizing many of them as prominent Hamilton businessmen. This fact was confirmed when the group, under the seal of the Invisible Empire, Knights of the Ku Klux Klan of Canada, Hamilton Clan No. 10 sent a statement to the Toronto *Globe* with their version of the affair. For their part, the Klan justified the raid by stating that Isobel Jones's mother had requested their help, and that the girl was being detained by "the negro" for a period of five nights alone in his parents' home. They had at no time "laid a hand upon the girl or the man," nor did they enter their home, and everyone had acted of their own free will. They were simply "endeavouring to maintain British justice in the promotion of law and order as set forth by our civil Government":

> Be it understood that we strenuously oppose the marriage between the white and colored races, regardless of nationality, on the ground of racial purity, and that we hold no grievance, grudge, malice or ill will against any person or people, provided that they maintain peace and harmony, and live up to the integrity and standards of Christianity, which we uphold and represent.[53]

The Klan in Canada, the statement continued, was not affiliated with the KKK in the United States and was not opposed to the "colored people." This was a "service" they were apparently providing to good and law-abiding British subjects regardless of colour or creed.[54]

Some newspaper accounts of the event were somewhat sympathetic to the Klan's actions. The *Toronto Daily Star* noted that at no time was violence used, and quoted Police Chief Kerr that the Klan's conduct was "all that could be desired."[55] The *Hamilton Spectator* concluded its initial report stating, "The citizens of Oakville, generally, seemed pleased with the work accomplished by the visit."[56] However, Blacks in Toronto came to the defence of the couple and their right to marry if they chose. Black lawyers E.L. Cross and B.J. Spencer Pitt were outraged and denounced the "lawlessness" of such an act. Dr. D.A. Wyke, graduate of the University of

Toronto and Reverend H. Lawrence McNeill of the First Baptist Church on University Avenue, also expressed great shock and concern.[57] A mass meeting was planned for March 4 at the First Baptist Church, at which time a resolution was passed to organize a delegation to bring the matter before the prime minister, attorney general, and minister of justice.[58]

No record exists of the reaction of Black Hamiltonians at the time to the existence of the Klan and its "operations" in the area. However, Ray Lewis later wrote that he attended the trial of three of the Klansmen, along with Reverend W. Constantine Perry, a pastor of the local AME Church, who had been scheduled to officiate at the wedding of the accused couple, and another man. Lewis also observed a man by the name of John Wallace, the "oldest Negro resident" in Oakville. Ira Johnson was also in attendance for part of the trial. It was a packed courthouse. Four men were charged with having their faces masked or otherwise disguised by night, without lawful excuse. This law was a carryover from an old English statute aimed at deterring house burglars. The accused were Dr. William Phillips, a Hamilton chiropractor; Ernest Taylor, a pastor at the Hamilton Presbyterian Church, as well as an interpreter for the local police court; Harold C. Orme, who worked as a chiropractic assistant; and William Maloney, of unspecified address and occupation.[59] Ray Lewis recalled that a friend of his, Dave Griffin, offered him a swig of gin behind the courthouse during a break in the trial. It belonged to one of the accused, who had asked Dave to hold it for him. How ironic, thought Lewis, that Dave, who happened to be Catholic, and Lewis, who was Black, "were drinking the 'borrowed' gin of a Klansman."[60]

Ultimately, only one of the four men was convicted of the charge. Maloney had disappeared and Taylor and Orme, based on testimony, were not wearing hoods. Dr. Phillips was fined only $50, to the dismay of Black and Jewish leaders. However, when he appealed the conviction, the five-judge panel not only upheld the conviction, but found the original sentence to be a "travesty of justice," and imposed a prison term of three months. Stunned, Phillips was taken into custody on April 23 and promptly began a hunger strike that lasted for thirteen days. The Klan's claims of upholding law and order and of not taking justice into its own hands were belied by subsequent troubling events: Ira Johnson's house was completely burned to the ground, although no one was in the house at the time. Black leaders were also targeted. Reverend McNeill received threatening phone calls and Lionel Cross received threatening and abusive calls and letters, signed "Member of the Ku Klux Klan."[61]

Some have pronounced the Oakville trial as the "symbolic death-knell for the KKK in Canada," whose growth was sapped by the "glare of publicity, the official intrusion into KKK affairs, and the ringing condemnation of Klan methods from senior governmental and judicial circles."[62] As for the couple at the centre of the storm, they wed on March 22, 1930, apparently with the blessings of both Jones's mother and the Johnsons. In another twist in the saga, Ira Johnson, who was very light-skinned, claimed after the initial incident that he had no African ancestry, but was rather of mixed "Indian" and white blood. Reverend Perry of the African Methodist Episcopal Church was replaced by an aboriginal, Reverend Frank Burgess of the United Church, as the officiating minister at his wedding. Interestingly, Ted Grayson, his Black friend from Toronto, was retained as the driver of the bridal party. The Johnsons then quickly receded from the glare of public scrutiny.[63]

The Klan gradually petered out as a force in Ontario, although it grew in Saskatchewan and Alberta, aided by the migration of key organizers in Ontario to that province. Hamilton-born J.J. Maloney became the driving force behind the Klan in Alberta, first joining the organization in Ontario and then Saskatchewan between 1926 and 1929.[64] By 1933, the Klan collapsed in Alberta, partly because of a scandal that erupted from Maloney's involvement in separate fraud, theft, vandalism, and slander cases, for which he served time. As in Ontario and elsewhere, the publicity of Klan violence and corruption in the United States was also a contributing factor.[65]

Chapter 7

Roadblocks Ahead: The Reverend Holland Years

In the 1930s and 1940s, living life in a Black skin was not for the faint of heart. Of course, during the Depression, the entire country was mired in a crisis. Some observers wrote that Hamilton suffered more than other cities in Ontario because of its dependence on heavy industry. Some plants closed, and others, like National Steel Car, Otis Elevator, and International Harvester, operated on a skeleton crew. Stelco and Dofasco functioned at 40–50 percent capacity. Construction projects came to a halt.[1] As one historian noted, in August 1929 the major Hamilton firms employed 40,632 people, but by May 1933 they employed only 21,800. In March 1933, nine thousand people were receiving relief assistance.[2] But at the height of the Depression, when many people were hurting badly, the old adage that Black workers were the "last hired and the first fired" was fitting.

Oliver Holland, son of respected minister and sleeping-car porter, Reverend John C. Holland, worked as a redcap at the Toronto Hamilton

& Buffalo (TH&B) railway station. He was interviewed for the *Hamilton Spectator* a year after graduating with a BA in political economy and history from McMaster University in 1936, making him one of the early African Canadians to graduate from that institution.[3] Summing up the dismal job prospects of African Hamiltonians, Holland was quoted as saying:

> Some people think our girls are fitted only for house-work, our men only to be bellhops, porters or labour-ers.... Of between 400 and 500 negroes in this city, only about half a dozen men are engaged in a profession or business other than labour. With the exception of those employed by our own people, the women who work are all employed at housework.[4]

Holland went on to study law at Osgoode Hall Law School and was called to the bar, but he would continue to take the lead on these issues in the years to come.

One of the only saving graces was that railway porters, in the one job that employed Black men exclusively, worked continuously throughout the Depression. Although a low-level service job, it gave Black families the ability to buy homes and put their children through university, even in hard times. Former union activist and citizenship court judge, Stanley Grizzle, wrote that sleeping car porters were the "aristocrats of African-Canadian communities."[5]

The church, always an important respite from racism and exclusion, continued to play a pivotal role in the lives of many a Hamilton congregant. Shirley Brown recalled her early experiences as a child at Stewart Memorial Church in the 1930s:

> Well, we did everything down there. We'd go to church ... we'd have our junior missionary meetings and Mrs. Holland always let us do crafts next door in the parson-age, and even when Reverend Holland married the sec-ond time after Mrs. Holland died, Rachel Holland would let us come there and do craftwork. We'd never have to

go home after school and be by ourselves — well, I was never by myself; I had a big family. It's just that everything was done in the church. We had picnics and we were able to play out in the back yard of the church and down in the basement of the church ... That was just our second home away from home.[6]

One of the best-known and most beloved ministers of Stewart Memorial was the Reverend John Christie Holland. Jessie Beattie,[7] in her biography entitled *John Christie Holland: Man of the Year*, featured the life of the man who was revered both within the Black community, as well as in Hamilton society as a whole. Beattie's biography, however, is a highly romanticized treatment of Holland's story and at times the particulars of her narrative are inconsistent with other available information.

Reverend Holland was born in Hamilton on Christmas Day, 1882. His parents carried on the tradition in many African cultures of naming the child on the basis of the day, or circumstances of birth. Holland had actually been christened John Christmas Holland. Years later, he legally changed his middle name to Christie. His father, Thomas John Holland, was a former slave from Sandy Spring, Montgomery County, Maryland, the fourth child of William Augustus Holland and Leatha Howard Holland.[8] According to Jesse Beattie, Thomas Holland escaped from slavery in the year 1860 and followed his brother to the Queen's Bush, where the elder William had fled several years earlier. Beattie also stated that Josiah Henson, the leader of the Dawn Settlement at Dresden, assisted the Hollands by travelling into slave territory and informing Thomas of his brother William's safety and whereabouts in Canada. The brothers eventually left the Queen's Bush and bought a small plot of land in Bronte, just outside of Oakville. William married and put down roots there, while Thomas decided to move to Hamilton. However, another version of the story obtained from his obituary and an article written at the time of his seventieth birthday suggest that Holland came to Canada from Washington D.C. *after* serving in the Civil War, and that he first moved to Bronte for six years, and then relocated to Hamilton, where he lived for his remaining fifty-two years. That means that he would have arrived in Canada in 1870, and that date, at least, is corroborated by the 1901 census, which reported the year of immigration of Thomas Holland as 1870, five years *after* slavery had already been abolished.[9]

In Jesse Beattie's account, the Holland brothers attended the AME Church when it was located on Cathcart Street in Hamilton and sang in the choir. They also visited the Mission Church on the Mountain where Tom met Henrietta Shortts. She was the Canadian-born daughter of an Irish father and Black mother who lived in Tapleytown, the latter also hailing from Maryland. Interestingly, further investigation reveals that Henrietta, who was born in 1855, was actually the adopted daughter of Isaac and Eliza Shortts. Isaac Shortts was a Kentucky-born Black farmer living in Saltfleet Township with his wife, Eliza, a Black woman from Chatham, Canada West. Henrietta, whose birth name was Cass, reported in the 1891 census that her biological father was indeed from Ireland and her biological mother from the United States, however. It appears that the Shortts adopted several other Black children as well — Mary Ann Giles, and John and Lewis Ryan.[10]

Tom decided to settle in Hamilton and open a flour-and-feed store on the corner of Gore and Mary Streets in Hamilton. Henrietta Shortts was now attending the church in downtown Hamilton, according to Beattie, and the two rekindled their romance. They married on December 28, 1875. George Morton and Lucinda Gwyder witnessed the ceremony. Lucinda was the eldest daughter of Richard Gwyder, one of the leaders of the effort to obtain a Black fire brigade. It is not known whether George Morton Sr. or Jr. was the other witness. The latter was also a well-known leader in the community, as we have seen.[11]

The newlyweds bought the brick house next to the store on Mary Street and started a family. Thomas had a gifted bass singing voice and was invited to join the original incarnation of the O'Banyoun Jubilee Singers, touring during the winter months to supplement the family income. The group toured across North America and in Europe. It was even reported to have given a command performance before Queen Victoria and her court at Buckingham Palace.[12] Henrietta ran the store in his absence and cared for her growing brood. She tended a stall at the market where she sold straw and goose down and feathers used to make pillows and bedding. As the children grew, they helped out in the store at noon hours, after school, and on Saturdays, filling sacks with hay and straw and assisting at the market stall. William later established a hay-pressing business that supplied the family business in Hamilton, and employed several men just outside Hamilton. John Christie was the fourth of nine children who survived to adulthood.[13]

In 1901, the family was the owner of a nine-room house on a lot with a store and barn at 253 Catherine Street North.[14] John was eighteen years old, reported no employment, and was out of high school. His sisters, Abigail and Florence, ages twenty-one and twenty, worked as a dressmaker and a tailoress respectively. Three younger siblings, Garnet, Rosetta, and Kathleen, aged eleven, ten, and eight, were still in grade school. The oldest brother, William, was twenty-four and did not report an occupation. Fourteen-year-old Arthur was neither in school nor employed. It is more than likely that William, John, and Arthur were helping out in the family business at that time. Baby Grace was just four years old. Although the family was far from wealthy, Thomas and Henrietta made sure that their children were well-rounded. It helped that they were talented. Kathleen studied piano and organ at the Hamilton Conservatory of Music. William took voice lessons from R. Thomas Steele and formed another group called the Canadian Jubilee Singers, who toured Ontario. An interesting piece in the December 19, 1914, issue of the *Canadian Observer* described the group: "Mr. W.H. Holland's company of jubilee and popular melody songsters ... is composed of some of the city's best talent. Large audiences greet the singers [in Hamilton and the surrounding country] and the receipts are very gratifying. On Tuesday of this week they gave a most successful concert in the Barton Street Methodist Church." Ultimately, however, William sought a bigger audience for his musical talents, and moved to New York, studying at the School of Musical Art there. He later joined several companies, including Connie Mack's Musical Comedy, as well as appearing on Broadway. Grace was given lessons in elocution and later joined the Twentieth Century Literary Association as secretary, where she undoubtedly showcased her talents as an elocutionist. The Association met every Thursday evening at 8:00 p.m. at St. Paul's AME. John Holland joined the

Courtesy of the Multicultural History Society of Ontario, Toronto.

Miss Kathleen Holland

Teacher of Piano and Theory

will resume teaching Monday, September 6, at her residence, 253 N. Catharine street, Hamilton.

The Canadian Observer, *September 4, 1915, page 3. Musical talent ran in the Holland family. John's sister Kathleen was a gifted pianist and organist. John's daughters, Gladys and Alfreda, studied at the Hamilton Conservatory of Music as had their aunt. John's son, Gilbert, became a professional singer like his uncle William and also moved to New York. According to Jessie Beattie, he later replaced Paul Robeson, the renowned singer and activist, in the London production of* Showboat.

church choir at age thirteen, but, as the scholar of the family, according to his sister Grace, he had decided early on to go to college and study for the ministry. As it turned out, it would be a long and arduous process.[15]

In the meantime, John Christie Holland met and fell in love with Josephine Idenia Johnson of Oakville. They married in 1901. Both worked various jobs so that John could save enough to study at university. He tried selling jewellery for Connors Brothers Jewelers at one point, according to the December 26, 1914, edition of the *Canadian Observer*, boasting "an up-to-date assortment ... for his customers' selection." They even lived and worked in New Jersey for several years, staying with John's brother William and his family. John had trouble finding decent work in Hamilton because of the racist hiring practices of many firms, and William got him work in New Jersey at much higher wages. But America would not be his destiny. The couple, with the addition of a son they named Gilbert, moved back to Hamilton, after which another three children were born: Gladys, Alfreda, and Oliver.[16]

In 1909, John Holland began working as a janitor at Westinghouse, doubling as a waiter at noon in the company's cafeteria. An executive of the company interviewed by Beattie stated that:

There was no doubt among us of John Holland's ability to do a factory job or even to do clerical work … but I doubt if it occurred to any one of us that we were denying him a place among us in industry because of his colour. We looked upon his occupation as suited to his race and yet, if we had given it a thought, we would have admitted that he ranked above most of us in intelligence and equaled us in culture.[17]

There is some question about exactly when he began working for the TH&B as a porter. Jessie Beattie stated that he began there in 1916, while the *Dictionary of Hamilton Biography* reported that he actually began as a janitor there in 1917, and two years later, was working as a porter for the company. In any case, according to Beattie, he advanced from porter at the station, to Pullman car attendant, and finally to the position of attendant on the private car that was used by the president of the company. His association with the company would last over thirty years. Holland also continued to study for the ministry by correspondence. He became an ordained minister in 1925 through the AME Conference at Payne Theological Seminary in Wilberforce, Ohio. He had been working part-time at Stewart Memorial on weekends, singing in the choir, teaching, and acting as superintendent in the Sunday school. He also preached when the regular pastor was absent. By all accounts, he made a tremendous mark on all those who

From Jessie Beattie, *John Christie Holland: Man of the Year* (Toronto: Ryerson Press, 1956), opposite page 16.

Reverend John Holland worked as a porter for the Toronto, Hamilton & Buffalo Railway for over thirty years while serving as the beloved pastor of Stewart Memorial Church.

knew him, from the young children who attended Sunday school, to the president of the railway company where he was an employee.[18]

Shirley Brown, speaking of Reverend Holland, remembered the man:

> Well, like I say, everybody liked Reverend Holland — everyone. I don't think I've ever heard, even to this day, anyone say anything bad about Reverend Holland. He was like a father figure to all the ones at Sunday school who didn't have a father, because there were a lot of us that grew up just with our mothers. But he was a very gentle, kind person — I don't think I could ever say enough about Reverend Holland. He was just a gentle, gentle man.[19]

As a young boy Joe Rhodes, the grandson of Wesley and Mary Rhodes, recalled the impact Reverend Holland had on him and that he was "just a tremendous human being":

> Well, I remember he was a very gentle, great man. Actually he was a major influence on my life because when I was five and six years old in the neighbourhood where I was living, the kids wanted to fight and be very abusive, and he would come actually to our home … and we would read the Bible and he would talk to us, and he just made us feel good about getting our life together and keeping our life together…. I don't remember all the words he said but he sort of reassured us that life was going to be okay. He reassured us that there are ways and means.[20]

Rhodes attested to the powerful sway that Reverend Holland and the church represented in his young life:

> Stewart Memorial was jam-packed at all times. The people were lined up outside when Reverend Holland was

there and we had just a tremendous choir, and he and the enthusiasm of the church were just exciting. He just made you feel good about yourself. And even though I was very young at the time, I could feel that … my mother thought … I was going to be a minister …[21]

Reverend Holland remained in an assistant role without pay until 1936. Reverend Claude Stewart from Barbados was the minister of the church from 1926–36. Just before his death in 1936, he summoned Reverend Holland to his side and begged him to take over the leadership of the struggling congregation. This Holland pledged to do. But it would not be easy. The church was deeply in debt, the building in a bad state of repair, and the church property was being listed for tax sale. Moreover, it was the height of the Depression. Many in the congregation were unemployed.[22]

Courtesy of Norval Johnson Heritage Library, Niagara Falls, Ontario.

AME Conference, 1945. Reverend Holland is in the front row, far right. Rachel Holland is in the second row, third from left.

Holland immediately approached the mayor and the business community of Hamilton. With his quiet power of persuasion, he enlisted the help of Hamilton's business elite, who organized a tag day to raise money for the church. The proceeds — over $1,500 — were enough to pay the tax arrears and the mortgage interest, with a small balance left for repairs to the building. Although this took care of the immediate problems, a longer-term solution was to establish a Visitors' Night on the first Sunday of every month when the business leaders and others from the wider community would attend the little church on John Street and add to the collection plate.[23] Visitors' Night was an important evening at Stewart Memorial and the choir became known far and wide for the beautiful spirituals it sang. Shirley Brown recounted her memories in the choir on Visitors' Night:

Stewart Memorial Church Choir, 1946. Front row (l–r): Margery Brown, Wilma Miller Morrison, Shirley Busby Heal, Shirley Wade Brown, Lois Wade Gaskin, Dorothy Hunt Parker, Leila Brown Dennis. Back row (l–r): Oliver Holland (director), Alfonso Allen, Byron Wade, William Brown, and Harrison Wade.

[E]verything was special. We would always come out from the back room and we would march around the front by the altar and up into the choir loft. And we only did it on the first Sunday of every month. And when church was over, we'd come down again, march in front, they'd say the closing prayer, we'd go in the back room and take our robes off.[24]

In 1937, St. Paul's AME Church severed ties with the AME body in the United States and became non-denominational. Its name was changed to Stewart Memorial in honour of Reverend Claude Stewart.[25]

Jessie Beattie's biography wrote of his quiet dignity and humanity, and of the very high regard in which Reverend Holland was held by virtually everyone in Hamilton who knew the man. However, her book did not address some of the important inroads made by the Hollands in the area of civil rights. According to Wilma Morrison, respected community leader in Niagara Falls who grew up in Hamilton, John Holland took a number of Black men down to Stelco and other steel factories in late 1939 and early 1940 and single-handedly got them work. He insisted that they be hired at a time when these companies were not hiring Blacks. "But this was the kind of man he was," insisted Wilma. "He would take on any task at all and just make it seem so easy." Of course, his action bore fruit because "the group was hired and, for the most part, most of them retired from the steel company."[26]

Courtesy of Norval Johnson Heritage Library, Dorothy Hunt Parker Collection, Niagara Falls, Ontario.

Garfield Parker moved to Hamilton from North Buxton and was one of the men who first got a job at Stelco through the efforts of Reverend Holland.

Not surprisingly, Stelco continued its racist hiring practices in other ways. Lincoln Alexander noted in his memoir that when he tried to get a job at Stelco with his fellow McMaster graduate buddies in 1949, he was offered a job, but not in the sales department like the other graduates. It was in the plant in the open hearth area: "The clear and unacceptable implication was that the company felt that having a black in sales would harm its image. There was not room for a black among the white-collar types, university education or not.[27] Alexander received the assistance of everyone from the university to the mayor of Hamilton in his attempt to get a job in sales, but Stelco would not budge. Ultimately, Lincoln did not take the job.

Courtesy of Hamilton Public Library, Special Collections.

Royal Connaught Hotel, 1937. On the site of the old Anglo American Hotel and later Waldorf Hotel, the Edwardian-style Royal Connaught was constructed and opened in 1916.

Some Hamilton companies not only refused to hire African Canadians, but also refused their business. These included theatres, hotels, and restaurants. Reverend Bob Foster, assistant pastor of Stewart Memorial Church in the 1980s and 1990s, once stated that he knew precisely where one could eat, drink, and get a room, and where one could not: "We had the people come here, such as Joe Louis.... He came here and could not get into the Royal Connaught Hotel.... [That was] in the 40s. They sent him to a hotel up on King Street. At one time you couldn't go into any of the beverage halls."[28]

Shirley Brown observed that one of the reasons the church was so important was because there were a lot of places Blacks couldn't go, such as the skating rink on James and the Royal Alexandra Theatre. She remembered that they would have to go into the back door to see her father perform at the Granada:

> My father was an entertainer. He sang and danced, and when he and my mother used to sing too, and my aunt and ... my uncle — the four of them used to go around and sing together. The Vagabonds they were called. But my father used to sing and dance on stage at the Granada Theatre, and we used to go to the back door in between Sunday School and church at night — we'd go to the backdoor of the Granada Theatre, and they would let us go in the back there and sit and listen to my father.[29]

Another elderly man described a typical encounter when he would try to eat in certain restaurants:

> You go in a restaurant, you sit there for ten minutes and then they'll come and ask you what you want. You tell them. Ten minutes later they'll come back and ask you

Vaudeville act (l–r): Byron Kenton Wade, Mabel Berry, Gladys Holland, Hazel Hicks Berry, Clayse Berry, (first name unknown) Holland, Hiram Berry (out front), Jo Holland, Grace Holland Tolliver, and Reverend John Holland.

what you want again. Ten minutes later, they'll come back and say, "You wanna take it out." You say no, I'll eat it here. They'll come back in another ten minutes and say, "We don't have any." This is what we've experienced. Now, it's hard and difficult for most people to believe this. But it is true. It was the same manner in the way of our churches.[30]

In his biography, Ray Lewis also commented on being refused service in restaurants:

> If you were Black, waiters and waitresses would head into the kitchen and try to wait you out if you sought service in a whites-only restaurant. Or they would circle around the restaurant, topping up coffee for other patrons, doing anything to avoid coming to your table, hoping that you would get tired and leave. The average Canadian grew up with a false sense of "we don't do that here" — but I experienced it many times over.[31]

Lewis also remembered how the Brant Inn, a popular supper club in Burlington, had a policy of not allowing Blacks to dance in their ballroom. They could get a meal, but would not be allowed on the dance floor. He described how his friend, Vince Bryant, had gone to the Brant Inn to celebrate his having coached Hamilton Technical School's high school football team to the city championships. When he went to join the others on the dance floor, he was tapped on the shoulder and told, "You're not allowed to dance here." He returned grim-faced to his table.[32] The Brant Inn was also known for booking great jazz musicians like Louis Armstrong and Count Basie. However, these bands could not stay there overnight. Mrs. Rachel Holland had a large house and she used to rent rooms where some of these artists stayed. Wilma Morrison stated that this was why people in the community got to meet many of the top artists. For example, the man who played trombone for Louis Armstrong stayed at Morrison's house on three different occasions. Morrison also noted that her mother worked at the Brant Inn, and she would go with her and sit in the washroom and listen to all the great acts.[33]

Ray Lewis added that this treatment was a family tradition. The father of the owner of the Brant Inn owned a pool room at one time on the corner of King and Wentworth in Hamilton. He once threw Ray Lewis's brother, Howard, out of his establishment for no other reason than that he was Black.[34]

In reminiscing about the late 1940s, Wilma Morrison recalled how the youth group of the church, led by Oliver Holland, held sit-ins in different Hamilton restaurants to combat segregated service. When confronted by an entire group of African-Canadian young people, these places generally caved to the pressure without incident. Thereafter, there were no reported incidents of lack of service to Black people, and the youth would test these restaurants every so often to make sure. However, the Alexandra Skating Rink, notorious for barring Black people on its premises, would not go down so easily.

As Wilma remembered it:

> We decided we would book [the skating rink]. Oliver Holland, who was Reverend Holland's son, booked it in the young people's names.... We decided that we would all meet at the church and we would go as a group together, and we arrived at the door and the poor doorman had a fit. "Oh," he said, "I think there's been some mistake," and Oliver said, "No, there hasn't been any mistake," — Oliver was a lawyer — and he said, "No, we booked for the young people's department and then we told him we would be here at 7 o'clock." "Oh," he said, "I'll have to call my boss." So he called his boss and she said, "Don't let them in." So he came back to us and said that the boss had said that we were not to be allowed in. So, I think they thought that we would just get up and go home, but we didn't. We stayed there, and every time someone opened the door to come in skating, we'd say, "Sorry, we're closed." And so they lost

Courtesy of Norval Johnson Heritage Library, Niagara Falls, Ontario.

AME Conference attendees, August 1941. Standing (l–r): Lillian Allen, Norma Lewis, (first name unknown) Berry, (name unknown), Dorothy Hunt Parker, (name unknown), Ellen Wade, Harrison Wade, Lois Wade, (name unknown). Seated (l–r): Hilbourne Berry, Byron Wade.

the business for that evening…. She paid a little bit of a price for being stupid.[35]

Eventually, the Alexandra came to its senses and opened its doors to Blacks. However, these incidents have gone undocumented in the history books.

John Holland was eventually given the highest honour of a Hamilton resident by being named Citizen of the Year for 1953. Wilma Morrison acknowledged that "we [in the Black community] were as proud as proud could be of him."[36] His greatest power was that he was somehow able to win over both the CEOs of the largest companies in Canada and the poorest people he came across through the sheer force of his grace, intelligence, and determination. Reverend Norman Rawson once wrote that John Holland made you forget the Black–white divide: "One never thought of it in his presence and I have often tried to analyze why it was.

It wasn't because he ever dodged it, or played it down. He was proud of his race, proud of his ancestry, proud of his humble beginnings ..."[37]

Most people assert that he genuinely cared about and was interested in all people. As Joe Rhodes put it:

> Unfortunately, Stewart Memorial at times overlooked the poor Blacks that were struggling, because they didn't attend the church, and because they didn't attend the church, the elders of the church kind of looked down on them — which was sad. But Reverend Holland, on the other hand ... would come into the Black community and actually come out and see people and speak with them, so that influence was always there.... I really enjoyed having that brief time that I did have with him, because he died, as you know, in 1954 ...[38]

Reverend Holland died just three months after receiving the highest accolade any Hamilton resident could receive. Reverend Rawson officiated at his funeral, which took place at Centenary Church in Hamilton. He noted: "In my day, I have conducted many funerals for people in all walks of life, but that service stands out in my memory. The great Church was filled to the doors, the humble, the poor, the rich, the socially elite, the politically famous were all there and sorrow was written on every face. We had all lost a beloved friend."[39]

When Canada entered the Second World War, officials again moved to bar Black men from any involvement. The latter protested, and in time, secured the right to enlist, and this time they fought alongside white soldiers.[40] Lincoln Alexander served in the Air Force, starting out as a wireless operator on the ground and rising to the rank of corporal. As the war continued, a draft was instated. Men from Jamaica and other Caribbean countries also enlisted in the Canadian armed forces. After the war, these soldiers were able to apply for landed immigrant status.[41]

Jackie Washington, born in 1919 into a very musical Hamilton family, was one of the many men who were drafted. His father, George Washington, was born *circa* 1873, the son of a slave from Virginia who had come north on the Underground Railroad. Raised just outside of Welland, he never learned to read and write, because, according to the family, Black and First Nations children were barred from the schools in the area. Jackie's mother, Rose Thompson, was an orphan and was raised as a domestic in Greensville, Ontario. They met and married in 1916 in Hamilton and began a family of what would become fifteen children. Jackie was the third-born and best-known sibling. However, the family was legendary in Hamilton, and entertained generations with their singing and music.[42]

William "Mickey" Berry, Second World War veteran, was a high school track and field star. During the war he won the Canadian Army Track and Field Championship. He went on to become the top Black furrier in Canada.

Courtesy of Robert Foster Jr., Kingston, Ontario.

Jackie's father, George, worked at the Overland Garage washing cars, then as a spare with the city doing jobs like cutting ice in the bay during the winter, cleaning sidewalks, opening sewers, and so forth. In time, he got a job as a garbage man. George was a talent in his own right, and could play the violin, accordion, harmonica, and "step dance." Jackie and his brother began to sing at school concerts from the ages of five and seven, and eventually were invited to sing at church socials and garden parties almost every weekend. They were paid in ice cream, candy, and maybe some change.

As they got older, the boys in the family formed a trio and then a quartet, with Ormsby, the oldest, Jackie, Harold, and Doc. They started out singing hymns and spirituals, and then styled themselves after the Mills Brothers. Later, the Washington girls became involved in various incarnations of the Washington singers. Shirley Brown recalled: "They

For decades the Washington Jazz Band entertained Hamiltonians with their musical talent.

sang all the time, and as each one started growing up, they automatically sang. They all sang, played the piano — they were just a really gifted family … and if they didn't know the tune, they made a tune up [and] put the words to it.[43]

Eventually, they gravitated to jazz. Despite the colour bar, they got in to see all the big bands and the great jazz artists of the day because the owner of one of the popular spots, Mrs. Hicks, invited the Washingtons to come and see all of the greats who came through: Duke Ellington, Count Basie, Benny Goodman, Artie Shaw, Glenn Miller, Earl "Fatha" Hines, and Tommy and Jimmy Dorsey. Jackie Washington met all the "girl singers" too, like Lena Horne, Dinah Shore, Sarah Vaughan, Ella Fitzgerald, Peggy Lee, and Carmen McRae. These were some of the great jazz artists of all time, but they always took time to show Jackie how to do something on the guitar or piano, or to offer some advice. Most ended up in the Washington family home. Some stayed there instead of at a hotel.

The quartet, not to mention the family, was dealt a huge blow when Ormsby drowned in Waubaushene, Ontario, in 1938. Following the tragedy, Jackie went to work as a porter with the CPR in 1939. He would often take the children from his railway car and the adjacent car and play guitar and sing songs with them and occupy their time on the train, with many thanks from their grateful parents. In 1941, however, Jackie was drafted into the Army, a time in his life he absolutely hated:

> For one thing, I was the only Black in that regiment ... The officers would come in every day ... We had a Captain and a Lieutenant and a 2nd Lieutenant, you know, but every time they came in, there was a joke about being Black ... about me. "Oh, I see it's going to rain." You know, those kinds of things. So I told them, I said, "Look, I don't like this."
>
> "Oh, we're just having fun."
>
> I said, "Yeah, you're just having fun at my expense. I don't like it." But it didn't stop them. They still thought they were smart. So I thought, "Well, I'm gonna be smart."[44]

His unit got the order to leave basic training and head for their next destination — Kingston. They arrived in Kingston on a very hot day, standing in the parade square with all their equipment on, and the army brass arrived to inspect the troops. When they got to the end of Washington's line, one made a remark about "Captain Black," alerting him to what was to come:

> "Washington."
>
> "Yessir?"
>
> "I see you're not well."
>
> "I beg your pardon, sir?"
>
> "I see you're not well. You're looking kind of pale."
>
> They all had a laugh. I laughed with them.
>
> After awhile, the regimental sergeant said, "Everybody for sick bay fall out over here."

Jackie fell out of line and was sent to the hospital. A week later, a nurse questioned him about his illness:

"Washington, I've got your chart here, and there doesn't seem to be anything wrong with you."

I said, "Well, I didn't say there was anything wrong with me."

"Well, how did you come to get in here?"

I said, "Well, Captain Black told me that I was sick, and he's a commissioned officer and knows far more than I'll ever know."

She said, "Oh, he was just joking. You're just swinging the lead. Get your things and get the hell out of here."[45]

This kind of harassment under the guise of having fun continued, however, until Washington decided he would get out of the Army, come hell or high water. He feigned illness by swallowing a handful of raisins. They showed up on the X-ray as stomach ulcers and he was immediately discharged. The date remained etched in his memory — September 8, 1943.

After his stint in the service, Jackie worked at a number of different jobs, building sidewalks for the city, and as a garbage man like his father, at National Steel Car, Otis-Fensom Elevator, and American Can. At American Can the personnel manager gave Jackie the usual brush-off by saying that he couldn't hire him because nobody would work with a Black person. Washington asked if they had ever had Black people working there before:

He said, "No."

"How do you know they won't work with me?"

He said, "You've got a good point. I tell you what. I'll give you a week's try here, and if you can prove that they'll work with you, you've got a job."[46]

At the end of the week, Washington not only proved they would work with him, he claimed that he was the most popular employee they ever had. By the end of the first month, they paid him extra to play the piano and sing at coffee breaks and noon hours. They held jitterbug contests, and had a great time. With American Can as his day job, Jackie could always perform at night. When the company asked him to do night shifts, he left.

In 1943, Jackie took up with a singer named Sonny Johnston, with whom he entertained around town. They also had a radio show on CKOC, and later joined a troupe show with dancing girls and different acts. In 1948, Jackie became a disc jockey at CHML. He also married for the first time, but it didn't work out. In the decades that followed, he did regular gigs at the Royal Connaught Hotel and the old Barton Street Forum. As a washroom attendant at Duffy's Tavern, he sometimes filled in when the featured acts didn't show up. In the 1960s and later, Jackie became a fixture on the folk-music circuit and at summer music festivals. Through it all, he became a national celebrity, but it was the mark he made on the city of Hamilton, in more ways than one, that spoke volumes.

The significance of the Washington family and Jackie Washington to Hamilton cannot be overstated. One article on the family noted the important contribution the Washingtons made for almost a century on the musical culture of the city. But the impact they had on race relations was also of significance:

> "We were the only black family in the north end," Rosemary [Washington] says. "The racism was there, but our parents were both very shrewd on how they handled that because they knew we were out in the public eye and that was part of our livelihood. So we were taught to sort of turn away from it, not acknowledge that it existed. As a result, we could go to a lot of places where a lot of coloured people could not."[47]

The article went on to state that this approach to desegregation was hardly radical, but that it helped people get accustomed to seeing people of colour performing in certain clubs in which only whites previously had performed, and it increased the tolerance and the acceptance of minorities throughout the city. Make no mistake, declared the article, "they became an integral part of the desegregation of Hamilton."[48] And

Courtesy of Hamilton Spectator Newspaper Collection, Hamilton Public Library, Special Collections.

Jackie Washington, the best-known of the Washingtons, was an affable, fun-loving character. When he died in June 2009, the last of the legendary Washington family passed into history. Photo taken in 1987.

Jackie Washington, through the force of his winning personality, was an important component of that process.

Along with his induction into the Canadian Jazz and Blues Hall of Fame and the Hamilton Gallery of Distinction, plus the receipt of an Ontario Arts Council Lifetime Achievement Award, Jackie Washington was given an honourary doctorate from McMaster University in 2003. Now there is even a park called the Jackie Washington Rotary Park, appropriately located at Wellington Street north of Barton in the North End where the musical icon grew up. Thankfully Hamiltonians came to recognize and thank Jackie and his family for their inestimable contributions to the community.[49]

The Second World War marked an important turning point in African-Canadian history, as it did in the history of African Americans. It is indeed ironic that Canada's entry into the war in 1939 first opened the doors of opportunity — if only just a crack — for Canadian women and minorities. Blacks, who had been shut out of industry after industry for decades, filled the positions left behind by servicemen who fought overseas. The Ford plant in Windsor, for example, hired its first full-time employees of African descent and Black women worked alongside white women in munitions plants across the country.[50] For the first time, many Black workers became members of labour unions, fighting for better wages and working conditions alongside their white counterparts.

As one older Hamiltonian remarked:

> The War changed so many things. I've used the terminology without endorsing it, but I'd have to say "Thank you, Mister Hitler." Manpower shortage happened here and that's how we got jobs we never got before ... It's a terrible thing to think that it took a war to open the doors for us job-wise ... You see, I've met people on trains — particularly when I was a railway porter, and that really was the only job we could get, and I've talked to them and I was offered a great many jobs — domestic jobs. I had [----] ask me to run his home in Winnipeg ... I said, "What I'd like to learn is merchandising in your store." He went on to tell me that he couldn't put me in the store because the other employees would not want to be on the same level with me and me on their level and perhaps use the same facilities. The war came along and they had to hire us to get help.[51]

Viola Berry Aylestock concurred: "I think the whole thing opened up with the war: more was demanded and consequently they had to have more people in jobs; this was the turning point for Blacks."[52]

Dionne Brand has made the point that "racism did not so much decrease as mobilization for the war effort made it expedient to do away with some of the more primitive racial restrictions in order to free all the productive forces in the service of winning the war."[53] Nevertheless, after the war, Blacks had gained an important foothold in industry, and once they were in, they would not again be excluded. As Brand phrased it, "... Black women (and men) in Canada grabbed onto the industrial wage and hung on for dear life."[54] This was coupled with the fact that

Black men returning from the European theatre were no longer willing to accept second-class citizenship. For it was after the war that the civil rights campaign was joined in Ontario, led, in part, by Blacks who had suddenly been thrust onto a more level playing field with whites that they were not going to readily abandon.

Some of the walls of discrimination crumbled fairly easily under the weight of a little publicity or protest, as was seen with the restaurants in Hamilton. The *Spectator* reported an incident in which a Black veteran, Danny Saunders, was refused entry into the Dundurn Park dance pavilion in 1948. Orchestra leader Morgan Thomas, in charge of the dances, was quite adamant when first interviewed that the policy would remain the same. "The practice in all dance halls, he said, was to 'keep them out,' and added: 'If I let one in, I'd have to let two in, and then more, and the crowd would fall off.'"[55] A few days later, however, he was forced to apologize to the Black community after Alderman Peter Dunlop threatened to picket the dance hall. Although Thomas fudged the truth when he stated that they had never practised discrimination, he added that he had "no feelings of racial superiority of any sort toward the coloured race," and that Blacks would be welcome at any time in the future provided they "conduct themselves as ladies and gentlemen."[56]

After that victory (of sorts), Alderman Dunlop took his stand against racial discrimination to city council. He put forward a motion "so that refusal of admission on the grounds of race, colour or creed [would] be impermissible at public amusements, entertainments and dance halls."[57] However, that proposal was attacked by Alderman Peter McCulloch as "nothing more than Communist propaganda" and, after a lengthy discussion in council, failed to pass.

However, the winds of freedom and anti-discrimination were blowing across the province. The world was waking up to the absolute insanity of what racial discrimination had wrought in Europe during the war. In southwestern Ontario, the National Unity Association was established in 1948 by Blacks in the Chatham, Buxton, and Dresden area who were fed up with discrimination in local restaurants, taverns, and hotels, as well as every other facet of life. Formed in 1948, it was led by a carpenter named Hugh Burnett. After returning home from the Second World

War, Burnett had filed a complaint in 1943 with the federal justice minister against Kay's Café in Dresden after he was refused service there. However, the government felt it could not act against businesses that discriminated. It was a departure from the traditional legal principle of freedom of commerce.[58]

After the NUA was formed, it launched a petition in Dresden, collecting the signatures of 115 people of both races asking the Dresden Town Council to prevent businesses from discriminating. When the town council refused, the town's citizens eventually voted in a referendum. On December 6, 1949, Dresden voters were asked the following question: "Do you approve the passing of legislation compelling restaurant owners to serve, regardless of race, creed or colour?" The results were: 517 against, 108 in favour. The National Unity Association lost this battle. However, the publicity from the event helped gain support for its cause.[59]

Hugh Burnett's moving stories of discrimination in Dresden prompted the Toronto Association for Civil Liberties, backed by the Canadian Jewish Labour Committee, to take the issue to Leslie Frost, the new Conservative premier of Ontario. A deputation of different ethnic organizations, trade unions, women's groups, and churches met with Frost on July 7, 1949, asking for passage of a Fair Employment Practices Act prohibiting discrimination in employment. The assembly also requested action on restrictive covenants and the ability to cancel the licences of any provider of public services that practised racial or religious discrimination. Frost politely told the group that he and his government would duly consider their discussion, but made no promises. Soon after the NUA's failed referendum in Dresden, however, another deputation met with Premier Frost, consisting of several hundred people representing 104 civil libertarian, church, labour, ethnic, and social welfare organizations. Blacks from Dresden were present, as well as a number of other Black groups: the Amherstburg Baptist Young Peoples Association, the Brotherhood of Sleeping Car Porters (BSCP), First Baptist Church of Toronto, the Toronto Negro Study Group, Toronto United Negro Association, and the Windsor Interracial Council. William Carter and Hugh Burnett of Dresden, Dr. Oscar Brewton and Reverend

N.J. Gonsalves of First Baptist Church, Harry Gairey of the BSCP, and Lyle Talbot of the Windsor Interracial Council all made presentations.[60]

Premier Frost passed the Fair Employment Practices Act in 1951, despite some opposition from his cabinet. This legislation banned discrimination in hiring or employment as well as in union membership. His government also passed the first female equal pay legislation, the Female Employees Fair Remuneration Act. Frost was not yet prepared to move on discrimination in public accommodation, however.[61]

Meanwhile, the following year after Dunlop's failed motion at city council, the movement against discrimination in public facilities in Hamilton gained momentum. The YWCA's public affairs committee decided to petition the city to pass legislation banning the owner of a public hall or amusement place from discriminating against a person on the basis of race, creed, or colour. At a symposium held in conjunction with Brotherhood Week February 1950, representatives of twenty civic organizations, including service clubs, labour unions, social agencies, and church groups got behind the move and stated their intention to sign a petition to that effect. Reverend Holland was one of the guest speakers at the event.[62]

Unfortunately, an incident involving renowned jazz pianist Oscar Peterson brought headlines charging racism in Hamilton. On May 4, 1951, Oscar Peterson and bassist Ray Brown, who were in town playing at Fischer's Hotel, went into the Commerce Barber Shop at 75 King Street West and tried to get a haircut. They were told the shop was closed. When Peterson returned later, he was again told the shop was closed. Just then someone else waltzed in, walked past him, and was served. Peterson returned to the hotel where he was staying and called the police. The police told him to go back and if refused again, to consult the Crown attorney, which is exactly what he did. In the *Spectator* article on the incident, Peterson told the reporter that he had boasted to his American colleagues that Jim Crow did not exist in Canada, "but when something like this happens to you, it almost makes you feel as though you are not a man … It hurt to watch that man walk past me and get served."[63] Mayor Lloyd Jackson was quoted as saying, "I am ashamed to think it would happen here. I never dreamed any one would refuse to cut the hair of a negro."[64]

Of course, many Black Hamiltonians were probably choking on their supper after they read the paper that evening, knowing full well that this had been going on for as long as anyone could remember. It was ironic, moreover, that a professional service that had once been dominated by Black men in the 1800s was now discriminating against Black men when they attempted to utilize the same service. Only a few months earlier, a petition signed by more than fifty Blacks, and another by more than fifty Jewish people, had been sent to the Board of Police Commissioners, requesting them to look into cases of discrimination in the entertainment field. They also asked that a city bylaw be drafted to ban discrimination in dance halls, theatres, and other places of amusement or risk losing their licence to operate. No action had been taken by the commission.[65]

Meanwhile, the owner of Commerce Barber Shop, Glen McQuaid, probably didn't do himself any favours when he appeared with his lawyer before Mayor Jackson to protest the unfavourable publicity he had received. Apparently McQuaid had personally given Ray Brown a haircut a day earlier, which is why Brown referred the shop to his partner. McQuaid himself was "qualified" to cut a Black person's hair, which he described as "an art in itself" because "you could break perhaps five combs if you didn't know how to do it." Therefore, if he was in the shop, any Black person could come in and get a haircut. His other barbers, on the other hand, not being qualified, had been instructed to deny the service. This wasn't discrimination, it was just lack of experience.[66]

But McQuaid was in danger of losing his business licence when it was learned that a 1947 city bylaw existed banning discrimination on the basis of race, colour, or creed by licensed barbershops, beauty and hairdressing salons, laundry and dry-cleaning establishments, massage parlours, et cetera. This bylaw had been put in place after a similar incident in an east-end shop at that time. It meant that any business owner of a barbershop, hair salon, or other similar service that discriminated could have their licence suspended or revoked. Peterson said that he would not press charges, however, as he felt he had done his job by bringing it to the attention of the public and the authorities.[67]

As more and more cases of outright discrimination in public accommodation became known to the Canadian public, some were hopeful that the government would act. In late 1953, however, Attorney General Dana Porter informed Hugh Burnett "that the province had no legal power to prohibit racial discrimination in cases where municipalities had refused to pass bylaws." Burnett then approached Donna Hill, recently appointed as secretary of the Toronto labour committee, who began putting together a policy network that would ask for a provincial Fair Accommodation Practices law.[68] Hill was a sociologist from the United States and married to sociologist and activist Daniel Hill, a transplanted African American who would become the first director of the Ontario Human Rights Commission. They were also the parents of noted singer-songwriter Dan Hill Jr. and renowned novelist Lawrence Hill. Donna Hill and Ben Kayfetz, the Toronto executive director of the Canadian Jewish Congress's Joint Public Relations Committee, along with its legal advisors, produced another brief.[69] A new deputation met with Premier Frost on March 24, 1954, and included, again, the Brotherhood of Sleeping Car Porters and First Baptist Church of Toronto, as well as the Home Service Association, the National Unity Association, and the Negro Citizenship Association among the numerous labour, ethnic, church and civic groups that assembled. Hugh Burnett and Donald Moore, the latter representing the Negro Citizenship Association, were among those who made presentations.[70] This time the situation in Dresden was a central issue in the brief and Hugh Burnett got the most publicity when he spoke, saying he was "ashamed to have to plead for his fundamental democratic rights."[71] Less than a week later, the Ontario government introduced the Fair Accommodation Practices Act. The law stated that no one can deny to any person or persons the accommodation, services, or facilities usually available to members of the public on the basis of race, creed, colour, nationality, ancestry, or place of origin. It was enacted April 6, 1954.[72]

This was a victory for the human rights campaigners and activists, but Dresden restaurant owners and some other businesses in the area continued to discriminate. The NUA tested the restaurants on numerous occasions, now in an atmosphere of glaring media publicity and heightened national awareness. Eventually, Kay's Café, owned by Morley McKay, was prosecuted. Kay's was convicted and fined, making it the first successful prosecution under the new law. On November 16, 1956, a test group from

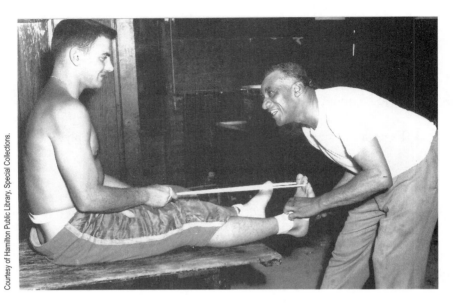

Courtesy of Hamilton Public Library, Special Collections.

Norman "Pinky" Thomas Lewis (1899–1977), an avid sportsman and, as mascot, player, manager, trainer, and coach, was involved with many hockey, football, and softball teams over the years, particularly youth teams. He became the Hamilton Ti-Cat trainer from 1952–62, and was named Canadian Trainer of the Year in 1969. Lewis was honoured with the title of Citizen of the Year in 1970. The Norman "Pinky" Lewis Recreation Centre on Wentworth Street North was named in his memory. Photograph by Lloyd Bloom.

the NUA went into the restaurant once again and was served, thus ending segregated service in Dresden.[73] The Mitchell's Bay Sportsman's Camp, a boat rental company at Mitchell's Bay, as well as other places of business, were also successfully prosecuted and convicted.[74]

During the heady days of these important developments in human and civil rights, Wilma Morrison said many years later that she didn't know where she got the *cajones* to go down to the Hamilton police department and protest the lack of hiring of Blacks there, but somehow she did:

> The young men who were coming out of school were saying that there were no Black police officers and the police department didn't hire Blacks and the fire department didn't hire Blacks, and they wanted to know why and what could be done about it. So with that, I made an appointment ... with the Chief of Police at that time.

> And so we sat down to talk and I told him … I won-
> dered why he didn't have any Black officers and would
> they hire Black officers. Back in those days there were a
> lot of stipulations that you had to be six feet tall, you had
> to be under thirty because of the pension plan …[75]

The police chief took the wind out of her sails with his reply:

> He said to me, "Miss Miller, I've been on the police force
> for almost thirty years, and to my knowledge, no Black
> person has ever applied …" I said, "Well, I'll apply." He
> said, "You're too short." So I said, "My girlfriend will
> apply," … because she's five foot eight and she would
> qualify. It turned out that she was two years too old. She
> was thirty-two at that time.[76]

Wilma did the same thing with the fire department, going down to
meet with brass and asking why there were no Black firemen in Hamilton.
She received the same response — no one had applied. Of course, this
was undoubtedly a cop-out, because if there was no specific recruitment
campaign that targeted minority groups, letting them know that the old
colour barriers were no longer in place, then Blacks and other groups
would not be inclined to apply for jobs for which they were certain to
be turned down. In any case, when she went back to the young people's
group, sure enough, no one had applied for these jobs. But Noel Wade
and Reginald Bryant applied some time thereafter and were hired by the
fire department.[77] This was in the early 1950s. More than sixty years after
George Morton, Hiram Demun, Richard Gwyder, and James Lightfoot
appeared before the Market, Fire and Police Committee, the community
had finally won a small victory. It was indeed a long time coming.

CHAPTER 8

New Pathways, Old Destination: Contemporary Fighters for Social Justice

Although the death of Reverend Holland was a great blow to the community, the realities of the mid-twentieth century worked to propel African Canadians in Hamilton forward. In the 1950s, shifts on the international front within the Black world ultimately would bring dramatic changes to the composition of the Black population of the area. It became increasingly evident, for example, that Caribbean countries were moving toward independence. The Canadian government began to realize that trade and both current and potential investment opportunities between Canada and the Caribbean region would be impeded with the continuing barrier to immigration from that region. A brief prepared for the government in 1951 by the Canadian Trade Commissioner in Trinidad brought the point home in stark terms:

> During the past year it has been becoming increasingly

apparent that in the minds of the public the convic-
tion is growing that Canadian immigration policy in
effect is based on a racial colour bar. This viewpoint
has been expressed by individuals both verbally and in
writing and in public by political leaders in Barbados
and Jamaica.... Canadian business has a big stake in
the British Caribbean built up over many decades.
Over 1500 Canadian firms have trading connections
in the colonies with a volume of exports which ... has
ranged between $30 and $80 million. In addition, mention should be made of the transportation investments
by Canadian National Steamships and Trans Canada
Airlines and such private investments as that of the
Aluminum Company of Canada in British Guiana and
Jamaica bauxite and public utilities in the same colonies.
Without going into details it is quite clear that the stake
is sufficiently large to warrant close attention to any
Canadian Government policy the operation of which
may affect its future security....[1]

From this brief, it becomes clear just how important the national-
ist and independence movements in Africa and the Caribbean were in
bringing down some of the most egregious racist policies and practices
of Western governments like Canada, such as Canada's immigration policy. The trade commissioner, T.G. Major, continued:

The colonies are moving rapidly towards self-gov-
ernment and a new British nation will emerge in the
foreseeable future. The leaders are arising from the
people of coloured racial origin. It is with such persons
and not with white British colonial officials and white
West Indians that Canadian officials and business men
increasingly will have to deal. Obviously it is important that the good will of the coloured peoples of the
British Caribbean should be maintained and cultivated

if future commercial relations are to be on a satisfactory basis.... The growing suspicion that Canada is operating a colour bar immigration policy, irrespective of personal qualifications, could mushroom very quickly and turn the present goodwill into dislike....[2]

In addition to the obvious pressures coming from these soon-to-be independent Black countries, the 1950s and early 1960s saw a movement of increasing protest within Canada against the blatant racism of Canadian immigration policy regarding people of colour from these parts of the world. Prior to Confederation in 1867, petitions or movements against Black immigration into the country did not gain traction because Canadians did not determine these policies without British approval. In 1830, for example a select committee of the Upper Canadian Assembly recommended restrictions on Black immigration after receiving petitions against it from whites in Gosfield and Colchester Townships. In the 1850s, Edwin Larwill was a vocal opponent of the Black settlement known as the Elgin Settlement (or Buxton) in Raleigh Township. Larwill trotted out every negative stereotype he could think of, even running for the Legislative Assembly partly on an anti-Black platform. The British government did not support these efforts, and Blacks voted in a block against his candidacy, helping to defeat him in two elections.[3] After Confederation, it was a different story. Beginning in the 1890s, when the Canadian government was advertising the Canadian West to prospective American settlers, it sent agents into the south to discourage Black settlers from coming. Those who got to the border were turned away and medical personnel were instructed to declare Black immigrants medically unfit. This unofficial policy was made law with the Immigration Act of 1910, when the government declared that it could "prohibit ... the landing in Canada of immigrants belonging to any race deemed unsuited to the climate or requirements of Canada, or of immigrants of any specified class, occupation or character."[4] One year later, an order-in-council prohibited for a period of one year "the landing in Canada ... of any immigrants belonging to the Negro race, which race is deemed unsuitable to the climate and requirements of Canada."[5] Although this order was repealed two months later, it revealed the extent to which the government might go to prevent Black immigration into the country. As late as 1952, the government passed an act that authorized the banning of immigrants on the grounds of their "ethnic group," "geographical area of origin," or "probable inability to become readily assimilated."[6] Obviously, the government had not heeded Trade Commissioner Major's warnings at that time.

Blacks challenged the law. In Toronto's Black community, a tailor originally from Barbados named Donald Moore and his organization called the Negro Citizenship Association, began to agitate for the liberalization of immigration laws so that people of African descent could be more readily admitted into Canada. Other organizations, like the Brotherhood of Sleeping Car Porters, also took up the mantle of challenging the immigration laws where people of colour were concerned. This pressure for change led to the formation of the West Indian Domestic Program in 1955, whereby Caribbean women could come and work as domestic servants in Canadian homes. While bringing in women of colour as servants was hardly a liberal program and had more to do with the need for cheap labour for upper-class Canadians, it did enable women, many of whom were educated professionals, teachers, secretaries, and the like, to enter the country and eventually become Canadian citizens. It also allowed for a number of educated people, such as nurses, to come under the "exceptional merit" clause of the Immigration Act.[7] More importantly, it set the stage for the opening up of Canada to people of all nations and races in the 1960s.

In addition to changes in the composition of the Black community over time, the political scene was slowly becoming more representative of its population. Ellen Fairclough became Hamilton's first female member of parliament in 1950 and later Canada's first female cabinet minister in 1957. At the provincial level, Hamilton's Ada Pritchard became the first female Conservative member of the Ontario legislature in 1963. In 1957, Hamilton East also sent the first Italian Canadian to Parliament: Quinto Martini.[8]

The eventual repeal of the Immigration Act in 1962 — brought about under Ellen Fairclough's leadership as minister of Citizenship and Immigration — and the new regulations devised in 1967 allowed people to immigrate on a points system, based on skills and education. The doors were then opened wider than they had been since the days of the Underground Railroad. Caribbean Blacks, in particular, began to come by the thousands, and although Toronto and Montreal were the primary destinations of many new immigrants, Hamilton and smaller cities received their share of these new Canadians. Not only were people voluntarily bringing their skills forward by immigrating here, but the separate school board in Hamilton also scouted for teachers in the Caribbean, especially Trinidad, and enticed several dozen teachers to immigrate to the area.

Dr. Gary Warner, now retired, but formerly of McMaster University, referred to this recruitment process as a "reverse flow of human resources from South to North."[9] Warner correctly pointed out that the conventional view of a flow of aid and resources from north to south was challenged by immigration from Africa and the Caribbean, such as the case of this teacher recruitment to Hamilton-Wentworth in the 1960s. The following brief biographies of some noted African Hamiltonians represent, in part, the contributions of Blacks to Hamilton since the 1960s. There are many paths that these notable individuals took to become leaders of the community, from the towers of some of the top colleges and universities, to being smuggled into the country in a picnic basket at the age of two months. Whatever their origin, their many contributions form part of a long history of community activism and struggle for social justice that has helped shape the twenty-first-century city.

Eleanor Wiltshire Rodney

Eleanor Wiltshire Rodney was one of the teachers recruited from the Caribbean to teach in Hamilton. Born in Trinidad in 1938 of a Grenadian mother and a Barbadian father, she attended Teacher's College in Port of Spain, and, after obtaining her teaching certificate, moved with her husband to Canada in pursuit of opportunity. He had been recruited to teach in the Hamilton Separate School Board in 1966. She followed him into the board one year later. However, as with many immigrants from this region, she did not rest on her laurels, but instead took the opportunity to obtain a Bachelor of Arts from McMaster University, a Master of Education from the Ontario Institute for Studies in Education, as well as specialist certificates in Religion, Language Arts, English as a Second Language (ESL), and Special Education.[10]

In addition to upgrading her own skills, Ms. Rodney became involved in an important initiative in the Black community in her role as a teacher and mentor. As she explained:

> For the first two years teaching in the Hamilton-Wentworth Separate School Board, I did not have Black kids in my classes, because most of the Black kids who came from the Caribbean at that time were in the *public* school system.... In the early seventies, somebody did a thesis at McMaster and recognized the fact that a lot of the Caribbean kids were not performing as well as they should in the public school system. So what they did is ask some of these teachers to volunteer some of their time in the summer to help these students.[11]

Just as in the nineteenth century when Black teachers fulfilled a need in their communities and set up ad hoc schoolrooms for newly arriving fugitive slave children, or taught Sunday school, lessons that often went far beyond the simple teaching of Bible Studies, Eleanor Rodney was part of a twentieth-century wave of teachers, primarily from the Caribbean, but also from Africa, who filled a need among immigrant children for mentors and role models to ease their integration into Canadian society. Rodney was one of the teachers involved in this remedial program:

> We found out at that time that it wasn't because the kids were below their intellectual level. It was because they were experiencing a sort of culture shock. The teachers were strange to them, they were strange to the teachers,

and many of them were streamed in the bottom level. So what we did at that time was we tested the kids first of all and those who were up to ... their grade level, we gave them work to help them proceed further in their new class that they would be going into in September. About three-quarters of them were not doing well and what we did is give them remedial activities in the summer to bring them up to the class level that they should be ...[12]

There were about thirty teachers involved in this program. Most of them taught in the Separate School Board, although the majority of the students were in the public school system. The program lasted about twelve years. Then, in 1991–92, the provincial government published a report about the high-school-dropout rates of African-Canadian children, particularly in centres like Toronto. As a result, Eleanor established the first African Language and Heritage Class for African-Caribbean children in Hamilton to help boost their self-esteem and to improve their acculturation into the Ontario school system:

We had to choose a language because, at that time, that's the only venue we had for getting Black kids together.... So we started this heritage class and we did the Swahili language — Gary Warner got somebody from McMaster University to come and teach Swahili — so we did that for about 50 percent of the time, but for the rest of the period, we told the kids about their Black history.[13]

Rodney remembered the tremendous impact the class had on many of the students: "I must say that it improved their self-esteem, their self-worth, and we found the kids blossomed.... As a matter of fact, about half of those kids who passed through our system became leaders in their schools."[14] Not only did some of the students go on to become leaders in their schools, but a number became John Holland Award winners, or won trustee awards. One of the students, Andrea Henry, became a "pop star," appearing in a television series about the making of the Canadian girl group, Sugar Jones. Another,

Kimahli Powell, won the very first national Mathieu Da Costa Award for the best essay on multiculturalism. In 1996, Rodney went a step further and founded the African Caribbean Cultural Potpourri Inc. (ACCPI), which gives awards to youth who have excelled not only academically, but also as leaders in the community. The annual Caribbean Potpourri charity variety show, perhaps her crowning achievement, is a showcase for promising talent and a fundraiser for several charities.

Rodney has had a tremendous impact both within the school system, as well as in the community. She pioneered the adult Canadian citizenship course for the Catholic school board, as well as helping to write its race relations policy. Through her tutoring and mentorship, numerous students have gone on to compete at district, regional, and provincial public-speaking contests. Among her literary achievements, she was one of the *Hamilton Spectator*'s first community editorial board members, where she wrote about racial and social issues. She was also the chief editor of *Nurturing the Trillium: The Contributions of African & Caribbean Educators to the Development of the Hamilton-Wentworth Region*, published in 2002.[15] This book stands as a lasting tribute to the teachers of the Hamilton-Wentworth region who have made important contributions to the lives of their students and the educational system as a whole.

Neville Nunes

Neville Nunes was another outstanding teacher who taught in the Hamilton-Wentworth District public-school system. What Rodney was doing from her vantage point in the separate schools, Nunes was echoing in the regular public-school system. Nunes received his early education in his native Jamaica, where he graduated from MICO Teacher's College with a diploma in education. After immigrating to Canada in 1959, he obtained a Bachelor of Arts from McMaster University and a Master of Sciences in Education from Niagara University in New York State.

Neville was active on a number of fronts — within the school he participated extensively in extracurricular activities such as coaching soccer, and at the board level, he contributed in a variety of ways, conducting workshops, presenting at conferences, publishing journal articles, and piloting several significant projects. One of these was the Multicultural Education Policy designed specifically for the Ainslie-Wood Vocational School. This policy was subsequently adopted and implemented by the school system.

Neville Nunes pioneered the Hamilton Board of Education's Black History Month celebrations beginning in 1988. As a member of the *Spectator*'s Community Editorial Board, Nunes wrote, or was featured in, countless articles on the need for more Black history in the schools. In February 1989, for example, Nunes was quoted as saying that "the number of black students in the schools is growing. We need black history so our black kids ... can learn more about themselves, can identify with the black community, can build self-esteem and can find role models."[16] In a 1997 article, Nunes, in his characteristic poetic eloquence, likened the drive to obtain enlightenment about Black achievements as walking through the dark night into the dawn of a new day. Vigilance was needed so that Black history would not be forgotten after February. "This celebration of the achievements of a proud people cannot possibly end when the sun sets on February 28. Ways must be found to make the dawn truly

Courtesy of Workers Arts and Heritage Centre, Hamilton.

African Canadian Workers' Committee at the launch of the travelling exhibit "... and still I rise: A History of African Canadians in Ontario, 1900–Present." (l–r): Carmen Henry, Adrienne Shadd, Fleurette Osborne, Gary Warner, Janice Gairey, Noreen Glasgow, Neville Nunes, and Maxine Carter.

a daily occurrence."[17] He was a founder of the Black Youth Achievement Organization, and, in 1993, developed an ESL handbook that provided guidelines for student placement in ESL programs.

Throughout the years, Neville also participated in many organizations, such as the Jamaican Association, the Alliance of Black Educators, the Settlement and Integration Advisory Committee for Organizational Change, and the John Howard Society. He has been recognized for his contributions as the recipient of a lifetime achievement award from the Jamaica Foundation, the African Canadian Cultural Association for continuing service, as well as a Certificate of Merit from the J.C. Holland Award for Educators. In 1993, he received an award for dedication to the needs of exceptional children from the Council of Exceptional Children and was a nominee for the World Citizenship Award.[18]

Dr. Gary Warner

A third educator made his mark at the university level as well as in the wider community. Dr. Gary Warner was born in Trinidad. After completing a Bachelor of Arts (Honours) in French from the University of London and a Ph.D. from the Université de Caen in France, Dr. Warner immigrated to Canada in 1967. Now retired, the McMaster University professor was chair of Romance Languages, associate dean of Humanities and director of the Arts and Science Program. He taught courses on French, African, and Caribbean literature, French language, and seventeenth-century literature, as well as on peace and international development.

As with all of the community activists presented in this chapter, Gary was not interested in simply making a mark in the classroom or through his work as an academic. He was and continues to be a dedicated community worker, committed to issues of international development, racism, human rights, and social justice. Warner co-founded McMaster's School for International Justice and Human Rights and did development work in Sierra Leone in the late 1970s. He chaired the board of the Settlement and Integration Services Organization (SISO), which helps new Canadians adapt to Hamilton. He also chaired the anti-racism group known as Strengthening Hamilton's Community Initiative (SHCI) and the African Caribbean Cultural Potpourri Inc. Scholarship Committee. Dr. Warner's service to the community has also included work with Amnesty International, Development and Peace, the Regional Advisory Committee on Immigration and Refugee Issues, and the Hamilton Board of Education Race Relations Steering Committee, among others.

Courtesy of Dr. Gary Warner.

Dr. Gary Warner, retired McMaster University professor, has a long record of community service and leadership on peace and social justice issues.

Since the 1990s, Professor Warner has been literally showered with awards, honours, and distinctions. In 1998, he received a J.C. Holland Award in the Professional category, and in March 2004, the McMaster Students Union Lifetime Achievement Award. The years 2005 and 2006 were particular banner years, when he received the Order of Canada and Hamilton's Citizen of the Year award, as well as being named to the Hamilton Gallery of Distinction. Like his predecessor, Reverend Holland, Dr. Warner was humbled by being named Citizen of the Year. When interviewed, he said, "It takes a whole community for one of us to receive an award like this."[19] Upon being named a Member of the Order of Canada, Warner reflected:

> [The Order of Canada distinction] represents for me recognition of the path that I have chosen, combining my academic interests with a strong commitment

to community service and to values of equity and social justice.... As an immigrant to Canada, I also see it as recognition of the positive contribution that immigrants and refugees make to this country, contrary to some negative stereotypes. And as an African Canadian, I see it as part of my mentorship role to youth in general, and to African Canadian and visible minority youth in particular.[20]

In 2007, Warner was inducted into the College of the Immaculate Conception (CIC) Hall of Fame in Port-of-Spain, Trinidad. CIC is otherwise known as St. Mary's College. His award was presented by the president of Trinidad and Tobago, George Richards. A colleague summed up his contributions as follows: "His whole life has been dedicated to the service of others. He has not restricted himself to the so-called ivory tower but has taken his knowledge and applied it in the larger community and then taken what he has learned in the larger community and brought it back to the classroom."[21]

Ladnor S. Phillpotts (Bill) De Lisser

Another dedicated mover and shaker in Hamilton is Bill De Lisser. Born in Jamaica, De Lisser came to Hamilton in the 1970s. He was a graduate in business administration from West London College in London, England. In 1978, he became a member of the newly formed Afro-Canadian Caribbean Association (ACCA), and served on the committee to develop the constitution and obtain approval of its charitable status. De Lisser was also instrumental in setting up the cultural arts section of ACCA and founded the Accamba Theatre Workshop and Accamba singers. These initiatives provided a wealth of enjoyment and education about Black and Caribbean culture for the citizens of Hamilton and region. Under the theatre umbrella, De Lisser wrote and produced two stage plays, *A Two-Way Street* and *Good-bye Brixton*. In addition, he wrote numerous skits, the most memorable of which was *Only for Five Years*, a musical story of the journey from one's homeland of birth to a new life in Canada. From 1989–96, Bill was president of ACCA.

Since his involvement with ACCA, Bill De Lisser has served on numerous boards and committees for the betterment of his community. From 1991–95, he was a member of the Mayor's Race Relations Committee, the Hamilton Firefighters' Committee (he helped to revise its recruitment process to include visible minorities in 1993), and, in the same year, founded and became

Courtesy of Bill De Lisser.

Among Bill De Lisser's goals has been to promote the recognition and appreciation of the contributions of Jamaican Canadians and Caribbean culture to Hamilton.

president of the Jamaica Foundation of Hamilton. The aim of this organization is to recognize the contributions of Jamaican Canadians living in Hamilton, and to provide assistance to Jamaicans at home and abroad as the need arises. He was a board member and past chair of the Hamilton Urban Core Community Health Centre, a member of the Community Advisory Board on Homeless Initiatives in Hamilton and board member and regional vice-president of the National Council of Jamaicans and Supportive Organizations in Canada. For his outstanding record of service to the community, Mr. De Lisser was a finalist for the Hamilton and District Citizen of the Year award in 1998, and he received a 2007 Spirit of the Community Award (Dinthill High School Canadian Chapter Alumni).[22]

Evelyn Myrie

There is no person in Hamilton who has done more to serve her community than Evelyn Myrie. She was born in Jamaica and immigrated to Windsor, Ontario, in 1974, arriving with her five sisters to join their mother, Deloris, who had come to Canada several years earlier on the West Indian Domestic Scheme. After studying communications at the University of Windsor, Evelyn got a job working for Women Working for Immigrant Women, which launched her career as an advocate for women's equity and immigrant issues.

In 1989, Evelyn moved to Hamilton and became a consultant for the Status of Women, Canada. In that position, she spent over ten years in program design and management. In conjunction with her job, she

Courtesy of Evelyn Myrie.

Evelyn Myrie, Chair, and the Hamilton Black History Committee spearheaded the 175th anniversary celebrations of the founding of Stewart Memorial Church in 2010.

also became the first Black woman to chair the city's Status of Women Subcommittee. She successfully lobbied city hall to establish a non-sexist language policy and introduced anti-racism training and a broader outreach into diverse women's communities. For example, for the first time, meetings were held at the Aboriginal Native Friendship Centre in Hamilton. Evelyn was also responsible for inviting Glenda Simms, the first guest speaker of colour at the annual awards dinner. At the time, Simms was the head of the Canadian Advisory Council on the Status of Women. Roberta Jamieson, a First Nations woman and Ontario Ombudsman, was another guest speaker in those years. These initiatives helped to sensitize the subcommittee to hearing the voices of marginalized and racialized minorities. Evelyn then made a move to the United Way in the Peel Newcomer Strategy Group where she was the director, again working more closely with new immigrants.

If Evelyn were to tally up all of her contributions in her work on women's and immigrant issues, she would be very proud of her many achievements. However, as with the other men and women on these pages, she has contributed so much more. As a founding member and chairperson of the Hamilton Black History Committee, Ms. Myrie has been another of the champions of the recognition of Black history in Hamilton. In 1996, the year of the City of Hamilton's 150th birthday celebrations, the committee organized the first John C. Holland Awards Dinner, named after the esteemed minister of Stewart Memorial Church. These annual awards are given out every year to worthy recipients at a gala dinner held appropriately in February. The event is now carried on Cable 14 and CHCH TV also provides significant coverage. Myrie also brought in the *Hamilton Spectator* newspaper as a key partner. This event is now one of the largest Black History Month celebrations in the Golden Horseshoe.

Evelyn was the driving force behind the establishment of the John Holland Institute for Leadership, an African-centred leadership and mentorship program for youth. Its home base is the renovated manse of Stewart Memorial Church where a homework club provides a space for students to come and get help with their school work. The "Lifting as We Climb" summer camp is run out of the institute, as well as a Big Sister and Big Brother mentoring program that offers positive role models for the youth.

Evelyn has also worked outside Hamilton, for example, as past chairperson of the African Canadian Legal Clinic in Toronto. In that capacity, she helped to expand the clinic's role in supporting African Canadians outside of Toronto. She represented the clinic at the United Nations World Conference Against Racism in Durban, South Africa, in 2001. She also continues her role as freelance writer for the *Spectator* newspaper, and knocked on the door of political office twice, running for city councillor in Ward 1 and seeking the provincial NDP nomination for Hamilton West in 2003.

But there is another aspect to Evelyn Myrie's life that should not go unmentioned. Evelyn is the creator of Eman Fine Art Prints & Tings, an online gallery of African art and the art of those of African descent. When she came to Hamilton in 1989, she says, there was nothing in the stores to reflect the diverse cultures of the city, whether this was in the form of greeting cards, art, or simply images around the city that acknowledged that people of colour lived there. "I decided to call some artists I knew in Detroit and carry their art cards and prints. I then began to organize home shows and I rented space in hotels and community centres for art shows."[23] Gradually, her collection came to include African masks, fabric, original paintings, and sculpture. At one point, she opened a store on Hamilton's trendy Locke Street. According to Evelyn, the public, particularly the 15,000 Blacks in the area, responded enthusiastically and there was a great demand for the work. "You're filling a gap, and they feel that's exciting."[24]

The Eman Fine Art Gallery is probably what gives her the energy and sense of balance to do all that she does. Incredibly, however, in addition to all the other things on her plate, Myrie was for many years a long-distance runner. She actually ran seven marathons, including those in London, England; Berlin; and in Pennsylvania and Detroit. As with everything, Myrie used these races to raise awareness and funds for broader issues confronting the community — sickle cell anemia research and violence against women projects in Hamilton. But we wouldn't expect her to do anything less.[25]

Garfield Parker

All of the men and women in this chapter had mentors and role models who helped shape them and make them conscious of the need to give back and to work on behalf of human rights and social justice issues. In the case of Garfield Parker, however, his ancestors went down in the annals of history as true freedom fighters who held their ground with firearms in their effort to live in freedom and dignity. William and Eliza

Parker were the heroes of the Christiana Riots of 1851, which some historians have hailed as the first salvo of the American Civil War.

Born a slave in Anne Arundel County, Maryland, around 1822, William Parker was first owned by Major William Brogden and then by his son David. Parker escaped in 1839 at the age of about seventeen and began living a life of freedom in Lancaster County, Pennsylvania. Because this was an area just across the border from Maryland where many fugitive slaves resided, there were many instances when white slave catchers would roam the area searching for escaped slaves. They would break into people's homes and drag them away, even when they were not the right individuals. Parker formed a Black self-defence organization comprised of Black men in the area. Parker himself was described as someone of intelligence and indomitable will who "possessed a strong social nature and … put his own body in danger to protect a friend. These qualities gained for him the respect of a very large class in that community."[26] Parker and his self-defence organization repeatedly foiled numerous kidnapping attempts. Years later a Quaker from the area stated that William Parker was viewed as the "Toussaint L'Ouverture of his people," who commanded the "universal respect of all of them who did not have occasion to fear him."[27]

On the fateful day of September 11, 1851, however, Parker, his wife Eliza, and his self-defence organization fought off a white posse determined to retrieve several former slaves who were holed up at the Parkers' home and return them to bondage in Maryland. Edward Gorsuch, the owner of the slaves, was killed in the melee and Gorsuch's son, Dickinson, and several others, were severely wounded. In the aftermath of the "riots," dozens of Black men and women were jailed and a treason trial was held. The fact that many whites in the area helped the Blacks in one way or another and refused to let the posse have their way was a huge affront to southern slaveholders.

Eliza and her sister Hannah Pinckney, who had played key roles in the resistance, were released from prison before the trial, but thirty-eight men, including four Quakers, were tried. They were all acquitted. Meanwhile, William Parker and three other key participants had escaped to Canada. After living for some several months just north of Toronto, where Parker was reunited with his wife Eliza, William Parker, his family, and Abraham Johnson settled in Buxton. Newspaper publisher Henry Bibb spoke for the entire anti-slavery movement when he wrote that "he is said to have carried out the sublime idea that 'resistance to tyrants is obedience to God.' This man, in our estimation, deserves the admiration of a Hannibal, a Toussaint L'Ouverture, or a George Washington. A nobler defence was never made in behalf of human liberty on the plains of Lexington, Concord, or Bunker Hill than was put forth by William Parker at Christiana ..."[28]

Garfield Parker was born in North Buxton in 1923. His father, Frances "Frank" Henry Parker, was the grandson of William and Eliza Parker. Frank Parker's father, Frances Merriam Parker, was born in 1864 to William and Eliza in Buxton, and was the sixth of ten children they had. Frank Parker's first wife and Garfield's mother was Mabel Elizabeth Jones, also from North Buxton.[29] Garfield's early life growing up in Buxton was vastly removed from the life and death struggle against tyranny that had been the existence of his great-grandfather. However, whatever compelled William Parker to thrust himself into the role of freedom fighter must also have been present in a young Garfield, because his selfless dedication and service to the community was an unwavering thread throughout his life.

Garfield Parker left for Hamilton at a very young age. In fact, Parker was one of the men that Reverend Holland took down to Stelco to get employment in 1939–40. Parker remained at Stelco for forty-three years, becoming a foreman in the blast-furnace area where the metal was poured. Parker married Dorothy Hunt, a hairdresser, who, in church historian Evie Auchinvole's words, was one of "the ambassadors of the community."[30] When newcomers came to her hair salon, she would invite them to Stewart Memorial, and that's how many people who were new to Hamilton became members of the church.[31]

The couple worked hand in hand in building up the membership and furthering outreach and the good works of the church. Garfield was the chairman of the Board of Trustees, which looked after all financial matters of the church *and* he was chairman of the Official Board, which comprised the members of all the other boards of the church. Parker's contributions to the church and the Masonic fraternity were his life's work.

He was a past master of Mount Olive Lodge #1, a grand worthy patron of the Grand Chapter of the Eastern Star. He also served as grand master of the Prince Hall Grand Lodge from 1960–63. Parker was the first grand master from Hamilton since Hiram Demun left office in 1900.[32]

Vince Morgan, chairman of the Official Board at Stewart Memorial in 2010, remembered that Parker was a man of great dignity and a "workaholic for the church," who, when there was handiwork to be done or something needed to be fixed, would literally do the work himself. During his tenure, he was very conscious of church affairs and accommodated the trustees by holding trustee meetings at his home because he often worked late and could not otherwise make the meetings.

In the mid-1980s, Vince Morgan was a youth chairman at the Mount Olive Lodge #1 and, according to Morgan, the church under Parker's leadership opened its doors to sixty-three youth of the community. Morgan remembered, "We formed a youth choir that was tremendous. We got invitations to sing all over the province. There was also a karate group that lasted for twelve years. Garfield had so much confidence in us that he allowed us to renovate the basement using church funds. There was a great community effort under his watch."[33] According to Morgan, Parker was also very generous to the church. "I remember that when we were short of cash, he would take his own money and loan it to the church. It was supposed to be hush hush. If we were short of funds, instead of cashing in the GIC, he would loan the church the money and ensure that the GIC was still intact."[34] Morgan stated that he was able to take over as chairman of the Official Board because he had such a close relationship with Parker, essentially shadowing him during his time at the helm.

In 1988, Garfield Parker died at the age of sixty-five after developing lung cancer. However, he left his mark on the church and the community, and the church was in a much stronger financial position because of him. "We were able to fund some major projects because of him, like when we renovated the outside brick of the church building. The outside was painted grey and we cleaned the brick and restored it to its original reddish colour.... They were here for a month working on it.... These are some of the reasons why Garfield Parker should get an honourable mention for his contributions."[35]

Reverend Robert (Bob) Foster

Robert "Bob" Foster ingrained in his children the idea that respect and responsibility are the two key qualities that a Foster should possess.[36] Bob Foster taught his children these principles not just through his words, but, more importantly, through the power of his example. According to his son Robert Foster Jr., his example also won him the respect and admiration of the entire Hamilton community.

Bob Foster was born in Louisiana in 1920. His stepfather died, and with no means of income or support, his mother Wilhelmina and two-month-old baby travelled up to the border to Canada in order to be with her mother and stepfather. However, immigration officials at the border would not allow her to enter the country. She sent word and a Black minister from Fort Erie came across on the ferry and smuggled the child back in a picnic basket. This is how Robert Michael Foster came to grow up in Hamilton, adopted and raised by his grandparents, George and Lucinda "Lucy" Lee Foster. Years later, he met his biological father Sam Clifton. Clifton played in the Negro Baseball Leagues.

Bob Foster followed in the footsteps of his adoptive father. George Foster was born in

Courtesy of Robert Foster Jr., Kingston, Ontario.

Reverend Robert Foster officiating at the wedding of his son Robert Foster Jr. to Bonita Bell in 1990. Robert Foster Jr. served in the Canadian Armed Forces from 1961 to 1981, and then became a correctional services officer, retiring in 2000.

Mississippi, and he and his brother, James, fled from the Ku Klux Klan there and moved to Louisville, Kentucky, where they obtained jobs at the racetrack. When a rich Canadian named George Henry invited Foster to come to Canada, he ended up in Hamilton working at the Hamilton Jockey Club racetrack. George met and married Lucinda Lee, and they subsequently purchased a home on Argyle Street in East Hamilton. George Foster started out doing laundry and other menial jobs, became a valet — the person who saddles the horses and looks after the jockeys — and then worked his way up to custodian of the jock's room, or someone who solely takes care of the jockeys. In the late 1800s, the jockeys were Black and the valets were Black. Later, there was the odd white jockey and they wanted to have white valets. Eventually, George was demoted to assistant custodian of the jock's room because of the changeover from Black to white jockeys.

In the meantime, Bob Foster began at the racetrack working as a valet, eventually becoming custodian of the jock's room in the 1950s. By this time, there was only one other Black valet and one other jockey out of perhaps twenty. He went from that to clerk of the scales, or someone who weighs the jockeys prior to a race. He did that job for a couple of years, and then became a racing judge. In addition, Bob Foster received his ordination in 1982 from McMaster Divinity College, which he had attended on a part-time basis. The Ontario Racing Commission approached him to become the chaplain for the racetrack as well as head of recreation. In these capacities, he married people, buried people, provided counselling services, and set up organized sports such as hockey teams and basketball teams. One of Foster's goals was to assist the poor people at the racetrack with services and to help provide them with a better quality of life, particularly as they were getting older. He worked with those in the "backstretch" — the people who walked the horses, and worked in the stables. In his own quiet, determined way, he broke barriers. Foster performed his many services at an office at Woodbine Racetrack, making him the first chaplain, not to mention the first Black chaplain, at the remaining two thoroughbred racetracks in Ontario — Woodbine Racetrack and Fort Erie.[37]

In addition to his work at the racetrack, Reverend Foster also had a business, which he had inherited from his father. This was a private laundry that looked after the clothing for the jockeys. He sold saddles and tacks, and hired a woman to sew the racing colours (uniforms) for the jockeys. At one time Mrs. Rachel Holland held the contract to sew the racing colours.

Sometimes Foster held three and four jobs to keep his household of six solvent. He married Barbara Berry, a granddaughter of Julia and Henry Berry, in 1940. She was the daughter of Hiram and Hazel Hicks Berry, but had been raised in part by Doll, Julia's daughter, after the death of her mother from tuberculosis in 1930. Bob and Barbara Foster had four children, Robert Jr., Rodney, Leslie, and Judith. Their home was always open to strangers. As his daughter Judith commented, "He reached into his pocket to help people without a loaf of bread. When people from the Caribbean came into town, they were given our father's name, because he was known in the community. There was always a stranger at our table during Thanksgiving, Christmas, and other occasions when we were growing up."[38]

As a younger man, Reverend Foster was an avid sportsman who ran track, played football, baseball, and boxed. Later on, he organized and coached teams and was involved with the Kiwanis Club and other sports clubs, particularly those that worked with low-income kids. Foster was also instrumental in forming and coaching the Sepia Queen's basketball team and Imperial Wizards Boys' team, the basketball teams that played out of Stewart Memorial Church. Foster naturally came to be seen as a leader, not just at the racetrack, but in his community overall. When there was talk of establishing a Black community centre for Hamilton in 1972, Bob Foster was one of the five-member committee formed to study its feasibility.[39]

Reverend Foster was an avid fraternity brother who was involved with the Shriners out of Buffalo, as well as Mount Olive Lodge #1, becoming grand master of the Prince Hall Grand Lodge from 1972–75. In her book on the Prince Hall Masons, Arlie Robbins stated, with tongue in cheek, that "Grand Master Foster came under some criticism for appointing a woman, sister Arlie C. Robbins, as Grand Lodge History Coordinator, for some of the brothers feared an attempt would be made to break the inner sanctum of the Grand Lodge. When this proved not to be the case, the brothers were agreeable for the most part."[40] He was a co-founder and first president of the Afro-Canadian Caribbean Association, a member of the Hamilton Race Relations Committee, and involved in numerous other initiatives. "He was certainly someone that I looked up to, along with everyone else," his son Robert declared.[41] "But the ministry was truly his calling," his daughter Judith emphasized.[42] In that regard, Foster became assistant pastor of Stewart Memorial Church in 1982 and remained in that position until his stroke some years later. In 2002, Reverend Foster passed away, leaving a huge void in the community. Black Hamilton in particular lost a beloved mentor and champion of human rights. "My father was someone who loved his race … who did everything in his power to move [the cause of Black people] along …" added his son. "If he could have been alive to see Barack Obama become president, that would have done it for him."[43]

Wilma Morrison

On her eightieth birthday, she received letters of congratulations from Prime Minister Stephen Harper and Premier Dalton McGuinty. The previous February, she was honoured at a special Black History Month event in Niagara Falls. The Nigerian-born editor of *Mosaic Edition* described this event for "Chief" *Iya Oge* or *Mother of Beauty of Niagara* as akin to a coronation in an African village.[44] She is the only Canadian woman to be given the Uncrowned Queens Culture Keeper Award for Preservation of Black History. This from the Uncrowned Queens Institute of Buffalo, New York, in 2005. She has bagged dozens of awards and honours over the years. Praise for this down-to-earth community stalwart and her many contributions is legion.

Wilma Morrison[45] was born Wilma Miller in London, Ontario, in 1929. She never knew her father, and was raised by her mother and grandmother. When she was ten, they moved to Hamilton. Wilma had originally wanted to become a teacher after she graduated from high school in 1947, but she would have had to study in the United States, which the family could not afford. The "normal schools" or teacher's colleges in the province did not accept Blacks at that time, although a group of Black women from Bermuda were permitted to attend as long as they left after graduation. It was the same in the nursing profession. Neither of the Hamilton hospitals were accepting Black women into their Registered Nurse training programs. "Then my friend, Doris Malott, from Brantford ... found she would be accepted in the Certified Nursing Assistant program and she came to live with my mother and I. The agency responsible for the program suggested it might be easier for her if a companion joined her in the program — and so I did!"[46] Upon graduation, they both applied to the Ontario Hospital, now the Hamilton Psychiatric Hospital, and were accepted to start work. Wilma worked there for nine years, and then left to work as a civil servant for the Royal Canadian Navy. She got to go aboard the yacht *Britannia* during the Queen's visit to open the St. Lawrence Seaway. It was at that time that her mother, Mabel Miller, died.

Wilma met Lorne Morrison, the son of Collingwood matriarch Rita Duvall Cummings, in 1950. They married on July 27, 1955. "Lorne had insisted that we stay in Hamilton as he felt it would be unfair to move [my mother] to the Falls where she would be among strangers. The sold sign went on the Rebecca Street house in Hamilton a month after Mom died ..."[47] In Niagara Falls, Wilma and Lorne worked and enjoyed life together. They were part of a close-knit group of friends who enjoyed vacations and socializing together and the Morrison home became a hub for family, friends, and good times throughout the years.

In 1987, Wilma was minding her own business when she got a call from a real estate agent who told her that the minister had called and said the church was for sale. Reverend Ernest Crawford had approached and received permission from the BME Conference without mentioning it to the last remaining members of the congregation. "I replied: 'It's not!' I told the agent ... that [it] was the only thing left in town that indicated the presence of Black people and their contribution to the development of the Niagara Falls community for over 200 years. My husband Lorne's comment on all this was: 'Well, mouth, you've got $1.98 in your pocket and now you've got a church!' 'Well,' I said, 'I have to try!'"[48]

Courtesy of Mrs. Morrison, Niagara Falls, Ontario.

Wilma Morrison inside the historic R. Nathaniel Dett Memorial BME Chapel, Niagara Falls, Ontario.

Thus, a new career, so to speak, was launched. Wilma's rationale was simple: "These places were built and left to us by folks who had suffered and had a lot less than we have today. Life is better for us because of them. I will always try to honour them for their foresight and try to pass it on to the next generation."[49] The first thing they did was hold a fundraising concert and the choir from the Collingwood BME Church came down to perform. This helped to pay the bills owed. They next set up a library in the Sunday School room of the church and named it the Norval Johnson Heritage Library, in memory of Norval Johnson, a tireless worker in the church. The Ontario Historical Society gave a $5,000 grant to this end. The library opened in March 1991. Next came the Niagara Freedom Trail tours that Morrison put together. These consisted of notable Black history sites around the region which she conducted in conjunction with the BME Salem Chapel in St. Catharines and Bertie Hall in Fort Erie. In 1999, the church began to rent the manse next door for $1 per annum so that the library could move into it.

Throughout the years, the church was renovated with grants from government and various agencies and organizations. Don Thomas, whose parents Mabel and Garnet Thomas had been church stalwarts, also did a lot of the interior restoration work. In 2000, the R. Nathaniel Dett Memorial Chapel (renamed for the famed composer and choir director in 1984) was designated a National Historic Site, and, in 2008, its refurbishment was complete.

Wilma has continued her work representing the church and library, conducting tours and going into the classrooms and community groups to give presentations on the region's Black history. She serves on numerous heritage boards and represents the Norval Johnson Heritage Centre on the Central Ontario Network for Black History, the Niagara Black History Association, and at Brock University through the African Students Association. Her work in commemorating new sites and locations pertinent to Black history is ongoing. "It has been a wonderful experience for me and I would not have traded it for the world." Besides, if she hadn't, she adds, "my mom would have reached down from Heaven and slapped me."[50]

Ray Lewis

Ray Lewis was born in Hamilton in 1910 at a time when the impediments to people of colour are almost unimaginable today. His mother, Emma Green, was born in Collingwood, Ontario, and his father, Cornelius, was from Simcoe. His ancestors were Underground Railroad alumni, and his parents worked hard in menial jobs to make ends meet.

Despite the odds, Lewis was able to excel in track and field. He distinguished himself as a sprinter early on, and his accomplishments are now legendary. However, Lewis decided that he was not going to "go along to get along." He spoke out against racism and discrimination, and was prepared to put his sprinting career on the line.

In the run-up to the 1930 British Empire Games, now known as the Commonwealth Games, Ray approached M.M. "Bobby" Robinson, the sports editor for the *Spectator* and the person responsible for reviving the games and bringing them to Hamilton that year. Lewis was a well-known and celebrated sprinter, and, even in those days, athletes were favoured for good jobs in any number of fields. However, when Lewis asked him about a job, Robinson told him there was nothing for him. Then Robinson asked him when he would start training for the Empire Games. According to Ray, he decided then and there: no job, no running.[51] As he explained:

> The first British Empire Games were then coming up here in Hamilton — they were around here — the first — and I didn't even try for the team, and I'm sure I would have made it because two years later, I made the Olympic team and came home with a medal. So I'm sure I would have made that first team. Of course, I was angry, and I just did not run.[52]

Ultimately Lewis got a job as a porter on the railway. However, he kept training. On trips back across the country without passengers, he would prepare for meets by running alongside the track when the train stopped to re-service:

> I had to train wherever I could run, and I trained out on the Prairies when I was on freight trains "deadheading" across the country. And every time the train stopped any length of time, I was out jogging beside the train. I guess those who saw me wondered, "What the hell is he doing?" … People would ask me, "What are you run-ning like that for?"
>
> "Oh, I just like to run." But they didn't know I had a hundred odd medals in my trunk at home.[53]

Ray Lewis was a world-class sprinter whose achievements reached the pinnacle of the athletic world. He won a bronze medal in the 4 x 400-metre relay race at the 1932 Olympic Games in Los Angeles, making him the first Canadian-born Black athlete to win an Olympic medal.[54] He went on to win a silver medal at the 1934 British Empire Games in

London, England. Each time he returned to Canada, however, he went right back to the railway. Working as a porter on the railway was an education in and of itself. Porters had to be very diligent in providing all the services that passengers requested, and they had to be polite at all times. Even so, there was a limit, and Lewis refused to be belittled, such as being called "boy," in spite of the fact that he was a grown man:

> I remember a man said, "Boy, boy...." He called me "Boy" about a dozen times, and I ignored him. Then he said, "Porter ..." and I said, "Oh, were you calling me?" and I smiled right in his face. He took a ginger ale and left, and he was on the train three days and never spoke to me anymore. You had to be careful, but it was an education. It was an education, railroading, you met them all![55]

Lewis worked on the railway during the crucial period when the Brotherhood of Sleeping Car Porters union was being formed. It was a very hush-hush operation, whose activities, had they been compromised, would have meant instant dismissal. Lewis described his involvement in its formation when he signed up members for the new union:

> We just had to be very quiet with the waiters who all happened to be white and you didn't know what they were blabbing.... I was chairman of the welfare committee that the CPR appointed me to and I was doing *my* work, not theirs, talking to people and getting our men lined up with the Brotherhood.[56]

According to Stan Grizzle, one of the union leaders from Toronto, Ray was a strong devotee of the Brotherhood. "He was one of our strong union supporters. He was never an officer, but he was always proud of the fact that he was a member."[57] In 1942, under the brilliant tutelage of the African-American labour leader A. Philip Randolph, the Brotherhood of Sleeping Car Porters was formed, establishing divisions in Montreal, Toronto, Winnipeg, and later Calgary, Edmonton, and Vancouver. On

May 18, 1945, the union signed its first collective agreement with CPR Rail, which obtained an increase in wages and time off, and an overall improvement in working conditions. It marked the first time that a trade union organized by and for Black men signed an agreement with a Canadian company and Ray had been part of it.

Ray was also proud of his rise in the Masonic fraternity. He was a thirty-third-degree Mason and past grand master of the Prince Hall Grand Lodge in Ontario from 1968–70. In 2001, he received the most distinguished honour a Canadian can receive — the Order of Canada. The Ray

Ray Lewis received a Black History Committee Award of Merit for 1999.

Lewis Public School on Hamilton Mountain opened posthumously in 2005. Its primary goal is preparing its students to "Pursue the Dream."[58]

Ray Lewis wrote about his many experiences in two memoirs, *Shadow Running* and *Rapid Ray*, both written with John Cooper.[59] In them he talked about his life growing up in Hamilton, his life on the railroad, about his running career, and the many triumphs and setbacks he faced over the years. His life is an inspiration to anyone who has to overcome obstacles to reach a goal.

Fleurette Osborne

Fleurette Osborne was always interested in politics, art, and social issues from the time she was a young girl in her native Barbados. After attending

St. Mathias Girls School and the St. Michael School, Fleurette graduated with a London matriculation and Cambridge School certificate, and then taught English, Geography, and History at the secondary-school level. She also taught in the elementary school system for a time.

It was a recurring inflammation of her right eye that, in part, brought Fleurette to Canada, which her Canadian doctor cleared up by putting her on a regimen of cortisone. However, she took the opportunity to attend Sir George Williams University (now Concordia University). Osborne obtained a Bachelor of Arts in Sociology, Philosophy, and Literature. While at university, she became involved with a group of women who met with domestic workers from the Caribbean on Thursdays and Sundays, the days these workers usually had time off from their live-in situations. Fleurette's group helped to provide skills training and counselled the women on life in Canada, since all were new immigrants to the country. Thereafter, organizing around women's issues became a central theme of her life.

Fleurette went on to obtain a master's degree in Social Work at McGill University, concentrating on the community organization/community development approach to problem solving. This led to a job in Toronto as a community development officer with the Department of Indian and Northern Affairs, where she helped to train aboriginal people to develop their job and leadership skills. It was about helping people to empower themselves, Fleurette says, which caused a run-in with the director and the end of her position there. A problem in finding an apartment in Toronto because of racist housing practices led to the Ontario Human Rights Commission becoming involved in her case, and ultimately resulted in Fleurette obtaining a job as an investigative officer with the commission, and later director of conciliation. Human rights also took Fleurette to Saskatchewan to help with the development of the Human Rights Commission there.

It was during her time in Saskatchewan that Fleurette became involved with the Congress of Black Women of Canada, attending the Fourth National Congress in Windsor, Ontario, in 1977. In 1981, Ms. Osborne became the first national president of the organization. Under her stewardship, the number of chapters jumped from four (Toronto, Montreal, Winnipeg, and Halifax) to fifteen, and eventually twenty-five across the country. This was the first of numerous times she was elected president of the organization. During her tenure, she criss-crossed the country to get input on the review of the constitution and also did a series of workshops on employment equity, in addition to lobbying the government on issues like employment equity and immigration. Because of her involvement with the Congress, Osborne also joined the National Action Committee on the Status of Women (NAC), first as a member-at-large and later as a board member. At NAC she chaired the Human Rights and Justice Committee and the Visible Minority Committee.

In 1993, Fleurette became a member of the Canadian coordinating committee to prepare for the Fourth World Conference on Women that was to be held in 1995 in Beijing. Through this endeavour, she became involved with the UN Commission on the Status of Women, at which she and other women of colour from London, Africa, South America, and the Caribbean also formed an International Women's Action Committee. They spent long hours preparing briefs that were presented to the UN Assembly around the global concerns of women, one of which was the issue of property rights for African women.

Locally, Fleurette Osborne had moved to Hamilton in 1986 and brought her experience at the national and international levels to good use in that city. She established a Hamilton chapter of the Congress of Black Women of Canada, and worked with Gary Warner on forming CARD, or Committee Against Racism and Discrimination. She was one of the voices that the media would consult when, for example, the government of Ontario introduced new employment equity legislation, and she could always be counted on to lend a hand on other projects and committees, such as the J.C. Holland Awards committee and the Workers Arts and Heritage Centre's consultative group for the "... and still I rise" travelling exhibit and education kit. Unfortunately, according to Fleurette, some of these important initiatives died out. Organizations that relied on government funding went under when their funds were cut. In particular, when Harper's government cut the funding of NAC, the agenda of many women's groups was seriously undermined. "But the issues haven't really changed over the years. What used to happen on the doorstep is now taking place behind the door."[60]

Lincoln Alexander

In his autobiography, *Go To School, You're a Little Black Boy*, the Honourable Lincoln Alexander declared that confronting racism was an enterprise that had engaged him his entire life, both personally and at the organizational level.[61] Perhaps the most important way that Alexander confronted racism was through the sheer force of his excellence and his personality, first as a student, then a corporal in the Royal Canadian Air Force, as a lawyer, member of Parliament for Hamilton West, cabinet minister, and as lieutenant-governor of Ontario. For much of his career, Alexander was a *first*. He was the first Black Canadian to be elected to the House of Commons and the first to be appointed to the vice-regal post of lieutenant-governor of Ontario. The list goes on.

Lincoln Alexander was born in Toronto in 1922, the son of Mae Rose Royale from Jamaica and Lincoln MacCauley Alexander Sr. from St. Vincent and the Grenadines. Alexander stated that his parents took the "default jobs for Blacks at that time." His father, a carpenter by trade, got a job as a porter on the railroad and his mother worked as a domestic. However, his parents provided the necessities of life as well as some great life lessons that stuck with him. It was his mother's constant chiding to "go to school, you're a little black boy," that was one of the most beneficial lessons he learned, and he learned it well. After serving as corporal in the Canadian Air Force, he attended McMaster University and then Osgoode Hall Law School in Toronto, obtaining his degree in 1953 with the help of the Army. They extended his veteran's benefits so that he could attend, with the proviso that he remain in the top quarter of his class.

Lincoln Alexander went into private practice, partly as a result of his negative experience with Stelco, where he was denied a job in sales like his fellow McMaster graduates because he was Black. He formed one of the first, if not *the* first, interracial law firm in the country, called Millar, Alexander, Tokiwa and Isaacs. Dubbed Hamilton's "United Nations" law firm, it included Jack Millar; Paul Yoshiharu Tokiwa, a

Japanese Canadian; and Peter Isaacs, a Native Canadian. They bucked the trend of the typical law firm that hired only well-connected white males. However, by the early 1960s, Lincoln began to develop an interest in running for office. After being tapped by Prime Minister John Diefenbaker to run for the Conservatives, Alexander initially waged a losing battle in Hamilton West in 1965. In 1968, he ran again, edging out the Liberal candidate by just 342 votes. Not only did Lincoln make history when he was elected to the House of Commons in Ottawa as the first Black MP, he was also the only Conservative candidate from an urban riding in all of Ontario.

"Linc," as he affectionately became known, was elected on June 25, 1968. As a Member of Parliament, he was, among other things, an observer to the United Nations and was appointed federal minister of labour in the Joe Clark government in 1979. The next year, Alexander accepted the position of chair of the Ontario Workers Compensation Board, and, in 1985, he was appointed the twenty-fourth lieutenant-governor of Ontario. In this role, Linc was greatly respected for the work he did toward the improvement of Canadian race relations. Throughout this time, he told it as he saw it. For example, there was the time Lieutenant-Governor Alexander prodded business leaders to create a subcommittee on the Toronto Board of Trade to study racial discrimination in the workplace, something that surprised many.[62] In 2002, he brought his personal reputation to bear on the problem of policing and the Black community in the aftermath of the *Toronto Star* study on racial profiling by calling a summit.[63] Three recommendations came out of this initiative: an amendment to the Police Services Act that made the complaint system more accessible for members of the public, the improvement of the training in race relations for new police recruits, and a greater access to provincial funding for communities who want to address these issues. Alexander helped senior politicians and the Toronto Police Services Board understand that this was indeed a problem that needed to be dealt with head on. Member of Provincial Parliament Alvin Curling also brought his knowledge of the issue to the table in this regard. Linc retired from his formal public career in 1991, although he served several stints as chancellor of the University of Guelph.

Courtesy of Hamilton Black History Committee.

The Honourable Lincoln Alexander after receiving a Black History Committee Award of Merit at the 1998 John Holland Awards Dinner.

Lincoln Alexander has been bestowed with many awards and honourary degrees, including a J.C. Holland Award, a Harry Jerome Lifetime Achievement Award, and a Companion of the Order of Canada in 1992. He was named chairperson of the Canadian Race Relations Foundation and honorary chief of the Hamilton-Wentworth Regional Police in 1998. He serves on the boards of the University of Guelph, Massey Hall/Roy Thompson Hall in Toronto, Doctor's Hospital, and the Shaw Festival in Niagara-on-the Lake. He also has three schools named after him: one in Hamilton, another in Ajax, and a secondary school in Mississauga. Lincoln Alexander was also voted the greatest Hamiltonian in a *Hamilton Spectator* contest.

In one profile written some years ago, Alexander named three key mentors in his life. They were his mother for her emphasis on education, his father because he taught him to respect people, and John Diefenbaker for his vision and approach to life and politics. Therefore, in explaining his own life trajectory, he stated that "I could admire other people's qualities and stop there, or I could build my life around action to emulate those qualities.... You can admire anyone you want, but I took it one step further: let me be like them."[64] The Lincoln M. Alexander Parkway (The Linc), after which this book was partially titled, opened in October 1997.[65]

The people discussed in this chapter are part of a long line of champions of equality and social justice, the struggle for which has been an important theme of this book. African Hamiltonians have petitioned and lobbied their government representatives, they have written letters to the editor and spoken out in the media, they have sent deputations to city hall, or delivered addresses in front of it, and they have waged their own solitary battles against racism and discrimination. Some were heavily involved in the church, the fraternal orders, and other important self-help organizations. They organized campaigns, held bazaars, and sold baked goods to raise money for their cause. They gave their all, and some their very lives, to ensure that Canada remained a country that honoured the principle of equality and justice before the law. They wanted respect, and the ability to live their lives in freedom and dignity, whether in 1793 or in 2010. They dreamed that their children would have better lives than they did.

This story of Blacks in Hamilton is also a story of their contributions to the building and development of the city as we know it. An enslaved population existed from the earliest days of settlement at the Head of the Lake. Although they comprised a vital element of the population, African Hamiltonians have not been recognized for the important role they played in the growth and expansion of the early metropolis. Blacks brought their talents as builders, skilled tradesmen and women, entrepreneurs and labourers, and made up an important segment of the labour force. Black women raised the children and did the work in the home, as well as waged work as washerwomen, domestic servants, charwomen, seamstresses, teachers — anything to augment the family income and get the household on a solid footing. Black men also dominated the barbering trade and were the waiters in city hotels.

Books about the history of Hamilton barely mention the African presence, or when it is mentioned, it is in the context of the Underground Railroad, when it was assumed that the city offered these refugees much more than what they gave in return. This was far from the case. When, in the 1930s, Mabel Burkholder was concocting a narrative of fugitive slaves on the Mountain as essentially beggars being given a free handout of plots of land in a community called "Little Africa," the true facts were that Blacks were buying their land at the going rate and creating a niche as market gardeners, carters, and providers of services such as carriages for hire. In contrast to Burkholder's assertion that the community disappeared as residents returned south, unable to make a go of the charity they had received, the vast majority remained in the Hamilton area, many moving downtown, and buying property there after having made a profit from the sale of their land on the Mountain.

By the late 1800s and early 1900s, Blacks in Hamilton, as elsewhere, were essentially pushed down to the bottom rungs of society, allowed to fill only the lowest-skill and lowest-income occupations. The perception was that they were incapable of doing otherwise, or didn't deserve better. Ironically, many found greater opportunity in a segregated America than they did in Canada. It took a war against Hitler, and a broad-based movement of protest, of which African Hamiltonians were a part, to remove some of these irrational barriers to human dignity and equality. It has been a long journey from the days when Julia Berry operated the tollgate at the top of James Street, to the opening of the scenic Lincoln M. Alexander Parkway along Hamilton Mountain from the Highway 403 to Mud Street. The over two-hundred-year journey of Blacks in Hamilton has been a fascinating and revealing ride. There have been many detours and roadblocks along the way. The next two hundred years will undoubtedly expose more bumps in the road. The journey continues.

APPENDIX A

Population Statistics, City of Hamilton, 1791–2001*

Year	Total Population	Black Population
1791	31 families	n.a.
1823	1,000	n.a.
1841	3,446	n.a.
1848	9,889	280
1851	14,112	244[1] (98)
1861	19,096	498[1] (347)
1871	26,880	354[1] (350)
1881	36,661	476[1]
1891	48,959	n.a.
1901	52,634	450
1911	81,969	304
1921	114,151	375
1931	155,547	337
1941	166,337	305

1951	196,246	n.a.
1961	273,991	470
1971	309,180	665
1981	303,405	760[2]
1991	318,499	5,830[3]
2001	490,268	10,460

Sources: *Censuses of Canada, 1665–1871*, Vol. IV (Ottawa: 1876), 164, 169, 254, 266; *Census of the Canadas, 1851–52*, Personal Census, Vol. I (Quebec: John Lovell, 1853), 307; *Census of Canada, 1870–71*, Vol. I (Ottawa: 1873), 258; *Fourth Census of Canada, 1901*, Vol. I: Population (Ottawa: 1902), 325; *Fifth Census of Canada, 1911*, Vol. II (Ottawa: 1913), 372; *Sixth Census of Canada, 1921*, Vol. I: Population (Ottawa: 1924), 489; *Seventh Census of Canada, 1931*, Vol. II: Population by Areas (Ottawa: 1933), 495; *Eighth Census of Canada, 1941*, Vol II: Population by Subdivisions (Ottawa: 1946), 512; *Ninth Census of Canada, 1951*, Vol. I: Population (Ottawa: 1953), 35–33; *1961 Census of Canada*, Vol. I (Part 2), 38–35, 38–36; *1971 Census of Canada*, Vol. I (Part: 3) Population (Ottawa: 1976), 5–7, 5–8; 1981 Census of Canada, Vol. 2, Provincial series (Ottawa: 1984), 2–5; *1991 Census*, Catalogue 93–315: Ethnic Origin, 38, 40; *2001, Profile of Census Divisions and Subdivisions in Ontario*, Vol. I (Ottawa: 2004), 240.*

Appendix B

Occupations of Black Males and Females in Hamilton, 1851–1901

Occupations of Black Males, Hamilton, 1851
Skilled/Semi-skilled Trades

7 shoemakers	1 cooper
5 barbers	1 gunsmith
5 cooks	1 root doctor
4 blacksmiths	1 dyer
3 ministers	1 town crier
2 carpenters	1 saloonkeeper
2 farmers	1 cab driver/owner of house of entertainment
1 wood sawyer	1 bricklayer

Total = 37 (44%)

Unskilled Trades

23 labourers	1 servant
5 waiters	1 chimney sweep

5 whitewashers	1 porter
3 butlers	1 driver
2 carters	1 sailor
1 steward	

Total = 44 (52%)
No Occupation Reported = 4 (5%)
Grand Total = 85 (101%)

1861

Skilled/Semi-skilled Trades

15 barbers	1 cab owner
7 shoemakers	1 grocer
6 carpenters	1 butcher
6 saloon owners/hotel keepers	1 gardener
5 bricklayers	1 fruit merchant
5 cooks	1 speculator
4 stonemasons	1 whitesmith
3 farmers	1 cooper
2 blacksmiths	1 wagon maker
2 ministers	1 tailor
2 plasterers	1 engineer

Total = 68 (43%)

Unskilled Trades

44 labourers
12 waiters
5 whitewashers
5 servants
4 porters
2 sailors/mariners
1 cab driver
1 teamster

Total = 74 (46%)
No Occupation Reported = 18 (11%)
Grand Total = 160 (100%)

1871

Skilled/Semiskilled Trades

15 barbers/hairdressers

15 tobacconists/cigar makers/tobacco strippers

10 plasterers

6 tailors

6 shoemakers

5 masons/stone cutters/bricklayers

3 cooks

2 carpenters

2 ministers

2 tavern keepers/owner of refreshment saloon

2 farmers

1 broker

1 cabman

1 livery stables owner

1 bookkeeper

1 wagon maker

1 wood dealer

1 mail carrier

1 cooper

1 printer

Total = 77 (64%)

Unskilled Trades

24 labourers

4 waiters

4 whitewashers

3 hucksters/peddlers

1 saw sharpener

1 food cutter

1 carter

1 messenger

Total = 39 (32%)
No Occupation Reported = 5 (4%)
Grand Total = 121 (100%)

1881

Skilled/Semi-skilled Trades

21 barbers	2 gardeners
9 tobacconists	1 restaurateur
9 plasterers	1 rope-maker
6 bricklayers/makers	1 hay merchant
4 shoemakers	1 stone cutter
4 ministers	1 pattern cutter
3 blacksmiths	1 clothes cleaner
3 carpenters	1 moulder
3 tailors	1 tinner
2 merchants	1 farmer
2 brokers	1 saloon keeper
2 clerks	1 storekeeper

Total = 81 (51%)

Unskilled Occupations

36 labourers	2 messengers
10 waiters	1 sailor
8 servants	
7 whitewashers	
3 teamsters	

Total=67 (42%)
No Occupation Reported = 10 (6%)
Grand Total = 158 (99%)

1901

Skilled/Semi-skilled Trades

6 barbers	2 clergymen
4 plasterers	1 tailor
3 merchants	1 brush-maker
3 cooks	1 clothier

2 carpenters	1 letter carrier
2 tobacconists	1 brick-maker
2 gardeners	1 book agent
2 cigar makers	1 printer

Total = 33 (32%)

Unskilled Occupations

27 labourers	2 fruit dealers
7 whitewashers	1 chimney sweep
7 tobacco workers	1 messenger
6 waiters	1 hotel employee
5 porters/hotel porters	1 railway porter
3 bellhops	1 butler
2 teamsters	

Total = 64 (63%)
No Occupation Reported = 5 (5%)
Grand Total = 102 (100%)

Occupations of Black Females, Hamilton 1851

Skilled/Semi-skilled Occupations
2 cooks
1 teacher
1 seamstress

Total = 4 (8%)

Unskilled Occupations
4 servants
3 housekeepers
1 stagecoach driver
1 washerwoman

Total = 9 (18%)

No Occupation Reported 36 (73%)
Grand Total = 49 (99%)

1861
Skilled/Semi-skilled Occupations
5 seamstresses
1 cook

Total = 6 (5%)

Unskilled Occupations
8 servants
6 laundresses
2 hucksters

Total = 16 (12%)
No Occupation Reported= 109 (83%)
Grand Total = 131 (100%)

1871
Skilled/Semi-skilled Occupations
6 seamstresses
2 cooks
1 grocer
1 innkeeper

Total = 10 (10%)

Unskilled Occupations
11 servants
6 washerwomen

Total = 17 (16%)
No Occupation Reported= 77 (74%)
Grand Total = 104 (100%)

1881

Skilled/Semi-skilled Occupations
19 seamstress/dressmakers/tailoresses
2 cooks
1 teacher
1 music teacher
1 storekeeper
1 employed by the city to keep 3 "foundlings"

Total = 25 (18%)

Unskilled Occupations
14 servants
13 washerwomen/laundresses
4 workwomen/factory hands
1 charwoman
1 housekeeper

Total = 33 (23%)
No Occupation Reported = 85 (59%)
Grand Total = 143 (100%)

1901

Skilled/Semi-skilled Occupations
11 dressmakers/tailoresses
3 vocalists
2 music teachers
1 teacher
1 pianist
1 cook

Total = 19 (18%)

Unskilled Occupations
13 domestic servants

6 washerwomen
1 tobacco worker
1 peddler
1 charwoman

Total = 22 (21%)
No Occupation Reported = 66 (62%)
Grand Total = 107 (101%)

Source: Manuscript *Censuses of Canada, City of Hamilton*, 1851, 1861, 1871, 1901.

N.B.: The census for 1891 did not ask the person's race or ethnicity and therefore is excluded from this survey. All percentages are rounded to the nearest whole number.

⇌ NOTES ⇌

Introduction

1. Karolyn Smardz Frost, "Communities of Resistance: African Americans and African Canadians in Antebellum Toronto," *Ontario History*, XCIX, No. 1 (Spring 2007): 48. Smardz Frost looked at what she referred to as "communities of resistance" in antebellum Black Toronto that depended upon the development of institutions, most notably the church, as well as the emergence of respected and charismatic leaders. Once these key components were in place, they facilitated the development of: 1. political and overt anti-slavery activism, 2. "practical abolitionism" involving fugitive slave reception and assistance, and 3. anti-racism/racial uplift activity.

2. Reverend W.M. Mitchell, *The Under-Ground Railroad* (1860; reprint, Westport, CN: Negro Universities Press, 1970), 133–34.

3. William Wells Brown, "The Colored People of Canada," in *The Black Abolitionist Papers, II: Canada*, (hereafter *BAP*), C. Peter Ripley, et al., (Chapel Hill, NC and London, UK: University of North Carolina Press, 1986), 463–64.

4. The only other centre that William Wells Brown visited in which he mentioned visual artists was Toronto, where he noted that there were forty-five "artists in water colors." *Ibid.*, 463. None of those listed in the Hamilton census reported occupations as artists, probably indicating that no one could live as an artist, and, as in any era, would have had other forms of employment.

5. Benjamin Drew, ed., *Refugees from Slavery: Autobiographies of Fugitive Slaves in Canada*, (1856; reprint, Mineola, NY: Dover Publications, 2004), 83.

6. Smardz Frost, "Communities of Resistance," 48.
7. Bill Freeman, *Hamilton: A People's History* (Toronto, ON: James Lorimer & Co., 2001), 40, 46–47.
8. Michael B. Katz, *The People of Hamilton, Canada West: Family and Class in a Mid-Nineteenth-Century City* (Cambridge, MA: Harvard University Press, 1975).
9. Robin Winks, *The Blacks in Canada: A History* (Montreal, New Haven, and London, UK: McGill-Queen's University Press and Yale University Press, 1971), 290.
10. *Ibid.*, 292.
11. *Hamilton Evening Times*, October 23 and October 27, 1866.
12. John Cooper, *Shadow Running: Ray Lewis, Canadian Railway Porter & Olympic Athlete* (Toronto: Umbrella Press, 1999).
13. Lincoln Alexander with Herb Shoveller, *"Go To School, You're a Little Black Boy" The Honourable Lincoln M. Alexander: A Memoir* (Toronto: Dundurn Press, 2006), 86.
14. Interview with Wilma Morrison, February 11, 2003.
15. A. Jeffers Toby, ed., *Hamilton: A Black Perspective. A History of Blacks and Their Contribution* (Hamilton, ON: Afro-Canadian Caribbean Association of Hamilton and District, 1991), 2.

Chapter 1— The Journey Begins: Slavery and Freedom at the Head of the Lake

1. James W. St. G. Walker, *The Black Loyalists: The Search for a Promised Land in Nova Scotia and Sierra Leone 1783–1870* (New York: Africana Publishing Company, 1976), 2.
2. Richard Martin died soon after the war ended. See "The Petition of Peter Martin," in *Ontario History*, 26 (1930): 243.
3. Ernest A. Cruikshank, ed., *The Correspondence of Lieutenant Governor John Graves Simcoe, with Allied Documents relating to His Administration of the Government of Upper Canada*, Vol. I (Toronto: Ontario Historical Society, 1923), 304.
4. Winks, 97.
5. *Ibid.*, 1–2; Daniel G. Hill, *The Freedom-Seekers: Blacks in Early Canada* (Agincourt, ON: Book Society of Canada, 1981), 3; Afua Cooper, *The Hanging of Angélique: The Untold Story of Canadian Slavery and the Burning of Old Montréal* (Toronto: HarperCollins, 2006), 70–71.
6. Marcel Trudel, *Dictionnaire des esclaves et de leurs propriétaires au Canada français* (LaSalle, QC: Hurtubise HMH, 1990), xv. Trudel's earlier opus had counted 3,604 slaves, both aboriginal and African. See Marcel Trudel, *L'Esclavage au Canada français: histoire et conditions de l'esclavage* (Quebec:

Les Presses de l'Université Quebec, 1960), 87–88.

7. Ernest J. Lajeunesse, ed., *The Windsor Border Region: Canada's Southernmost Frontier* (Toronto: Champlain Society for the Government of Ontario and Unversity of Toronto Press, 1960), lxvii–lxviii. See also the Tables for 1750, 1773, and 1782, 54–56, 82 and 69–73.

8. Trudel, *Dictionnaire des esclaves*, xix.

9. Michael Power and Nancy Butler, *Slavery and Freedom in Niagara* (Niagara-on-the-Lake, ON: Niagara Historical Society, 1993), 13–15.

10. Library and Archives Canada, B168, 42, cited in William Renwick Riddell, "The Slave in Canada," in *Journal of Negro History*, V, No. 3 (July 1920): 294.

11. Christine Mosser, ed., *York, Upper Canada Minutes of Town Meetings and Lists of Inhabitants, 1797–1823* (Toronto: Metropolitan Toronto Library Board, 1984), 9–37.

12. Winks, 26.

13. "Memoirs of Colonel John Clarke, of Port Dalhousie, C.W.," *Ontario Historical Society Papers & Records*, 7 (1906): 187.

14. Richard D. Merritt, "The Davis Family of Mount Albion: A Loyalist Sketch," *Wentworth Bygones* 7 (1967): 35.

15. Bruce Pettit Davis and Carroll Langstaff Davis, *The Davis Family and the Leather Industry, 1834–1934* (Toronto: Ryerson Press, 1934), Chapter 3; Merritt, "The Davis Family of Mount Albion," 33–37.

16. Davis and Davis, 52.

17. Executive Committee of the British American Institute to the Editor, October 4, 1847, *The National Era*, November 18, 1847; William Thomas was the mill-wright in question. He married Elizabeth Henson, daughter of Josiah Henson. 1861 Census of Canada, Canada West, Kent County, Township of Camden.

18. Agreement of sale between Street & Butler and Adam Crysler regarding sale of slave, Sarah, November 6, 1786, Archives of Ontario (hereafter AO), Crysler Family fonds F4421-2-0-28; Agreement of sale between Adam Vrooman and Adam Crysler regarding sale of slave named Tom, August 25, 1792, AO, Crysler Family fonds, F4421-2-0-39.

19. John Morden Crysler, *Crysler and Other Early Settlers in the Township of Niagara* (Niagara-on-the-Lake, ON: John M. Crysler and the *Niagara Advance*, n.d.), 17–25.

20. From a list of Black privates in the War of 1812, originally taken from Alan Holden's Military History Collection (St. Catharines Historical Society) and reprinted in "Black History in the Niagara Peninsula," a list of documents and information compiled by Maggie Parnall in 1996, 15. I am thankful to Wilma Morrison and the Norval Johnson Heritage Library, Niagara Falls, for providing me with a copy of this document.

21. Census of Canada, 1851, Canada West, Wentworth County, Township of Ancaster, 22.

22. 1861 Census, Canada West, Township of East Flamborough, Ward 1, 6. There is no description of the house or land on which they lived, but it appears they owned a cow valued at $20. The 1864 Assessment Roll for Flamborough East lists James Chrisler (*sic*), Labourer, aged 40, on Concession 1, Lot 2. He was on the 1st Class Militia Roll and owed or had provided two statute days of labour. I checked the Assessment Rolls for Flamborough Township and between 1841–65 and this was the only listing for James Crysler found.

23. Deborah Gray White, *Ar'n't I a Woman? Female Slaves in the Plantation South*, (New York and London, UK: W.W. Norton, 1985), 38–44; Jacqueline Jones, *Labor of Love, Labor of Sorrow* (New York: Vintage Books, 1986), 12.

24. Crysler, 34, Document 32, 126.

25. Power and Butler, 26, 39.

26. Lois C. Evans, *Hamilton: The Story of a City* (Toronto: Ryerson Press, 1970), 17–23; Freeman, 9–10.

27. Nicholas Leblovic, "The Life and History of Richard Beasley, Esquire," in *Wentworth Bygones*, 7 (1967):10, 16fn70; *Dictionary of Hamilton Biography* (hereafter referred to as *DHB*), Vol. 1 (Hamilton: W.L. Griffin, 1981), 18.

28. Nicholas Leblovic, 16fn70. This account was provided by Margaret Beasley, the great-granddaughter of Richard Beasley.

29. Richard Butler, "When Slaves Were Owned in Upper Canada," *Hamilton Spectator*, April 29, 1916, in Butler Scrapbook, *Saturday Musings: A Series of Weekly Articles from the Spectator Dealing with the Early History of the City of Hamilton*, Vol. 1, 28, Hamilton Public Library, Special Collections; *DHB*, Vol. 1, 18.

30. Charles Durand, *Reminiscences of Charles Durand of Toronto, Barrister* (Toronto: Hunter, Rose Co., 1897–99), 10–11.

31. *Ibid.*, 10–11, 443.

32. Charles and James C. Thomas, "Reminiscences of the First Settlers in the County of Brant," in *Ontario Historical Society Papers and Records*, XII (1914): 58–59, 66–67.

33. For example, Daniel Hill claims that Brant owned thirty to forty African slaves. Hill, *Freedom-Seekers*, 13. Other sources, such as the *Dictionary of Canadian Biography Online* (hereafter *DCB Online*) state that the number was about twenty. See "Thayendanegea," at *www.biographi.ca*, referenced October 19, 2008.

34. Patrick Campbell, *Travels in the Interior Inhabited Parts of North America in the Years 1791 and 1792*, edited with an Introduction by H.H. Langton (1793; reprint, Toronto: The Champlain Society, 1937), 167.

35. *Ibid.*, 164.

36. Drew, 135–37; See also Jane Mulkewich, "Sophia Pooley's Story," *www.unityserve.org/dundashistory/articles*, referenced September 21, 2008. Some of the estimated dates in Mulkewich's account of Pooley differ from my own.

37. Drew, 135.

38. *Ibid.*

39. *Ibid.*, 136.

40. Jeromus Johnson to William L. Stone, 1 December, 1837, in William L. Stone, *Life of Joseph Brant — Thayendanegea: Including the Border Wars of the American Revolution, and Sketches of the Indian Campaigns of Generals Harmar, St. Clair, and Wayne, and Other Matters Connected with the Indian Relations of the United States and Great Britain, From the Peace of 1783 to the Indian Peace of 1795*, Vol. 2 (Buffalo, NY: Phinney & Co, 1851), Appendix XVI, xliv.

41. Drew, 137.

42. Sophia Burthen Pooley stated that at twelve years of age she was sold to Samuel Hatt, but, based on the date that Hatt arrived in Upper Canada, this would not have been possible. Mulkewich believes that this date may have been in October 1807, the year Hatt married Margaret Thompson and a month before Brant's death. Mulkewich, "Sophia Pooley's Story"; *DHB*,Vol. I, 100.

43. "The Petition of Richard Hatt and Family," in *Ontario Historical Society Papers & Records*, XXIV (1927): 77–79.

44. *DHB*, Vol. 1, 96–100.

45. Deposition of George Rousseau, made before Mathew Crooks, justice of the peace for Gore District, March 31, 1821, Jean Baptiste Rousseau family fonds, AO, F 493-1, Microfilm MS 7294.

46. When the Earl of Selkirk visited the Hatt establishment in 1804, he noted in his diary that they employed three or four coopers, paying them each wages plus board. It is not likely, therefore, that if the people who removed the oak from Rousseau's property were coopers, that they were also slaves. Thomas Douglas, Earl of Selkirk, *Lord Selkirk's Diary, 1803–1804: A Journal of His Travels in British North America and the Northeastern United States*, Patrick D.T. White, ed. (Toronto: Champlain Society, 1958), 301.

47. Again, Pooley stated that she remained with Hatt for seven years. However, if she in fact remained with him until 1834, when the British Emancipation Proclamation came into effect, freeing slaves across the Empire, then she would have remained with him for at least thirty years, which seems unlikely.

48. Drew, 137.

49. Richard Butler, "When Slaves were Owned in Upper Canada," 29.

50. For more information on the life of James Crooks, see "Crooks, James," *DCB Online, www.biographi.ca*, referenced in October 14, 2008.

51. Power and Butler, 20.

52. A large body of literature exists on slave resistance, beginning in the 1940s, and ranges from discussions of slave revolts and uprisings to the more common, everyday types of resistant behaviour that is for the most part addressed in this chapter. An excellent discussion of everyday resistance is found in such studies as Herbert G. Gutman, *The Black Family in Slavery and Freedom, 1750–1925* (New York: Vintage Books, 1976); Eugene Genovese, *Roll, Jordan, Roll: The World the Slaves Made* (1974; reprint, New York: Vintage Books, 1976); John Blassingame, *The Slave Community: Plantation Life in the Antebellum South* (New York: Oxford University Press, 1972); and George P. Rawick, *From Sundown to Sunup: The Making of the Black Community* (Westport, CT: Greenwood Press, 1972). There are also some excellent studies of female slavery that discuss this topic, for example, Deborah Gray White, *Ar'n't I a Woman? Female Slaves in the Plantation South* (New York and London: W.W. Norton, 1985), 60, and Elizabeth Fox-Genovese, *Within the Plantation Household: Black and White Women of the Old South* (Chapel Hill, NC and London, UK: University of North Carolina Press, 1988). For an example of larger slave uprisings, see the landmark work by Herbert Aptheker, *Negro Slave Revolts* (1943; reprint, New York: International Publishers, 5th ed., 1983).

53. Cooper, *The Hanging of Angélique*.

54. Stuart Family fonds, 1778–1833, AO, F 966, 112–13, cited in Sherry Edmunds, "Slavery in the Kingston, Ontario and Bay of Quinte Region" (master's thesis, University of California, Los Angeles, 1988), 56.

55. Henry Lewis to William Jarvis, 3 May 1798, William Jarvis Papers, S 109 B55, 56–57, Toronto Reference Library Special Collections, Baldwin Room, Archive and Digital Collections.

56. *Ibid.*

57. *Ibid.*

58. Quarter Session Court Records (1790), Queen's Archives, Queen's University, Kingston, cited in Edmunds, 41.

59. "Civil and Provincial Secretary Lower Canada," "S" Series, 1760–1840, Library and Archives Canada, RG 4, A1, Vol. 33, Microfilm C-300Z, 10753, cited in *ibid.*, 52.

60. Russell Papers, cited in Edith G. Firth, *The Town of York, 1793–1815* (Toronto: The Champlain Society for the Government of Ontario, University of Toronto Press, 1962), 243.

61. Cooper, *The Hanging of Angélique*, 96.

62. Gray White, 77.

63. *Ibid.*, 70–76.

64. Indenture of Eli Brackenridge, January 25, 1810, Jean Baptiste Rousseau family fonds, AO, F 493–1, Microfilm MS 7294.

65. "An Act to provide for the Education and Support of Orphan Children," Upper Canada, *Statutes*, 1799, 39, Geo.3, c.3. See Charlotte Neff, "Pauper Apprenticeship in Early Nineteenth Century Ontario," *Journal of Family History*, 21, No. 2 (1996): 144–71.

66. Indenture of Ann Thayer, March 5, 1803, Jean Baptiste Rousseau family fonds, AO, F 493–1, Microfilm MS 7294.

67. *Ibid.*

68. Neff, Fn 20. According to Neff, of the seventeen examples of pauper apprenticeships she found in the nineteenth century, all required that the children be given a basic education, even if only for one year, which was often the length of education received in the early days of provincial education.

69. Indenture of Ann Thayer.

70. Winks, 97–98. The entire act can be found in Power and Butler, Appendix A: 36–39. It is also online on several websites.

71. Janet Carnochan, *History of Niagara*, cited in Power and Butler, 29; Winks, 98.

72. François-Alexandre-Frédéric La Rochefoucault-Liancourt, *Travels Through the United States of North America: The Country of the Iroquois, and Upper Canada, in the Years 1795, 1796, and 1797*, Vol. 1, Herman Neuman, trans. (London, UK: R. Phillips, 1799), 254–55.

73. Power and Butler, 30–31.

74. "The Petition of Peter Martin," in *Ontario History*, 26 (1930): 243; The "Negroe Boy named George" was actually bequeathed to Butler's grandson, John Butler. Will of John Butler, Esquire, Newark, 11 June, 1796, AO, RG 22–155, MS638, Reel 41.

75. "Black History in the Niagara Peninsula," compiled by Maggie Parnall from Alan Holden's Military History Collection, St. Catharines Historical Society, 15.

76. Peter and David Meyler, *Searching for Richard Pierpoint: A Stolen Life* (Toronto: Natural Heritage Books, 1999), 105–06.

Chapter 2 — Routes to Freedom

1. Census of Canada, 1851 (hereafter 1851 Census), Canada West, City of Hamilton, St. Andrew's Ward, 85.

2. *Ibid.*, St. Andrew's Ward, 508.

3. *Ibid.*, St. Lawrence Ward, 9.

4. *Ibid.*, St. Lawrence Ward, 317; "Slave's freedom document awakens search for roots," *Hamilton Spectator*, March 15, 1979; "Family Tree of the Bryant Family," genealogy document. I am grateful to Corinne (Bryant) Chevalier,

great-great-granddaughter of Abraham Bryant, for providing me with these documents. Mrs. Chevalier now has possession of the "freedom papers," which are mounted along with the tin box, on her wall against a cork background in a gold box frame.

5. *Ibid.*, St. George's Ward, 305.

6. *Ibid.*, St. Lawrence Ward, 369.

7. *Ibid.*, St. Patrick's Ward, 258; Slavery in Ohio was abolished in 1802, and it is possible that Joseph and Elizabeth Kere were slaves at some point in their lives, since they were eighty and sixty years of age, respectively, in 1851 and therefore born before slavery ended there in 1802.

8. 1851 Census, Canada West, City of Hamilton, St. George's Ward, 202. Brown's biography can be found in *DHB*, Vol. 1, 27–28.

9. *The Gore Gazette, and Ancaster, Hamilton, Dundas, and Flamborough Advertiser* was published in Ancaster by George Gurnett. The petition was also reprinted as "A Petition of the People of Color at Ancaster," *Journal of Negro History*, 15, No. 1 (1930): 115-116.

10. Upper Canada Land Petitions "B" Bundle 15, pt. 2, 1820–1829, 115f, 115g, Library and Archives Canada, RG1, L3, Vol. 50, accessed on microfilm at the Archives of Ontario, Reel C-1628.

11. *Ibid.*

12. *Ibid.*; Gary E. French, *Men of Colour: An Historical Account of the Black Settlement on Wilberforce Street and in Oro Township, Simcoe County, Ontario, 1819-1949* (Stroud, ON: Kaste Books, 1978), 10–18.

13. Upper Canada Land Petitions "B" Bundle 15, pt. 2, 1820–1829, 115f, 115g, Library and Archives Canada, RG1, L3, Vol. 50, accessed on microfilm at AO, Reel C-1628.

14. *Ibid.*, 115c, 115d.

15. *Ibid.*, 115d.

16. *Ibid.*, 117, 117a, 117b, 117e. The Civil Secretary's correspondence also contains a shortened copy of this petition from which the numbers of people signing from the various localities were listed. Civil Secretary's Correspondence, Upper Canada Sundries, November-December 1828, Library and Archives Canada, RG5, A1, Vol.91, 50676-50678, accessed on microfilm at AO, Reel C-6866, 50676-50678. This document indicated many more people interested in settling in such a community than did the one in the Upper Canada Land Petitions already referenced, although there are more names written out in the latter document than in the former. Either the land petition document did not represent everyone who was willing to relocate or the petition in the Civil Secretary's correspondence overstated the numbers.

17. *Ibid.*, 117c.

18. Upper Canada Land Petitions "J" Bundle 16, 1829–1931, 5, 5a, 5c, 5d, 5f, Library and Archives Canada, RG1, L3, Vol. 259, accessed on microfilm at AO, Reel C-2111

19. Fred Landon, "The History of the Wilberforce Refugee Colony in Middlesex County," in *Ontario's African-Canadian Heritage: Collected Writing by Fred Landon, 1918–1967*, Karolyn Smardz Frost, Bryan Walls, Hilary Bates Neary, and Frederick H. Armstrong, eds. (Toronto: Dundurn Press, 2009), 76.

20. *Ibid.*, 75–77; Drew, 171–72; French, 23–29; Marilyn Bailey, "From Cincinnati, Ohio to Wilberforce, Canada: A Note on Antebellum Colonization," *Journal of Negro History*, 58, No. 4 (October 1973): 427–32; See also William and Jane Pease, *Black Utopia: Negro Communal Experiments in America* (Madison, WI: State Historical Society of Wisconsin, 1963), Chapter 3 and Nikki M. Taylor, *Frontiers of Freedom: Cincinnati's Black Community, 1802–1868* (Athens, OH: Ohio University Press, 2005), Chapter 3.

21. W.V. Uttley, "Woolwich Township — Its Early Settlement," *Waterloo Historical Society* (Annual Volume), 21 (1933): 10–11, 13; *www.woolwich.ca/en/tourism/EarlyHistory.asp* (accessed September 7, 2009); "James Crooks," *DCB Online, www. biographi.ca* (accessed January 19, 2009); Linda Brown-Kubisch, *The Queen's Bush Settlement: Black Pioneers, 1839–1865* (Toronto: Natural Heritage Books, 2004), 27.

22. Assessment Rolls, District of Gore, Township of Woolwich, 1831.

23. Benjamin Lundy, "The Diary of Benjamin Lundy Written During His Journey Through Upper Canada, January 1832," in *Ontario Historical Society Papers and Records* XIX (1922): 116, 122.

24. Joseph Mallot, Solomon Connaway, Daniel Banks, and Griffith Hughes were not on the December 1828 list of petitioners. Assessment Rolls, District of Gore, Township of Woolwich, 1832; Upper Canada Land Petitions "B" Bundle 15, Part 2, 117a, 117b, 117e, 1820–1829, Library and Archives Canada, RG1, L3, Vol. 50, accessed at AO, microfilm reel C-1628.

25. Assessment Rolls, District of Gore, Township of Woolwich, 1833; 1851 Census, Canada West, City of Hamilton, St. George's Ward, 202.

26. Assessment Rolls, District of Gore, Township of Woolwich, 1837.

27. *Ibid.*, 1840.

28. Brown-Kubisch, 29–31.

29. Brown-Kubisch, 31, believed that the Connaways must have moved to the Queen's Bush because Solomon Connaway signed the 1843 petition of the inhabitants of the Queen's Bush. However, evidence in Chapters 3 and 4 reveals that the family was actually living in the Hamilton area.

30. Brown, "Circular Address to the Free People of Color," *Liberator*, October 27, 1832; Waterloo County Land Registry Records, Abstract Index Books,

ca. 1800–1958, Woolwich Township, Vol. 1-2, AO, reel GSU 169995. Further attempts to find out what might have happened to the settlement by searching the Commissioner of Crown Land correspondence or the Court of Quarter Sessions of the Peace for the district were unsuccessful.

31. Austin Steward, *Twenty-Two Years a Slave, and Forty Years a Freeman: Embracing a Correspondence of Several Years, While President of Wilberforce Colony, London, Canada West* (1857; reprint, New York: Negro Universities, 1968); Nikki Taylor, in *Frontiers of Freedom* (77–78), provides Lewis's side of the story, which was that he was not fundraising for Steward's group anymore, but rather for a newer organization that was dissatisfied with the latter's leadership. Therefore, he was no longer answerable to them.

32. Drew, 93.

33. *Ibid.*, 83.

34. *Ibid.*, 83–84.

35. 1851 Census, Canada West, City of Hamilton, St. Andrew's Ward, 459.

36. Drew, 85.

37. William Wells Brown, "The Colored People of Canada," 463.

38. *Ibid.*, 461, 463–64.

39. Drew, 89.

40. *Ibid.*, 90.

41. *Ibid.*

42. *Ibid.*

43. Pease had likely already gone into business for himself by 1861, as he invested $200 in a barbershop at that time. By 1875, however, he was clearly listed at a different address than Bland in the city directory, located at 2 Hughson Street. *1858 City of Hamilton Directory Containing a Full and Complete List of Householders, A Classified List of Trades and Professions, Together with Statistical and Other Information, Local and Provincial, and Advertisements of the Principal Business Houses* (Hamilton, ON: William A. Shepard, 1858), 231; *McAlpine's Hamilton City and County of Wentworth Directory, 1875, Containing an Alphabetical Directory of Hamilton, Dundas, Waterdown, Ancaster, Lynden, Copetown, East and West Flamborough, Bullock's Corners, Aldershot and Greensville, with a Street & Business Directory of Hamilton City* (Montreal, Toronto, Hamilton, London, Ottawa, Halifax, N.S. and St. John, N.B.: McAlpine, Everet & Co.,1875), 201; 1861 Census of Canada, Canada West, City of Hamilton, St. Lawrence Ward, District 1, 62; 1871 Census of Canada, Province of Ontario, City of Hamilton, St. Lawrence Ward, Div. 1, 75; 1881 Census of Canada, City of Hamilton, Ward 6, Div. 1, 71; 1901 Census of Canada, Province of Ontario, Wentworth County, City of Hamilton, Ward 6, Subdivision 1, 2; Probate of the Will of John Henry

Bland, AO, RG 22-204, Vol. P., G.S. 2, Reel 229 #179.

44. Drew, 91.

45. William Still, *Underground Rail Road Records, Revised Edition, with a Life of the Author, Narrating the Hardships, Hairbreadth Escapes and Death Struggles of the Slaves in Their Efforts for Freedom, Together with Sketches of Some of the Eminent Friends of Freedom, and Most Liberal Aiders and Advisers of the Road* (Philadelphia, PA: William Still, 1883), 512–14. On the constraints of flight for slave women, see Gray White, 70–74; Adrienne Shadd, "The Lord Seemed to Say 'Go': Women and the Underground Railroad Movement," in *"We're Rooted Here and They Can't Pull Us Up": Essays in African Canadian Women's History*, Peggy Bristow, Dionne Brand, Linda Carty, Afua Cooper, Sylvia Hamilton, and Adrienne Shadd, eds. (Toronto: University of Toronto Press, 1994), 42–48.

46. Still, 292.

47. *Ibid.*, 293.

48. *Ibid.*, 271.

49. The 1875 city directory shows Reverend Robert Jones living at 103 James Street North, having left the Reddick household. *McAlpine's Hamilton City Directory 1875,* 144; 1861 Census, City of Hamilton, St. Andrew's Ward, 398; 1871 Census, City of Hamilton, St. Andrew's Ward, Div. 1, 22; 1881 Census of Canada, City of Hamilton, Ward 2, Div. 2, 10; *1858 City of Hamilton Directory*, 199.

50. The following life story of Henry Criel can be found in "Escaped from Slavery: Interesting Incident in the Life History of a Man Who Still Resides in Hamilton," *Hamilton Herald*, August 23, 1902, in Tinsley Scrapbook, Vol. 8, 145–47, Hamilton Public Library, Special Collections.

51. Wentworth County Land Registry Office Records (hereafter WCLRO), Lot 9, Concession 4, Deed No's 292 and 1724, for the years 1867 and 1874 respectively.

52. "Escaped from Slavery," Tinsley Scrapbook, Vol. 8; The 1851 and 1861 Censuses listed Criel as a sailor and that he was living with Irish-born Jane Criel. By 1871 he was a widower in St. Mary's Ward, Div. 1, 52, and working as a waiter. Delila Scott, a thirty-two-year-old African-Canadian servant born in Ontario, was also living in the household. She was described as deaf and dumb.

53. 1881 Census, Province of Ontario, City of Hamilton, Ward 5, Div. 2, 73.

54. "Henry Criel Dead: Well-Known Citizen Passes Peacefully to the Great Beyond," *Hamilton Spectator*, October 17, 1904.

55. Wentworth County Estate Files, AO, RG 22-205, Grant No. 5981, November 2, 1904, MS 887, Reel 1917.

Chapter 3 — On Course: Settling in by the Bay

1. Lundy, 119–20.
2. *Ibid.*, 120–21.
3. Jermain Loguen, *The Rev. J.W. Loguen, as a Slave and as a Freeman: A Narrative of Real Life* (1859; reprint, New York: Negro Universities Press, 1968), 339–41.
4. *Ibid.*, 341–43; See also the Circle Association's African-American History of Western New York State, 1831–1865, *www.math.buffalo.edu/~sww/0history/loguen.jermain.wesley.html*, (accessed January 20, 2009).
5. The account in *Ancaster's Heritage* states that Griffin was born in Delaware. However, the 1861 census names Virginia as his place of birth. This and subsequent information on Enerals Griffin comes from the files of the Fieldcote Memorial Park and Museum/Griffin House. I am indebted to Lois Corey, site supervisor, and Anne Jarvis, historical interpreter at Griffin House for getting this information to me in short order.
6. T. Roy Woodhouse, "History of Ancaster Village," in *Ancaster's Heritage: A History of Ancaster Township*, compiled by J. McCormack (Ancaster, ON: Ancaster Township Historical Society, 1973), 135.
7. *Ibid.*
8. Reverend Hiram Wilson to Brother Wright, April 27, 1837, reprinted in *The Emancipator*, June 15, 1837.
9. Enerals Griffin files, Fieldcote Memorial Park and Museum/Griffin House; *www.findlaymarket.org/gen_james_findlay.htm* (accessed February 23, 2010); Melissa Zielke, "Go Down Moses: The Griffin House and the Continuing Struggle to Preserve, Interpret and Exhibit Black History," *Material History Review/Revue d'histoire de la culture matérielle*, 55 (Spring 2002): 41–52.
10. City Council minutes, December 13, 1834, RG1, January 8, 1833–July 11, 1849, 46, Hamilton Public Library Special Collections.
11. *Ibid.*, June 33 (*sic*), 1835, 63.
12. Dorothy S. Shreve, *The AfriCanadian Church: A Stabilizer* (Jordan Station, ON: Dorothy Shadd Shreve, 1983), 79; Hamilton City Council Minutes, October 22, 1838, 141.
13. Steward, 301.
14. *Ibid.*, 302–03.
15. Smardz Frost, "Communities of Resistance," 48. See Smardz Frost's discussion of the development of "communities of resistance" in antebellum Black Toronto. She explains that the development of a mature, well-developed community in Toronto depended upon the establishment of an institutional infrastructure and a cadre of charismatic leaders which, once in place, facilitated

political and anti-slavery activism, "practical abolitionism" involving fugitive slave reception and assistance, and anti-racism/racial uplift activity.

16. Colonial Office Papers (hereafter C.O.), Library and Archives Canada MG11, C.O. 42 Series, Vol. 439, August 14, 1837, 181–182, accessed at AO, Microfilm Reel B342.

17. *Ibid.*, J. Mackenzie Leask, "Jesse Happy, A Fugitive Slave from Kentucky," in *Ontario History*, 54, No. 2 (June 1962): 87.

18. David Murray, *Colonial Justice: Justice, Morality, and Crime in the Niagara District, 1791–1849*, Osgoode Society for Canadian Legal History (Toronto: University of Toronto Press, 2002), 197–216; Karolyn Smardz Frost, *I've Got a Home in Glory Land: A Lost Tale of the Underground Railroad* (Toronto: Thomas Allen, 2007), 243.

19. Smardz Frost, *Home in Glory Land*, 222–25.

20. C.O. 42 Series, Vol. 439, Petition of the persons of colour resident of the Town and Township of Niagara, September 2, 1837, 195–96.

21. Janet Carnochan, "A Slave Rescue in Niagara Sixty Years Ago," Niagara Historical Society, Paper No. 2 (1897), 8–18.

22. *Ibid.*, 11–15. See also Anna Jameson, *Winter Studies and Summer Rambles in Canada* (1838; reprint, Toronto: McClelland & Stewart, 1923), 98–99; Shadd, "The Lord Seemed to say 'Go,'" 59–61. Jameson did not mention stone-throwing, but rather emphasized that the women had persuaded their "husbands, brothers, and lovers, to use no arms, to do no illegal violence, but to lose their lives rather than see their comrade taken by force across the lines."

23. C.O. 42 Series, Vol. 439, September 7, 1837, 182–83.

24. *Ibid.*, 189.

25. C.O. 42 Series, Vol. 439, n.d., 184–85, AO Microfilm Reel B342; Hamilton City Council Minutes, October 22, 1838, 141.

26. *Ibid.*

27. *BAP*, Vol. II, 231–32, footnote 4.

28. C.O. 42 Series, Vol. 439, n.d., 185–86, AO Microfilm Reel B342.

29. *Ibid.*, 187–88.

30. *Ibid.*, 190–92.

31. Sir Francis Bond Head to Lord Glenelg, October 8 1837, *ibid.*, 170–74; Leask, 91.

32. "Fight for Freedom," *Hamilton Spectator*, August 17, 1963.

33. *Ibid.*

34. Leask, 92.

35. Roman J. Zorn, "Criminal Extradition Menaces the Canadian Haven for Fugitive Slaves, 1841–1861," *Canadian Historical Review* 38 (December 1957): 284–94; Smardz Frost, *Home in Glory Land*, 246–50.

36. Smardz Frost, *Home in Glory Land*, 247–48.

37. *National Anti-Slavery Standard*, October 20, 1842.

38. Sir George Arthur to Airey, November 21, 1838, in Charles Sanderson, ed., *The Arthur Papers Being the Canadian Papers Mainly Confidential, Private, and Demi-Official of Sir George Arthur, K.C.H. Last Lieutenant-Governor of Upper Canada, Volume I: 1822–1838*, (Toronto: Toronto Public Libraries and University of Toronto Press, 1957), 384. This statement was made almost a year after the outbreak of hostilities, but reflected the sentiment of the colonial authorities in employing Native and Black soldiers to assist in quelling the rebellion during all phases of the conflict.

39. The letter was reprinted in the *Quarterly Anti-Slavery Magazine* 2, No. 4 (July 1837): 350–51, and referenced in Landon, "Social Conditions Among the Negroes in Upper Canada," 183–84.

40. George Coventry, "A Contemporary Account of the Rebellion in Upper Canada, 1837," in *Ontario Historical Society Papers & Records*, XVII (1927): 148.

41. Loguen, 344.

42. Sir Francis Bond Head, *A Narrative* (1839; reprint, Toronto: McClelland & Stewart, 1969), 172–73.

43. Ernest Green, "Upper Canada's Black Defenders," *Ontario Historical Society Papers and Records*, XXVII (1931): 379. The discussion of the Coloured Corps raised during the Rebellion and their activities appears on pages 370–83.

44. Paola Brown, *An Address Intended to be Delivered in the City Hall, Hamilton, February 7, 1851, on the Subject of Slavery* (Hamilton, ON: Printed for the Author, 1851), 28.

45. *Ibid.*, 62.

46. Steward, 300.

47. Militia Papers, U.C. M.D., 45, cited in Green, 379.

48. *Ibid.*

49. French, 64–65; Gary French notes that a William Allen married Sarah Mandigo at Niagara. She was likely the widow or relative of William Mandgo or Madijo who served in the Coloured Corps during the War of 1812. See also Upper Canada Land Petitions "A" Bundle 13, 1819–1823, Library and Archives Canada, RG1, L1, Vol. 8, May 21, 1821, accessed at AO. Reel C-1611; Crown Lands Department, Military Settlement: Soldiers and Emigrants, 1816–1828, Library and Archives Canada, RG 1-158-0-3, 39, accessed at AO, MS 693, Reel 120; Crown Land Department Schedule of Locations, 1816–1828, Library and Archives Canada, RG-174-0-5, accessed at AO, MS 693 Reel 158.

50. French, 64–65.
51. Wayne Edward Kelly, "Race and Segregation in the Upper Canada Militia," *Journal of the Society for Army Historical Research* 78, No. 316 (Winter 2000): 266–67, 273.
52. Loguen, 345.
53. Josiah Henson, *An Autobiography of the Rev. Josiah Henson ("Uncle Tom") From 1789 to 1883* (London, UK: Christian Age Offices, 1882), 176.
54. Quoted from the *St. Catharines Journal* of February 27, 1838, and cited in Green, 380.
55. Sophia MacNab, *The Diary of Sophia MacNab*, edited by Charles Ambrose Carter and Thomas Melville Bailey (Hamilton, ON: W.L. Griffin, 1968), 54.
56. Green, 383–85.
57. Quoted in *ibid.*, 384.
58. *Ibid.*, 385–86.
59. Kelly, 277; quote is from "The Jubilee History of Thorold," in Green, 388.
60. Still, 272.
61. French, 64–65; Executive Council Minute Books for Land Matters, 1787–1867, RG 1, L1, Land Book U, Upper Canada, 25 June 1840–6 February 1841, Vol. 39, 469, accessed at AO, Reel C-107 and Land Book A, 15 March 1841–22 December 1842, Vol. 40, 22, AO. Reel C-107.
62. Reverend Amsted Brown to Sir Charles Metcalfe, October 4, 1843, Ontario Department of Education, Incoming Correspondence, AO RG2–12, Container 2.
63. Hamilton Assessment Rolls, 1848–9, AO D 205, Microfilm GS 1567; 1851 Census, Canada West, City of Hamilton, St. Andrew's Ward, 85.
64. Shreve, 43–44.
65. Donald G. Simpson, *Under the North Star: Black Communities in Upper Canada* (Trenton, NJ: Africa World Press, 2005), 198. This is a publication of the Harriet Tubman Resource Centre on the African Diaspora, York University, Toronto.
66. Shreve, 62–63.
67. Petition of the Coloured People of Hamilton, October 15, 1843, Ontario Department of Education, Incoming Correspondence, AO, RG2–12, Container 2. This petition can also be found in *BAP*, Vol. II, 97–98.)
68. *BAP*, Vol. II, 98fn2.
69. Reverend Robert Murray to George S. Tiffany, October 19, 1843, Ontario Department of Education, Incoming Correspondence, AO, RG2-12, Container 2.
70. *Ibid.*, George S. Tiffany to Reverend Robert Murray, November 9, 1843.
71. Mitchell, 133.

72. Freeman, 50.

73. William P. Newman, "The Colored People in Canada," *Oberlin Evangelist*, August 30, 1848. This survey can also be found in Brown-Kubisch, 112–13; See also William Wells Brown, "The Colored People of Canada," in *BAP*, Vol. II, 463.

74. Winks, 368–69.

75. Paola Brown, *Address*, 24–25. In *The Blacks in Canada*, Robin Winks (p. 376) states, incorrectly, that an unofficial separate school remained open in Hamilton until 1895. However, he based this statement on an article in the *Hamilton Spectator* of November 15, 1947, which referred to the Mission Church and School, located on the Mountain on Concession just west of 23rd Street on the south side. This school was never a separate school or unofficial separate school, but rather one which was open to all races and walks of life. The Black population living on the Mountain made full use of this school, attending both during the day and at night.

76. 1851 Census, Canada West, City of Hamilton, St. George's Ward, 210. The Brices are not listed in the 1861 Census for Hamilton.

77. *Voice of the Fugitive*, December 2, 1852.

78. Drew, 82.

79. Samuel Gridley Howe, *Report to the Freedmen's Inquiry Commission 1864: The Refugees from Slavery in Canada West* (1864; reprint, New York: Arno Press and the New York Times, 1969), 47.

80. "A.M.E. Conference for the Canada District," *Voice of the Fugitive*, August 12, 1852; August 26, 1852 .

81. Drew, 85.

Chapter 4 — Gathering Speed: Anatomy of a Community

1. "Colored Immigration to Canada," *Voice of the Fugitive*, May 20, 1852. See also Samuel Ringgold Ward to Henry Bibb, *ibid.*, March 11, 1852 and June 17,1852.

2. *Ibid.*, "Great Anti-Slavery Meeting in Toronto," *Voice of the Fugitive*, April 9, 1851.

3. *Ibid.*, William Still to Henry Bibb, December 15, 1851; January 1, 1852; January 15, 1852.

4. It should be noted that not all escaped slaves were assisted by the "organized" portion of the Underground Railroad. Some escaped unassisted by travelling known routes and reaching freedom primarily on their own steam. See, for example, James W. St. G. Walker, *A History of Blacks in Canada* (Hull, QC: Minister of Supply and Services, 1980), 48–50; and Larry Gara, *The Liberty Line: The Legend of the Underground Railroad* (Lexington, KT:

University of Kentucky Press, 1967), particularly Chapter 3. William Still's
Underground Rail Road Records (Philadelphia, PA: William Still, 1883)
and Bryan Prince's *A Shadow on the Household: One Enslaved Family's
Incredible Struggle for Freedom* (Toronto: McClelland & Stewart, 2009) provide examples of the organized part of the Underground Railroad and the
myriad methods used to help the enslaved reach freedom. These works also
clearly demonstrate that the activists planned their charges' passage right
into Canada.

5. Fred Landon, "The Negro Migration to Canada After the Passing of the
Fugitive Slave Act," in *Ontario's African-Canadian Heritage: Collected
Writings by Fred Landon, 1918–1967*, Smardz Frost et al, eds., 241.

6. "Proceedings of the North American Convention," in *BAP, Vol. II*, 149–69.
Russel (*sic*) and Burns's names are on page 150. The desire of some to have
the convention in Hamilton was mentioned by Hiram Wilson in Hiram
Wilson to Henry Bibb, July 8, 1851, *Voice of the Fugitive*, July 16, 1851.

7. "Call for the Convention," *Voice of the Fugitive*, August 13, 1851.

8. 1851 Census, Canada West, City of Hamilton; "AME Conference for the
Canada District," *Voice of the Fugitive*, August 26, 1852.

9. Burns can be found in the 1861 Census, St. Patrick's Ward, District 1, 390;
Richard Butler, "When Slaves Were Owned in Upper Canada," *Hamilton
Spectator*, April 29, 1916, in Butler Scrapbook, Vol. 1, 29, Hamilton Public
Library, Special Collections.

10. "Proceedings of the North American Convention," *BAP*, Vol. II. The quoted
resolutions can be found on pages 152 and 154.

11. Afua Cooper, "Political Organizing: The North American Convention of
Colored People, September 1851," Unpublished Report for Parks Canada,
2001, 3–4.

12. *Ibid.*, 4–5.

13. *The Second Annual Report Presented to the Anti-Slavery Society of Canada*
(Toronto: Brown's Printing, 1853), 8. Details about the Hamilton branch,
including who was involved and how long it was active, are not known.

14. *BAP*, Vol. II, 21.

15. *Voice of the Fugitive,* July 15, 29, 1852; Mary Ann Shadd to George Whipple,
July 21, 1852, American Missionary Association (AMA) Archives, Amistad
Research Center, New Orleans (on microfilm at AO). Proceedings of the
Public Meeting held at Windsor, Canada West, July 20, 1852, AMA. See
also Jane Rhodes, *Mary Ann Shadd Cary: The Black Press and Protest in
the Nineteenth Century* (Bloomington, IN: Indiana University Press, 1998),
53–59, 67–68, 70–74.

16. *Provincial Freeman*, April 15; April 22, 1854.

17. *Ibid.*, August 19, 1854. The Provincial Union was set up as an antidote to the Anti-Slavery Society of Canada, which failed to properly support the *Freeman* in Mary Ann Shadd's view. See Rhodes, 94.

18. City Council Minutes, July 31, 1837, 119, RG 1, January 8, 1833–July 11, 1849, Hamilton Public Library, Special Collections.

19. "Local and Miscellaneous Items — Emancipation," *Daily Spectator and Journal of Commerce*, August 3, 1853.

20. "Celebration a Disgraceful Scene," *Hamilton Herald*, August 4, 1853.

21. *Provincial Freeman*, August 5, 1854.

22. *Ibid.*, "Emancipation," August 22, 1857.

23. "Celebrations of the Anniversary of Emancipation," *The Daily Spectator and Journal of Commerce*, August 2, 1859. This was the only time the event took place at Claremont Park upon the invitation of Sir Isaac Buchanan. I am indebted to Tracy Warren for providing me with her paper entitled "Imagining, Remembering, Forgetting: Emancipation Day Celebrations in Hamilton-Niagara 1834–2008," unpublished paper submitted to Dr. H. V. Nelles, History Department, McMaster University, 2008.

24. 1851 Census, Canada West, City of Hamilton. These statistics represent the author's examination of the census. The location of the churches was found in *1856 The City of Hamilton Directory, Containing a Full and Complete List of Householders, Together with Statistical and Other Information and Advertisements of the Principal Business Houses* (Hamilton: William A. Shepard, 1856), 9; *1858 City of Hamilton Directory*, 23.

25. 1861 Census, Canada West, City of Hamilton and Barton Township, Wentworth County. Again, these statistics represent the author's count of the Black population of that year. The city of Hamilton count is slightly higher than Michael Wayne's number of 476 in "The Black Population of Canada West on the Eve of the American Civil War: A Reassessment Based on the Manuscript Census of 1861," *Social History*, XXVIII, No. 56 (November 1995), Appendix A: 485. The number for Barton Township is the same as Wayne's count.

26. Samuel Ringgold Ward to Henry Bibb, January 21, 1852, in *Voice of the Fugitive*, February 12, 1852.

27. Drew, 83.

28. 1851 Census, Canada West, City of Hamilton, St. George's Ward, 122.

29. 1851 Census, Canada West, City of Hamilton.

30. 1861 Census, Canada West, City of Hamilton, St. Andrew's Ward, 366; 1856 City of Hamilton Directory, 145; 1858 City of Hamilton Directory, 235.

31. 1861 Census, Canada West, City of Hamilton, St. Patrick's Ward, 292.

32. *Ibid.*, St. Andrew's Ward, 155; *1858 City of Hamilton Directory*, 195.

33. 1861 Census, Canada West, City of Hamilton; Herald Scrapbook, Vol. G1, Part 2, 4, Hamilton Public Library, Special Collections.

34. Douglas Bristol Jr., "Outposts to Enclaves: A Social History of Black Barbers from 1750 to 1915," *Enterprise & Society* 5, No. 4 (2004): 595.

35. Douglas Bristol, Jr., "Outposts to Enclaves,": 594–606, and "Regional Identity: Black Barbers and the African American Tradition of Entrepreneurialism," *South Quarterly*, 43 (Winter 2006): 74–96.

36. 1861 Census, Canada West, City of Hamilton. These statistics represent the author's examination of the census and documentation of occupations.

37. There were forty-nine women eighteen years of age or over who were counted as either having a job or having no listing. There was one female stagecoach driver, whom the author also placed in the labouring or working class.

38. Freeman, 56–62.

39. Drew, 93; *1856 City of Hamilton Directory*, 165.

40. Michael B. Katz, *The People of Hamilton, Canada West,* 68. Katz's analysis of Black employment in Hamilton stated that the proportion of Blacks in semi-skilled and unskilled employment declined from 47 to 38 percent between 1851–61, and those in the skilled trades rose from 37 to 49 percent. In addition, Katz stated, the proportion in commerce and the professions increased from 8 to 14 percent (68). This means that those engaged in the skilled trades and in businesses or professions represented 45 percent in 1851 and 63 percent in 1861, even greater percentages than in this study. However, Katz looked at heads of households as opposed to all adults with an occupation, which helps to explain the discrepancy.

41. "Number of Coloured Persons Resident in Toronto, 25 July 1840," cited in Dan Hill, "The Blacks in Toronto," in *Gathering Place: Peoples and Neighbourhoods of Toronto, 1834–1945* (Toronto: Multicultural History Society of Ontario, 1985), 82.

42. Jonathan W. Walton, "Blacks in Buxton and Chatham, Ontario, 1830–1890: Did the 49th Parallel Make a Difference?" (Ph.D. diss., Princeton University, 1979).

43. Walton, 62, 125n; *Censuses of Canada, 1665 to 1871*, Vol. IV, (Ottawa: 1876), 164, 169, 254, 266.

44. Wayne, Appendix A. Chatham's population in 1861 was 1,252, compared with Toronto (987), Colchester (937), St. Catharines (609), Windsor (533), Hamilton (476), and Amherstburg (373). The only place that had a higher population than Chatham was Raleigh Township, which included the rural Black settlement of Buxton (1,310). On Chatham's prominence, see Adrienne Shadd, "Celebrating the Legacy: Chatham's Black Heritage," unpublished paper produced for the revised exhibit *Black Mecca* at the Heritage

Room, W.I.S.H. Centre, Chatham, 2004; also Gwendolyn and John W. Robinson, *Seek the Truth: A Story of Chatham's Black Community*, Chatham, ON: (self-published),1989.

45. Walton, 62, Table 3.1, 263.
46. *Ibid.*, Table 4.4, 289.
47. *Ibid.*, 63, and Table 3.3, 265; Table 4.6, 291.
48. *Ibid.*, 64–65. Walton cited studies for the year 1850 showing that in New York the percentage of Black workers in skilled/semi-skilled jobs was 18, in Washington 18 percent, in Pittsburgh 17 percent, and in Cincinnati 20 percent. In contrast, Detroit's percentage in skilled/semi-skilled percentage was 52 percent. Nikki Taylor, in *Frontiers of Freedom* (Appendix A, 206) indicated that the skilled/semi-skilled ratio in Cincinnati was much higher than was reported by the earlier study, with over 34 percent of Black men in skilled jobs, compared with 21 percent in unskilled jobs in 1850.
49. John W. Blassingame, ed., *Slave Testimony: Two Centuries of Letters, Speeches, Interviews, and Autobiographies* (Baton Rouge, LA: Louisiana State University Press), 370.
50. *Ibid.*, 429; 1851 Census, Canada West, City of Hamilton, St. Mary's Ward, 174; 1861 Census, Canada West, City of Hamilton, St. Andrew's Ward, 100.
51. Blassingame, 430.
52. *Ibid.*
53. *1856 City of Hamilton Directory*, 114; *1858 City of Hamilton Directory*, 193.
54. 1861 Census of Canada West, Barton Township, County of Wentworth, District 1, 6. This was in Lot 10, Concession 2, Barton Township; Martha McCray's relationship to Rosetta was found in the 1850 United States Federal Census, State of Virginia, City of Petersburg on *www.ancestry.com* (accessed March 3, 2010).
55. Samuel Gridley Howe published an account of the Black people living in Canada West, and included Hill and his favourable view of Hill's establishment in his book. Howe, 73–75.
56. Blassingame, 428.
57. *Ibid.*, 428–29.
58. 1861 Census, Canada West, Barton Township, District 1, 43; Still, 200–03. John Hill had a brother, James, who also escaped from slavery. Still did not mention that James Hill came to Canada. However, a James Hill of African descent was living in Barton Township in 1871 with a wife, Marva, and daughter Lucinda E. It is possible that Hill's brother James also lived in the Hamilton area for a time. According to Still, James Hill eventually relocated to Boston. 1871 Census, Canada West, Barton Township, Div. 1, 34.

59. Still, 191–203; *BAP*, Vol. II, 347fn3.
60. This autobiography of Dr. Nathan Mossell is located at the University of Pennsylvania Archives and can be found online at *www.archives.upenn.edu/people/1800s/mossell_nathan_f.html* (accessed February 3, 2009).
61. *Ibid.*, 1–2.
62. *Ibid.*, 3.
63. *Ibid.*, 7; 1856 *City of Hamilton Directory*, 136.
64. "An English Opinion of the 'Ambitious City,'" *Hamilton Spectator*, October 20, 1860, 2.
65. "Autobiography of Dr. Nathan Mossell," 4.
66. *Ibid.*, 3–4.
67. *Ibid.*, 4.
68. Philip Girard, "British Justice, English Law, and Canadian Legal Culture," in Phillip Buckner, ed., *Canada and the British Empire* (Oxford, UK, New York, NY: Oxford University Press, 2008), 265.
69. Wentworth County Land Registry Records (hereafter WCLRO), Barton Township, Lot 21, Concession 2, Deed Nos. B881, B885 and D525, registered February 23, 1856, and May 17, 1864; 1861 Census, Canada West, Barton Township, District 2, 58, 63. Interestingly, the terms of repayment of the mortgage are not written out in the document, and may have been cause for a misunderstanding between the parties. However, the exact nature of what took place will probably never be known.
70. See Mossell's biography on the website of "Penn Biographies" at *www.archives.upenn.edu/people/1800s/mossell_nathan_f.html* (accessed February 3, 2009).
71. "Mossell, Gertrude E. H. Bustill" in *Dictionary of American Negro Biography*, Rayford W. Logan and Michael R. Winston, eds. (New York and London, UK: W.W. Norton, 1982), 457. One of Gertrude Mossell's works, Mrs. N.F. Mossell, *The Work of the Afro-American Woman*, originally published in Philadelphia in 1908, is a survey of the achievements of Black women in American history and was republished as part of the *Schomburg Library of Nineteenth-Century Black Women Writers* series edited by Henry Louis Gates Jr. (New York and Oxford, UK: Oxford University Press, 1988).
72. Memoir of Dr. Nathan Mossell, 8; "Mossell, Nathan Francis," *Dictionary of American Negro Biography*, 457–58.
73. 1861 Census, Wentworth County, Township of Barton, District 1, 39.
74. Blassingame, 426.
75. *Ibid.*, 426–27.
76. 1861 Census, Barton Township, District 1, 39.
77. 1871 Census, Barton Township, District 1, 1871, 43.
78. Email communication with great-great-grandson Howard Charles Green,

December 20, 2007, and March 10, 2009; WCLRO, Barton Township, Lot 9, Concession 4, AO, Abstract Index Books, Vol. 2.

79. WCLRO, *ibid.*; Adrienne Shadd, "'Little Africa' Revisited: Tracing Hamilton Mountain's Black Community," Report to the Culture Division, Community Services Department, City of Hamilton, March 3, 2010, 8–10.

80. *1856 City of Hamilton Directory*, 89; *1858 City of Hamilton Directory*, 160. WCLRO, Barton Township, Lot 9 Concession 12, Deed Nos. B780, C58, C259, C738, 623, and 624 registered in the years 1855–69. Charles J. Carter and family were found in the 1840 United States Census for West Brunswick, Schuylkill County, Pennsylvania, in the section for "Free persons of colour." See *www.ancestry.com* (accessed January 18, 2010).

81. Shadd, "'Little Africa' Revisted," 9; These transactions and the corresponding deeds can be found in WCLRO, Barton Township, Lot 9, Concession 4, Abstract Index Books, Vol. 2, 1810–1865, 1866–1900.

82. William Kirkendall was likely the relative of Samuel Kirkendall, another Hamilton farmer and lumber merchant whose parents, David and Rhoda Kirkendall, came from the Delaware Valley, New Jersey, in 1800. *DHB*, Vol. I, 117; The land transactions and corresponding deeds are found in WCLRO, Barton Township, Lot 12, Concession 4, Abstract Index Books, Vol. 2, 1801–1865, 1866–1900.

83. Shadd, "'Little Africa' Revisited," 4–5; 1861 Census, Barton Township, District 1, 38; "Former Coloured Colony on Mount Dubbed Little Africa," *Hamilton Spectator*, July 15, 1936; *DHB*, Vol. I, 110. In 1859, William Calamese took out a mortgage on the church property with Joseph Williams for $125, and, in 1863, the property was reclaimed by Williams for non-payment of the mortgage. It is unclear at this juncture what became of the church.

84. See the 1861 Census, Barton Township. On Julia Berry, see 1881 Census of Canada, Province of Ontario, Wentworth County, Barton Township, District C, Div. 2, 54; Dionne Brand, *No Burden to Carry: Black Working Women in Ontario, 1920s to 1950s* (Toronto: Women's Press, 1991), 89.

85. "Jacob Burkholder," DHB, Vol. I, 38.

86. "Former Coloured Colony on Mount Dubbed Little Africa," *Hamilton Spectator*, July 15, 1936.

87. "Mission School, Frame Church, Toll Gates," *Hamilton Spectator*, November 15, 1947. See also Mabel Burkholder, *The Story of Hamilton* (Hamilton, ON: Davis-Lisson, 1938), 144–46; *Barton on the Mountain* (Hamilton, ON: 1956), 27–29; and *Out of the Storied Past* (Hamilton, ON: 1968), 146–48.

88. Efajemue Etoroma, "Blacks in Hamilton: An Analysis of Factors in Community Building," (Ph.D. diss., McMaster University, 1992), 94–95.

89. Brand, *No Burden to Carry*, 89.

90. Berry family history and interview with Robert G. Foster Jr., August 24, 2009. I am indebted to Mr. Foster for providing me with a detailed family history of the Berrys.

91. The connection to Daniel Servos and the Niagara area is from Walter Kern, *Reclaiming Your Heritage*, 1985 (booklet in the Niagara Public Library), as cited in Power and Butler, 48; Henry Berry's death record states that he was born in Virginia in 1845. Death Registration for the year 1912, AO, Schedule C, #34028, Wentworth County, City of Hamilton. The location of the residence in Barton Township, Lot 10, Concession 4, comes from the birth certificate of Julia Elizabeth Berry, who was born on January 88, 1880, and who died at an early age. This document is in the family records held by Robert Foster Jr. See also the 1881 Census, Barton Township, District C, Div. 2, 54–55.

92. "The Walls of the City: A Chat with a Tollgate Keeper About Tolls," *Hamilton Spectator*, January 23, 1884; Mabel Burkholder, "The Barton Road Company," *Out of the Storied Past, from the Hamilton Spectator Articles*, Vol. 4, 277–78; "Smith's Sister Ran Tollgate," *Out of the Storied Past*, Vol. 4, 151; "Records Show Toll Roads Paid Owners Handsomely," *Out of the Storied Past*, Vol. 4, 187–88; "Toll Gates: At First Considered a Boon, Were Later a Nuisance," *Out of the Storied Past*, Vol. 1, 133–34. Burkholder's articles from her column *Out of the Storied Past* are in bound volumes in the main Hamilton Public Library Special Collections.

93. Berry family history documents; Letters of Administration of Property of Henry Franklin Berry, Surrogate Court Files, County of Wentworth, City of Hamilton, AO, RG 22-205, Grant #8165, 1912, MS887, Reel #1934.

94. Ann Harcus, "A Personal Search That Became a Life's Work," *The Teaneck Suburbanite*, July 11, 1984, 3, 7; additional information obtained from Viola Berry Aylestock and Robert Foster Jr.

95. "Is Mountain Mission Hall About to Change Hands?" *Hamilton Spectator*, October 24, 1941, from *Mountain Mission Scrapbooks*, Vol. 1, Hamilton Public Library, Special Collections; Jane Mulkewich, "Little Africa: Settlement Goes Back to 1850s," in *Vanished Hamilton II*, Margaret Houghton, ed., (Burlington, ON: North Shore Publishing, 2006), 104.

96. WCLRO, Barton Township, Deed Nos. A173, C851, C905, Will D26; D116, D117, registered from 1849–1861; 1851 Census, Barton Township, District 1, 29; 1861 Census, City of Hamilton, St. Mary's Ward, 125. In the 1861 census, Rosanna was recorded as *Susanna* Spellman.

97. WCLRO, Barton Township, Deed No. 2836, registered May 20, 1880.

98. WCLRO, Barton Township, Deed No. 4626, registered March 5, 1886; Surrogate Court, Wentworth County Estate Files, AO, RG 22-205, Vol. R, 1890-1893, Letters of Administration, Grant #3436, GS1, Reel #623.

99. WCLRO, Barton Township Deed Nos. C895, 1514, registered September 27, 1856, and March 13, 1874; 1871 Census, Province of Ontario, City of Hamilton, St. Lawrence Ward, Div. 1, 9; Wentworth County Surrogate Court Index to the Estate Files, RG 22-205, 1877, 435–36.

100. WCLRO, Barton Township, Deed Nos. 623 and 624, registered August 28, 1869, and September 4, 1869.

101. *British Colonist*, June 10, 1840, cited in Hill, "The Blacks in Toronto," 86.

102. Hill, "The Blacks in Toronto," 86.

103. "An Outrage Upon Society: Petition From the Coloured Citizens of Hamilton," *Hamilton Evening Times*, October 23, 1866.

104. "A Whitewashing Proceeding," *Hamilton Evening Times*, October 27, 1866.

105. *Ibid.*; Hill, "The Blacks in Toronto," 86.

106. Drew, 83–84.

107. *Ibid.*, 84.

108. *Ibid.*

109. *Ibid.*

110. *Ibid.*, 94.

111. *Ibid.*

112. William Wells Brown, "The Colored People of Canada," 463–64.

113. Mitchell, 133–34.

114. *Ibid.*, 133; William Wells Brown, 464.

115. 1861 Census, City of Hamilton, St. Mary's Ward, 76. The street address comes from *1858 City of Hamilton Directory*, 216.

116. *The National Era*, May 26, 1859; *Provincial Freeman*, August 12, 1854; Rhodes, 94.

117. Interview with Tom Brooks, October 2009. Although he does not like the term "expert," Tom Brooks is an authority on Canadians who fought in the Civil War. He states that upwards of fifty thousand Canadians fought, the vast majority on the Union side. His self-published book on the Civil War is under the name Thomas Walter Brooks, and entitled *Lee's Foreign Legion: A History of the 10th Louisiana Infantry* (Gravenhurst, ON: 1995).

118. Rhodes, 152–55.

119. The number 1,300 comes from Tom Brooks, who looked at the original rosters of regiments housed at the National Archives in Washington, D.C. It represents men who stated they were born in Canadian cities or localities such as Upper Canada or Canada West, Lower Canada, Canada East or Quebec, Nova Scotia, New Brunswick, Prince Edward Island, British North America, or simply Canada. The number of 348 sailors comes from the Civil War Soldiers and Sailors website, *www.civilwar.nps.gov*, referenced July 16, 2009. Two hundred and twenty-two of them stated they were born

in Canada, Canada East (Quebec) or Canada West (Ontario); forty-nine were from New Brunswick, seventy-four from Nova Scotia, and three from Prince Edward Island.

120. See *www. civilwar.nps.gov* (accessed July 19, 2009). Although Douglas was the only sailor who listed his place of birth as Hamilton, Canada West, he is probably not the only one from Hamilton who enlisted in the Navy.

121. I am indebted to Bryan Prince for his list of Civil War soldiers from Hamilton. Bryan's list comes in part from Tom Brooks's research, to whom I am also deeply indebted.

122. Tara Chanel Scott, "How We Came to Be: The Legacy of Mary Roth and Wesley Rhodes," unpublished history prepared for the Rhodes Family Reunion August 4–5, 2006, Detroit, Michigan. I am indebted to Jouvane "Joe" Rhodes and Tara Scott, descendants of Mary Roth and Wesley Rhodes, for this information.

123. Jessie L. Beattie, *John Christie Holland: Man of the Year* (Toronto: Ryerson Press, 1956), 27; "Thomas J. Holland is Called to Rest," *Hamilton Herald*, June 11, 1928. Bryan Prince's list includes a John Holland who joined the 102nd Regiment, United States Colored Infantry, Company A on September 23, 1863. It is not clear whether this Holland was related to Thomas Holland, or was perhaps the same person.

124. Nelson Stevens's name was obtained by Bryan Prince from historian Robin McPhee, who was responsible for his belated recognition in November 2007. See *www.usembassy.gov* (accessed October 28, 2009).

125. "Mrs. J. Diggs has Joined the Great Majority," *Hamilton Herald*, November 20, 1919. A search of the Civil War Soldiers and Sailors website (*www.civilwar.nps.gov*) did not result in a match for the name William Diggs.

126. Richard Butler, "When Slaves Were Owned in Upper Canada," in Butler Scrapbook, Vol. 1, 30, Hamilton Public Library, Special Collections.

127. Colonel W. Mallory, *Old Plantation Days* (Hamilton, ON: s.n., 1902), 3, 5, 14–16. The quotation is found on page 16 and the complete text can be found on the website entitled "Documenting the American South" at *http:// docsouth.unc. edu/neh/mallory.html* (accessed May 12, 2002). Mallory claimed that after a period of time as a private, he was promoted to colonel. However, a search of the Civil War Soldiers and Sailors website found two William Mallorys in Black regiments: one was in the 15th United States Colored Infantry, Company E, organized in Nashville, Tennessee, and the other in the 109th United States Colored Infantry, Company I, organized in Louisville, Kentucky. Both remained privates throughout their stint in the army. More research would be required to determine which one was our protagonist from Hamilton.

128. Mallory, 16–17; 1871 Census, Province of Ontario, City of Hamilton, St. Patrick's Ward, Div. 1, 10; 1881 Census, Province of Ontario, City of Hamilton, Ward 2, Div. 1, 61; *McAlpine's Hamilton City Directory, 1875*, 163; WCLRO, Barton Township, Deed Nos. 2670, 3217, registered in 1879–81.

129. Mallory, 17, 36–38; 1901 Census, City of Hamilton, Ward 2, Subdivision 4,3; Schedule C, AO, Death Registration for the year 1907, #32738, City of Hamilton, County of Wentworth.

Chapter 5: Eyeing the Summit, 1870–1900

1. Freeman, 63.
2. *Ibid.*, 64–67, 84.
3. Lerone Bennett, Jr., *Before the Mayflower: A History of the Negro in America, 1619–1964* (Baltimore, MD: Penguin Books, 1966), Chapter 8: "Black Power in Dixie."
4. For example, see *BAP*, Vol. II, 39–46; Winks, *The Blacks in Canada*, 289–90.
5. Still, 203; John Henry Hill's naturalization papers, Series II, Estate Correspondence and family documents, Box 2, Acc. 1956-13, Special Collection and Archives, Johnson Memorial Library, Virginia State University, Petersburg, Virginia. I would like to thank Karolyn Smardz Frost for alerting me to Hill's naturalization document and the existence of the Colson-Hill Family Papers.
6. 1871 Census of Canada, Province of Ontario, County of Wentworth, City of Hamilton. Again, these statistics derive from my own analysis of the census and the occupational breakdown for Black men and women.
7. Wayne found 17,053 Blacks in the 1861 census (although he estimated that the real number may have been as high as 20,000–22,500). However, the average figure given by contemporary observers was between 30,000–40,000. The 1871 census counted 13,500 Africans, indicating a drop of 3,500 or 20 percent compared to 55–66 percent if the larger estimates are used. Michael Wayne, "The Black Population of Canada West on the Eve of the American Civil War: A Reassessment Based on the Manuscript Census of 1861," *Social History* XXVIII, No. 56 (November 1995), 470–71.
8. Adrienne Shadd, "Deborah Brown and Black Settlement in York Township West, 1860–1870," unpublished paper presented to Parks Canada, April 2001. My analysis of the Black population in York Township West, Ward 3, of York County — the one with the largest number of residents of African descent in the Township — found that over the ten-year period from 1861 to 1871, 64 percent were still living in the county in 1871, although some had moved into the City of Toronto proper, or other townships in the county. Of the 36 percent who were no longer resident in York County, a number had passed away

and others were unaccounted for. Some had probably moved to other locales in the province, and, of the rest, many probably left for the United States.

9. The other ads were placed by Mary A. Glancford and David Goodler.

10. 1861 Census, City of Hamilton, St. Lawrence Ward, Div. 3. 651.

11. 1871 Census, Province of Ontario, City of Hamilton.

12. Walton, Tables 5.8 and 5.9: 326–67.

13. 1871 Census.

14. See Bennett, Chapter 9: "The Birth of Jim Crow."

15. 1881 Census of Canada, Province of Ontario, City of Hamilton.

16. Walton, Table 5.20, 340. Walton used information from the *Planet Directory of the Town of Chatham, 1882* (Chatham: Planet Steam Printing, 1882) to obtain information about male employment. However, city and town directories did not always mention who was Black and who was not, so Walton's sample in this case was just a subset of the more accurate number of Black heads of household in Chatham that he would have found if the 1881 census had been available at the time of his study.

17. Constance McLaughlin Green, *The Secret City: A History of Race Relations in the Nation's Capital*, cited in Walton, 210–11.

18. Kenneth Kusmer, *A Ghetto Takes Shape: Black Cleveland, 1870–1930*, cited in *ibid.*, 213.

19. David Katzman, *Before the Ghetto: Black Detroit in the Nineteenth Century*, in *ibid.*, 214–16.

20. Emma Lou Thornbrough, *The Negro in Indiana: A Study of a Minority*, cited in *ibid.*, 217–19.

21. "Coloured Men in Essex in Convention," *Missionary Messenger*, December 1, 1877, cited in Walton, 196–97; "The Reform Demonstration," *Missionary Messenger*, August 1, 1874; E.C. Cooper, "The First of August," *Chatham Banner*, August 7, 1876; "The First of August," *Missionary Messenger*, 1876. These articles are cited in Walton, 197, and are all located in the Abbott Papers, Toronto Public Library (TRL), Baldwin Room, S 90.

22. Adrienne Shadd, "No 'Black Alley Clique': The campaign to desegregate Chatham's public schools, 1891–93," *Ontario History* XCIX, No. 1 (Spring 2007): 77–95.

23. Shreve, 81; Winks, 356.

24. British Methodist Episcopal Church Conference Committee on Education, "Education of the Coloured People in Canada," *Journal of Education* 21 (1868): 151. Buxton was actually in a different situation in that while it had started out as a school for Black children, its standards were so high that white children in the vicinity began to attend it rather than the common school in the area, which closed as a result.

25. "Market, Fire, Police: The Colored Citizens Present Their Rightful Claims," *Hamilton Herald*, December 25, 1889.

26. *Ibid.*

27. Freeman Campbell, 149–51. Freeman Campbell traces the beginnings of the modern fire department with the appointment of Chief Alexander Aitchison in 1879, under whose tenure the policies were revised. On the career of Chief Aitchison and the history of the fire department, see also Reginald Swanborough, "The Early History of the Hamilton Fire Department, 1816–1905," *Wentworth Bygones* 8 (1969): 23–33.

28. "Market, Fire, Police: The Colored Citizens Present Their Rightful Claims," *Hamilton Herald*, December 25, 1889.

29. 1871 Census, City of Hamilton, St. Patrick's Ward, Div. 2, 14–15; 1881 Census, City of Hamilton, Ward 5, Div. 2, 12. In 1871, Richard Gwyder was listed as a broker, and, in 1881, as a whitewasher. Surrogate Court Files, County of Wentworth, City of Hamilton, AO, RG 22-205, Grant #3784, 1894, G.S. 1, Reel #627; Death Registration for 1894, AO. Schedule C #19766, County of Wentworth, City of Hamilton. At the annual meeting in Hamilton, August 1892, Gwyder was elected grand guard of the organization. *Chatham Daily Planet*, August 20, 1892.

30. "In Brotherhoods Bonds: Echoes from the Several Local Lodge Rooms," *Chatham Daily Planet*, August 24, 1892. Demun was elected grand captain of the host chapter in August 1892. Arlie C. Robbins, *Prince Hall Masonry in Ontario, 1852–1933*, (Chatham, ON: self-published, 1980); *Hamilton City Directory 1901: Embracing An Alphabetical List of All Business Firms and Private Citizens; A Classified Business Directory; A Miscellaneous Directory, Also A Complete Street Guide* (Hamilton: Might Directories, 1901), 203; Death Records for 1902, Schedule C, AO, #27999, County of Wentworth, City of Hamilton. Information about Demun's African origin derives from his death registration.

31. *McAlpine's Hamilton City Directory* 1875, 187; 1871 Census, City of Hamilton, St. Mary's Ward, Div. 1, 16; 1881 Census, City of Hamilton, Ward 3, Div. 1, 31; "Colored Oddfellows," *Hamilton Spectator*, August 28, 1884; "In Brotherhood's Bonds: Echoes from the Several Local Lodge Rooms," *Chatham Daily Planet*, November 18, 1893; Adrienne Shadd, "'Little Africa' Revisited," 25–26; George Morton to Editor, "Justice is Not Blind: The Color Line Drawn Even at the Sacred Altar," Hamilton Herald, December 27, 1889, 2.

32. 1871 Census, City of Hamilton, St. Mary's Ward, Div. 1, 16; *McAlpine's Hamilton City Directory*, 1875, 157; 1881 Census, City of Hamilton, Ward 5, Div. 2, 54; "Colored Oddfellows," *Hamilton Spectator*, August 28, 1884; Robbins, 119.

33. Professor J. Gant to Editor, "Prof. Gant's Say," *Hamilton Spectator*, October 23, 1884; D. Taylor to Editor, "Going for Gant," *Hamilton Spectator*, October 23, 1884; Professor J. Gant to Editor, "Gant's Ultimatum," *Hamilton Spectator*, October 24, 1884.

34. "Market, Fire, Police: The Colored Citizens Present Their Rightful Claims," *Hamilton Herald*, December 25, 1889, 1.

35. "What the Firemen Think. A Mean Insinuation Against the Colored Brethren's Staying Powers," *Hamilton Herald*, December 26, 1889, 1.

36. "The Colored Brigade," *Hamilton Herald*, December 26, 1889, 2.

37. "The Proposed Colored Brigade: It is Opposed by Prof. Gant, Who Gives His Reasons," *Ibid.*, 3.

38. "The Colored Fire Brigade. A Corps of Sixteen Men Suggested For the Job," *Hamilton Herald*, December 27, 1889, 1.

39. George Morton to Editor, "Justice is Not Blind: The Color Line Drawn Even at the Sacred Altar," *Ibid.*, 2.

40. "The Color Line," *Ibid.*

41. "The Colored Fire Brigade: Chief Aitchison Declines to Give an Opinion on the Subject," *Hamilton Herald*, December 28, 1889, 1.

42. I checked the minutes dating from December 9, 1889, through March 31, 1890, and no mention was made of the Black community's request. City Council Minutes, 1888–1890, on microfilm, Hamilton Public Library, Special Collections. The sixteen names of Black men put forward for jobs with the fire department were: David Jackson, S. Hart, J.L. Lightfoot, William McComas, Jacob Thompson, A. Pinkston, Charles Workman, F. Lightfoot, W.T. Cary, William Lewis, J. Cockburn, George Crawford, A. Talbot, Louis Bennett, John Burns, and John Slaughter. "The Colored Fire Brigade: A Corps of Sixteen Men Suggested For the Job," *Hamilton Herald*, December 27, 1889, 1.

43. Tara Scott, "How We Came to Be: The Legacy of Mary Roth & Wesley Rhodes," unpublished history prepared for the Rhodes Family Reunion August 4–6, 2006, Detroit Michigan.

44. Edwin S. Redkey, ed., *A Grand Army of Black Men: Letters from African-American Soldiers in the Union Army, 1861–1865* (New York: Cambridge University Press, 1992), 119–120.

45. 1901 Census, City of Hamilton, Ward 1, Subdivision 2, 2–3.

46. Tara Scott, "How We Came To Be," 3.

47. *Ibid.*, 2–3; E-mail communication with Tara Scott, November 6, 2009.

48. 1851, 1861, 1871, 1881 Censuses of Canada West and Ontario, Flamborough Township, Wentworth County. Henson conducted Samuel Jackson Lightfoot, Thomas Jefferson Lightfoot, and two other brothers and a nephew of James Lightfoot out of bondage. Their trip on the Underground Railroad

was chronicled by Henson in his autobiography: Henson, Chapters XVI and XVII. Robbins, in *Prince Hall Masonry in Ontario*, 35, states that James L. Lightfoot was the son of James L. Lightfoot Sr. However, Laurie Lightfoot Sexton's research on the Lightfoots states that he was the son of Samuel Jackson Lightfoot. This research can be found at *http//:freepages.genealogy rootsweb. ancestry.com/~lightfoot/index.html*, (accessed August 4, 2009).

49. Adrienne Shadd et al., *Underground Railroad*, 64; 1881 Census, Province of Ontario, Flamborough Township, Wentworth County. In the 1881 census, Levi Lightfoot is listed with Hannah, two young children and Thomas Casey, aged seventy-eight. There were five additional Lightfoot households in Flamborough Township in 1881.

50. The Hubbards and the Douglasses attended an Abbott, Hubbard, and Lightfoot family reunion in Dundas in 1904. Catherine Slaney, *Family Secrets: Crossing the Colour Line* (Toronto: Natural Heritage Books, 2003), 192–93.

51. "New Barber Shop," *Hamilton Spectator*, November 1, 1875.

52. There are at least thirty-five articles, letters to the editor, or notices of upcoming events in which he was involved that are listed in the card catalogue of Hamilton Public Library, Special Collections, or that I found independent of that resource. This does not include all the articles written about him since his death as one of the "colourful characters" of Hamilton in the latter nineteenth century.

53. "Professor Jesse Gant: A Man Whose Genius is Many-Sided," *Hamilton Herald*, November 2, 1895; *DHB, Vol. II: 1876–1924*, 55.

54. "Ended in a Free Fight: Watermelons in the Air at Last Night's Dundurn Show," *Hamilton Spectator*, August 20, 1896.

55. "John and Little Oscar: Professor Gant the Plaintiff in an Amusing Case," *Hamilton Herald*, July 28, 1890. In 1901, the Gants were listed in the census living in Ward 1, Subdivision 5 at 324 King Street East. At the age of seventeen, Gant's oldest son Oscar also worked as a barber with his father, while the younger sons, Harry and Joseph, aged fourteen and eleven respectively, were attending school all year round.

56. "Razors in the Air: Prof. Gant's Barber Shop Bombarded," *Hamilton Spectator*, February 12, 1883.

57. "Prof. Gant Makes a Call: He Conveys the Regards of the Coloured Citizens to Lord Aberdeen," *Hamilton Spectator*, September 19, 1890; Information about Lord and Lady Aberdeen can be found at *www.gg.ca* under "Roles and Responsibilities," (accessed December 11, 2009).

58. Toby, 29.

59. *DHB, Vol. II*, 80–81; Annual BME Church Conference minutes from 1875–79 indicate that Johnson withdrew from the church amid charges

of maladministration, causing him to resign in in June 1879. There were numerous complaints against him on the part of parishioners and ministers in those years. British Methodist Church of Canada fonds (53), Annual Conference Minutes, 1875–1884, United Church Archives, Reel 1, 57, 58, 59, 76, 77, 80, 81, 130, 133, 145; Some examples of Johnson's lectures are reported in "The Sun Do Move: Astronomical Opinions of Prof. Johnson, of Hamilton," *Hamilton Spectator*, January 10, 1882; "The Sun Do Move: Reconstruction of the Sciences of Geography and Astronomy by a Hamilton Preacher," *Hamilton Spectator*, May 8, 1882; "Doomed to Destruction: The Earth to Come to an End in Fifty Years — A Modern Edition of Mother Shipton," *Hamilton Spectator*, November 2, 1883; "C. Astronomical Johnson Talks Wisdom to the Benighted People of St. Kitts," *Hamilton Spectator*, March 6, 1897.

60. 1881 Census, City of Hamilton, Ward 3, Div. 1, 31–32.

61. "The British Lion," *Hamilton Spectator*, October 12, 1883; "Astronomical Johnson," *Hamilton Spectator*, August 29, 1884. Robin Winks states that the *British Lion* began in 1881, although his sources indicated 1883 as the year that the paper began publication. The final year of publication, according to Winks, was 1892, although I found evidence that it was still being published in 1897, located on 44 Wilson Street. Robin Winks, *Blacks in Canada*, 398; C.A. Johnson to Editor, "Mr. Johnson Mops the Floor with the Spectator," *Hamilton Spectator*, March 8, 1897.

62. "In a New Role: Prof. and Col. C.A. Johnson Announces a Startling Machine," *Hamilton Spectator*, July 20, 1885.

63. "Brer Johnson's Latest: Full Text of His Remarkable Address to Sir John Macdonald," *Hamilton Spectator*, February 13, 1890; "Her Majesty's Loyal Negroes: Editor Johnson Assures the Queen of Their Unswerving Devotion," *Hamilton Herald*, February 12, 1890, 4.

64. "On Earthquakes: Fourth Lecture by the Rev. C. Astronomical Johnson," *Hamilton Spectator*, August 6, 1887; "A Joke on Astronomical Johnson," *Hamilton Spectator*, August 23, 1887; "Readers Lacking Brains: Prof. Johnson's Flight into the Future," *New York Times*, March 31, 1888.

65. Robbins, *Prince Hall Masonry in Ontario*, 22; Arlie C. Robbins, *Legacy to Buxton* (Chatham, ON: self-published, 1983), 38–39; Joyce Shadd Middleton, "Abraham D. Shadd," unpublished article in possession of the author.

66. Robbins, *Prince Hall Masonry in Ontario*, 23; On Edmund Crump, see Robbins, *Prince Hall Masonry in Ontario*, 32; also 1851 and 1861 Censuses, City of Hamilton, St. Andrew's Ward, 324 and District 2, 303 respectively; *1858 City of Hamilton Directory*, 168.

67. Robinson and Robinson, 69–70; Shreve, 80–81.

68. *Ibid.*, 23; 1861 Census, Hamilton City, St. Lawrence Ward, District 1, 193.

69. Robbins, *Prince Hall Masonry in Ontario*, 27–28. Philip Broadwater is listed in the 1851 Census for Hamilton, and the 1861–1871 censuses for Barton Township. Henry Fields, grand sword bearer, was a farmer originally from Virginia, but who had more recently lived in Buffalo, New York. The origins of him and his family were discussed in Chapter 2. 1861 Census, City of Hamilton, St. Lawrence Ward, District 3.

70. Robbins, *Prince Hall Masonry in Ontario*, 35.

71. *Ibid.*, 28.

72. *Ibid.*, 29, 36.

73. *Ibid.*, 40.

74. *Ibid.*, 29–32, 36–37. They included Hamilton's Mount Olive #1 and Olive Branch #3, which had been transplanted from Windsor, plus Victoria #2 of St. Catharines, Shaftsbury #6 of London, Kinnard #7 of Ingersoll, Lincoln #8 of Amherstburg, North American #9 of Windsor, King Hiram #4 of Toronto, and Mount Carmel #10 of Buxton. Prince Hall #5 of Chatham had been charged with insubordination and expelled.

75. *Ibid.*, Chapter 6. Robbins also concluded that the formation of the Dominion of Canada from several colonial provinces had an impact on the desire for amalgamation, as well as the rise in anti-Black sentiment after emancipation, when whites wanted these Black Canadians to "go home," 6.

76. *Ibid.*, 76, 119.

77. Robinson and Robinson, 117; Robbins, *Prince Hall Masonry in Ontario*, 131–34. After five years, Ontario and Michigan separated into two jurisdictions. Robbins's account of the Order of the Eastern Star is far less detailed than that of the Prince Hall Masons, and she does not mention the early Hamilton women who were associated with the order. An article in the *Chatham Daily Planet*, August 22, 1892, stated that a meeting of the Grand Chapter in Hamilton reported there had been an increase of three chapters in the past year, bringing the number of chapters to fifteen, with a total membership of three hundred. No Hamilton women were listed as being elected to the Grand Chapter, but Brother G.H. Hughes from Hamilton was elected grand warden. The Order of the Eastern Star was described as the "ladies branch of the Knights Templar."

78. Robinson and Robinson, 117–18. Robert G. Foster and Judy Morgan informed me that Julia Berry had been a member of the Order of the Eastern Star's Esther Chapter #3. A subsequent email communication of March 22, 2010, from Robert Foster Jr., included the additional tidbit that at an Eastern Star celebration in Hamilton in early 2010 it was reported that Julia Berry had been elected to represent her chapter at the province-wide meeting to establish the new order on August 30, 1889.

79. *Chatham Daily Planet*, August 4, August 17, August 20, August 22, 1892.

80. My research on Chatham informs me that the Chatham Oddfellows, at least, were resurrected and became an active branch of the Black Oddfellows by the early 1890s.

81. 1851 Census, City of Hamilton, St. Andrew's Ward, 516.

82. "The Minstrels Move: O'Banyoun's Jubilee Singers Reorganize for the Season," *Chatham Daily Planet*, October 14, 1892.

83. See *www.nyfiskalumni.com/history.htm* (accessed April 22, 2010).

84. *Ibid.*; 1881 Census, City of Hamilton, Ward 6, 44. "Colored People Congregate: Business and Pleasure Judiciously Blended," *Chatham Tri-Weekly Planet*, August 3, 1891. Reverend O'Banyoun spoke at Chatham's 1891 Emancipation Day ceremonies and noted that he was from Brantford. Peter O'Banyoun's biography can be found in C. Peter Ripley, *BAP*, 231-2fn4.

85. "The Minstrels Move: O'Banyoun's Jubilee Singers Reorganize for the Season," *Chatham Daily Planet*, October 14, 1892.

86. Lynn Abbott and Doug Seroff, *Out of Sight: The Rise of African American Popular Music, 1889–1895* (Jackson: University of Mississippi, 2002) 176–77; Daniel Hill, *Freedom-Seekers*, see photograph on page 181; Census of Canada, 1891, Hamilton, Ontario, Ward 5, Div. 4, 43. James E. Lightfoot, son of James L. Lightfoot, was born in Hamilton in approximately 1872. In 1891, James E. Lightfoot was nineteen years old, and his older brother Charles F. was twenty-six. He had two sisters, Ida M. and Lena. Their mother, Elizabeth, was deceased. The information on James E. Lightfoot and the Williams and Walker Glee Club comes from Lynn Abbott and Doug Seroff, *Ragged but Right: Black Travelling Shows, "Coon Songs," and the Dark Pathway to Blues and Jazz* (Jackson: University Press of Mississippi, 2007), 63.

87. Abbott and Seroff, *Out of Sight*, 176–77; 1901 Census, City of Hamilton, Ward 5, Subdivision 4, 19.

88. Abbott and Seroff, *Out of Sight*, 177. Abbott and Seroff quote a column called "The Stage," in the *Indianapolis Freeman* of July 31, 1897, and May 11, 1907, for these references on the duration of the group's seasons.

89. Hill, *Freedom-Seekers*, photograph on page 181; *Songs Sung by the Famous Canadian Jubilee Singers, The Royal Paragon Male Quartet and Imperial Orchestra* (Hamilton, ON: Duncan Lith Co., n.d.). I am indebted to Eugene Miller of Toronto, a prodigious collector of early jazz and African-Canadian memorabilia, for providing me not only with the photographs of the front and back covers of the songbooks, but also for photocopying the table of contents of both.

90. "The Stage," *Indianapolis Freeman*, September 8, 1906, quoted in Abbott and Seroff, *Out of Sight*, 177.

Chapter 6: At a Crossroads: The Turn of a New Century

1. "Professor Gant Dead: Well-known Barber Succumbed to Bright's Disease This Morning," *Hamilton Spectator*, January 18, 1905. It should be noted that his obituary in the *Hamilton Evening Times* of the same date reported that Oscar was living in Hamilton.

2. My own population count of the manuscript census was 353. However, there were some pages that were so faint that they were virtually unreadable. The birthplace percentages are based on my count of the number of Blacks in Hamilton rather than the figure of 450 reported in the published census. The omission of the 1891 census is accounted for by the fact that racial and ethnic origin was not asked in that year.

3. Walker, *A History of Blacks in Canada*, 67.

4. Brand, *No Burden to Carry*, 101.

5. Robbins, *Prince Hall Masonry in Ontario*, 103.

6. This biographical outline is derived from several sources: Charles Victor Roman, *Meharry Medical College: A History* (Nashville, TN: Sunday School Publishing Board of the National Baptist Convention Inc., 1934). In this book, Roman discusses his own story at some length; his entry in Rayford Logan and Michael Winston, eds., *Dictionary of American Negro Biography*, 532–3; his obituary in *Journal of Negro History* 20, No. 1 (January 1935): 116–17; William Montague Cobb, "Medical History," *Journal of National Medical Association*, 45, No. 4 (July 1953): 301–05; "From a Dundas Cotton Mill Boy to Become Noted for his Science as a Medical Expert," Hamilton Public Library, Special Collections Clipping File. Where discrepancies exist in the facts of Dr. Roman's life, I have either left them out, or relied on Dr. Roman's own account. For example, one source states that Roman had no children, and another that he had a son who became a doctor and settled in Canada. This I left out completely. There was a Dr. Charles Lightfoot Roman who obtained his medical degree from McGill University and practised in Montreal. This man was born in 1889 in Port Elgin, Ontario, of the union of James Ferdinand Roman and Fannie Lightfoot. He became a grand master of the Masonic Lodges of Quebec in 1952, an unusual feat for a Black man at that time. It turns out that he was also the great nephew of James L. Lightfoot, brother of Dr. Charles Lightfoot Roman's grandmother. Robbins, *Prince Hall Masonry in Ontario*, 72.

7. Roman, 85.

8. *Ibid.*, 51.

9. *Ibid.*, 52.

10. Cobb, 301.

11. *Dictionary of American Negro Biography,* 532; Obituary in *Journal of Negro History:* 116–17. "From a Dundas Cotton Mill Boy."

12. Cobb, 303.

13. *Ibid.*

14. *Ibid.,* 304.

15. *Ibid.*

16. Ida Greaves, *The Negro in Canada* (Montreal: McGill University Economic Studies No. 16, 1930), 57.

17. Again, these statistics represent my own tabulation of occupations based on the manuscript census, and from the 353 Blacks that I found. This number is lower than that of the published census, and is at least partly the result of the fact that some of the pages of the manuscript census were simply unreadable.

18. Mrs. A.M. Waters to the editor, *Hamilton Evening Times,* May 15, 1894; "Jesse Gant," *DHB II,* 55. I could not find Gant's letter, although it is referred to in the *Dictionary of Hamilton Biography* just referenced. No mention of Police Matron Lewis was made in the City Council Minutes, April through July 1894.

19. "G. Morton Dead: He Was Letter Carrier and on Local Staff for 36 Years," *Hamilton Herald,* August 20, 1927.

20. Winks, 325–26.

21. Ray Lewis, as told to John Cooper, *Shadow Running: Ray Lewis, Canadian Railway Porter & Olympic Athlete* (Toronto: Umbrella Press, 1999), 12–15.

22. Interview with Shirley Brown, July 2, 2003. All information about the Wade family comes from this interview.

23. *Ibid.*

24. 1901 Census, Province of Canada, City of Hamilton, Ward 6, Subdivision 3.

25. Lewis, *Shadow Running,* 17. Another book aimed at a younger audience was published by John Cooper under the title *Rapid Ray: The Story of Ray Lewis* (Toronto: Tundra Books, 2002).

26. Stewart Memorial Board Minute Book, 1910–1935, Stewart Memorial Church Archives, John Holland Centre for Leadership Training.

27. Calvin Ruck, *The Black Battalion, 1916–1920: Canada's Best Kept Military Secret* (Halifax: Nimbus Publishing, 1987), 6.

28. Arthur Alexander to Minister of Militia and Defence, November 7, 1914, reprinted in *ibid.,* 90.

29. George Morton to Sir Sam Hughes, September 7, 1915, Records of the Department of National Defence, cited in *ibid.,* 8.

30. W.E. Hodgins to J.L. Stewart, October 16, 1915, in *ibid.*

31. *Ibid.,* 6–7.

32. *Ibid.,* 13.

33. *Ibid.*, 9–13, Appendix A: 85–86.

34. *Ibid.*, 20–21.

35. Robbins, *Prince Hall Masonry in Ontario*, 28, 34, 40.

36. Robin Winks, *The Blacks in Canada*, 298.

37. James W. St. G. Walker, *"Race," Rights and the Law in the Supreme Court of Canada* (Toronto: Osgoode Society for Canadian Legal History and Wilfrid Laurier University, 1997), 124–25.

38. The history of the Ku Klux Klan and its emergence in Canada is reviewed in Constance Backhouse, *Colour-Coded: A Legal History of Racism in Canada, 1900–1950* (Toronto: Osgoode Society for Legal History and the University of Toronto Press, 1999), 181–93.

39. *Ibid.*, 184–85. Winks, *The Blacks in Canada*, 320, states that there may have been some followers in the counties of Leeds and Grenville in Ontario, but finds little other evidence of its existence prior to the 1920s. Backhouse, 183, cites a case in London in the 1880s, when the home of Richard B. Harrison was burned to the ground by a group calling itself the "Klux Clan." Fortunately, the family had moved to Windsor only two days earlier, so no one was harmed. Then a teenager of seventeen, Harrison went on to become a celebrated actor on the Broadway stage. He recalled the incident fifty years later when he returned to his home town of London to great acclaim by the local who's who. "Father and Mother Arrived in London as Runaway Slaves; Distinguished Actor Who Was Born in the City, and Spent Boyhood Here, is Officially Honored with Freedom of City at Rotary Club Luncheon," *London Advertiser*, October 30, 1937.

40. "Klansmen of Hamilton Defend Their Conduct in 'Raid' at Oakville," *Toronto Globe*, March 3, 1930; Backhouse, 186.

41. Martin Robin, *Shades of Right: Nativist and Fascist Politics in Canada, 1920–1940* (Toronto: University of Toronto Press, 1992), 13.

42. Backhouse, 186–87.

43. *Hamilton Herald*, March 25, 1935; Brian Henley, "For a time, the Klan Reared its Ugly Head," *Hamilton Spectator*, June 22, 1991.

44. "Ku Klux Klan Rears Head in City of Hamilton with 32 Initiations," "A Klan of his Own," and "Detective Warned in Note Signed K.K.K.," *Toronto Globe*, November 19 and 22, 1924, Backhouse, 187. In the article, an amount of $200 was mentioned for the two fiery crosses, but an editorial in the *Toronto Globe* of November 20, 1924, stated that it was $20, a more likely amount for this item.

45. "Detective Warned in Note Signed K.K.K.," *Toronto Globe*, November 22, 1924. Another recently organized fraternal order, the Most Noble Order of Crusaders, had no problem with the Klan. Describing the Crusaders as

an "Empire organization" that sought to uphold British ideas, a spokes-man stated that "the Klan in Canada, as far as I can learn, seems to be keeping within bounds." See "Ku Klux Klan: Crusaders Have No Feeling Towards the Order," *Hamilton Spectator*, March 27, 1925. However, a for-mer Hamilton reporter who covered a march of the Klan in Hamilton in 1929 stated that the organization was held with an offhand contempt by the public. "The Klan didn't cut any ice ..." See "A Flashback to 1930: The Klan's March Through Oakville," *Hamilton Spectator*, December 26, 1960.

46. "Klan Organizing in this District," *Hamilton Spectator*, February 18, 1925.

47. "Ladies Klan Would March to City Hall: Mrs. E. Miller Declares K.K.K. Has 1000 Members Here," *Hamilton Herald*, March 20, 1925.

48. "Three Must Appear in Oakville Court Because of 'Raid,'" *Toronto Globe*, March 8, 1930.

49. Robin, 14.

50. Toby *et al.*, 59.

51. Lewis, *Shadow Running*, 24–25; 32–33.

52. "Klan Took Oakville Girl from Negro Home; Hooded Ordered (*sic*) Foils Black-White Romance," *Toronto Daily Star*, March 1, 1930, 1–2; "Klan Separates Oakville Negro and White Girl," *Hamilton Spectator*, March 1, 1930, 1; "Klansmen of Hamilton Defend Their Conduct In 'Raid' at Oakville," *Toronto Globe*, March 3, 1930, 1–2; Backhouse, 173–74. The details of the story differ slightly from one version to the next, so I have used statements from the eye witnesses, including Ira Johnson and his mother as well as the Klan's own statement of what occurred, where they coincide.

53. "Klansmen of Hamilton Defend Their Conduct in 'Raid' at Oakville," *Toronto Globe*, March 3, 1930, 2.

54. *Ibid.*

55. "Klan Took Oakville Girl from Negro Home; Hooded Ordered (*sic*) Foils Black-White Romance," *Toronto Daily Star*, March 1, 1930, 1.

56. "Klan Separates Oakville Negro and White Girl," *Hamilton Spectator*, March 1, 1930, 1.

57. "Klan Took Oakville Girl from Negro Home; Hooded Ordered (*sic*) Foils Black-White Romance," *Toronto Daily Star*, March 1, 1930, 2.

58. "All Negro Population to Protest Klan Act," *Toronto Daily Star*, March 3, 1930.

59. Backhouse, 193–94, 199; Lewis, *Shadow Running*, 40.

60. Lewis, 40.

61. Backhouse, 199–224.

62. *Ibid.*, 224. Backhouse cites Julian Sher, *White Hoods: Canada's Ku Klux Klan* (Vancouver: New Star, 1983), 60, and Winks, 324–25.

63. "Couple Parted by K.K.K. Wed by Indian Pastor," *Toronto Daily Star*, March 24, 1930, 1; "Johnson Claims Indian Descent: No Negro Blood in Him, Klan Victim States," *Hamilton Spectator*, March 6, 1930.

64. Howard Palmer, *Patterns of Prejudice: A History of Nativism in Alberta* (Toronto: McClelland & Stewart, 1982), 101–02.

65. *Ibid.*, 142.

Chapter 7 — Roadblocks Ahead: The Reverend Holland Era

1. Freeman, 35.

2. Evans, 190.

3. *DHB*, Vol. IV, 134.

4. "States Racial Prejudice Here Hurts Negroes," *Hamilton Spectator*, January 16, 1937.

5. Lewis, *Shadow Running*, 56; Stanley G. Grizzle (with John Cooper), *My Name's Not George: The Story of the Brotherhood of Sleeping Car Porters in Canada* (Toronto: Umbrella Press, 1998), 37.

6. Interview with Shirley Brown, July 2, 2003.

7. Jessie L. Beattie, *John Christie Holland: Man of the Year* (Toronto: Ryerson Press, 1956).

8. "Thomas J. Holland is Called To Rest: Was Last Surviving Member of Noted O'Bannyon [*sic*] Jubilee Singers," *Hamilton Herald*, June 11, 1928; "70th Birthday," The *Canadian Observer,* January 2, 1915; Eleventh Howard-Holland Family Reunion Booklet, July 18–21, 2002. The *Hamilton Herald* states that his date of birth was 1845, while the family reunion booklet contends that Holland was born in 1843.

9. "Thomas J. Holland is Called To Rest," *Hamilton Herald*, June 11, 1928; Beattie, 21–24; 1901 Census, City of Hamilton, Ward 6, Subdivision 8, 1. Beattie also suggested that Holland's parents were still living when he escaped to Canada, and that after serving in the Civil War, Holland attempted to find them, only to discover that his mother had died, and his father had been sold to a Kentucky planter as punishment for his escape (p. 27). The *Canadian Observer* article of January 2, 1915, on the other hand, stated that he suffered the loss of his parents early in life. Holland family information notes that William Augustus Holland died about 1850 and that Leatha Holland was manumitted in 1856 and remarried Josiah Webster of Mt. Zion, Maryland, giving birth to two more children. Although her birth year is 1816, no year of death is given. Eleventh Howard-Holland Family Reunion Booklet, July 18–21, 2002.

10. 1851 Census, Canada West, County of Wentworth, Saltfleet Township, 44; 1871 Census, County of Wentworth, Saltfleet Township, Div. 1, 35; 1891

Census, City of Hamilton, Ward, 6, District 3, 49; Ontario Marriages, 1801–1930, Schedule B, Registration #10402, No. 275, County of Wentworth, City of Hamilton. At the bottom of their marriage registration, it is revealed that "The Bride was adopted by Isaac + Eliza Shortt [*sic*]."

11. Ontario Marriages, 1801–1930, AO, Schedule B, Registration #10402, No. 275. Beattie, 27, states that Thomas and Henrietta married in 1873.

12. Eleventh Howard-Holland Family Reunion Booklet, July 18–21, 2002.

13. Beattie, 28–30, 33; 1901 Census, City of Hamilton, Ward 6, Subdivision 8, 1. William Holland's hay-pressing business was mentioned in the *Canadian Observer* of December 26, 1914, under "Hamilton" news.

14. 1901 Census, Province of Ontario, City of Hamilton, Ward 6, Subdivision 8, 1.

15. Beattie, 30–36; Grace Holland's membership in the Twentieth Century Literary Association was recorded in African Canadian newspaper, the *Canadian Observer*, where the organization placed ads beginning January 9, 1915. She served as secretary of the organization for several months of that year. Mr. R. Hammond was listed as president. Not surprisingly, the eloquent George Morton succeeded as president by May 1, 1915 and Mina Lucas became secretary. The *Observer* was an African Canadian paper published weekly by American-born J. R. B. Whitney, and ran from December 12, 1914 through June 14, 1919.

16. *Ibid.*, 63–67.

17. *Ibid.*, 69–70.

18. *Ibid.*, 72, 88–92; *DHB*, Vol. IV, 133.

19. Interview with Shirley Brown, July 2, 2003.

20. Interview with Jouvane "Joe" Rhodes, December 1, 2003.

21. *Ibid.*

22. Beattie, 97–99, 101.

23. *Ibid.*, 103–105, 109.

24. Interview with Shirley Brown, July 2, 2003.

25. Beattie, 109.

26. Interview with Wilma Morrison, February 11, 2003.

27. Alexander, *Go to School*, 56.

28. Toby, 60.

29. Interview with Shirley Brown, July 2, 2003.

30. Efajemue E. Etoroma, "Blacks in Hamilton: An Analysis of Factors in Community Building," (Ph.D. diss., McMaster University, 1992, 101–02.

31. Lewis, *Shadow Running*, 59.

32. *Ibid.*, 75.

33. Interview with Wilma Morrison, February 11, 2003.

34. Lewis, *Shadow Running*, 75.

35. Interview with Wilma Morrison, February 11, 2003.
36. *Ibid.*
37. Beattie, vii.
38. Interview with Jouvane "Joe" Rhodes, December 1, 2003.
39. Beattie, viii.
40. Winks, 420–21; Interview with Jim Braithwaite, February 19, 2003. Mr. Braithwaite told the story of his brother, Danny Braithwaite, of Toronto, who attempted to join the Air Force, but was never called. He was later accused of refusing to be drafted into the regular Army. He never did get into the Air Force, but served in the Army. Other men, like Lincoln Alexander, did join the Air Force, however.
41. See Charles Roach interview in *Identity: The Black Experience in Canada* (Toronto: Ontario Educational Communications Authority and Gage Publishing, 1979), 43. Neville Nunes also made this point during the time that I worked as a curator for "… and still I rise," the travelling exhibit for the African Canadian Workers Advisory Committee and the Workers Arts and Heritage Centre, 2001–03.
42. Interview with Jackie Washington, September 10, 2003. The information about Jackie Washington's life comes from this interview, and is supplemented by two articles: Mark McNeil, "The Legend of the Washingtons," *Hamilton Spectator*, March 28, 1987, C3, and Ric Taylor, "Jackie Washington," *View*, June 12–18, 2003, 11, 14.
43. Interview with Shirley Brown, July 2, 2003.
44. Interview with Jackie Washington, September 10, 2003.
45. *Ibid.*
46. *Ibid.*
47. Al-X, "Hamilton's First Family of Jazz and Blues," *View*, September 20–27, 1995, 9.
48. *Ibid.*
49. Ric Taylor, "Jackie Washington," *View*, June 12–18, 2003, 14.
50. Brand, *No Burden to Carry*, 96, 184, 215, 243, 277. Not only were some Black women now working in munitions plants, but they often found themselves in the dirtiest or most dangerous sections of the plant.
51. Etoroma, 102.
52. Brand, *No Burden to Carry*, 96.
53. Dionne Brand, "'We weren't allow to go into factory work until Hitler started the war,'" in *"We're Rooted Here and They Can't Pull Us Up": Essays in African Canadian Women's History*, Peggy Bristow *et al.*, eds. (Toronto: University of Toronto Press, 1994), 180.
54. *Ibid.*, 188.

55. "Negro Veteran Denied Admission to Dundurn Dance," *Hamilton Spectator*, July 7, 1948, in Discrimination Scrapbook, Vol.1, 1926–1989, 3, Hamilton Public Library, Special Collections .

56. "Apology Made, Colour Incident Is Now Closed," *Hamilton Spectator*, July 13, 1948, Discrimination Scrapbook, Vol.1, 1926–1989, 4, Hamilton Public Library, Special Collections.

57. "Racial Discrimination Motion Lost in Council," *Hamilton Spectator*, September 1, 1948, in Discrimination Scrapbook, Vol.1, 1926–1989, 5, Hamilton Public Library, Special Collections.

58. Arlie Robbins's History of the National Unity Association, 1983, Buxton National Historic Site and Museum, NUA Files, 2000, 6, 7–5; Ross Lambertson, "The Dresden Story: Racism, Human Rights and the Jewish Labour Committee," *Labour/Le Travail*, No. 47 (Spring 2001): 14. This is available online at *www. historycoop.org/journals/llt47/03lamber.html*, referenced August 26, 2002. Walker, *"Race" Rights and the Law*, 19–20, 144. See also Sue Ferguson, "A Town Divided: Racism Once Flourished in the Town of Dresden, Ont.," *Maclean's*, September 10, 2001.

59. Lambertson, "Dresden Story," Ferguson, 43.

60. *Ibid.*; Herbert Sohn, "Human Rights Legislation in Ontario: A Study of Social Action," (Ph.D. diss., University of Toronto, 1975), Appendix H: The 1950 Community Deputation.

61. Lambertson, 19.

62. "Groups Support Y.W.C.A. in Anti-Discrimination," *Hamilton Spectator*, February 23, 1950, in Discrimination Scrapbook, Vol. 1, 1926–1989, 8, Hamilton Public Library, Special Collections.

63. "Refused Haircut Here, Famed Pianist Charges: Oscar Peterson Makes Complaint; Warrender Seeks Test of By-Law," *Hamilton Spectator*, May 5, 1951, in Discrimination Scrapbook, Vol. 1, 1926–1989, 9, Hamilton Public Library, Special Collections.

64. *Ibid.*

65. "'No Discrimination' Clause Clear, Board to Be Advised," *Hamilton Spectator*, May 7, 1951, in Discrimination Scrapbook, Vol. 1, 1926–1989, 13, Hamilton Public Library, Special Collections.

66. "Barber Protests Publicity in Noted Pianist Incident: Employees Not Qualified to Cut Negro's Hair, Mayor Is Told," *Hamilton Spectator*, May 7, 1951, in Discrimination Scrapbook, Vol. 1, 1926–1989, 11, Hamilton Public Library, Special Collections.

67. "'No Discrimination' Clause Clear, Board to Be Advised," *Hamilton Spectator*, May 7, 1951, in Discrimination Scrapbook, Vol.1, 1926-1989, 13, Hamilton Public Library, Special Collections.

68. Lambertson, 20.
69. *Ibid.*
70. Sohn, Appendix I: The 1954 Community Deputation.
71. Lambertson, 20.
72. *Ibid.*
73. *Ibid.*, 21–28.
74. Fair Accommodation Practices Act Complaint filed against Mr. and Mrs. Leo Loudenslager, July 28, 1957, NUA Papers, 2000, 6, 180, Buxton National Historic Site and Museum. Also, interview with Ed Shadd, September 18, 2009.
75. Interview with Wilma Morrison, February 11, 2003.
76. *Ibid.*
77. *Ibid.*

Chapter 8 — New Pathways, Old Destination: Contemporary Fighters for Social Justice

1. "Immigration from the British Caribbean," Brief by T.G. Major, Canadian government trade commissioner in Trinidad, August 31, 1951, Library and Archives Canada, RG 76, Vol. 830, File 552-1-644 (Pt. 1), 1–2; Agnes Calliste, "Canada's Immigration Policy and Domestics from the Caribbean: The Second Domestic Scheme," *Socialist Studies/Etudes Socialistes* 5 (1989): 139–40.
2. *Ibid.*, 2–3; Calliste, "The Second Domestic Scheme," 139.
3. Walker, *History of Blacks in Canada*, 79, 94; Winks, 212–15.
4. Walker, *History of Blacks in Canada*, 94; For a very thorough discussion of the movement of Oklahoman Blacks into the Canadian prairies and the Canadian government's efforts to keep them out see R. Bruce Shepard, *Deemed Unsuitable: Blacks from Oklahoma Move to the Canadian Prairies in Search of Equality in the Early 20th Century Only to Find Racism in Their New Home* (Toronto, Umbrella Press, 1997).
5. Walker, *History of Blacks in Canada*, 94; Shepard, 100.
6. Walker, *History of Blacks in Canada*, 94; Winks, 437–38.
7. Donald Moore, *Don Moore: An Autobiography* (Toronto: Williams-Wallace, 1985). See Chapters 11 and 12 in particular; Winks, 438–39; Agnes Calliste, "Women of 'Exceptional Merit': Immigration of Caribbean Nurses to Canada," *Canadian Journal of Women and the Law*, 6, No. 1 (1993).
8. Alexander, 91–92. Another first for Fairclough was her position as deputy prime minister from February 19–20, 1958. It was fitting, therefore, that Fairclough was the person who nominated Kim Campbell as leader of the Progressive Conservative Party, after which Campbell became Canada's first woman prime minister in 1993.

9. See Eleanor Wiltshire Rodney, ed., *Nurturing the Trillium: The Contributions of African & Caribbean Educators to the Development of the Hamilton-Wentworth Region*, (Hamilton, ON: Seldon Griffin Graphics, 2002), 9.

10. *Ibid.*, 39.

11. Interview with Eleanor Rodney, May 12, 2004.

12. *Ibid.*

13. *Ibid.*

14. *Ibid.*

15. Rodney, ed., *Nurturing the Trillium.*

16. "History of Blacks in Area Said Thin," *Hamilton Spectator*, February 6, 1989, in Hamilton Blacks Scrapbook, Vol. 1, 11, Hamilton Public Library, Special Collections.

17. Neville Nunes, "Vigilance Needed to Keep Black History Central," *Hamilton Spectator*, February 21, 1997, in Hamilton Blacks Scrapbook, Vol 1, 9, Hamilton Public Library, Special Collections.

18. Rodney, 58; Dawn Williams, *Who's Who in Black Canada: Black Success and Black Excellence in Canada, a Contemporary Directory* (Toronto: d.p. williams & associates, 2002), 274.

19. Matthew Kwong and Daniel Nolan, "Promoter of Peace, Citizen of the Year: Gary Warner," *Hamilton Spectator*, January 31, 2006.

20. "Two McMaster Professors Named to Order of Canada," *McMaster Daily eNews*, August 30, 2005.

21. Material on CIC Hall of Fame Inductees from Dr. Gary Warner. See also Rodney, 63.

22. Information provided by Bill De Lisser.

23. Interview with Evelyn Myrie, August 29, 2009.

24. "Gallery an Outlet for Black Artists," *Hamilton Spectator*, n. d., Hamilton Special Collections Clipping File.

25. This brief biography of Evelyn Myrie is partially based on an article written about her entitled "Art: The Mirror on the Wall," in *The Power of Story: A Kindergarten to Grade Eight Resource*, Vol. 2 (Toronto: Elementary Teachers' Federation of Ontario, 2004) 196–99. Information also comes from an interview with Evelyn on August 29, 2009, and other materials that she kindly provided, plus articles from the the Hamilton Public Library Special Collections Clipping File.

26. R.C. Smedley, *History of the Underground Railroad in Chester and the Neighbouring Counties of Pennsylvania* (1883; reprint, Mechanicsburg, PA: Stackpole Books, 2005), 108.

27. Jonathan Katz, *Resistance at Christiana: The Fugitive Slave Rebellion, Christiana, Pennsylvania, September 11, 1851* (New York: Thomas Y. Crowell, 1974), 34.

28. Editorial by Henry Bibb, *Voice of the Fugitive*, June 3, 1852.

29. Ella Forbes, *But We Have No Country: The 1851 Christiana, Pennsylvania Resistance* (Cherry Hill, NJ: Africana Homestead Legacy Publishers, 1998), 48. The information on Garfield Parker's date of birth and death was provided by the Hamilton Black History Committee.

30. Interview with Evie Auchinvole, September 4, 2009.

31. *Ibid.*

32. Arlie Robbins, *Prince Hall Masonry in Ontario*, 119.

33. Interview with Vince Morgan, September 4, 2009.

34. *Ibid.*

35. *Ibid.* See also Obituaries, *Hamilton Spectator*, December 8, 1988, C4.

36. This brief biography of Reverend Foster was told by his son, Robert George Foster Jr., and his daughter, Judy (Foster) Morgan. Interview with Robert G. Foster, August 24, 2009; interview with Judy Morgan, August 29, 2009.

37. The Hamilton Jockey Club, located on Barton Street in Hamilton, closed down in 1952. It is currently the site of the Centre Mall.

38. Interview with Judith (Foster) Morgan, August 29, 2009.

39. "Blacks to Study if Centre Wanted," *Hamilton Spectator*, February 15, 1972, in Hamilton Blacks Scrapbook, Vol. 1, 5–6, Hamilton Public Library, Special Collections. The other members of the committee were Reg Bryant, Sandra Bell, Steve Brown, and Courtney Blair.

40. Robbins, *Prince Hall Masonry in Ontario*, 116.

41. Interview with Robert Foster Jr., August 24, 2009.

42. Interview with Judith (Foster) Morgan, August 29, 2009.

43. Interview with Robert Foster Jr., August 24, 2009.

44. Edward Akinwunmi, "Niagara Community Honours Wilma Morrison," *Mosaic Edition*, 2008 (n.d.).

45. This short biography is derived primarily from "Wilma's Story," the unpublished memoir of Wilma Morrison, Norval Johnson Heritage Centre, and from Joe Hvilivitzky, "Preserver and Teacher of Local Black History," *Niagara Magazine* (Winter 2006): 37–40. In addition to Wilma Morrison, I would like to thank Lyn Royce for assisting in getting this and many additional newspaper clippings and documents to me.

46. Wilma Morrison, "Wilma's Story."

47. *Ibid.*

48. *Ibid.*

49. *Ibid.*

50. Email communication from Wilma Morrison, July 20, 2009.

51. Lewis, *Shadow Running*, 33–34.

52. Interview with Ray Lewis, February 20, 2003.

53. *Ibid.*

54. Phil Edwards, from Guyana, won a bronze medal in the 4-metre x 100-metre relay race in the 1928 summer Olympics in Amsterdam.

55. Interview with Ray Lewis, February 20, 2003.

56. *Ibid.*

57. Telephone conversation with Stanley G. Grizzle, November 24, 2009.

58. See the Hamilton-Wentworth District School Board listings at *www.hwdsb. on.ca/schools/school_listing.aspx?school=raylewis* (accessed November 24, 2009).

59. Ray Lewis with John Cooper, *Rapid Ray: The Story of Ray Lewis* (Toronto: Tundra Books, 2002). *Rapid Ray* is essentially the same text as *Shadow Running*, except that it is written for a younger audience.

60. Interview with Fleurette Osborne, May 2, 2010; also "Equity Bill 'Triggers Navel Gazing' Doubtful Minority Groups Argue," *Hamilton Spectator,* June 26, 1992, in "Hamilton-Economic Conditions Scrapbook," Vol. 6, 53 and "Black women try for national voice," *Hamilton Spectator,* July 27, 1987, in "Hamilton Blacks Scrapbook," Vol. 1, 92, Hamilton Public Library, Special Collections.

61. Alexander, 22.

62. "Business accepts challenge to fight racism," *Toronto Star*, January 25, 1989, A3.

63. Alexander, 208–10.

64. Conchita Tan-Willman with Shiu Loon Kong, *Canadian Achievers & Their Mentors*, Vol. I (Toronto: PRIME Mentors of Canada, 1994), 123.

65. Alexander's biographical information comes primarily from Lincoln Alexander, *"Go to School, You're a Little Black Boy."* See also W.P. Holas, *Millennium Minds: 100 Black Canadians* (Ottawa: Pan-African Publications, 2000), 39 and Conchita Tan-Willman and Shiu Loon Kong, *Canadian Achievers & Their Mentors*, 122–123.

BIBLIOGRAPHY

Primary Sources

Archives of Ontario

American Missionary Association Archives, Amistad Research Center, New Orleans (on microfilm at the Archives of Ontario).

Colonial Office Paper.

Crown Lands Department.

Death Registrations.

Department of Education, Incoming Correspondence.

Manuscript Censuses for City of Hamilton, Barton Township, and Wentworth County, Upper Canada, Canada West and Ontario, 1851–1901.

Jean Baptiste Rousseau fonds, F 493-1.

Ryerson Papers, Department of Education.

Surrogate Court Records for Wentworth County re: Papers of Administration of Henry Berry, John Johnson; Wills of John H. Bland, John Butler, Henry Criel, Pompey Lewis, Jesse Gant, Richard Gwyder.

Tax Assessment Rolls for City of Hamilton, 1837–1861.

Tax Assessment Rolls, District of Gore, Woolwich Township, 1831–1840.

Upper Canada Land Petitions

Upper Canada Sundries, Civil Secretary's Correspondence

Wentworth County Land Registry Office Abstract Index Books and various handwritten copies of deeds.

Baldwin Room, Toronto Public Library
Anderson Ruffin Abbott Collection.
William Jarvis Papers.
Negroes in Ontario, 1963 exhibit materials.
Elizabeth Russell Diary.

Buxton National Historic Site and Museum
National Unity Association Files.

Fieldcote Memorial Park and Museum/Griffin House
Enerals Griffin biographical research and related materials.

Hamilton Public Library, Special Collections
Butler Scrapbook, Saturday Musings: A Series of Weekly Articles from the
    Spectator, Vol. 1.
City Council Minutes, 1833–94.
Clipping Files.
Discrimination Scrapbook, 1926–1989, Vol. 1.
Gardiner Scrapbooks, Vols. 113, 215, 273.
Hamilton Blacks Scrapbook, Vols. 1–2.
Hamilton-Economic Conditions Scrapbook, Vol. 6.
McCullough, Famous People, Landmarks, Events Scrapbook, Vol. 3.
Mountain Mission Scrapbook, Vol.1.
Out of the Storied Past, bound articles from the *Hamilton Spectator* by Mabel
    Burkholder, Vols. 1 and 4.
Tinsley Scrapbooks, Vol. 8.

Hamilton-Wentworth Land Registry Office
Various deeds of property.

Johnston Memorial Library Special Collections and Archives, Virginia State
    University
The Colson-Hill family papers.

Multicultural History Society of Ontario
The *Canadian Observer* newspaper on microfilm.

Norval Johnson Heritage Centre
"Black History in the Niagara Peninsula," a list of documents compiled by
    Maggie Parnall, 1996.

Various newspaper clippings on Wilma Morrison.

Various photographs of Blacks in Hamilton.

"Wilma's Story," Unpublished memoir by Wilma Morrison and timeline of R. Nathaniel Dett B.M.E. Chapel and Norval Johnson Heritage Library.

Stewart Memorial Church Archives, John Holland Centre for Leadership Training
Stewart Memorial Board Minute Book, 1910–1935 and other church records.

United Church Archives, Toronto
BME Church Annual Conference Minutes, 1875–1884

Interviews
Evie Auchinvole, September 4, 2009
Jim Braithwaite, February 19, 2003
Tom Brooks, October 18, 2009
Shirley (Wade) Brown, July 2, 2003
Corinne (Bryant) Chevalier, December 2003
Robert Foster Jr., August 24, 2009
Stanley G. Grizzle, November 24, 2009
Ray Lewis, February 20, 2003
Judith (Foster) Morgan, August 29, 2009
Vince Morgan, September 4, 2009
Evelyn Myrie, August 29, 2009
Fleurette Osborne, May 2, 2010
Jouvane "Joe" Rhodes, December 1, 2003
Eleanor Rodney, March 12, 2004
Ed Shadd, September 18, 2009
Doris (Washington) Skorpid, January 23, 2003
Wilma Morrison, February 11, 2003, November 1, 2003, July 4, 2008
Jackie Washington, September 10, 2003

Newspapers
The *Canadian Observer* (Toronto, Ontario, 1914–1919)
Chatham Banner (Chatham, Ontario)
Chatham Planet (Chatham, Ontario)
Christian Recorder (Philadelphia, Pennsylvania, 1854–1902)
Colonial Advocate (Queenston and Toronto, Upper Canada, 1824–34)
The *Emancipator* (New York, New York, 1833–48)
The *Liberator* (Boston, Massachusetts, 1831–65)
Missionary Messenger (Chatham, Ontario)

National Anti-Slavery Standard (New York, New York, 1840–71)

New National Era (Washington, D.C., 1870–74)

Provincial Freeman (Windsor, Toronto, and Chatham, Canada West, 1853–60)

Upper Canada Gazette or *American Oracle* (Niagara and Toronto, Upper Canada, 1793–1849)

Voice of the Fugitive (Sandwich [Windsor], Canada West, 1851–53)

Secondary Sources

Books, Articles, and Monographs

Abbott, Lynn and Doug Seroff. *Ragged but Right: Black Traveling Shows, "Coon Songs," and the Dark Pathway to Blues and Jazz.* Jackson, MS.: University Press of Mississippi, 2007.

———. *Out of Sight: The Rise of African American Popular Music, 1889–1895.* Jackson, MS.: University Press of Mississippi, 2002.

Akinwunmi, Edward. "Niagara Community Honours Wilma Morrison," *Mosaic Edition*, date unknown.

Alexander, Lincoln M., with Herb Shoveller. *"Go to School, You're a Little Black Boy": The Honourable Lincoln M. Alexander, a Memoir.* Toronto: Dundurn Press, 2006.

Al-X. "Hamilton's First Family of Jazz and Blues," *View*, September 20–27 (1995): 9.

Aptheker, Herbert. *Negro Slave Revolts* 5th edition. 1943. Reprint. New York: International Publishers, 1983.

"Art: The Mirror on the Wall." In *The Power of Story, Vol. 2. A Kindergarten to Grade Eight Resource*, Vol. 2. Toronto: Elementary Teachers' Federation of Ontario: 196–99.

Backhouse, Constance. *Colour-Coded: A Legal History of Racism in Canada, 1900–1950.* Toronto: Osgoode Society for Legal History and the University of Toronto Press, 1999.

Bailey, Marilyn. "From Cincinnati, Ohio to Wilberforce, Canada: A Note on Antebellum Colonization," *Journal of Negro History*, 58, No. 4 (October, 1973): 427–40.

Bailey, Thomas Melville, ed. *Dictionary of Hamilton Biography.* Vols.1–4. Hamilton: W.L. Griffin, 1981.

Beattie, Jessie. *John Christie Holland: Man of the Year.* Toronto: Ryerson Press, 1956.

Bennett Jr., Lerone. *Before the Mayflower: A History of the Negro in America, 1619–1964.* Baltimore, MD: Penguin Books, 1966.

Blassingame, John W. *The Slave Community: Plantation Life in the Antebellum*

South. New York: Oxford University Press, 1972.

Blassingame, John W., ed. *Slave Testimony: Two Centuries of Letters, Speeches, Interviews, and Autobiographies.* Baton Rouge, LA: Louisiana State University Press, 1977.

Boyce, Debra. "Equity Bill 'Triggers Navel Gazing' Doubtful Minority Groups Argue." *Hamilton Spectator,* June 26, 1992.

Brand, Dionne, ed. *No Burden to Carry: Narratives of Black Working Women in Ontario 1920s to 1950s.* Toronto: Women's Press, 1991.

_____. "'We weren't allowed to go into factory work until Hitler started the war': The 1920s to the 1940s." In *"We're Rooted Here and They Can't Pull Us Up": Essays in African Canadian Women's History.* Edited by Peggy Bristow, Dionne Brand, Linda Carty, Afua Cooper, Sylvia Hamilton and Adrienne Shadd. Toronto: University of Toronto Press, 1994: 171–91.

Bristol, Douglas, Jr. "From Outposts to Enclaves: A Social History of Black Barbers from 1750 to 1915." *Enterprise & Society* 5, No.4 (2004): 594–606.

_____. "Regional Identity, Black Barbers and the African American Tradition of Entrepreneurialism." *Southern Quarterly* 43 (Winter 2006): 74–96.

British Methodist Episcopal Church Conference Committee on Education, "Education of the Coloured People in Canada," *Journal of Education* 21 (1868): 151.

Brooks, Thomas Walter. *Lee's Foreign Legion: A History of the 10th Louisiana Infantry.* Gravenhurst, ON: self-published, 1995.

Brown, Paola. *An Address Intended to Be Delivered in the City Hall, Hamilton, February 7, 1851 on the Subject of Slavery.* Hamilton: Printed for the Author, 1851.

_____. "Circular Address to the Free People of Color Throughout the United States," *The Liberator,* October 27, 1832.

Brown, William Wells. "The Colored People of Canada." In *The Black Abolitionist Papers, Volume II: Canada, 1830–1865.* Edited by C. Peter Ripley et al. Chapel Hill, NC and London, UK: University of North Carolina Press, 1986, 461–98.

Brown-Kubisch, Linda. *The Queen's Bush Settlement: Black Pioneers 1830–1865.* Toronto: Natural Heritage Books, 2004.

Burkholder, Mabel. *Barton on the Mountain: A Short History of that part of Barton Township Which is Situated on the Mountain Above the City of Hamilton from Days of Early Settlement to the Opening Years of the Twentieth Century.* Hamilton, ON: self-published, 1956.

_____. *The Story of Hamilton.* Hamilton, ON: Davis-Lisson, 1938.

_____. *Out of the Storied Past.* Hamilton, ON: n.p., 1968.

Calliste, Agnes. "Canada's Immigration Policy and Domestics from the Caribbean: The Second Domestic Scheme." *Socialist Studies/Etudes Socialistes* 5 (1989): 133–165.

_____. "Women of 'Exceptional Merit': Immigration of Caribbean Nurses to Canada." *Canadian Journal of Women and the Law* 6, No. 1 (1993): 85–102.

Campbell, Marjorie Freeman. *A Mountain and a City: The Story of Hamilton.* Toronto: McClelland & Stewart, 1966.

Campbell, Patrick. *Travels in the Interior Inhabited Parts of North America in the Years 1791 and 1792.* Edited with an introduction by H.H. Langton. 1793. Reprint, Toronto: The Champlain Society, 1937.

Carnochan, Janet. "A Slave Rescue in Niagara Sixty Years Ago." Niagara Historical Society, Paper No. 2 (1897): 8–18.

Chatham Daily Planet, October 14, 1892, "The Minstrels Move: O'Banyoun's Jubilee Singers Reorganize for the Season."

Chatham Tri-Weekly Planet, August 3, 1891, "Colored People Congregate: Business and Pleasure Judiciously Blended."

"Memoirs of Colonel John Clarke, of Port Dalhousie, C.W." *Ontario Historical Society Papers & Records* 7 (1906): 157–93.

Cobb, William Montague. "Medical History," *Journal of National Medical Association* 45, No. 4 (July 1953): 301–05.

Cooper, Afua. "Black Women and Work in Nineteenth-Century Canada West: Black Woman Teacher Mary Bibb." In *"We're Rooted Here and They Can't Pull Us Up": Essays in African Canadian Women's History.* Edited by Peggy Bristow, Dionne Brand, Linda Carty, Afua Cooper, Sylvia Hamilton, and Adrienne Shadd. Toronto: University of Toronto Press, 1994, 143–70.

_____. "In Light of New Evidence … Mary Bibb: Pioneer, Abolitionist, Educator, Publisher, And A Place in History." Unpublished paper in possession of the author.

_____. "Political Organizing: The North American Convention of Colored People, September 1851." Unpublished Report for Parks Canada, 2001.

_____. *The Hanging of Angélique: The Untold Story of Canadian Slavery and the Burning of Old Montréal.* Toronto: HarperCollins, 2006.

Coventry, George. "A Contemporary Account of the Rebellion in Upper Canada, 1837," *Ontario Historical Society Papers & Records* XVII (1919): 113–48.

Cruikshank, Ernest A., ed. *The Correspondence of Lieutenant Governor John Graves Simcoe, with Allied Documents relating to His Administration of the Government of Upper Canada,* Vol. I. Toronto: Ontario Historical Society, 1923.

Crysler, John Morden. *Crysler and Other Early Settlers in the Township of Niagara.* Niagara-on-the-Lake, ON: John M. Crysler and the *Niagara Advance,* n.d.

Daily Spectator and Journal of Commerce, August 3, 1853, "Local and Miscellaneous Items — Emancipation."

The Daily Spectator and Journal of Commerce, August 2, 1859, "Celebrations of the Anniversary of Emancipation."

Davis, Bruce Pettit and Carroll Langstaff Davis. *The Davis Family and the Leather Industry, 1834–1934.* Toronto: Ryerson Press, 1934.

Douglas, Thomas, Earl of Selkirk. *Lord Selkirk's Diary, 1803–1804: A Journal of His Travels in British North America and the Northeastern United States.* Edited with an introduction by Patrick C.T. White. Toronto: Champlain Society, 1958.

Drew, Benjamin, ed. *Refugees from Slavery: Autobiographies of Fugitive Slaves in Canada.* 1856. Reprint. Mineola, NY: Dover Publications, 2004.

Durand, Charles, *Reminiscences of Charles Durand of Toronto, Barrister.* Toronto: Hunter, Rose Co., 1897–99.

Edmunds, Sherry. "Slavery in the Kingston, Ontario and Bay of Quinte Region." Master's thesis, University of California, 1988.

1856. The City of Hamilton Directory, Containing a Full and Complete List of Householders, Together with Statistical and Other Information and Advertisements of the Principal Business Houses. Hamilton, ON: William A. Shepard, 1856.

1858 City of Hamilton Directory Containing a Full and Complete List of Householders, A Classified List of Trades and Professions, Together with Statistical and Other Information, Local and Provincial, and Advertisements of the Principal Business Houses. Hamilton, ON: William A. Shepard, 1858.

Etoroma, Efajemue E. "Blacks in Hamilton: An Analysis of Factors in Community Building." Unpublished Ph.D. diss., McMaster University, 1992.

Evans, Lois C. *Hamilton: The Story of a City.* Toronto: Ryerson Press, 1970.

Executive Committee of the British American Institute to the Editor, October 4 1847, *The National Era*, November 18, 1847.

Ferguson, Sue. "A Town Divided: Racism Once Flourished in the Town of Dresden, Ont.," *Maclean's*, September 10, 2001: 42–43.

Firth, Edith G., ed. *The Town of York, 1793–1815.* Toronto: The Champlain Society for the Government of Ontario, University of Toronto Press, 1962.

Forbes, Ella. *But We Have No Country: The 1851 Christiana, Pennsylvania Resistance.* Cherry Hill, NJ: Africana Homestead Legacy, 1998.

Fox-Genovese, Elizabeth. *Within the Plantation Household: Black and White Women of the Old South.* Chapel Hill, NC and London, UK: University of North Carolina Press, 1988.

Freeman, Bill. *Hamilton: A People's History.* Toronto: Lorimer, 2001.

French, Gary E. *Men of Colour: An Historical Account of the Black Settlement on Wilberforce Street and in Oro Township, Simcoe County, Ontario, 1819–1949.*

Stroud, ON: Kaste Books, 1978.

Gara, Larry. *The Liberty Line: The Legend of the Underground Railroad.* Lexington, KY: University of Kentucky Press, 1967.

Genovese, Eugene. *Roll, Jordan, Roll: The World the Slaves Made.* New York: Vintage Books, 1976.

Girard, Philip. "British Justice, English Law, and Canadian Legal Culture." In Phillip Buckner, ed. *Canada and the British Empire.* Oxford UK and New York: Oxford University Press, 2008: 259–78.

Greaves, Ida. *The Negro in Canada.* McGill University Economic Studies, No. 16, 1930.

Green, Constance McLaughlin. *The Secret City: A History of Race Relations in the Nation's Capital.* Princeton, NJ: Princeton University Press, 1967.

Green, Ernest. "Upper Canada's Black Defenders." *Ontario Historical Society Papers and Records* XXVII (1931): 365–91.

Grizzle, Stanley G. (with John Cooper). *My Name's Not George: The Story of the Brotherhood of Sleeping Car Porters in Canada.* Toronto: Umbrella Press, 1998.

Gutman, Herbert G. *The Black Family in Slavery and Freedom: 1750–1925.* New York: Vintage Books, 1976.

Hamilton City Directory 1901 Embracing an Alphabetical List of All Business Firms and Private Citizens; A Classified Business Directory; A Miscellaneous Directory, Also a Complete Street Guide. Hamilton, ON: Might Directories, 1901.

Hamilton Evening Times, October 23, 1866, "An Outrage Upon Society: Petition From the Coloured Citizens of Hamilton."

Hamilton Evening Times, October 27, 1866, "A Whitewashing Proceeding."

Hamilton Herald, August 4, 1853, "Celebration a Disgraceful Scene."

Hamilton Herald, December 25, 1889, "Market, Fire, Police: the Colored Citizens Present Their Rightful Claims."

Hamilton Herald, December 26, 1889, "Colored Brigade."

Hamilton Herald, December 26, 1889, "The Proposed Brigade: It is Opposed by Prof. Gant, Who Gives His Reasons."

Hamilton Herald, December 26, 1889, "What the Firemen Think, A Mean Insinuation Against the Colored Brethren's Staying Powers."

Hamilton Herald, December 27, 1889, "The Colored Fire Brigade. A Corps of Sixteen Men Suggested for the Job."

Hamilton Herald, December 27, 1889, "Justice Is Not Blind: The Color Line Drawn even at the Sacred Altar."

Hamilton Herald, December 28, 1889, "The Colored Fire Brigade: Chief Aitchison Declines to Give an Opinion on the Subject."

Hamilton Herald, February 12, 1890, "Her Majesty's Loyal Negroes: Editor Johnson Assures the Queen of their Unswerving Devotion."

Hamilton Herald, July 28, 1890, "John and Little Oscar: Professor Gant the Plaintiff in an Amusing Case."

Hamilton Herald, November 2, 1895, "Professor Jesse Gant: a Man Whose Genius is Many-Sided."

Hamilton Herald, August 23, 1902, "Escaped from Slavery: Interesting Incident in the Life History of a Man Who Still Resides in Hamilton."

Hamilton Herald, January 18, 1905, "Prof. Gant Dead: Best Known Colored Resident of City Passes Away."

Hamilton Herald, August 24, 1907, "Bicycle Thief Got One Year: Coloured Youth, With a Past, Sent to Central Prison by Police Magistrate."

Hamilton Herald, November 20, 1919, "Mrs. J. Diggs has Joined the Great Majority."

Hamilton Herald, March 20, 1925, "Ladies Klan Would March to City Hall: Mrs. E. Miller Declares K.K.K. Has 1000 Members Here."

Hamilton Herald, August 20, 1927, "G. Morton Dead: He Was Letter Carrier and on Local Staff for 36 Years."

Hamilton Herald, June 11, 1928, "Thomas J. Holland is Called to Rest: Was Last Surviving Member of the Noted O'Bannyon (*sic*) Jubilee Singers."

Hamilton Spectator, October 20, 1860, "An English Opinion of the 'Ambitious City.'"

Hamilton Spectator, November 1, 1875, "New Barber Shop."

Hamilton Spectator, January 10, 1882, "The Sun Do Move: Astronomical Opinions of Prof. Johnson, of Hamilton."

Hamilton Spectator, May 8, 1882, "The Sun Do Move: Reconstruction of the Sciences of Geography and Astronomy by a Hamilton Preacher."

Hamilton Spectator, February 12, 1883, "Razors in the Air: Prof. Gant's Barber Shop Bombarded."

Hamilton Spectator, October 12, 1883, "The British Lion."

Hamilton Spectator, November 2, 1883, "Doomed to Destruction: The Earth to Come to an End in Fifty Years — A Modern Edition of Mother Shipton."

Hamilton Spectator, January 23, 1884, "The Walls of the City: A Chat With a Toll-Gate Keeper About Tolls."

Hamilton Spectator, August 28, 1884, "Colored Oddfellows."

Hamilton Spectator, August 29, 1884, "Astronomical Johnson."

Hamilton Spectator, October 23, 1884, "Prof. Gant's Say."

Hamilton Spectator, October 23, 1884, "Going for Gant."

Hamilton Spectator, October 24, 1884, "Gant's Ultimatum."

Hamilton Spectator, July 20, 1885, "In a New Role: Prof. and Col. C.A. Johnson Announces a Startling Machine."

Hamilton Spectator, August 6, 1887, "On Earthquakes: Fourth Lecture by the Rev. C. Astronomical Johnson."

Hamilton Spectator, August 23, 1887, "A Joke on Astronomical Johnson."

Hamilton Spectator, February 13, 1890, "Brer Johnson's Latest Full Text of His Remarkable Address to Sir John Macdonald."

Hamilton Spectator, September 19, 1890, "Prof. Gant Makes a Call: He Conveys the Regards of the Coloured Citizens to Lord Aberdeen."

Hamilton Spectator, August 20, 1896, "Ended in a Free Fight: Watermelons in the Air at Last Night's Dundurn Show."

Hamilton Spectator, March 6, 1897, "C. Astronomical Johnson Talks Wisdom to the Benighted People of St. Kitts."

Hamilton Spectator, March 8, 1897, "Mr. Johnson Mops the Floor with the Spectator."

Hamilton Spectator, October 17, 1904, "Henry Criel Dead: Well-Known Citizen Passes Peacefully to the Great Beyond."

Hamilton Spectator, January 18, 1905, "Professor Gant Dead: Well-known Barber Succumbed to Bright's Disease This Morning."

Hamilton Spectator, March 27, 1925, "Ku Klux Klan: Crusaders Have No Feeling Towards the Order."

Hamilton Spectator, February 18, 1925, "Klan Organizing in this District."

Hamilton Spectator, March 1, 1930, "Klan Separates Oakville Negro and White Girl."

Hamilton Spectator, March 6, 1930, "Johnson Claims Indian Descent: No Negro Blood in Him, Klan Victim States."

Hamilton Spectator, July 15, 1936, "Former Coloured Colony on Mount Dubbed Little Africa."

Hamilton Spectator, January 16, 1937, "States Racial Prejudice Here Hurts Negroes."

Hamilton Spectator, July 15, 1946, "Mountain Section Early Settlement."

Hamilton Spectator, November 15, 1947, "Mission School, Frame Church, Toll Gates."

Hamilton Spectator, July 7, 1948, "Negro Veteran Denied Admission to Dundurn Dance."

Hamilton Spectator, July 13, 1948, "Apology Made, Colour Incident Is Now Closed."

Hamilton Spectator, September 1, 1948, "Racial Discrimination Motion Lost in Council."

Hamilton Spectator, February 23, 1950, "Groups Support Y.W.C.A. in Anti-Discrimination."

Hamilton Spectator, May 5, 1951, "Refused Haircut Here, Famed Pianist Charges: Oscar Peterson Makes Complaint; Warrender Seeks Test of By-Law."

Hamilton Spectator, May 7, 1951, "Barber Protests Publicity in Noted Pianist Incident: Employees Not Qualified to Cut Negro's Hair, Mayor is Told."

Hamilton Spectator, May 7, 1951, "'No Discrimination' Clause Clear, Board to be Advised."

Hamilton Spectator, June 4, 1955, "Smith's Sister Ran Toll-gate."

Hamilton Spectator, December 26, 1960, "A Flashback to 1930: The Klan's March Through Oakville."

Hamilton Spectator, August 17, 1963, "Fight for Freedom."

Hamilton Spectator, February 15, 1972, "Blacks to Study if Centre Wanted."

Hamilton Spectator, February 6, 1989, "History of Blacks in Area Said Thin."

Harcus, Anne. "A Personal Search That Became a Life's Work." *The Teaneck Suburbanite*, (July 11, 1984): 3, 7.

Head, Sir Francis Bond. *A Narrative*. 1839. Reprint. Toronto: McClelland & Stewart, 1969.

Henley, Brian. "For a Time, the Klan Reared its Ugly Head," *Hamilton Spectator*, June 22, 1991.

Henson, Josiah. *An Autobiography of the Rev. Josiah Henson ("Uncle Tom") from 1789 to 1883*. London, UK: Christian Age Offices, 1882.

Hill, Daniel G. "The Blacks in Toronto." In *Gathering Place: Peoples and Places of Toronto, 1834–1945*. Edited by Robert F. Harney. Toronto: Multicultural History Society of Ontario, 1985, 75–105.

_____. *The Freedom-Seekers: Blacks in Early Canada*. Agincourt, ON: Book Society of Canada, 1981.

Holas, W.P. *Millennium Minds: 100 Black Canadians*. Ottawa, ON: Pan-African Publications, 2000.

Howe, Samuel Gridley. *Report to the Freedmen's Inquiry Commission 1864: The Refugees from Slavery in Canada West*. 1864. Reprint. New York: Arno Press and the New York Times, 1969.

Hvilivitzky, Joe. "Preserver and Teacher of Local Black History." *Niagara Magazine* (Winter 2006): 37–40.

Jameson, Anna. *Winter Studies and Summer Rambles in Canada*. 1838. Reprint. Toronto: McClelland & Stewart, 1923.

Jones, Jacqueline. *Labor of Love, Labor of Sorrow: Black Women, Work and the Family, from Slavery to the Present*. New York: Vintage, 1986.

Katz, Jonathan. Resistance at Christiana: The Fugitive Slave Rebellion, Christiana, Pennsylvania, September 11, 1851. New York: Thomas Y. Crowell, 1974.

Katz, Michael B. *The People of Hamilton, Canada West: Family and Class in a Mid-Nineteenth-Century-City*. Cambridge, MA: Harvard University Press, 1975.

Katzman, David. *Before the Ghetto: Black Detroit in the Nineteenth Century*. Urbana, IL: University of Illinois Press, 1973.

Kelly, Wayne Edward. "Race and Segregation in the Upper Canada Militia." *Journal of the Society for Army Historical Research* 78, No. 316 (Winter 2000): 264–77.

Kern, Walter. *Reclaiming Your Heritage*. Booklet in the Niagara Public Library, 1985.

Kusmer, Kenneth. *A Ghetto Takes Shape: Black Cleveland, 1870–1930*. Urbana, IL: University of Illinois Press, 1976.

Kwong, Matthew and Daniel Nolan. "Promoter of Peace, Citizen of the Year: Gary Warner," *Hamilton Spectator*, January 31, 2006.

Lajeunesse, Ernest J., ed. *The Windsor Border Region: Canada's Southernmost Frontier*. Toronto: Champlain Society for the Government of Ontario and University of Toronto Press, 1960.

Landon, Fred. "The History of the Wilberforce Refugee Colony in Middlesex County," in *Ontario's African-Canadian Heritage: Collected Writings by Fred Landon, 1918–1967*. Edited by Karolyn Smardz Frost, Bryan Walls, Hilary Bates Neary and Frederick H. Armstrong. Toronto: Dundurn Press, 2009: 75–94.

_____. "The Negro Migration to Canada After the Passing of the Fugitive Slave Act," in *Ontario's African-Canadian Heritage: Collected Writings by Fred Landon, 1918–1967*. Edited by Karolyn Smardz Frost, Bryan Walls, Hilary Bates Neary and Frederick H. Armstrong. Toronto: Dundurn Press, 2009, 240–52.

_____. "Social Conditions Among the Negroes in Upper Canada Before 1865," in *Ontario's African-Canadian Heritage: Collected Writings by Fred Landon, 1918–1967*. Edited by Karolyn Smardz Frost, Bryan Walls, Hilary Bates Neary and Frederick H. Armstrong. Toronto: Dundurn Press, 2009, 169–92.

Leask, Mackenzie. "Jesse Happy, a Fugitive Slave from Kentucky." *Ontario History*, Vol. 54, No. 2 (June 1962): 87–98.

Leblovic, Nicholas. "The Life and History of Richard Beasley, Esquire." *Wentworth Bygones*, 7 (1967): 3–16.

Lees, Janet. "Black Women Try for National Voice." *Hamilton Spectator*, July 27, 1987.

Lewis, Ray, with John Cooper. *Rapid Ray: The Story of Ray Lewis*. Toronto: Tundra Books, 2002.

_____. As told to John Cooper. *Shadow Running: Ray Lewis, Canadian Railway Porter & Olympic Athlete*. Toronto: Umbrella Press, 1999.

Logan, Rayford, W. and Michael R. Winston, eds. *Dictionary of American Negro Biography*. New York and London, UK: W.W. Norton, 1982.

Loguen, Jermain. *The Rev. J.W. Loguen, as a Slave and as a Freeman: A Narrative of Real Life*. 1859. Reprint. New York: Negro Universities Press, 1968.

London Advertiser, October 30, 1937, "Father and Mother Arrived in London as Runaway Slaves. Distinguished Actor Who Was Born in the City, and Spent Boyhood Here, Is Officially Honored with Freedom of City at Rotary Club Luncheon."

Lundy, Benjamin. "The Diary of Benjamin Lundy Written During His Journey Through Upper Canada, January 1832." *Ontario Historical Society Papers and Records* XIX (1922): 110–33.

Mallory, Col. W. *Old Plantation Days*. Hamilton, ON: s.n., 1902.

McAlpine's Hamilton City and County of Wentworth Directory, 1875, Containing an Alphabetical Directory of Hamilton, Dundas, Waterdown, Ancaster,

Lynden, Copetown, East and West Flamborough, Bullock's Corners, Aldershot and Greensville, With a Street & Business Directory of Hamilton City, Also Each Township Arranged with P.O. Address, Concession and Lot of All Persons Holding Property in the County with an Appendix Containing Full Information. Montreal, Toronto, Hamilton, London, Ottawa, Halifax, N.S. and St. John, N.B.: McAlpine, Everet, 1875.

McMaster Daily eNews. "Two McMaster Professors Named to Order of Canada," August 30, 2005.

MacNab, Sophia. *The Diary of Sophia MacNab.* Edited by Charles Ambrose Carter and Thomas Melville Bailey. Hamilton, ON: W.L. Griffin, 1968.

McNeil, Mark. "The Legend of the Washingtons." *Hamilton Spectator*, March 28, 1987.

Merritt, Richard D. "The Davis Family of Mount Albion: A Loyalist Sketch." *Wentworth Bygones* 7 (1967): 33–41.

Meyler, Peter and David. *Searching for Richard Pierpont: A Stolen Life.* Toronto: Natural Heritage Books, 1999.

Mitchell, Reverend W.M. *The Under-Ground Railroad.* 1860. Reprint. Westport, CT: Negro Universities Press, 1970.

Moore, Donald. *Don Moore: An Autobiography.* Toronto: Williams-Wallace, 1985.

Morgan, Huw. "Slave's Freedom Document Awakens Search for Roots." *Hamilton Spectator*, March 15, 1979.

Mossell, Mr. N.F. *The Work of the Afro-American Woman.* 1908, Reprint. New York and Oxford, UK: Oxford University Press, 1988.

Mosser, Christine, ed. *York, Upper Canada Minutes of Town Meetings and Lists of Inhabitants, 1797–1823.* Toronto: Metropolitan Toronto Library Board, 1984.

Mulkewich, Jane. "Little Africa: Settlement Goes Back to 1850s," in *Vanished Hamilton II.* Edited by Margaret Houghton. Burlington, ON: North Shore Publishing, 2006, 103–04.

Murray, David. *Colonial Justice: Justice, Morality, and Crime in the Niagara District, 1791–1849.* Osgoode Society for Canadian Legal History. Toronto: University of Toronto Press, 2002.

Neff, Charlotte. "Pauper Apprenticeship in Early Nineteenth Century Ontario." *Journal of Family History* 21, No. 2 (1996): 144–71.

New York Times, March 31, 1888, "Readers Lacking Brains: Prof. Johnson's Flight into the Future."

Newman, William P. "The Colored People in Canada." *Oberlin Evangelist*, August 30, 1848.

Nunes, Neville. "Vigilance Needed to Keep Black History Central." *Hamilton Spectator*, February 21, 1997.

Ontario Educational Communications Authority. *Identity: The Black Experience in Canada*. Toronto: Ontario Educational Communications Authority and Gage Educational Publishing, 1979.

Palmer, Howard. *Patterns of Prejudice: A History of Nativism in Alberta*. Toronto: McClelland & Stewart, 1982.

Pease, William and Jane. *Black Utopia: Negro Communal Experiments in America*. Madison, WI: State Historical Society of Wisconsin, 1963.

"A Petition of the People of Color at Ancaster." *Journal of Negro History* 15, No. 1 (1930): 115–16.

"The Petition of Richard Hatt and Family." *Ontario Historical Society Papers & Records* XXIV (1927): 77–79.

"The Petition of Peter Martin." *Ontario History*, Vol. 26 (1930): 243.

Planet Directory of the Town of Chatham, 1882. Chatham, ON: Planet Steam Printing, 1882.

Power, Michael and Nancy Butler. *Slavery and Freedom in Niagara*. Niagara-on-the-Lake, ON: Niagara Historical Society, 1993.

Prince, Bryan. *A Shadow on the Household: One Enslaved Family's Incredible Struggle for Freedom*. Toronto: McClelland & Stewart, 2009.

Rawick, George P. *From Sundown to Sunup: The Making of the Black Community*. Westport, CT: Greenwood Press, 1972.

Redkey, Edwin S., ed. *A Grand Army of Black Men: Letters from African-American Soldiers in the Union Army, 1861–1865*. New York: Cambridge University Press, 1992.

Rhodes, Jane. *Mary Ann Shadd Cary: The Black Press and Protest in the Nineteenth Century*. Bloomington, IN: Indiana University Press, 1998.

Riddell, William Renwick. "The Slave in Canada." *Journal of Negro History* V, No. 3 (July 1920): 261–377.

Ripley, C. Peter *et al.*, eds. *The Black Abolitionist Papers, Volume II: Canada, 1830–1865*. Chapel Hill, NC and London, UK: University of North Carolina Press, 1986.

Robbins, Arlie C. *Prince Hall Masonry in Ontario, 1852–1933*. Chatham, ON: 1980.

Robin, Martin. *Shades of Right: Nativist and Fascist Politics in Canada, 1920–1940*. Toronto: University of Toronto Press, 1992.

Robinson, Gwendolyn and John W. *Seek the Truth: A Story of Chatham's Black Community*. Chatham, ON: Gwendolyn and John Robinson, 1989.

Rochefoucault-Liancourt, François-Alexandre-Fréderic La. *Travels Through the United States of North America: The Country of the Iroquois, and Upper Canada, in the Years 1795, 1796, and 1797*, Vol.1. Translated by Herman Neuman. London, UK: R. Phillips, 1799.

Rodney, Eleanor Wiltshire, ed. *Nurturing the Trillium: The Contributions of African & Caribbean Educators to the Development of the Hamilton-Wentworth*

Region. Hamilton: Seldon Griffin Graphics, 2002.

Roman, Charles Victor. *Meharry Medical College: A History*. Nashville, TN: Sunday School Publishing Board of the National Baptist Convention Inc., 1934.

"Charles V. Roman Obituary," *Journal of Negro History* 20, No. 1 (January 1935): 116–17.

Ruck, Calvin W. *The Black Battalion, 1916–1920: Canada's Best Kept Military Secret*. Halifax, NS: Nimbus Publishing, 1987.

Sanderson, Charles, ed. *The Arthur Papers, Being the Canadian Papers Mainly Confidential, Private, and Demi-Official of Sir George Arthur, K.C.H. Last Lieutenant-Governor of Upper Canada, Volume I: 1822–1838*. Toronto: Toronto Public Libraries and University of Toronto Press, 1957.

Scott, Tara. "How We Came to Be: The Legacy of Mary Roth & Wesley Rhodes." Detroit, MI: Unpublished history prepared for the Rhodes Family Reunion, August 4–6, 2006.

The Second Annual Report Presented to the Anti-Slavery Society of Canada. Toronto: Brown's Printing, 1853.

Shadd, Adrienne. "Celebrating the Legacy: Chatham's Black Heritage." Unpublished paper produced for the revised exhibit *Black Mecca: The Story of Chatham's Black Community*, Chatham-Kent Black Historical Society, Heritage Room, W.I.S.H. Centre. Chatham, 2004.

_____. "Deborah Brown and Black Settlement in York Township West, 1860–1870," Unpublished paper presented to Parks Canada, April 2001.

_____. "'Little Africa' Revisited: Tracing Hamilton Mountain's Black Community." Report to the Culture Division, Community Services Department, City of Hamilton, March 3, 2010.

_____. "'Little Africa': Where Do We Go From Here?" Report to the Culture Division, Community Services Department, City of Hamilton, April 2009.

_____. "No 'Black Alley Clique': The Campaign to Desegregate Chatham's Public Schools, 1891–93." *Ontario History* XCIX, No. 1 (Spring 2007): 77–95.

_____. "The Lord Seemed to Say 'Go': Women and the Underground Railroad Movement." In *"We're Rooted Here and They Can't Pull Us Up:" Essays in African Canadian Women's History*. Edited by Peggy Bristow, Dionne Brand, Linda Carty, Afua Cooper, Sylvia Hamilton and Adrienne Shadd. Toronto: University of Toronto Press, 1994, 41–68.

_____, Afua Cooper and Karolyn Smardz Frost. *The Underground Railroad: Next Stop, Toronto!* Toronto: Natural Heritage Books, 2002.

Shepard, R. Bruce. *Deemed Unsuitable: Blacks from Oklahoma Move to the Canadian Prairies in Search of Equality in the Early 20th Century Only to Find Racism in their New Home*. Toronto: Umbrella Press, 1997.

Sher, Julian. *White Hoods: Canada's Ku Klux Klan.* Vancouver: New Star, 1983.

Shreve, Dorothy S. *The AfriCanadian Church: A Stablizer.* Jordan Station, ON: Dorothy Shadd Shreve, 1983.

Simpson, Donald G. *Under the North Star: Black Communities in Upper Canada.* A publication of the Harriet Tubman Resource Centre on the African Diaspora, York University. Trenton, NJ: Africa World Press, 2005.

Slaney, Catherine. *Family Secrets: Crossing the Colour Line.* Toronto: Natural Heritage Books, 2003.

Smardz Frost, Karolyn. "Communities of Resistance: African Americans and African Canadians in Antebellum Toronto." *Ontario History* XCIX, No. 1 (Spring 2007): 44–63.

_____. *I've Got a Home in Glory Land: A Lost Tale of the Underground Railroad.* Toronto: Thomas Allen, 2007.

Smedley, R.C. *History of the Underground Railroad in Chester and the Neighbouring Counties of Pennsylvania.* 1883. Reprint. Mechanicsburg, PA: Stackpole Books, 2005.

Sohn, Herbert. "Human Rights Legislation in Ontario: A Study of Social Action." Unpublished Ph.D. diss., University of Toronto, 1975.

Steward, Austin. *Twenty-Two Years a Slave, and Forty Years a Freeman; Embracing a Correspondence of Several Years, While President of Wilberforce Colony, London, Canada West.* 1857. Reprint. New York: Negro Universities Press, 1968.

Still, William. *Underground Rail Road Records, Revised Edition: With a Life of the Author, Narrating the Hardships, Hairbreadth Escapes and Death Struggles of the Slaves in their Efforts for Freedom, Together with Sketches of Some of the Eminent Friends of Freedom, and Most Liberal Aiders and Advisers of the Road.* Philadelphia, PA: William Still, 1883.

Stone, William L. *Life of Joseph Brant — Thayendanegea: Including the Border Wars of the American Revolution, and Sketches of the Indian Campaigns of Generals Harmar, St. Clair, and Wayne, and Other Matters Connected with the Indian Relations of the United States and Great Britain, from the Peace of 1783 to the Indian Peace of 1795,* Vol. 2. Buffalo, NY: Phinney & Co, 1851.

Swanborough, Reginald, "The Early History of the Hamilton Fire Department, 1816–1905," *Wentworth Bygones* 8 (1969): 23–33.

Tan-Willman, Conchita with Shiu Loon Kong. *Canadian Achievers & Their Mentors.* Vol. I. Toronto: PRIME Mentors of Canada, 1994.

Taylor, Nikki, *Frontiers of Freedom: Cincinnati's Black Community, 1802–1868.* Athens, OH: Ohio University Press, 2005.

Taylor, Ric. "Jackie Washington." *View,* June 12–18, 2003.

Thomas, Charles and James C., "Reminiscences of the First Settlers in the County of Brant." *Ontario Historical Society Papers and Records* 12 (1914): 58–71.

Thornbrough, Emma Lou. *The Negro in Indiana: A Study of a Minority*. Bloomington, IN: University of Indiana Press, 1993.

Toby, A. Jeffers, ed. *Hamilton: A Black Perspective. A History of Blacks and Their Contribution*. Hamilton: Afro-Canadian Caribbean Association of Hamilton and District, 1991.

Toronto Daily Star, March 1, 1930, "Klan Took Oakville Girl from Negro Home: Hooded Ordered [*sic*] Foils Black-White Romance."

Toronto Daily Star, March 3, 1930, "All Negro Population to Protest Klan Act."

Toronto Daily Star, March 24, 1930, "Couple Parted by K.K.K. Wed by Indian Pastor."

Toronto Globe, November 19, 1924, "Ku, Klux, Klan Rears Head in City of Hamilton with 32 Initiations."

Toronto Globe, November 19, 1924, "A Klan of His Own."

Toronto Globe, November 22, 1924, "Detective Warned in Note Signed K.K.K."

Toronto Globe, March 3, 1930, "Klansmen of Hamilton Defend Their Conduct in 'Raid' at Oakville."

Toronto Globe, March 8, 1930, "Three Must Appear in Oakville Court Because of 'Raid.'"

Toronto Star, January 25, 1989, "Business Accepts Challenge to Fight Racism," A3.

Trudel, Marcel. *Dictionnaire des esclaves et de leurs propriétaires au Canada français*. LaSalle, QC: Hurtubise HMH, 1990.

_____. *L'Esclavage au Canada français: histoire et conditions de L'esclavage*, Quebec, QC: Les Presses de l'Université Laval, 1960.

Union Publishing Co.'s farmers and business directory for the Counties of Brant, Halton, Waterloo and Wentworth, 1884–5. Ingersoll, ON: 1884.

Walker, James W. St. G. *The Black Loyalists: The Search for a Promised Land in Nova Scotia and Sierra Leone 1783–1870*. New York: Africana Publishing Company, 1976.

_____. *A History of Blacks in Canada: A Study Guide for Teachers and Students*. Hull, QC: Minister of Supply and Services Canada, 1980.

_____. *"Race," Rights and the Law in the Supreme Court of Canada*. Toronto: Osgoode Society for Canadian Legal History and Wilfrid Laurier University, 1997

Walton, Jonathan. "Blacks in Buxton and Chatham, Ontario, 1830–1890: Did the 49th Parallel Make a Difference?" Unpublished Ph.D. diss., Princeton University, 1979.

Warren, Tracy. "Imagining, Remembering, Forgetting: Emancipation Day Celebrations in Hamilton-Niagara 1834–2008," Unpublished paper for Dr. H.V. Nelles, McMaster University, 2008.

Wayne, Michael. "The Black Population of Canada West on the Eve of the American Civil War: A Reassessment Based on the Manuscript Census of 1861." *Social*

History/Histoire Sociale XXVIII, No. 56 (November 1995): 465–85.

White, Deborah Gray. *Ar'n't I a Woman? Female Slaves in the Plantation South*. Markham, ON: New York and London, UK: W.W. Norton, 1985.

Williams, Dawn P. *Who's Who in Black Canada: Black Success and Black Excellence in Canada, a Contemporary Directory*. Toronto: d.p. williams & associates, 2002.

Winks, Robin. *The Blacks in Canada: A History*. Montreal, QC, and New Haven, CT: McGill-Queen's Press and Yale University Press, 1971.

Woodhouse, T. Roy. "History of Ancaster Village." In *Ancaster's Heritage: A History of Ancaster Township*. Compiled by J. McCormack. Ancaster, ON: Ancaster Township Historical Society, 1973.

Zielke, Melissa, "Go Down Moses: The Griffin House and the Continuing Struggle to Preserve, Interpret and Exhibit Black History, *Material History Review/Revue d'histoire de la culture matérielle* 55 (Spring 2002): 41–52.

Zorn, Roman J. "Criminal Extradition Menaces the Canadian Haven for Fugitive Slaves, 1841–1861." *Canadian Historical Review* 38 (December 1957): 284–94.

Websites

On the Earl and Lady Aberdeen, see *www.gg.ca* under "Roles and Responsibilities" (accessed December 11, 2009).

The Civil War Soldiers and Sailors website can be found at *www.civilwar.nps.gov*.

A guide to the papers of the Colson-Hill Family Collection can be found at *http://ead.lib.virginia.edu/vivaead/published/vsu/vipets00050.xml.frame* (accessed April 20, 2010).

"James Crooks," "Thayendanegea." Dictionary of Canadian Biography Online, *www.biographi.ca* (accessed October 19, 2008 and November 2, 2008).

A biography of General James Findlay of Cincinnati can be found at *www.findlay-market.org/gen_james_findlay.htm* (accessed February 23, 2010).

Lambertson, Ross. "The Dresden Story: Racism, Human Rights and the Jewish Labour Committee," *Labour/Le Travail*, No. 47 (Spring 2001): 14. This is available online at *www.historycoop.org/journals/llt/47/03lamber.html* (accessed August 26, 2009).

Information about the Ray Lewis Public School can be found on the Hamilton-Wentworth District School Board listings website at *www.hwdsb.on.ca/schools/school_listing.aspx?school=raylewis* (accessed November 24, 2009).

The Lightfoot genealogy can be found at *http://freepages.genealogy.rootsweb.ancestry.com/~lightfoot/index.html* (accessed August 4, 2009).

Biography of Jermain Loguen is on the website of the Circle Association's African American History of Western New York State, 1831–1865, at *www.math*.

buffalo.edu/~sww/0history/loguen.jermain.wesley.html (accessed January 20, 2009).

Colonel W. Mallory's narrative, entitled *Old Plantation Days* (Hamilton, ON: s.n. 1902), can be found on the website entitled "Documenting the American South" at *http://docsouth,unc.edu/neh/mallory.html* (accessed May 12, 2002).

Dr. Nathan Mossell's memoir is on the website of "Penn Biographies" at *www. archives.upenn.edu/people/1800s/mossell_nathan_f.html* (accessed February 3, 2009).

Mulkewich, Jane. "Sophia Pooley's Story." See *www.unityserve.org/dundashis-tory/articles* (accessed September 21, 2008).

On the early history of Woolwich Township, see *www.woolwich.ca/en/tourism/ EarlyHistory.asp* (accessed September 7, 2009).

Nelson Stevens's tombstone dedication can be found on the United States embassy website by clicking on Toronto, Canada, then "Headlines Archives." The event occurred November 3, 2007. www.usembassy.gov (accessed October 28, 2009).

INDEX

ABOUT THE AUTHOR

Adrienne Shadd hails from North Buxton, Ontario, one of the original stops on the Underground Railroad. She is the co-author of *We're Rooted Here and They Can't Pull Us Up: Essays in African-Canadian Women's History* and *The Underground Railroad: Next Stop, Toronto!* Adrienne has curated exhibits on African-Canadian history in Toronto, Hamilton, Chatham, Dresden, and online with the Virtual Museum of Canada. In 2009, she received the City of Toronto's William P. Hubbard Award for Race Relations. She lives in Toronto with her daughter.

Also by Adrienne Shadd

The Underground Railroad
Next Stop, Toronto!
Adrienne Shadd, Afua Cooper, and
Karolyn Smardz Frost
978-1-55488-429-2
$16.99

This richly illustrated book not only
traces the story of the Underground
Railroad itself and how people
courageously made the trip north
to Canada and freedom, but it also
explores what happened to them after
they arrived. And it does so using
never-before-published information on
the African-Canadian community of
Toronto. This volume offers new insights
into the rich heritage of the Black people
who made Toronto their home before
the Civil War. It portrays life in the
city during the nineteenth century in
considerable detail.

Of Related Interest

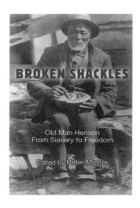

Broken Shackles
Old Man Henson from Slavery to Freedom
John Frost, edited by Peter Meyler
978-1-89621-957-8
$22.95

In 1889, *Broken Shackles* was published in Toronto under the pseudonym of *Glenelg*. Chronicling the recollections of Old Man Henson, this was one of the very few books that documented the journey to Canada from the perspective of a person of African descent. Henson's spark of life shines through as he describes the horrors of slavery and his goal of escaping its tenacious hold. The stories of his family, friends, and enemies will both amuse and shock readers.

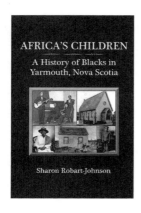

Africa's Children
A History of Blacks in Yarmouth, Nova Scotia
Sharon Robart-Johnson
978-1-55002-862-1
$28.99

Recalling the history of Black families of the Yarmouth area of Nova Scotia, *Africa's Children* is a mirror image of the hopes and despairs and the achievements and injustices that mark the early stories of many African Canadians. Robarts-Johnson traces the lives of those people, still enslaved at the time, who arrived with the influx of Black Loyalists and landed in Shelburne in 1783, as well as those who had come with their masters as early as 1767. Their migration to a new home did little to improve their overall living conditions, a situation that would persist for many years throughout Yarmouth County.

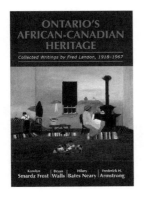

Ontario's African-Canadian Heritage
Collected Writings by Fred Landon, 1918–1967
Karolyn Smardz Frost
978-155002-814-0
$28.99

The collected works of Professor Fred Landon, who for more than sixty years wrote about African-Canadian history. The selected articles have, for the most part, never been surpassed by more recent research and offer a wealth of data on slavery, abolition, the Underground Railroad, and more, providing unique insights into the abundance of African-Canadian heritage in Ontario.

"Go to School, You're a Little Black Boy"
The Honourable Lincoln M. Alexander:
A Memoir
Lincoln M. Alexander with Herb Shoveller
978-1-55002-663-4
$40.00

From facing down racism to challenging
the postwar Ontario establishment,
becoming Canada's first Black member
of Parliament, entertaining royalty as
Ontario's lieutenant-governor, and serving
as chancellor of one of Canada's leading
universities, Lincoln Alexander's is the
ultimate, uplifting Canadian success story,
the embodiment of what defines Canada.

Available at your favourite bookseller.

DUNDURN PRESS
www.dundurn.com

What did you think of this book? Visit *www.dundurn.com*
for reviews, videos, updates, and more!